D1234633

110TH AAA:
DRIVING HITLER'S CRAWLIN' COFFIN

110TH AAA:
DRIVING HITLER'S CRAWLIN' COFFIN

A Young G.I.'s Account of WWII from D-Day to the Rhine

LONNIE R. SPEER

To order additional copies of this book, contact:
Xlibris Corporation
1-888-795-4274
www.Xlibris.com
Orders@Xlibris.com
32397

CONTENTS

DEDICATION

For Glen
and
all the other former members of
the 110th AAA Gun Bn.
who shared so many of their memories and personal feelings with me

and
to all the other young men of that time who naively crossed the ocean
and grew up over night

ACKNOWLEDGMENTS

As usual, there has been a lot of help in the production of this book. I am very grateful for all of the sincere interest and support from archivists Richard J. Sommers, Rick Baker and JoAnna M. McDonald of the U.S. Army Military History Institute; the helpful staff of the National Archives and the Library of Congress; the interest, caring, and very diligent hard work of Colleen O'Donnell, Research Assistant, National D-Day Museum; Joel K. Thiele, Special Collections Librarian, Malden (MA) Library; Rachel B. Galan, Linda Reynolds, and Anne Kendall of the Stephen F. Austin State University, East Texas Research Center; Diane M. Ranney, Assistant Director of the Bourne (MA) Library; Meg, Debbie, and Sally of the East Branch, Falmouth (MA) Library as well as Kathie Glynn and Adrienne Latimer, the Falmouth Library Research Assistants; Helene DeFore, Janet, Lauren, and Susan, the excellent and helpful staff of the Mashpee (MA) Public Library; Iona Reiver, for all of the wonderful photographs and information she provided, Maxine Edmondson for all of her help and photos, Vivian Lashier for her interest and time in providing information and photographs, Joy Knollman Hunter, Historian for Battery-B, 110th AAA Gun Bn.for her information; Bob Fitzpatrick, Falmouth (MA) Historical Society; Tony Honeyman of Nettlebed, (UK) for the excellent detailed information he researched and provided from the other side of the ocean; Edward Sheary, Director, and Philip Banks, Research Assistant, Pack Memorial Library of Asheville (NC); Joan Sandin and Anne Butler of the Black Mountain (NC) Public Library; and Ariel Gurrea and Jeanette Raffinan, Sherwin Soy, Danessa Alinsug, and Jay Rosales of Xlibris.

I also want to thank the late Betty Speer for her constant interest and help in this endeavor as well as Patricia and Tom Baker, the late Merle Spear, Christine, Candace and Glen Spear, Eddie, Jackie and Wendy Spear, J. R., Cindy, Jillian, and Eddie Speer, Steve, Tye and Amanda Bjork, Randy and Merlinda Speer, Melba Speer, Maxine and the late Richard Jones, Arlette Greenlee Moore, Collette Greenlee Rickert, Roy and Linda Greenlee, Ray and Betty Greenlee, and David and Shirley Greenlee, for all of *their* constant support and encouragement.

PROLOGUE

It was nearly 11:00 in the morning, Tuesday, June 6, 1944, as a line of LSTs slowly plowed through the water on yet another trip toward Omaha Beach, Normandy, France. While heavy bombardment could be seen and heard on the beach ahead of them, several young men assigned to Battery-D of the 110th Anti-Aircraft Artillery Gun Battalion, attached to the 29th Infantry Division, stood on the deck of their landing craft and looked out at the awe-inspiring array of ships positioned all around them. What they saw—an unprecedented number of battleships pounding strategic positions on shore with heavy artillery and a wide variety of landing craft and supply ships, with barrage balloons attached and floating in the air above them— as far as the eye could see.

"Surely we saw there before us more ships than any human being had ever seen before at one glance," Ernie Pyle, a Scripps-Howard war correspondent, riding in another LST nearby, correctly realized. "As far as you could see in every direction the ocean was infested with ships. There must have been every type of ocean-going vessel in the world . . . . There were battleships and all other kinds of warships clear down to patrol boats. There were great fleets of Liberty ships. There were fleets of luxury liners turned into troop transports, and fleets of big landing craft and tank carriers and tankers. And in and out through it all were nondescript ships—converted yachts, river boats, tugs, and barges."[1]

Few of the men in Battery-D realized, or even cared at this point, that what they were witnessing, what they were on their way to take part in, was the greatest amphibious assault force that had ever been assembled in the history of warfare and that what they were doing was making unprecedented history.

"What we saw," recalled then nineteen year old Ivan Glen Speer, one of the young men in Battery-D, "was unnerving. The entire area where we were assigned to go, [code-named] Dog Green Omaha, was under constant bombardment by both the American ships and the German artillery."[2]

"Although we arrived just on time," Ernie Pyle reported in agreement, "they weren't ready for us on the beaches and we spent several hours weaving in and out among the multitude of ships just off the beachhead. Finally we just settled down to await our turn . . . . Shells from battleships were whamming over our heads, and occasionally a dead man floated face downward past us. We could stand at the rail and see both our shells and German shells exploding on the beaches, where struggling men were leaping ashore, desperately hauling guns and equipment through the water."[3]

At Omaha Beach, between Vierville-sur-Mer and Colleville-sur-Mer, American troops—most of whom had landed a mile south of their original objective because of the strong wind and high waves—faced the fiercest fighting of D-Day. The ocean, close to shore, seemed to be a sea of floating dead as each wave washed more corpses up onto the beach.

"About 200 or 300 yards from shore we encountered the first enemy artillery fire," reported nineteen-year-old J. Robert Slaughter, a Heavy Weapons Sergeant from Roanoke, Virginia, serving in Company-D, 1st Battalion, 116th Infantry, 29th Division, riding in a landing craft toward the beach earlier that morning. "Near misses sent water skyward, and then it rained back on us . . . . About 150 yards from shore I raised my head despite the warning from someone to 'Keep your heads down!' I could see the craft to our right taking a terrific licking from small arms fire. Tracer bullets were bouncing and skipping off the ramp and sides as [German gunfire] zeroed in on the boat, which touched down a few minutes before we did . . . . As we approached the beach [our] ramp was lowered. Mortar and artillery shells exploded on land and in the water. Unseen snipers concealed in the cliffs were shooting down at individuals, but most havoc was from automatic weapons. The water was turning red from the blood. Explosions from artillery gunfire, the rapid-fire rattle from nearby MG-42s, and naval gunfire firing inland was frightening . . . . We knew then that this was not going to be a walk-in [but] no one thought that the enemy would give us this kind of opposition on the water's edge."[4]

"[O]n D-Day we thought we were going to run up on the beach and keep on going," admitted twenty-one year old Bob L. Sales of Company-B, 116th Infantry, 29th Division, originally from Madison Heights, Virginia. "[T]he coxswain [of the landing-craft] said he couldn't go in any further. He dropped the ramp and when you open up the ramp on a landing craft, that's when the machine guns open up on you."[5]

Many men later recalled their landing experience on Omaha Beach as comparable to becoming part of some macabre amusement park shooting gallery. In an effort to avoid the gunfire many men jumped off the ramp into deep water, only to sink out of sight under the heavy load of equipment in their back pack. Others, who could, removed their equipment in order to make it to shore. All around the area there were dead men floating in the water and live men acting dead, letting the tide take them in.

"You're so scared," Sales continued. "Anyone who says he wasn't scared isn't telling the truth. But we knew what we had to do and we just did our best."[6]

"Some wet their breeches, others cried unashamedly," admitted Slaughter, "and many just had to find it within themselves to get the job done. This is where the discipline and training took over."[7]

Eighteen year old Vincent Dougherty of Lee County, Virginia, remembered jumping off his landing craft as soon as the front ramp dropped and wading toward the beach under heavy gunfire. As he reached knee-deep water he began running in a crouched position but dropped his rifle in the ankle-deep water as he neared the shore. Stopping, he quickly reached down and grabbed the weapon only to drop it again. While dodging constant machine-gun fire and nearby explosions, he reached down into the water a second and third time before he finally noticed the thumb of his right hand had been shot off. Retrieving the rifle with his left hand, he continued his run up onto the beach where he hunkered down behind a seawall.

"I started to run toward the seawall under a deafening row of explosions and bullets," recalled Warner Hamlett, Company-F, 116th Infantry. "I heard a shell coming in and dove into the sand, face down. Shrapnel rose over my head and hit all around me, blowing me three or four feet. My rifle was [blown] from my hand and my helmet went twenty-five or thirty feet in front of me [as the] Germans began firing mortars, trying to knock out those few of us who had made it across the beach and were waiting behind the seawall."[8]

"We went across the beach in a weapons carrier which became bogged in the embankment on the sand," complained Alfred Lang of Linwood, New Jersey, who came ashore with the Headquarters Battery of the 110th Field Artillery Division. "German artillery fire was pounding the area and snipers were holding out and taking pot shots at [us]."[9]

Pinned down and unable to move forward or back, such scenes continued all day long but eventually, the progression of American troops began to slowly creep forward.

During this day, the Allies proceeded to put some 175,000 men ashore at Normandy. Casualties ran extremely high, estimated at 10,274, including 2,132 killed in action. Allied ships had originally off-loaded the assault troops into landing crafts—LCAs and LCVPs—eleven miles from the shore.

Many of these had sank or were grounded on sandbars before arriving on the beach to drop their ramps. Coxswains of others became panicked in the midst of the heavy bombardment and prematurely dropped ramps in an effort to quickly vacate the area. In both cases soldiers, many sea-sick, confused, off-course and disoriented had scrambled off the landing crafts into deep water, only to sink and drown under the weight of their seventy-pound packs while many others, exhausted or wounded by the terrifyingly heavy machine-gun, mortar, and artillery fire, had been unable to out-crawl the swiftly rising tide and had drowned within ten yards of the beach. In addition, thirty-two Duplex Drive amphibious tanks had been launched five-thousand yards from shore but twenty-seven of them had immediately sank with the loss of nearly all of their crews while forty out of seventy-two boats carrying artillery pieces had capsized.[10]

Slowly, American troops pressed inland across the 200-yard-wide beach and up over the heavily fortified bluffs under constantly heavy bombardment all through that day and night. During some of the heaviest fighting, three companies of the 2nd Ranger Battalion had scaled the sheer 100-foot cliffs of Pointe du Hoc on the west side of Omaha Beach on ropes. By the end of the day nearly 34,250 American troops had come ashore at Omaha Beach with another 35,250 at nearby Utah Beach along with 20,000 paratroopers. Further down, nearly 83,115 British and Canadian troops came ashore in their assigned sectors. The initial Allied invasion of Normandy involved a total of nearly 185,000 troops, 18,000 paratroopers, 13,175 aircraft, 4,066 landing ships, 745 large ships, and 20,000 vehicles. Within two weeks of this assault, by D-Day plus eleven, exactly 487,653 men and 89,728 vehicles would be landed on the continent.[11]

The reinforcements began coming in at dawn on June 7. Although the majority of the fighting had moved further inland by this time—in fact, some of the bloodiest fighting began to unfold at the beginning of D-Day Plus One—unyielding sporadic artillery shelling and intermittent sniper fire from Germans still holding various positions along the bluff continued as the reinforcements and equipment came up onto the beach.[12]

Speer was part of the long procession of equipment that landed on the Normandy beach once the troops had established a foothold. The 110th AAA Gun Battalion was originally scheduled to land during the mid-morning and afternoon hours of D-Day but because of the intense fighting, all landings onto Omaha beach were delayed. Although it had seemed to everyone involved as one long continuous operation as part of the original D-Day landing, the exact time that Speer and his equipment had drove up onto the beach was officially designated "D-Day Plus One." In fact, Speer was part of the first wave of heavy support equipment to hit the beach, arriving within 24 hours after the last initial wave of ground troops, but the raging battle and the constant stream of men and equipment moving onto the beach provided many of these men years later, including Speer, the mistaken impression that it had all taken place throughout the long day of June 6. "Time ceased to have a measured cadence," one soldier would later marvel. "Morning, afternoon, evening and nighttime simply blended together in a jumble of action and exhaustion." Even German Field Marshall Erwin Rommel, in command of the enemy forces at Normandy, was in agreement when he referred to June 6 and 7 as *The Longest Day.*[13]

An in-depth look at the 110th AAA reveals what really carried this nation to victory in World War II—the individual efforts of the common soldier—the unsung heroes often skipped over or reduced to footnotes in the massive volumes of war history—working together as a team as part of a larger team. But, individually or as a team, the American soldier has never been "common." From the Revolutionary War through the Civil War, and all the others that followed, the American soldier has always proved to be anything but common. In this aspect and many others, the 110th AAA serves as a prime, text-book, example. Like thousands of individuals in other units in this war, each of its men added to the success of D-Day and, later, the Battle of the Bulge, using their own initiative, ideas, and individual courage. These men not only inspired each other but others around them as well. Their undaunted courage and individual efforts made combat leaders famous. There is no doubt men like General George S. Patton, Jr. of the U.S. Third Army Division and General Omar N. Bradley of the U.S. First Army Division were great leaders who inspired their men into action, but if it wasn't for the individual efforts of these so-called common soldiers, those great leaders would be nothing more than footnotes in history, themselves.

Like so many other units, the 110th AAA was made up of young men in their late teens to early twenties who were plucked from family farms and small towns all across America. They were quickly trained and shipped to Europe and thrown into the greatest, most devastating conflict the world had ever known. Except for their training, all they knew about war was what their fathers and their uncles had told them about World War I— and many of those men had been reluctant to talk much about that war by the time this conflict had begun—or what they might have read in the books and newspapers about it up until their departure.

Understandably experiencing a fear of the unknown, these young men entered the conflict in the midst of an all-out, highly pitched battle, immediately baptized by fire with no opportunity to gradually become accustomed to warfare. But, as one soldier would later observe, "[I]t was better this way. There's no way to become accustomed to something like this."[14] These young men quickly learned that. They hit the beach as teenagers and by nightfall they had become men.

"Hitler's Crawlin' Coffin" was an eighteen-ton M-4 high-speed artillery tractor that crept up out of the surf onto Omaha Beach that day hauling a 90mm anti-aircraft gun and its crew during the afternoon hours of D-Day Plus One. Named and operated by nineteen year old Ivan Glen Speer, the tractor would go on to successfully push through France, enter Paris, break through the Bulge in Belgium, and slowly climb its way into Germany in an attempt to find its namesake.

Ivan Glen Speer was my uncle. To me, of course, he was a hero. To everyone else he was just a typical American G.I. who did what he had been assigned to do. This, then, is his story.

CHAPTER 1

South-central Iowa:
The Home Front

In 1941 people all across America were just beginning to recover from the economic depression that had dominated the 1930s. Although nearly 30.25 million people still lived or did their work on farms, many were acquiring electricity and indoor plumbing for the first time while many others were just beginning to replace draft animals with tractors. By 1941, there was 1,665,000 tractors in the United States, or about one per every four farms. Slowly, all across the nation, the average American lifestyle was being revolutionized. The automobile, quickly becoming a necessity too, was being acquired by more and more citizens and over 85-percent of America's households had radios. In fact, 57 million radios served 29 million homes by 1941, while nearly 14 million sets were sold in that year alone.[1]

The most common leisure activities during this time included board games such as checkers, dominoes, or Chinese checkers, all sorts of card games, and working jigsaw puzzles. The majority also hunted, fished, attended church and community gatherings, and often spent their Sunday afternoons visiting family and friends.

Cultural life was undergoing various changes too. Big bands and ballroom dancing had become a national craze, the jitterbug had become popular with teens and nearly every town had its own local dance band. Professional sports was dominated by such names as Joe DiMaggio, Bob Feller and Joe Lewis. The movies were dominated by such names as Lana Turner, Bette Davis, Gary Cooper, and Clark Gable. And for news and current events, Americans turned to the weekly magazines of *Time* or *Newsweek* and the ever popular periodicals of *Life* and the *Saturday Evening Post*, while their daily news and entertainment was quickly becoming dominated by radio, of which the Columbia Broadcasting System led the way with news correspondents William L. Shirer, Eric Sevareid, and Edward R. Murrow.

For the most part, the Speer family of Wayne County, Iowa, could be considered an average American farm family of this period. Forty-three year old Dewey Oliver Speer and his thirty-nine year old wife, Elsie Mariah Greenlee Speer, and their two sons, Ivan Glen Speer, 17, and Lloyd Rex Speer, aged 11, had recently moved from a larger farm near Millerton to a smaller 100-acre farmstead just west of the county seat of Corydon. Although the total acreage of the new place was smaller, it had better advantage of location and possessed a big white two-story country-style house with electricity and indoor plumbing. In addition, the family owned a car, a 1939 Chevrolet, a floor-model Philco radio, and a Maytag wringer-type washing machine powered by a small gasoline engine. Shortly afterwards, Dewey would acquire a big red Farmall tractor to do the work of his two huge Belgian draft horses and, except for a few odd jobs, they would then be used solely for exhibitions and horse-pull competitions at county fairs. Glen, as Ivan was more commonly known among family and friends, had graduated from high school in June of that year but had remained on the family farm since then to help out. In addition, Glen did a lot of work for others on neighboring farms as well, and because he was a sincere young man who possessed a natural charm, he was well-liked and respected throughout his community.

Glen first heard about the Japanese attack on Pearl Harbor when he turned on the radio at about 2 P.M. on Sunday afternoon, December 7, 1941. "I was laying on the floor of the front room with my eleven year old brother and [my cousins]," he recalled. At the news, his parents entered the room to listen to all the details. "We were shocked," recalled Glen. "We were all stunned at the report." However, being only seventeen years old at the time, Glen didn't give much thought to how this event might personally involve him, but perhaps his father—who Glen remembered seeing having a serious, worried look on his face—did: The United States would surely go to war—and within a short time Glen would be draft age.[2]

The following Monday morning, 11 A.M. on December 8, the family gathered around the radio and heard their President, Franklin Deleno Roosevelt, address the Congress of the United States. It only took Roosevelt ten minutes to deliver the speech in which he referred to the "day that will live in infamy" and asked Congress to declare war. Three days later, on December 11, Germany and Italy, in support of their Axis Pact with Japan, declared war on the United States.

By this time, however, the draft was already in place. Because of the enactment of the Selective Service Act the previous year, American men between the ages of twenty-one and thirty-five had already began registering for the draft. With these new developments, the minimum draft age was soon reduced to eighteen. Within days of his eighteenth birthday, Speer registered under the new law. Within nine months, Ivan Glen Speer received his draft notice.

"Greetings," announced the form letter. "Having submitted yourself to a local board composed of your neighbors for the purpose of determining your availability for training and service in the armed forces of the United States, you are hereby notified that you have been selected for training and service in the Army." It then ended with instructions on when and where to report.

Ormal V. Bott, who owned the farm nearest to the Speer property, came over a few days after learning Glen had received his draft notice. Glen had done a lot of work on the Bott and other farms, assisting in the shucking, husking, and harvesting of corn, the cutting, raking, and putting up of hay, and the annual threshing of wheat. Ormal informed Glen and his father that he was there representing the entire farming community. According to Ormal, they had all agreed to draw up a petition requesting Glen's exemption from military service because he was a well-respected, hardworking, dependable worker who was desperately needed on the neighborhood farms.

Mr. Bott's proposal was entirely legitimate and quite conceivable. During World War II draft deferments were obtained for a variety of reasons, including conscientious objection, economic dependency, and employment in an essential occupation such as farming. By 1944 nearly two-million farm workers had been given occupational deferments based upon the idea that their employment and farming experience was essential to the nation's economy and its national defense.[3]

Glen was deeply touched by Bott's offer, and although he was somewhat apprehensive about the possibility of going to war, he wanted a good excuse to get away from the farm as well. He thanked Mr. Bott for the offer but politely turned it down.

"I didn't want to work for Ormal and the other farmers all my life," admitted Speer. "At the age of eighteen you begin to kinda think about wantin' to leave the farm—and this was my perfect chance to leave—so I chose to be inducted."[4]

For days afterward Glen noticed that his mother, normally a very strong and independent woman, seemed easily upset and on edge. He later learned from his father that she often paced the floor at night and had been unable to sleep since the day Glen received his draft notice. He further learned she was now going to bed saying that she "wished she could just go to sleep and *never* wake up." Dewey attributed his wife's condition to perhaps going through "the change of life" and assured Glen there was no need for him to worry. However, Glen eventually learned that his mother remained depressed and easily upset for quite some time. Although Elsie *was* able to eventually cope and endure, her anxiety and insomnia was more probably the result of her fears about Glen and the previous loss of her first son Gerald. He had died in 1932 at the age of twelve after a bout of what was later determined to be rheumatic fever. With the loss of her first son eleven years earlier, the raging war in Europe now, and Glen's recent induction into the service, there is little doubt her anxiety was caused by worry and the fear of possibly losing her second son.

A number of Wayne County boys had received draft notices that same week, including Speer's best friend Wayne Edmondson. Although Wayne had attended a rival high school at nearby Lineville and he and Glen had competed against each other on their school's baseball and basketball teams, the two had remained good friends ever since their sophomore year back in 1939. On Friday morning, March 26, 1943, Glen and Wayne proceeded to Corydon's First National Café, on the town square across from the county court house, to report in for a bus trip to the induction center. A neighbor of the Speer family, Geraldine Warren, worked at the draft board office and offered her apologies to the boys. As the paperwork began, Glen and Wayne assured her that they completely understood.

North side of the square, Corydon, Wayne County, Iowa
looking west toward Hwy. 14. (Author's collection)

"The Selective Service office was located in an upstairs room on the northeast side of the square," recalled Speer. "Geraldine had sent out the notices because she did the office work for the draft board. We had attended school together and played together as kids."[5]

After all the paperwork was processed, the boys were led out with others to a waiting bus for a nearly three hour trip to the state's main induction center at Camp Dodge. By this time parents, friends, and relatives had gathered around the bus to bid the boys good-bye.

"I remember the morning we left on the bus," advised Glen. "Quite a lot of people had gathered there to watch us board and to say good-bye."[6]

Such occasions had indeed become big events in many small towns all across America. Large crowds of parents, relatives and friends of the boys would gather to see them off but often times so did hundreds of others. After all, nearly everyone in town knew these boys who were boarding this bus to go off to war. These were boys who had attended school with their children. These were boys who had played—and lettered—on the local high school football, basketball, track, and baseball teams; boys that they had chaperoned at the school dances and parties, who had dated their daughters, had done yard work and odd jobs for them, had bagged their groceries at the local grocer, had escorted them to their seats at the local theater, had serviced their car at the local gas station, or had helped them in their farming. Everyone in town knew these boys or knew their family. And all of these boys, they no doubt felt, were going off to represent all of them and their community in the far off fight against oppression and in the fight for liberty.

"A lot of the people cried," recalled Glen in thinking back about the crowd that had gathered around the bus, "but I never knew that my dad could cry. I had never seen him cry."[7]

Glen remembered that his mother, Elsie, was terribly upset and crying about his leaving but he had come to expect such behavior from her. His father, on the other hand, had always seemed to be a serious, hardworking, strict disciplinarian who Glen believed, was a completely unemotional man.

"I had never seen him cry," Glen repeated, "but the bus cranked up and made a U-turn and went to the Highway 14 stop sign [at the other end of the square] and as we turned north at that corner, where many of the people had gone up to [to see us one last time], I saw my dad cry— standing there crying—that was really something to me. It made a deep impression."[8]

Camp Dodge was located on the northwest side of Des Moines, Iowa— the state capitol—about one-hundred miles northwest of Corydon.

Established in 1909 and named in honor of the state's Civil War General Grenville M. Dodge, the camp served as the state's annual two-week training center for the Iowa National Guard. The facility had been a regional training center during World War I and it was here that Glen's uncles received their basic training before being shipped off to Europe to fight the Kaiser's German Army. Back then Camp Dodge consisted of 1,872 buildings to accommodate 40,000 men—although the most ever maintained was 23,000 in September, 1917—but by the time Glen arrived in 1943 the camp had about one-fourth as many buildings on its 2,690 acres and had been converted into a 1,250 man induction center for the state's new recruits. As bus loads of young men rendezvoused here from all over the state, they endured batteries of medical examines and tests over a three day period before being shipped out to various basic training centers across the nation.

The Camp Dodge Induction Center near Des Moines
(Author's Collection)

Escorted off the bus by uniformed military personnel, the recruits were sworn in and lectured. They then spent the remaining two days standing in long lines to be interviewed, fingerprinted, given physical exams, inoculated from both sides as they shuffled along, and eventually ended up at the barber's shop where they received the standard military haircut that the recruits referred to as "chili bowls"—hair sheared off close around the ears and up around the side of the head leaving the maximum length of one and one-half inches around the crown.

This was all a new experience for many of these boys. Many had never been so far away from home and many of them had never been compelled to spend so much time with others in such large groups. What's more, many of these mid-west farm boys had never taken a shower before.

"I was very fortunate to live in a home with running water," said Glen, "and I had taken tub baths all the time but I had never taken a shower.... And to be inducted into the Army with a whole bunch of guys and have to go shower in a group shower with [them] was very intimidating... it was extremely embarrassing for an old farm boy to undress and shower in front of others!"[9]

By March 28, their first Sunday at the Camp Dodge induction center, the boy's families were allowed to visit. All of the preliminary tests and medical exams had been completed and this group of recruits was scheduled to be trained out the following day to the various basic training camps.

"One of my first disappointments," Glen later pointed out in thinking about his life, "came that first Sunday. Quite a few of the boys' parents came up to see 'em. And of course there were quite a few of us Wayne county boys who went up there together."[10]

Understandably, for each of these young men to see their families one more time before they left was a welcome sight. Many of the boys were uneasy, nervous, or apprehensive. They didn't know what to expect or what the future might hold for them. Glen enjoyed visiting with many of his Wayne County acquaintances who made the trip, but surrounded by so many friends, he still felt unbelievably lonely.

"[My friends'] parents came up to visit," Glen continued, to this day still unable to hold back his tears, "and I often thought about how great they must have felt to be able to spend that time with them... and how disappointed I was that my folks couldn't come. Even after all these years I still get very emotional when I talk about this stuff."[11]

All the visiting parents were required to leave later that afternoon. The next day, Monday March 29, the recruits were escorted to a waiting train that headed out eastbound away from Camp Dodge. "Everything was a big secret," advised Glen, "and you had no idea where you were going. They wouldn't tell us. Most of the train travel was during the night, for the most part, and we just kept wondering where we were going. We knew we were going east but we didn't know exactly to where."[12]

The train traveled under war-time blackout conditions, operating after dark with no outside lights and having heavy black shades drawn over all windows. As it continued eastbound through the night, most of these boys sat quietly. Some played cards, some slept, and some just sat and talked.

To still others, like Glen, it seemed like an eerie trip—traveling in the darkness to who-knew-where and with military officials on board refusing to tell or give any information at all—and nothing to do but sit and think and reflect.

"The railroad cars [we were on]," complained Glen, "were not very nice. The straight-back seats were upholstered with some kind of green felt or something—not velvet—and the soot, the old coal soot, blowing back along the cars from the train engine would come right through the closed windows. And you would have to brush your clothes off about every so often." [13]

He passed the night quietly and, although the train was crowded and he was surrounded by friends, Glen couldn't help but feel depressed and all alone.

Departures are often emotional events and some, of course, are more difficult than others. Still, it is said there are only several hundred events that will live in a man's mind forever. For Speer two of those events occurred in March 1943. The first was seeing his strong, intransigent father cry as he left for the war and the second was the failure of his parents to come visit him before he was to be shipped off to unfamiliar places with an uncertain destiny. As the train rocked along through the darkness, he thought of those events throughout the night and he would sometimes find himself reflecting on those two events many years later.

CHAPTER 2

A Farm Boy's First Trip Away From Home: Training At Camp Edwards, Mass.

As the first light of dawn crept above the horizon, Speer and a number of the others noticed a signpost for "Pittsburgh" as the train quickly passed it by.

"[E]very time we went through a town," complained one young G.I., "the M.P.s would come in and pull the shades or blinds so no one could see in and we would not see out. In Pittsburgh, one of our companions peeked out through the blinds."[1]

Still not knowing where they were going, they at least had gained some idea of their general locality. Immediately this caused great excitement and discussion as a number of the boys began to speculate out loud where they thought the train might be heading. Some believed they were enroute to Fort Dix in New Jersey while others argued their destination was perhaps one of the military camps within the state of New York—or possibly even Governor's Island in New York City, itself. But, after several more hours of travel the troop train finally came to a halt later that evening on a side track at Camp Edwards, Massachusetts.

"The train creaked slowly through a maze of tracks before stopping in a burst of steam," recalled another teenage recruit. "We grabbed our heavy [duffel] bags, stepped off the train, and looked around all wide-eyed." Being dark there was little to see. The new arrivals were marched a quarter-mile to the base Reception Station.[2]

Main Gate, Camp Edwards 1943 (Courtesy Terry Bye)

Camp Edwards was located in the upper Cape Cod region along the eastern tip of Massachusetts, just east of the town of Pocasset in Barnstable County. It was named in honor of Maj. Gen. Clarence R. Edwards, a well-known Massachusetts resident who became commander of the 26th (Yankee) Division in World War One. The base housed a total of 34,108 enlisted men and 1,945 officers. In addition to being a large basic training post, the camp served as the Army's Anti-Aircraft Training Center as well as its specialized Amphibious Training School.[3]

Shortly after their arrival these new recruits were assigned sleeping quarters adjacent to the reception center and bedded down for the night. The next day they awoke to predawn bugles and, after hours of lectures, more exams and some additional vaccinations, they were assigned to a training company and issued uniforms and equipment.

Generally, each inductee was issued three suits of khakis, two sets of fatigues, five pairs of summer underwear, four pairs of socks, two pairs of shoes, two wool winter uniforms, two sets of winter (long) underwear, a canvas field pack, a mess kit, a canteen, a steel helmet, a rifle, and other equipment including a webbed cartridge belt having a canvas cover for the canteen, an entrenching tool, and a scabbard for a bayonet attached. Quietly, many recruits complained—mostly among themselves—that a lot of the clothing didn't fit very well. Quite often these new soldiers were measured for clothing *over* their own clothing. Equally strange and unconventional, upon being fitted for shoes they were instructed to hold two fifty-pound buckets of sand. This, they later learned, was to flatten their feet to help simulate the weight of wearing a full backpack. However, it caused many recruits to receive shoes much larger than they normally wore. Consequently, when they weren't wearing a backpack, their feet slid around inside their shoes as they walked. Glen and many of the others quickly found out that the Army didn't care to hear about their personal concerns or opinions about this or any other matter. The Army, they were told, had a logical reason for everything even if it made no sense to any of them. What's more, they were informed, there was now three ways to get something done: There was a right way, a wrong way, and the Army way— and no matter what, it would be done the Army's way from now on. "A score of fitters measured necks, waists, inseams, heads, and feet," reported one new G.I. to illustrate the point. "My shoe size, a clerk yelled down the line, was ten and a half. 'I beg your pardon,' I prompted, 'I wear a size nine.' 'Forgive me,' he replied, a trifle weary, 'I believe the expression is 'I *wore* a size nine.'"[4]

Next the inductees were escorted down the street and assigned company barracks. Most of these buildings, situated on the west side and south end of the base, were all one story white painted wood structures housing fifty men. More recently built barracks of two stories and housing 100 men occupied the entire northwest section of the camp. These new arrivals were escorted to this area and became some of the first recruits assigned to the two-story wood structures. Once inside the recruits were given "bedding cards" to fill out with their names, and assigned a bunk, locker, and storage area for their newly issued clothing and equipment, and then escorted out to the bedding-supply warehouse. There, lined up single file with their arms stretched straight out in front of them and their bedding cards in their left hand, they were marched through the building as a Supply Sergeant, behind a counter, tossed a comforter, blanket, two sheets, and a pillow-case onto their outstretched arms and ordered them out the opposite door. The procedure was over within a minute.[5]

Returning to their barracks, the inductees were taught the proper bed-making procedure required by the Army. All folds had to be clean-cut with hospital corners. The top blanket and sheet had to be rolled back together in an eight-inch fold, four inches from the pillow and tucked in all around. In addition, the comforter had to be folded back from under the pillow an exact width of fifteen inches. "If it wasn't," complained one of the new recruits, "they'd just take it all and throw it out in the middle of the floor." Within days all the troops had learned the Army way of making their beds—drawing and tucking the covers over their bunks so tight that a quarter bounced when tossed upon it. "I finally got my bed to where it would pass inspection," admitted John A. "Jack" Forman. "And, you know, I never slept on that bed all the time I was there. I left it just like that and slept on the floor."[6]

For these new recruits, such fear was understandable. "If any person's bunk is out of order or there is anything wrong with the whole barracks or latrine," marveled one G.I. in a letter he wrote home to his parents, "the whole gang stays here. One guy can put the whole company on K.P."[7]

Camp Edwards was originally established in 1935 to serve as the annual training site for the Commonwealth of Massachusetts National Guard. It was taken over by the Federal Government on September 4, 1940, to serve as a basic training center for new recruits and at that time additional buildings, including two story barracks, were constructed. By 1943 the base consisted of 21,322 acres bordered by the towns of Pocasset, Bourne, Sagamore, Sandwich, Mashpee, and North Falmouth, covering nearly 34 square miles of upper Cape Cod. Glen and many of the other recruits were amazed that the base actually functioned as its own small independent city. Along with its own police force and fire department it had its own postal facilities (three), its own banking facilities (two), four telephone centers, two telegram facilities and one main telegraph office, thirteen chapels, two libraries, twenty-two stores—called post exchanges or PX for short—a barber shop in each PX, an enlisted men's clothing store, an Officers' Post Exchange, an Officers' Club, an Officers' restaurant, six Non-Commissioned Officers' Clubs, eight beer halls—each promoting a different atmosphere inside, various service clubs, four movie theaters, an outdoor amphitheater, a Sports Arena and Bowling Alley and *The Camp News*, its own newspaper. *The Camp News*, averaging twelve 11" X 17" pages of news, observations, rumors, gossip, speculation, and comments, was published weekly in a newspaper office located on the base.[8]

During the first few days at the camp the new recruits learned how to scrub the barracks while being taught a few basics about formations, saluting, and marching. On their fourth day each of the new arrivals were issued two rectangular, stainless steel identity labels referred to as "dog tags," strung onto beaded metal chains. Instructed to wear them around their necks at all times, the recruits saw that five lines of typescript had been stamped into each dog tag that consisted of their name—first name, middle initial and last name—on the first line, their assigned Army identification number, last two digits of the year of their last tetanus shot, and their blood type stamped into the second line, and then the name, home address, city and state of their next of kin made up the third, fourth and fifth lines.[9]

Over the next several days these young recruits fell into a normal daily routine of rising before dawn, washing up and shaving, going to breakfast in the mess hall, returning to sweep, dust, and straighten up their barracks, marching and drilling, returning to the barracks to wash up and stand in line for lunch (called "dinner"in the Army), waiting outside the orderly room for mail call before marching to the field again for drill, returning to the barracks to wash up for the evening ("supper") meal, honoring the lowering of the flag at the retreat ceremony in late afternoon by standing at attention wherever they happened to be when the bugle call sounded, returning to the barracks for showers at the end of the evening and preparing for the nightly bed check, and finally collapsing into their bunks at 11:00 P.M. as the CQ, or Charge of Quarters, turned the barracks' lights out just before the bugler played taps over the Public Address system.

"A tight schedule has been set up which requires that you eat at the time designated or else the whole thing will go haywire," warned a Camp information booklet issued to each new recruit. "For later meals a mess schedule is posted in your barracks. Enlisted men will take with them their [mess kit] knife, fork and spoon. Officers will not need them—but we will collect "two bits" on the line before each meal from them."[10]

At the same time, these new soldiers began to pick up a new vocabulary that included terms such as "on the double" for hurry, "fall in" meaning form up and come to attention, "AWOL" for absent without leave, "S-O-P" meaning "standard operating procedure," "SNAFU" which stood for "situation normal—all fouled up," and many other military terms. They also learned military slang that included "can" or "head" for bathroom or latrine, "little Abners" for shoes, "blanket drill" for sleep, "bunky" for buddy or friend, and "chow" for food.

In addition, they were taught the Army's phonetic alphabet, using words in place of the letters to prevent similar sounding ones from being misunderstood over the field radio. Thus, for these new recruits the alphabet was now Able, Baker, Charlie, Dog, Easy, Fox, George, How, Item, Jig, King, Love, Mike, Now, Oboe, Peter, Queen, Roger, Sugar, Tare, Uncle, Victor, William, X-ray, Yoke, and Zebra.

Nor was time in the Army measured as it was in civilian life. Military time numbered the hours of the day separately from one to twenty-four to differentiate between A.M. and P.M. Thus, 0100 was one o'clock in the morning while 1300 was one o'clock in the afternoon; 0900 was nine in the morning; 2100 was nine in the evening, and so on.

Every aspect of their lives, it seemed, was becoming affected by the Army.

Within a week their typical day had evolved into rising with "First Call" at 05:50 A.M., reveille and roll call ten minutes later, washing-up, shaving, and getting dressed, making their bunks, and falling into line for the five minute march to the mess hall for breakfast at 06:30 A.M. Allowed twenty minutes to eat, they were then marched back to the barracks where they arranged their clothing and prepared their equipment, and fell in to march to their training site. This usually consisted of one hour of calisthenics, two hours of drill, two hours of lectures including first aid training, map reading, weapons familiarization and a host of other courses, a break for dinner—always marching to and from the mess hall—another half-hour of drill, a double-time march to the rifle range for two hours of training and firing, double-time back to the barracks, washing up and preparing to attend supper, and so on.

Basic Training consisted of thirteen weeks of intense physical conditioning and fundamental military indoctrination to prepare the individual civilian inductees for the demands of military life. The first week concentrated on whipping the recruits into top physical condition with intense exercising and running programs while getting them acquainted with their new "best friend," the M-1 .30-caliber Garand rifle. In addition, they learned how to pull guard duty, how to prepare for inspections, and began their Basic Rifle Marksmanship course. The second week continued to focus on physical training with additional exercises and increases in running distances while their rifle course evolved into learning a variety of range and shooting procedures, firing positions, and the use of scorecards as well as some bayonet procedures and associated movements. They also began to prepare for troop formation inspections. The third week concentrated on getting the recruits ready for rifle qualification by focusing on firing from all positions, rapid fire and reloading, sight adjustments, moving with loaded weapons, and firing at moving and pop-up targets while their physical exercises developed into hand-to-hand combat training and grass drills. Inspections of troop ranks without weapons also began. In the fourth week the recruits qualified with their M-1s, made tactical daylight marches, learned security, dispersion and discipline procedures, practiced guerrilla tactics, and more advanced hand-to-hand combat training. At the same time they underwent more intensive running and exercise programs while going through daily inspections, in ranks, with weapons. To the individual inductees, these first four weeks seemed the worst. Although the training would intensify during the following nine, the first four were spent getting into shape and was said to be the "hardening period"—the roughest.[11]

"For those first three—or possibly four—weeks you will bear the greatest part of the painful process of adjusting yourself to an altogether new routine," agreed one old soldier. "In those first three weeks you will get almost the full required dose of confusion and misery. You will be afraid to leave your barracks lest the full wrath of the War Department fall upon you. You will find yourself unbelievably awkward and clumsy when you try to lean the drills and the knowledge of this awkwardness will make you even more awkward. Unless you relax you can be very unhappy during those first three or four weeks."[12]

And unfortunately many were. A number of new recruits wrote of hearing muffled sobs those first few nights at Basic Training. "You would hear crying during the night," agreed Speer. "It was something you tried not to think about but a lot of us were scared and homesick and you would hear muffled crying that would then make you feel sorry for whoever it might be, and it would then cause you to think about home."[13]

Slowly these new recruits grew accustomed to their new existence. According to many trainees, the best practical advise offered by the old soldiers was to read the bulletin board often, keep your eyes open and your mouth shut. Another expanded on that by saying, "Watch your attitude, do your work, respect your superiors, try to get along with your fellow soldiers, keep yourself and your equipment clean at all times, and behave yourself. Do these and you won't have any trouble with the Army."[14]

"Camp Edwards was an all new experience for a boy like me," admitted Speer. "I enjoyed a lot of things about it. It was an all new adventure. I didn't mind getting up for roll call and gettin' up [early]. And people complain about the food—shoot, [I thought] the food was good enough for an ol' farm boy like me."[15]

Needless to say, it was a unique experience for all of these new recruits. Military life and discipline had been alien to many of these boys. Although far from home, Glen was doing his basic training with several other Wayne County, Iowa, boys including Junior Annis, Kermit Hart, Tom Wolverton, Bob Cook, Dick Wilty, and his best friend Wayne Edmondson. He also knew recruit Carl Dunshee from nearby Chariton, Iowa, and several other Lucas County boys. In that aspect at least, he was fortunate. Despite the fact that this group also consisted of a number of boys training together from St. Louis County, Missouri, fifteen from Manchester, New Hampshire, and nearly fifty from the Middlesex County area of Connecticut, most of these young men were drawn from many different states and from many different backgrounds and had been thrown together for the first time. The barracks contained fifty young recruits on each floor, quite often from a wide mix of cultures, backgrounds, and personalities and it took getting used to. Many were still uncomfortable so far away from home. One inductee later recalled he hadn't so much as slept overnight at a friend's house by the time he was sent to basic training, let alone live and get along with fifty other boys who had never met.[16]

Once again, adding to everyone's discomfort was the lack of privacy—sleeping in your underwear in bunk beds arranged in the barracks in double rows with no partitions between the beds, toilets having no partitions between the bowls and located directly across from the sinks and mirrors where others stood shaving, and having to strip down and go into room-size showers with crowds of men. To many of these new recruits it was initially humiliating.

"[T]he best temporary strategy," insisted one new recruit, too embarrassed to use the toilet, "was to wait until taps and lights out.... [but] after a few weeks of community ablutions, I hardly noticed or cared what happened around me."[17]

Within days, their Army life was becoming routine.
(Courtesy Terry Bye)

Slowly, everyone began to become accustomed to their surroundings and to each other. Before long, these farm boys and city boys had all learned to wake up by the bugle, to go to sleep by the bugle, to eat at a certain time, to complete their meal by a certain time, who to salute, when to salute, to keep in step and keep up with others while wearing full field packs on early morning marches, to strip and reassemble a rife both in the daylight and while blindfolded, and at the same time they learned to endure such things as bayonet practice, grenade throwing practice, and constant drilling. In addition they learned how to quickly and efficiently clean and maintain their barracks, the fastest and best shoe or boot shining methods, proper care of their uniforms, proper care and repair of their equipment, proper display of their clothing and equipment, proper procedure for open foot locker inspections, and seemingly endless falling in, falling out, running, hiking, marching, exercising, and calisthenics.

"We have nothing to do until 07:30," complained one recruit, about getting up so early, "so we just sit around and scrub toilets, mop the floors, wash the windows and pick up all the matchsticks and cigarette butts within a radius of 2,000 feet of the barracks."[18]

"It was awfully hard to fall out on time," Joseph H. Scarangella, later assigned to Battery A of the 137th Gun Battalion, agreed. "Making bunks, getting into those leggings, and handling the many small barracks duties constituted a big job to be done by breakfast, [so] we got up earlier and earlier to finish everything."[19]

But within weeks all of these jobs seemed easier and were completed much faster as the recruits became more and more experienced with their daily duties.

Army drill sergeants taught the new recruits the rudiments of military discipline, familiarized and trained them in the use of their weapons and equipment, and motivated them to become highly efficient soldiers. Although it sometimes seemed drill sergeants used some harsh methods, their ultimate goal had several purposes. The tough rudiments of close-order drill instilled discipline and cohesion among the troops, the intense physical training toughened the recruits minds and bodies, and the strict inspections taught the new soldiers Army discipline while promoting camaraderie among them.[20]

These inspections were formal and strict. The inductees were required to lay their equipment and clothing out on top of their beds, arranged in proper order and at precise distances, the items in their footlockers had to be arranged in a particular pattern, and their clothes and equipment in their wall lockers had to be arranged on the shelves and hangers in an exact sequence—Again, the Army had a logical reason for this, even if it made no sense to these young recruits.[21]

"It's typical of army life," insisted one recruit who was getting used to the routine. "You have something to do and you [just] do it. It's dreary and thankless, but not torturous. You are told how to do it and given enough time. While doing it you laugh and talk and swap lies with someone who is just as new to the experience as you are." So together, and working with each other, these recruits learned the basics on how to properly roll a field pack, including bedrolls, and how to properly display their clothes and equipment at the Saturday morning inspections.[22]

"None of us thought of cleaning our bayonets," complained one young G.I. after his first Saturday morning inspection, "so all except two or three were "gigged" on that. So, at eight this a.m. we [all] had to have our rifles torn down to the fifteen main parts and cleaned and inspected [as punishment]."[23]

Physical conditioning, too, got easier as time went on. "[E]very morning we did calisthenics for an hour," recalled recruit Henry Peterson, a Camp Edwards trainee, "[and] every Sunday we marched for 25 miles with full field packs."[24]

"[T]he army has done some good," one trainee reluctantly admitted, "because I didn't even notice the forty or fifty pounds strapped on me for the whole twenty-five miles."[25]

"I weighed 131 pounds when I left home," insisted another G.I. "Carrying my *light* pack, I weigh 217 pounds!"[26]

"A gas mask, full canteen, bayonet, blanket, overcoat and raincoat, tent half and entrenching tools, sox and underwear, pegs and rope, toilet articles, First Aid pack, mess kit, and rifle makes quite a little pack," acknowledged one of the other new recruits.[27]

Of course, the units gradually worked up to packing such heavy loads on those kind of marches. Speer's battalion made longer and longer treks each week during their basic training. They started out with three to five mile hikes. On Tuesday May 25 they made their first thirteen mile hike, covering the distance between Camp Edwards and Scorten Neck, Massachusetts, on foot for their first bivouac. On June 2 they returned to Camp Edwards, making another thirteen mile hike. They continued making thirteen mile hikes each Saturday afterwards. Then on Friday July 16, they made their first 25 mile march by hiking from Camp Edwards to Scorten Neck and back. After that, the 25-mile hikes became weekly events.[28]

"There were some aching muscles in those first few weeks," recalled another Camp Edwards recruit. "Some of the hikes were pretty grueling, and the feet and legs got stiff [but] all in all we did get in shape, and the hikes and exercises grew easier."[29]

"There was an ambulance that followed us [on those hikes]." agreed Speer, "and picked up some of the guys who couldn't make it. But basically it was no big deal. A young man in good shape could hike twenty-five miles [with a heavy pack] with no trouble."[30]

In addition to the morning calisthenics and the weekly 25-mile hikes, the recruits learned to march in close order drill at a cadence of 128 steps per minute. A variety of special cadence counts and chanting in rhythm with their steps—sometimes musically and sometimes in syncopation—was also used to help them endure the tedious drilling. Counting cadence while marching kept the men in step and helped break the monotony.

Another component in their physical training and the Army's toughening process, was the "obstacle course." The recruits had to run the entire circuit in groups of four wearing light equipment—meaning uniform, field jacket, helmet, and heavy boots. It included "besides simple obstacles and rough terrain," reported the *Falmouth* (MA) *Enterprise*, whose reporter was allowed to witness one such class, "crawling under barbed wire, a seven-foot ramp, a long swing hand-over-hand, a 12-foot fence, and a four-foot chasm to leap with aid of a swinging rope. One or two sturdy souls make the leap without touching the rope, and brag a little afterward. The course ends with a nice simple 12-foot pit, to be escaped up a rope. The boys climb out and drop on pine-needles under the trees, panting a little, ready and willing to [good naturedly] criticize the performers who follow them." In the following weeks, as the recruits got in better shape and the course became easier for them, the army made it more difficult. "Next time you see them," the newspaper noted, "they will be zipping around the course with field packs and rifles, which is considerably more of a trick, and maybe the officers will be timing them."[31]

As if all of this wasn't enough—the grueling exercise programs, the conditioning marches and close order drill, the innumerable humiliating inspections, the strenuous work details that included KP duty, trash hauling, toilet scrubbing, floor mopping, window washing, and policing the buildings and grounds—these young recruits endured many additional hours of classroom instruction, lectures, and movies.

Weeks of classroom training consisted of a variety of subjects. Six total hours of instruction were devoted to military courtesy, discipline, and the Articles of War, ten hours were given to sanitation, first aid, and sexual hygiene, three hours to the protection of military information, an hour on Army organization, and seven total hours of "Indoctrination," explaining the nation's war aims along with presenting the latest information on the progress of the war. Other classroom training involved the practical aspects of soldiering such as seven hours of training on "equipment," covering everything from uniforms to pitching tents, eight hours of map and aerial photograph reading, eight hours of lectures regarding field fortification and camouflage, twelve hours of defense training against chemical attack, thirty-six hours of physical hand to hand training, a total of twenty hours training and lectures covering marches and bivouacs, and four hours covering guard duty, twenty hours of drill, and eighteen hours of inspections. The troops also had classes that taught them about night fighting, "dirty" fighting, mines and booby traps. Not all of these classroom sessions were lectures. By late 1943 over 400 training films, many of them high-quality Hollywood productions, were available to the instructors.[32]

Along with a lot of these classes the recruits often received a variety of technical manuals, referred to as TMs, and field manuals, referred to as FMs, while stationed at the base. In fact, it seemed the Army had a booklet for everything. When they first arrived a booklet titled *Welcome to Camp Edwards* was handed out that explained the rules and regulations of the base with a map showing the location of all the important buildings, another titled *So You've Got a Furlough* was later handed out to explain that procedure, as well as booklets on how to avoid venereal disease, intoxication, frivolous spending, con-men, being swindled, and women looking for an easy mark. "Don't mistake that gleam in her eye for love," warned that booklet, "when it may only be anticipation of [getting your] nice fat Government Allotment check." There were also booklets about their steel helmets and how to properly affix the helmet liner, booklets explaining the various chevrons and ribbons they would see others wearing, and booklets that explained who must be saluted and when they must be saluted. "You get a swell feeling inside when you toss a snappy 'highball' at an officer and he tosses one right back at you," the booklet informed the reader. "It makes you feel part of the same swell team." And further noted, "We insist on military courtesy on this Post to help you 'get in the 'groove' right away."

On the range, within just a few days of Basic Training's beginning, the dry-fire drills gave way to live fire practice. The M-1 rifle, which weighed 9 ½ pounds and was 43 inches long—59 inches with the bayonet attached— had an effective combat shooting range of 400 to 700 yards. It was loaded with an open block clip of eight cartridge-shells and fired semi-automatic, meaning the trigger had to be pulled for each shot. Training involved learning to clean, disassemble, reassemble both in the light and in the dark, and to learn to shoot under any conditions, in any weather and under any kind of stress or circumstances. The recruits spent two hours a day at the range firing their assigned M-1 at targets at distances of 100, 300, and 500 yards. Upon qualification Speer received "sharpshooter" which meant he was able to put eight of every ten shots into the bull's-eye circle. "I did pretty good with the rifle," Speer admitted, "but I didn't really like the rifle."[33]

Qualification with the M-1 eventually gave way to qualification or familiarization with machine guns, 45-caliber pistols, Browning Automatic Rifles (BARs) and later grenades, mortars and, for some, artillery.

"An obstacle course was set up on the firing range for the sub-machine gun," advised Glen. "You would walk through a brushy area and silhouettes of men would pop up at you as you walked [along] with that machine gun by your hip." The rapid-fire 45 cal. Machine gun added to Glen's confidence and he made "expert marksman" with it during qualification. "Boy I really did like that Thompson sub-machine gun," professed Speer, who was later issued the weapon and carried it throughout the war. "I really loved that thing and felt safe with it."[34]

Like everything else, grenade practice began with classroom training learning all about the object and the proper form for throwing them— facing the enemy, standing at an angle to control trajectory. The recruits were then taken to the grenade range, where they ran the course one at a time. "We ran relay form," advised one recruit, "starting from a prone position and throwing into a shell hole ahead. Then we'd throw at the next shell hole and repeat the charge and so on for five holes [and] then throw through a hole in a [simulated] building."[35]

Training on the mortar gun was just as detailed. "The whole afternoon was spent in four classes on the sixty millimeter mortar," complained one new recruit. "Whenever we study this stuff we have to learn everything." The first class consisted of teaching the recruits about the weapon's sight, learning all of its parts and their functions. Then, they practiced setting up the sight according to their classroom training. The second class was all about the mortar itself, its parts and their functions, and how to disassemble, clean, pack, and set up the mortar for action. The third class was all about the mortar's shell or ammo, its different parts and their functions and, finally, the fourth class was conducted at the mortar range with hands on experience. "This is a gas pipe with a couple legs," the recruit continued, trying to simplify all the detailed training. "You just drop a shell in it and the shell flies across the country and does a pretty good job where it hits."[36]

Familiarization and training on the big artillery guns was conducted in a similar manner. "The army has an effective (if unflattering) method of teaching us how to do things we were sure we couldn't do," admitted one inductee. "Everything seems to be based upon the theory that all of us have mentalities of only twelve-year-olds."[37]

Hands-on artillery training began with learning how to set up the guns.
(Author's Collection)

Eventually recruits were exposed to a different kind of danger far worse than they had ever known. They were taught to dodge live bullets in simulated combat and to hug the ground and move forward under live machine gun fire. "When the sergeant said to keep your head down [here]," recalled Speer, "you had no problem understanding that."[38]

As they crawled through these "infiltration courses," live machine gun bullets whizzed over them in a steady stream, thirty inches above their heads. In other exercises these recruits fired live ammo at "buttoned up" tanks and flattened themselves out in foxholes as those same tanks rolled over their position. The army did not hesitate to make their training as realistic as possible. Between 1942 to 1944 the Army Ground Forces used 240,000 tons of ammunition and explosives in their training exercises. During that same time there were also a number of accidental casualties.[39]

"While machine gun bullets whizz over plenty close (ever so many are tracers so we could see them)," admitted one army engineer assigned to conducting the course, "they crawl over rocks and through brush, around shell holes and under barbed wire strung everywhere. And to make [their] life more miserable we throw hunks of dynamite out in shell holes and when they get close, we set it off."[40]

"That [course] was a powerfully scary thing," admitted Speer. "I'll never forget that."[41]

Just as memorable or perhaps just as scary for many of these young G.I.s was the treatment they received from their drill instructors. While some of the cadre easily gained the respect and admiration of these new recruits, many others were regarded as some of the most demeaning, foul-mouthed individuals ever to walk the earth.

"Sergeant [John William] Sites was such a mean fella," recalled Speer in thinking back about his Camp Edwards drill instructor. "His favorite saying was 'I'll knock your damn teeth down your throat!'"[42]

"His bark was worse than his bite once you knew him," offered Clyde Libby, a young recruit assigned to the same company as Speer.[43] But although Libby might have had Sites figured out, most of these young recruits had never been exposed to the kind of verbal and mental abuse commonly practiced by some of these drill instructors. While most of the G.I.s eventually learned to tolerate being screamed at by them, the acrimonious methods of many drill sergeants drew the ire of many recruits. A number of them wrote home about their hatred for their Drill Instructors and one G.I. cleaned up, but illustrated quite effectively in a letter home to his parents just how his D.I. often came into the barracks at night and "*asked*" his recruits to "*please* quiet down:"

"If youse blankety-blanked little dash-dashes don't shut your cuss-cuss yaps and get the blankety-blank to sleep," he would scream, "I'm gonna come back up here and make yez scrub the whole blankety-blanked dash-dash cuss-cuss floor with a blankety-blank toothbrush. Now shaddap!"[44]

At the same time, some company cadre NCOs went out of their way to frighten the young recruits physically as well as verbally. Speer vividly recalled how his Camp Edwards' D.I.'s frequently enjoyed causing physical torment as well. "My bed was the bottom bunk right next to the door where you entered the latrine and I often read the Bible and had it on my pillow on my bed," he related. "Anyhow, those sergeants would go out drinkin' every night and come in and begin throwing bayonets at the latrine door [next to where I was laying]. Those bayonets would hit that door and penetrate up to five inches or so and, of course, it was powerfully scary and hard to stay in my bunk but I knew what I would have to go through if I jumped up and ran. So I just laid there trying to ignore them as I read my Bible and pretended it didn't bother me. Then ol' Sergeant Sites would come walkin' over to get their bayonets and would start rubbin' the top of my head and say 'Whats sa maat-ter Private? . . . Ya sca-a-ared?' [but] I wouldn't say nothin'! I knew better."[45]

Glen and many of the other Wayne County boys who were transported out to Camp Edwards that first week of April were all assigned to batteries of the 110th Anti-Aircraft Battalion being formed at that time. This battalion was made up of five companies, or batteries,—designated Headquarters, A, B, C, and D—and each lettered company had four 90mm guns— designated Gun #1, Gun #2, and so on. Generally, 16 men were assigned to each gun—although in some cases only 13 were assigned. Thus, in the case of the 110th AAA Gun Battalion, there was a total of 256 men manning 16 guns in the battalion plus 50 men in Headquarters Battery handling those duties and another 15 men in a "medic" medical detachment. Originally, the 110th AAA had been activated on January 20, 1943, starting out as the 110th Coast Artillery Corps (CAC) when about one-hundred men of the 406th CAC were transferred in from Fort Sheridan, Illinois. By February 10 the battalion, referred to by then as an Anti-Aircraft (AA) Battalion, was brought close to full strength as more men were transferred in from Fort Eustis, Virginia, and from the Army's specialized Anti-Aircraft training school of Camp Davis, North Carolina and its Electrical (training) School of Chicago, Illinois. The battalion then became known as an Anti-Aircraft Artillery (AAA) Battalion, one of the first formed as a 90mm Gun Battalion, as more trainees were brought in from Fort Devens, Massachusetts, around April 8. Most of these were inductees from Maine, New Hampshire, Vermont, Connecticut, and Rhode Island, as well as Massachusetts. During that same time and through April 11, more inductees arrived from the west and mid-west bringing recruits from the states of Kansas, Nebraska, Colorado, North and South Dakota, Minnesota, Wisconsin, Missouri, Illinois, and Iowa.[46]

Speer and his best friend Edmondson were assigned to D-Battery of the 110th AAA, Kermit Hart to A-Battery, Tom Wolverton to Headquarters Battery and a number of others, including Junior Annis, Bob Cook, and Dick Wilty, to C-Battery. Although Glen and Wayne quickly formed a close friendship with Battery-D inductees Bob Lewis of Rapid City, South Dakota, Clyde Libby of Lincoln, Maine, Ray Brassard of New Hampshire and Grayson Tackitt of Kentucky, it was through their C-Battery buddies that they soon became acquainted with a group from St. Louis, including Elmer Potzmann, Harold Mueller, and twins Henry and Walt Thake, in addition to Terry Bye of Rapid City, through his friendship with Lewis.

Each battery of the battalion was housed in separate barracks situated side-by-side along the same side of the street. Thus on the 110th's AAA Battery Street, Headquarters Battery was in one building, A-Battery was housed in the barracks next-door, B-Battery in the neighboring building, C-Battery in the next building, and D-Battery the next building over. In the next successive barracks buildings down that side of the street was the batteries of the 549th AAA Battalion—a unit of 40mm Bofors.[47]

The two-story white-painted wood barracks contained 25 double (bunk) beds on each floor arranged in two rows with a wide aisle down the center of the room. At one end of the barracks was the latrine with its row of toilets opposite a row of wash basins and large shower room, and at the other end of the barracks was the private quarters of the non-commissioned officer in charge—the drill sergeant.

According to a number of inductees, once lights were out there was always the usual attempts to get laughs. "Imitation burps, synthetic breaking of wind, and the whistle-snore routine were just a few of the things tried," recalled one inductee.[48] But the ground floor of D-Battery barracks had its own denizen entertainer. Every group, every training session it seems, had someone who eventually became the most memorable. Someone—whether for being really good or for being really bad, whether for being extremely energetic or for being a gold—bricker— who would eventually stand out in everyone's memory years later. In this group it was a young, some-what comical inductee remembered by nearly everyone only by his nick-name "Peter Rabbit."

"Peter Rabbit had a small pointy face," recalled Glen, "that reminded many of us of a [large] mouse face . . . . but he was funny and everyone liked him, so you never thought much about his looks."[49]

Peter Rabbit's real name was actually Otto Charles Richts from St. Louis. Within the first few weeks of Basic Training Richts had firmly established his memorable reputation among the recruits as well as the drill sergeant.

"Many a night, after lights out in the barracks, he would tell us stories using a Donald Duck voice," related Speer, "and he really sounded like [Walt Disney's cartoon character] Donald Duck and of course we would all lay there in the dark and begin to laugh." After several minutes into the story, the volume of the laughter intensified and became increasingly uncontrollable. "Finally, the door at the far end of the barracks would fly open," remembered Glen, "and Sergeant Sites would come stormin' into the room demanding to know what we were laughing about and yelling at us to stop immediately." These boys got by with this on several different occasions but finally they reached their Sergeant's limit. "One night," recalled Speer, "he came stormin' out of his quarters raising so much cane with us that he ended it by threatening 'If I hear any more noise you'll all be up scrubbin' the barracks!' and as he abruptly turned to head back to his room we all heard Peter Rabbit in a very low Donald Duck voice count off: 'Hut— two-three-four—hut.' Boy! Sites went berserk! He ran over screaming at us as he turned on the lights, ran up and down the isle between the rows of bunks ranting and raving and getting into every one's face ordering each and every one of us out of our bunks. We were up all that night in our underwear scrubbing the barrack's floors with toothbrushes."[50]

What was most remarkable was the fact that no one, other than Sergeant Sites, ever got angry at Richts. None of the recruits remember ever getting mad at him. They took everything he did in stride, including even the punishment he often caused them.

"At first everyone thought he was dumb because he was always getting into trouble,"remembered Speer. "Before we would go out on [those twenty-five mile] hikes, Peter Rabbit would always do something and get put on KP. And as we marched out past the mess hall there would be Peter Rabbit standing in the doorway, smiling real big and waving goodbye to us. After a while we all began to realize Peter Rabbit might be smarter than we were."[51]

Perhaps one benefit of Richts' behavior was that he often drew the drill sergeant's anger and attention away from the others. "He had the nerve to do things we wouldn't do," insisted Glen. Every time Sites got mad or upset with a trainee, he would get up in the recruit's face and, as he clenched his teeth tightly together and glared at them, threaten with his favored line, "I'll knock your damn teeth down your throat."

"It would scare all of us recruits except the one known to everyone as Peter Rabbit," recalled Speer. "Peter Rabbit would stand up to Sergeant Sites, sometimes nose to nose, and say 'Go ahead. I dare ya!'" But the Sergeant would ignore him and, with a scowl, walk away. "Peter knew more about the military than the rest of us," noted Glen, "and he was smart enough to have Sites court-martialed if he ever did hit him." Peter Rabbit was also well aware of a notice on the company bulletin board which forbid noncommissioned officers from physically harming, or even touching, soldiers under their command. But the other recruits weren't as convinced their sergeant remembered, or had even read, that bulletin. "Peter Rabbit had the nerve to do things we wouldn't do," Speer repeated, "and it was often something funny. He kept us entertained."[52]

Although "Peter Rabbit" helped break the monotony of their existence, the same general training routine continued day in and day out. Typically, the arduous training day ran from 05:50 to 22:00 but could sometimes be longer when they drew K.P. duty, a coal detail or some other special assignment such as the company bugler. "I'm the first one up (the cooks wake me up) and the last one to bed," complained Ed Kosicki, bugler for Battery-B of the 110th AAA. "I play 'Reveille,' 'Assembly,' and 'Taps.' Big Mistake! I never should have mentioned that I could play trumpet.[53]

"There were nice things about training [at Camp Edwards]," recalled recruit Joseph Eckenrode, assigned to Battery-D, 110th AAA, "especially the weekends. The boys from New England were the luckiest. A weekend pass was just like a furlough to them. They would go home. For the gang who couldn't go home there was plenty to do in Falmouth, Buzzards' Bay, Onset, New Bedford, Providence, and Boston."[54]

"The very first leave we ever got from Camp Edwards," recalled Speer, "I and Wayne Edmondson and some of the other boys, we called for a taxi and here come a 1941 Ford, a blue one, and we piled in there and told him we wanted to go to Malden, Massachusetts."[55]

Malden was a suburb on the north side of Boston. East of there was the community of Revere, the boy's true destination, where the Revere Beach Amusement Park, one of the oldest in America, was located. Speer and Edmondson climbed into the front seat of the cab next to the driver as Lewis, Brassard, and Tackitt piled into the back. "So we got into this '41 Ford and headed for Boston," advised Glen, "and we were all happy and excited."[56]

The distance between Camp Edwards and Revere, Massachusetts, is about sixty miles and the sleek-looking fancy cab seemed to be covering those miles much too slow for these boys. "So we asked the driver if he could speed it up a little," remembered Speer, "and he said he didn't know if he could. So somebody in the backseat said 'well if we take up a little bit of money among us, you think you could step on it' and he thought maybe he could. So we did and he did and I know we made the rest of that trip at seventy miles an hour."[57]

Although gas was being "war rationed" at the time causing the taxi driver to demand dearly for the extra that he burned with the increased speed, the boys thought it was well worth the money. "We shouldn't have been doing something like that," admitted Speer, "but we were so thrilled to have that first leave from Camp Edwards and wanted to enjoy as much of it at the amusement park as possible."[58]

Revere Beach was a three-mile long stretch of wide, broad beach that was lined with hundreds of amusements, entertainment halls, fun houses, and food stands. In operation since the 1890s, the park was widely known for its Cyclone roller coaster and other rides such as the Virginia Reel, the Wild Mouse, its Dodgem Cars, and the Hippodrome Carousel as well as Bluebeard's Funhouse, among many others. Immense crowds played on the beach or strolled through the many blocks of shops and entertainment while all the time accompanied by the strains of laughter and talking, loud music, carnival barkers, and the roller coasters and other rides in continual operation throughout the area.

"You see," advised Glen, "I was a born-again Christian at the age of sixteen and at eighteen I still believed in living in a Christian way so I [and my friends] didn't go out and drink [and gamble] like a lot of the others did. I and Wayne Edmondson always used our leaves and passes to go to amusement parks, the beach, sight-seeing, drinking malted milks, and such. At [Revere Beach] we got fried clams and French fries—an all-new experience for Iowa farm boys."[59]

When there was not enough time to go to the Boston area for entertainment, the trainees found plenty to do on the base. Some of the latest motion pictures were shown at the theaters on the post. The cost of admission was fifteen cents. "We also can get gum (three cents), and candy and ice cream and all such stuff at our P.X. all day, every day," offered one recruit. The nearby U.S.O. Club at Buzzards Bay had a soda fountain, sandwich counter, a barber and shoe shine shop, novelty and magazine stands, and it provided lots of magazines, games, books and writing tables for those who just wanted to hang out. "They will loan you cameras, wrap and mail packages, give free movies and refreshments, and pass out stacks and stacks of writing paper," advised one draftee. A chaplain at the center was always ready to talk or to listen upon the request of any soldier, and there were places to make a three-minute recording or to get a portrait to send home. "They have such stuff for anyone," noted a recruit, "plenty of swell things to do . . . just no time to do them."[60]

The United Service Organization, more commonly referred to as the USO, had established a large recreation hall at Buzzards Bay, Massachusetts, across the Cape Cod Channel from the base, to "get the boys off the street corners," "counsel homesick youngsters," and "plan for them morale boosting recreation" according to the organization's pamphlets. The USO center was located at 239 Main Street and it was here that young soldiers came to dance, relax, write home, and pass the time. Milkshakes here cost a dime, so Glen and his friends came here whenever possible.[61]

"Camp Edwards was a real nice place in the summer time," remembered Speer. "We would go to the U.S.O. to get away from everything or we would go to the beach. I went to the ocean quite a few times. I and Wayne Edmondson would sometimes go and lay on the beach, look up at the sky, and talk about home, the Army, the war, and other things, and talk about what bothered us and what didn't."[62]

It helped being from the farm-country of the mid-west to make being stationed at Camp Edwards something special to these boys. Not all of the recruits, however, shared Glen and Wayne's appreciation for the resort qualities of the area. "Basic training at Camp Edwards on Cape Cod sounds [great] right?" Franklin Johnson, a draftee from Naugatuck, Connecticut assigned to B-Battery of the 110th AAA, noted rather wryly. "[Well] its [just] sand, loaded with sand! Every place you went you [got sand all over you] and your barracks would be filled with sand that had blown in."[63]

Their training continued and intensified through the following weeks. "[It] was drill, drill, drill in the gun park and maintenance until we thought we would rub the surface off the guns," complained one Camp Edwards artillery trainee. "Other subjects were taught too, and there was night training, but we were doing things in a bigger way . . . . We began to dig in our equipment and started to fill sandbags with the hard Massachusetts earth."[64]

The first time the guns were taken out on a bivouac—towing them to an area other than the artillery range and putting them in place, digging them into position to shoot—called "boogying down"—it became a much more complicated process than expected. "These guns we have are seven and a half tons and you would have to jockey that gun around through the sand," declared Johnson of Battery-B.[65]

"A six-ton Corbitt truck is what we pulled them with," advised Speer. "[When] we got out there in the Massachusetts back country, in the scrub brush, the gun emplacements were already dug." The guns just had to be pulled to the site and backed into the pit. Sergeant Sites was in charge of Glen's crew. "[T]he driver of our truck was just having a horrible time getting that gun backed into place," recalled Speer. "The other three guns had all been backed into position while ours hadn't been yet and the Sergeant was standin' there shoutin' and hollerin' and the Captain was yelling and getting upset about that gun not getting backed in there. Finally, bein' just an ol' farm boy who had worked around different kinds of equipment all his life, I stepped up to the Captain and said 'Sir, I can back that gun up in there for ya' and he stopped yelling and said 'What'd you say soldier?' and I repeated 'I can back that up in there for ya.' He glared at me a moment and then hollered over at Sergeant Sites, 'Get that driver down out of there and let this boy back that in there.' So I climbed up into the truck and started backing it. 'Course I'd stop every ten or twelve feet and look back to see how I was doin' and luckily I backed it right into place on my very first time. I climbed down out of the truck and walked back over to where I had been, and thought nothing more about it."[66]

Several days later all the troops were individually called into the Captain's office to be assigned specific jobs or responsibilities on the gun crews. As Speer entered and stood at attention his Captain, Julius Reiver, sitting behind a big wooden desk, asked Speer what job he wanted on the gun crew. "I was scared to tell the Captain this," Speer later recalled, "but he asked, so I said 'Sir, I don't want none, Sir.'"

Calmly, Reiver sat there somewhat sympathetic and asked Speer what he meant by that. "Because," Glen answered, "that gun just simply scares me."

"It had a recoil," Speer later recounted, "of about 29-inches, I think. It was right near a yard, it seems to me. Anyway, it was just a powerful [and] pretty scary thing to me."[67]

Harold Mueller, assigned to the motor pool division of C-Battery and who pulled Gun #2, agreed. "Shooting that gun in the dark," he noted years later, "you *had* to know just how far that gun recoiled or else it would kill you."[68]

Captain Reiver sat there a moment looking at Speer without a word. "Aren't you that boy that backed the gun in for me the other day?" he finally asked.

"Yes Sir," answered Speer.

"How would you like to report to the motor pool in the morning?" asked Reiver.

"I would like that very much, Sir," responded Glen. So, with the stroke of a pen, Ivan G. Speer was reassigned to the motor pool division of the 110th AAA Gun Battalion.

As part of D-Battery, Speer was assigned to pull Gun #3. By that evening he found out that his friends, Wayne Edmondson and Junior Annis had also gotten assigned to the motor pool.

"Since we were [assigned] to a ninety-millimeter anti-aircraft gun crew," revealed Speer, "we all thought that would be a pretty safe outfit. Anti-aircraft fire, and all, we thought, would probably be back there behind the lines somewhere."[69]

"After countless tedious hours of aiming and sighting practice, triangulation and dry runs," recalled one of the trainees, "we took to the range." The 110th's first practice exercise with live ammo came at the camp's common range, about a mile north of Camp Edwards. Then they were off to the artillery field at Wellfleet. "Camp Wellfleet and the sand dunes," recalled another trainee, "where the wind howled in off the ocean, and tent pegs refused to stay rooted in the sand."[70]

"It was a great sight," recalled Mueller, "with sixteen guns and their support equipment and vehicles moving in a convoy up the main road on the Cape." Each of the four batteries took all four of their guns and once at the site, began to set the guns up to begin firing exercises and to bivouac for several days. Here the boys also found their physical training of equal importance. "One tent after another went flying off into the windswept

---

country side," complained a recruit, "with its owners chasing after it." Finally the cadre taught the boys to use sandbags to hold their tents in place.[71]

Wellfleet was 54 miles northeast of Camp Edwards on the opposite side of the crescent-shaped Cape Cod peninsula in the area commonly referred to as the Lower Cape. The artillery range was established one mile east of South Wellfleet on a bluff overlooking the sea. It was here that the recruits began hearing such terms as "ack-ack boys" in reference to the gun crews, "puttin' steel on target" when talking about firing the 90mm guns, and "runnin' gun" in reference to transporting or hauling the 90mm between the range and the camp. The slang-terms of "boogying down," in reference to digging the guns into place and lowering its metal platform and outrigger legs to ready it for firing and "boogying up" in reference to folding the platforms up to their towing positions to ready it for moving to another location, also became common usage among many of the crew after being here. Tow planes flew out over the ocean past the site pulling large red cloth banners, called sox or sleeves by the artillery crews, as targets for the guns. "We'd shoot at those socks," recalled Speer in amazement. "I always wondered if those guys flying those airplanes ever realized just how dangerous it was what they were doing!"[72]

These targets had copper wires woven into their fabric so the gun-laying radar could detect them but the gun crews also used optical sights to track the targets as well, using directors and plotting boards. A mechanical computer computed the fuse settings for the fuse cutters while the gunnery units learned how to fire at a variety of aerial targets including crossing, diving and incoming aircraft, as well as in both high and low altitude paths. The machine gun operators assigned to each battery also practiced firing their guns here at balloons, target missiles, and towed sleeves.

The established anti-aircraft procedure was to set the battery's four guns up in a diamond pattern in order to "box-in" or "bracket" any passing enemy airplane with artillery fire. Each gun was dug in at a different point of the pattern and, terrain permitting, each AAA battalion was dug in or set out in four diamond arrangements. One day, on Tuesday July 20, while firing at these targets during a training exercise, all four guns of Battery-C were firing at the moving artillery sock at the same time. At one point, as the other guns fired over Gun #1, an explosion occurred that sent shrapnel in all directions. "It must of been faulty [ammo] or the fuse malfunctioned," reported Harold Mueller, nearby at Battery-C's Gun #2. "It was a terrific explosion," added Elmer Potzmann, also standing nearby. "At about 30 or 40 yards out [after being fired], [the round] exploded. I was close enough that I was deaf for about five days." Recruit Harvey

Edds of B-Battery, set up a short distance away, was sitting on his machine gun watching the exercise when the premature explosion occurred. "My machine gun was a water-cooled type," he advised, "with a two gallon [water] tank [and] a 15-foot hose attached. I was sitting on the tank when a piece of shrapnel hit near me and cut the hose in two." Several men on C-Battery's Gun #1 were injured, including a good friend of Mueller's— Don Simons of Winsted, Connecticut who was hit in the face by shrapnel that nearly tore his upper lip off. Also injured was Lieutenant Charles Salidas, who suffered a severe wound to the neck, and Bill Stroud of Marceline, Missouri, who was hit in the foot by shrapnel that tore off his toe. The Gunnery Sergeant, Joseph Andrews, was killed outright. "You could of put a canteen cup into the hole in his back [made] from the shrapnel," reported Mueller after examining him.[73]

Finally, after thirteen weeks, basic training came to an end for this group and the entire battalion scattered to all parts of the country. Between August 29 to September 12 the Wayne County boys all went home to Iowa on furlough. "We took trains back then," advised Speer. "We [Edmondson and I and the others] took a train into Chicago where we had to switch and I remember switching trains there and [to catch] the next train out we had to run [several blocks] all the way across Union Station, but we made all of our connections."[74]

Glen home on leave, September 1943. L-R, his mother Elsie Speer, brother L. Rex, Glen, and his father Dewey Speer.

By mid-September all of the battalion had returned to Camp Edwards to begin their advanced training. "Advanced training seemed like basic training all over again," complained one of the recruits. "We learned how to drive trucks [and] some of us specialized [in] radio, radar, machine guns, and the 90s," another agreed. "Gradually we became experts, tactically on field problems and as artillerymen."[75]

Commander of the Camp Edwards post was Maj. Gen. Francis P. Hardaway, transferred in from the Army's west coast Anti-Aircraft Replacement Training Center at San Diego's Camp Callan in April, 1943. Second in command, in charge of daily administrative and day to day operations, was Col. Roy W. Smith, who came from the Camp Davis, North Carolina, Anti-Aircraft Training School in June of 1943. When the 110th CAC was originally organized at Camp Edwards that previous January, the battalion had been placed under the command of Lieutenant Colonel Supple. The following April, when the battalion was re-designated the 110th Anti-Aircraft Artillery, it was placed in command of Major (later Lt. Col.) William F. Curren Jr. of Columbia, South Carolina. Captain Theodore (Ted) H. Silverman of Boston was placed in command of A-Battery, Captain James E. Chase of Elgin, Illinois, was placed in command of B-Battery, Captain Lester K. Born of New York's Columbia University, was placed in command of C-Battery, and D-Battery was placed under the command of Captain (later Lt. Col.) Julius Reiver of Wilmington, Delaware. Later it would become apparent that Battery-D would have an advantage over the other batteries. Its commander would prove to be much more aggressive and outspoken than the other battery commanders and a whole lot more political.

After graduating from Basic Training Speer was promoted to Tec 5—Technician Fifth Grade with two stripes over a "T" on his sleeve—and with his return to the base his education became more highly specialized. "[Our] training grew more advanced as we shifted into regular jobs," explained one of the newly graduated G.I.s "Some became cannoneers, some communications men, others trackers and radar operators. The bulk of our training from this point on was in our own jobs." This also included members of the gun crew specializing as observers, trackers and plotters. Others as ammo carriers, loaders, and shooters, and still others as drivers, machine-gunners, and radio men.[76]

In the Army's Driving and Mechanics School Glen learned automotive repair, advancing through a Primary course, a Basic course, and an Advanced Automotive course. He also learned such strange terms as "the grandma gear," as military slang for low gear and the "Rachel gear" as slang for high. And, as a mechanic, he was taught the basics of working on both diesel and gasoline engines.

"While working under the big trucks," Speer admitted, "sometimes I would [attach] a good-sized wrench on a big nut or bolt and I'd be laying underneath there sleeping. The Sergeant would walk by and see me laying under the truck and think I was busy working. I got a lot of extra rest that way."[77]

Staff Sergeant Walter R. Pettyjohn headed up the motor pool for D-Battery and Buck Sergeant Ernest L. Francisco was second in command. Each battery's motor pool consisted of four six-ton Corbitt prime movers to tow the four guns, seven two-and-a-half-ton 6X6 trucks, two three-quarter-ton Dodge weapons carriers, two ammo trailers, four jeeps, and a large amount of miscellaneous gear such as camouflage netting and sandbags.

In the battalion's advanced training there were many more dry runs in the gun park, gun crew members practicing their procedures, machine gunners practicing theirs, drivers learning how to drive and maneuver their trucks and prime movers, getting their military license, and more bivouacs. "[M]y first trip in an army truck," recalled one young recruit, "was an experience that I shall never forget. . . . It is fairly decent riding when we are going along a paved road, but when we leave the road, as we often do, and cross over open fields and through woods you get shaken and knocked around until you are actually dizzy. . . . The commands 'Truck and Detruck' were new ones to me, but I [quickly became] used to them."[78]

Over and over during the next several weeks the battalion would go out and move into position, set up, and make many more dry runs until everyone's duties were performed automatically and all the procedures had become etched into their minds.

One of the most memorable aspects of bivouacking for these boys was living in tents and eating out of cans—a part of Army life they would always remember with disdain. On such outings they were provided a wide range of food possibilities that they would eventually learn to accept and get used to. A and B rations were prepared in mobile kitchens and was hot food similar to what could be obtained back at the base. Combat rations consisted of U-rations, sometimes called the 5-in-one and later the 10-in-one ration, that provided a day's ration for five, or later ten, men. It was the bulky U-rations that were issued to the armor and artillery units. Most of the food in a U-ration case was packed in various sets of cans providing five different meals. More practical were the C-rations, a flat tin containing a set of six small cans. Two of the cans provided the soldier with breakfast, two contained staples for a midday meal and two provided him supper. Although the sets of C-ration contents varied, the favorite was one having baked beans and chunks of meat and vegetables and another that contained a can of candy and crackers. D-rations was an emergency ration of small blocks of chocolate fortified with vitamins, sometimes called a D-bar. Although the C and D rations were popular under most circumstances, the K-rations were probably the most popular of all.

K-rations came in three small convenient boxes containing a can for each meal—meat and egg for breakfast, processed cheese for mid-day, and meat for supper—with biscuits, crackers, dextrose tablets, a soluble coffee packet, a fruit bar, a chocolate bar, bouillon, lemon juice crystals, sugar tablets, a stick of chewing gum, and a pack of four cigarettes.

Needless to say, these teenage troops began to appreciate the food back at the base and, in fact, seemed to crave it in some cases. "Down in one area of Camp Edwards," noted Glen, "there was a place to get pork chop sandwiches. They were so-o-o good and s-o-o thick." It started out with someone in the D-Battery motor pool hearing about the pork chop sandwiches and sending a driver down there in a jeep one day to pick some up for the crew at lunch time. Discovering how good they were and finding out they could get these sandwiches throughout the day, a driver would make a number of runs down there at mid-morning and again at mid-afternoon. Once word got around to the other batteries, they were sending drivers down to do the same. "You'd see Battery-A down there in a 6X6," said Speer, "and as time went on we were running three or four rigs down there to get pork chop sandwiches." The motor pool boys eventually admitted the situation seemed to be getting out of hand. At any one time there were more vehicles down there than at the maintenance shop. "Finally," confessed Speer, "Sergeant Pettyjohn and [the other commanding officers] began to notice the problem and orders were issued that no more [Army] vehicles could be used to go down to the pork chop place."[79]

"You see," admitted Glen, "us Wayne County boys [and the others] all tried to have fun wherever we were. We tried not to worry about what might happen [to us in the war] and [we] tried to enjoy each day that was there."[80]

Another enjoyable aspect found with the motor pool assignment was their freedom to take vehicles out for test drives whenever they took a notion. "After working on them," admitted Glen, "Wayne and I would tell the Sergeant we had to take the jeeps out on a test drive. Well, there was a sand pit at one end of Camp Edwards where [military] prisoners worked loading sand onto trucks with shovels. Wayne did most of the driving then and I would get into the passenger side and we would go out toward the pit and make that jeep perform just like you see in the movies [today]."[81]

The two boys would drive down the road past the sand pit so fast that the jeep would hit a big drop in the road near there, bounce out, and go airborne past the area. "We could get goin' fast enough," advised Speer, "that we could airborne it for quite a ways."[82]

Edmondson and Speer performed their aerial acrobatics with a jeep opposite the pit every day. "It got so the prisoners would come to expect it," noted Glen. "They would look for us, see us commin' and stop work in order to watch us perform." This continued for quite some time with no repercussions. "One day," advised Speer, "we airborned a jeep and when it [came down] the engine was still runnin' full-bore, or wide open, and we shucked out or hauled the inserts out of it—nearly blew the engine. When we got back with the jeep we told Sergeant Francisco about the [engine] problems but said we had no idea what might have caused them. He just couldn't understand what had happened to it—it had been runnin' so good when we left, he said."[83]

That incident brought the aerial acrobatic performances and some of their other shenanigans to an end. "We were kinda scared about that one," admitted Glen. "Had they known some of the things we done, why we would have been court-martialed forever."[84]

The Air Corps has nothing on us

This cartoon by Pvts. Harry Hogan and Don McGrath of Camp Edwards first appeared in *The Camp News*. Quite possibly it was inspired by the antics of Speer and Edmondson. (*This Army Stuff*)

Late in the fall of 1943 the 110th AAA got another leave but not with enough time for the Wayne County boys to go back home to Iowa. "So I had a friend," said Speer, "Clyde Libby of Lincoln, Maine, who wanted me to go home with him to visit his home and family."[85]

The battalion only got a three day pass. It was just enough time for the New Englanders to go home. "[So I] asked him to come up to Lincoln with me," advised Clyde. "My brother Floyd Libby took a day off from work and went hunting with Glen and me and we got a deer."[86]

"[Clyde] was from a fine family of folks," remembered Glen. "They seemed to live a good life and we all sat around talking about [deer hunting], eating apple pie, and drinking coffee. It was a very enjoyable time; a very enjoyable trip."[87]

After all the recruits had returned to Camp Edwards they were instructed to mail out their insurance forms and wills. Glen, along with the others, had filled out his insurance papers and will the previous September 22, listing his 13-year-old brother Lloyd Rex Speer as benefactor and his father Dewey O. Speer as executor of the will. These forms were mailed to Iowa on December 3, 1943.

"We are not having these documents made out with the thought of their ever being needed," Captain Reiver assured his recruits' parents in an enclosed letter. "They are merely part of the normal administration work of the Army . . . . Please keep them in a safe place."[88]

Three days later the 110th AAA Gun Battalion was ordered to Camp Kilmer, New Jersey, a known staging area for troops being shipped overseas.

L-R: Joe Adamowicz, O. Charles Richts [Peter Rabbit], Bill Clear, Ed Abate, Ernest Francisco, and August Tidlund in front of the D-Battery office. (Courtesy of Julius & Iona Reiver)

Back row L-R: Sgt. Bill Nelson, Harold Dunlap, Leo Clegg, Henry Omen, Glen Speer, unkn., Wayne Edmondson, unkn., Lloyd Noteboom. Front row L-R: Tom Monahan, Stan Pycior, George Slaven, Bernard Picinisco, George Peikett, Deryl Wergin, Gerald Fullington outside the battery's barracks. (Courtesy of A. William Nelson)

CHAPTER 3

A Trip to Europe at Uncle Sam's Expense: Aboard the *Queen Mary*

Camp Kilmer was a 1,544 acre site outside of Stelton, New Jersey, first activated in June of 1942 as a military staging area for the New York Port of Embarkation. Consisting of several hundred barracks, 29 mess halls, six telephone centers, five chapels, five PXs, five theaters, a large commissary, a full-size hospital and a wide variety of other buildings, the base housed 35,386 enlisted men along with 2,074 officers. The encampment was named in honor of Joyce Kilmer, a thirty-one year old soldier and renowned poet killed in France during World War I, who was born and raised at the nearby New Jersey town of New Brunswick.

Main Gate, Camp Kilmer, New Jersey 1943. (Author's Collection)

The battalion was trained out to this New Jersey site on the afternoon of December 6 and arrived later that evening. Throughout the day additional units arrived at this location from various nearby military bases, including Fort Dix, Fort Devens, and a number of others.

Although no military authorities would tell them, the boys knew they were probably getting pretty close to being shipped overseas. Camp Kilmer was the nation's busiest departure station. Its main function was to prepare and equip the troops for overseas transit and the authorities there were giving out two-day weekend passes like tissue paper.

The base was thirty miles south of New York City and fifty-five miles northeast of Philadelphia with bus and rail service to both points. The cost of a round-trip bus or train ticket to the city of New York was one dollar. The guys went there on many of these passes to take in all of the tourist sites they had heard or read about. On his first pass, Glen was craving ice cream and wanted a chocolate sundae. He and Edmondson went out and ate hot dogs, fried steaks, and topped it all off with huge chocolate sundaes on their way into the big city.[1]

"I and Wayne and some of the others went into New York and saw the Empire State Building, the museums, and Radio City Music Hall," declared Speer.[2]

During their first two weeks at Camp Kilmer all the units stationed there received refresher training and prepared for intra-company competitive drills. They practiced daily in close order and manual of arms drill. To help them prepare for their impending trip overseas, the Army passed out another pamphlet. Titled *A Short Guide To Great Britain*, the 38-page booklet briefed the servicemen with some historical background on the country along with its customs, its monetary system, and some of its more popular slang terms. It ended with a three-page glossary of language differences that exist between the Britons and Americans explaining: "The accent will be different from what you are used to and many of the words will be strange . . . but you will get used to it."[3]

Troops were instructed to keep their equipment packed and ready to go. Then, on December 21 the battalion was restricted to barracks. Meanwhile, in a radio address President Roosevelt assured all the mothers throughout America that none of their sons—no American soldier—would be going overseas during the Christmas holiday season.[4]

As newspapers repeated FDR's pledge in the following days, all of the 110th AAA and thousands of other soldiers at Camp Kilmer were loaded onto trains in full gear sometime around 02:30 on December 23 and transported to Hoboken. "After walking three blocks with full field pack and a duffle bag," reported Sergeant Eckenrode, "the battalion boarded a ferry."[5]

The group marched from the train depot to the New Jersey docks at Weehawken where they boarded a number of small vessels for a trip across the Hudson River to the New York passenger ship terminals. There, they were directed to board the *Queen Mary*.

"Now that was a huge thing to look at," noted Glen. "For us farmboys who had never seen a ship, loading cranes, or harbors, [this] was all a huge, awesome, scary sight. Many of us had never seen the ocean or any big ocean liner. It had a tremendous affect." In fact, many of these small-town country boys were absolutely stunned at the length and height of the great ocean liner when they first saw it. "I remember thinking this ship will never sail," recalled Lester Cohen of B-Battery, and for some time afterward he remained convinced the ship was so big it would surely sink.[6]

The troops were directed off the small ferry boats and over to the Pier 90 Terminal building by the Transportation Corps—soldiers identified by their red and gold armbands—who then chalked a number onto the helmets of the new arrivals. As the boys were lined up inside the building, a slightly festive atmosphere was created by a military band playing World War I tunes such as the "U.S. Field Artillery March," Over There," and the "Liberty Loan March," while Red Cross volunteers handed out cloth "overseas bags" filled with a variety of toiletries, a sewing kit, and other necessities, and served coffee and doughnuts.

"I couldn't believe that they charged us for the doughnuts," one G.I. bitterly complained. The sewing kits and other items were handed out free. "It was all that I got free from the Red Cross," complained another.[7]

The British registered Cunard-White Star Liner *Queen Mary* was the fastest ship in the world at the time. At 1,019 feet in length and 81,235 tons, the giant ocean liner nonetheless had broken the North Atlantic crossing record in 1938. It was the desperate need for troop transports during World War II that made it necessary to use a wide variety of vessels. In addition to old military ships and freighters, prewar passenger liners had to be requisitioned and converted over for use. Among these were a number under American registry, British registry, and vessels under the registry of other friendly nations such as French and Dutch liners. To obtain the maximum capacity space, these ships were stripped out and all comforts and luxuries were removed. In addition, they were painted a dull misty gray to help it blend in with the distant horizon. These fast passenger liners were able to complete their journey across the Atlantic in five to seven days, depending upon the weather. Such speed allowed these ships to dispense with the slower convoy procedures necessary for most other vessels. At Britain's offer, the U.S. Army began using the *Queen*

Mary, which could carry up to 15,000 soldiers on a single voyage, as their preferred troop ship carrier in January of 1942.

For the most part, the units conducted their movements from Camp Kilmer to the harbor under cover of darkness. The great ship was moored at Pier 90, on Manhattan's west side at 12th Avenue and 50th Street. Boarding was done by the numbers chalked onto the G.I.s' helmets. As the numbers were called out, each man then came forward, his last name was called and he answered with his first name and middle initial. As his name was checked off the boarding list he was directed forward and struggled up the steep gangplank fully equipped wearing his helmet, backpack and his cartridge belt with his bayonet, canteen, and gas mask attached, and his rifle slung over his shoulder, dragging his 120-pound barracks bag. Once on board he was handed a small blue card that informed him of his room or bunk assignment and he was then led or directed straight to his berth.

Loading of this big ship was accomplished in as little as five hours— from the time the first troops arrived at the pier to the time the last soldier passed over the gangway. To accomplish such a fast embarkation, the established procedure was to direct the troops straight to their quarters as each crossed over the gangway. Upon arriving at his compartment the soldier was then instructed to arrange his equipment as tightly as possible in his limited assigned space and then to crawl up into his bunk and remain there until the announcement that embarkation had been completed. There was to be no wandering around, getting in the way, or doing anything that might impede the billeting of the continuing arrival of troops. To enforce this procedure, M.P.s closely patrolled the decks.[8]

"Our tiny cabin would comfortably accommodate two tourists in twin beds," complained one G.I., "but now fifteen soldiers were to sleep in racks of five bunks each stacked against three walls." Speer and Edmondson also recalled a room full of men in their tiny cabins but, according to Sergeant Eckenrode the men of Battery-D, 110th AAA, were somewhat fortunate. They were all assigned to state rooms. "[I] slept in the library, along with umpteen hundred other guys," complained Leslie Lyon of Battery-B, while others of his battery were assigned to another large room on a different deck. "We were on the top deck in the old children's playroom," advised Frank Wisniewski [9]

The *Queen Mary* had 776 first class suites and state rooms, 784 tourist or 2nd class cabins, and 579 third class (steerage) cabins. They were all fitted out with "standee bunks," a rectangular frame of tubular steel, mounted on hinges and bolted to the bulkhead that supported three, five, or six canvas stretchers that would accommodate three, five or six sleeping soldiers. These hanging bunks or hammocks were strong and lightweight making it possible to pack many more men into the available space. In addition, in some areas—mostly the lounges, gyms, pool areas and auditoriums—three men were assigned to each canvas to sleep in rotating shifts or eight hours each over a twenty-four hour period. G.I.s referred to these as "hot bunks" because they were always occupied. As soon as one soldier woke up and crawled out, another soldier was scheduled to crawl in. Troops billeted in these areas used the centrally located public restrooms. Those housed in the third class cabins shared bathroom facilities with a number of other third class rooms down the hall from their cabins and those rooming in the first and second class staterooms had a restroom connected to each cabin.

Each of the ship's cabins was fitted out with 15 to 18 triple-tiered standee bunks. In addition to the individual rooms, the Observation Lounge and Midshipman's Bar was converted into a maze of five-tiered, and the bottoms of the boarded-over swimming pools was filled to capacity with a forest of seven-tiered frames. The standee bunks were also collapsible, or folded up, to facilitate more space during the daytime or for cleaning of the rooms.[10]

These canvas bunks sagged when occupied thereby allowing only about two feet of space between each bunk for sleeping. They allowed little room for tossing and turning, and gently swayed with the ship's motion. The tendency for most G.I.s when they first entered their assigned quarters was to choose the bottom "rack," as the standee bunks were soon dubbed. But many soldiers quickly learned that the best rack was the top one. Although more difficult to climb into, there was no low-hanging swag over you and no one above you getting seasick. "We were herded in there like a bunch of cattle," complained Glen. The rooms were crowded, stuffy, and full of equipment and most of them were located below the water level, scaring many of the mid-westerners. In fact, Battery-D was assigned rooms on E-Deck, just four levels above the bottom of the ship. "I just knew," worried Speer, "that if we were torpedoed they would hit our room and if they didn't, there would be a big enough hole made that they would have to close off all the doors to the stairways and [leave us down there to our fate]."[11]

Although they were fortunate to have a cabin, Speer and the others in D-Battery were actually in the least desirable part of the ship. While First Class cabins occupied the central part of the vessel and Second Class was in the stern, their Third Class room was in the bow. Those in the bow always felt the most motion of the ship at sea. In addition, those in cabins toward the rear of the bow had the additional annoyance of the ship's propeller vibrations. Still, they were thankful. It was better than being assigned to sleeping quarters in the public areas where the troops were sleeping in shifts in the "hot bunks."

Sometime during the embarking procedure, each soldier was given what appeared to be a letter from President Roosevelt on White House stationery that read, in part, "You are a soldier of the United States Army. You have embarked for distant places where the war is being fought." Copies of the ship's Standing Orders were also handed out. These explained emergency procedures in the event of an air attack, what to do if abandon-ship orders were given, and precautions to take to prevent fire. In addition, the troops were informed that Daily Orders would be posted throughout the ship each morning and that it would be their responsibility to check these for information on work assignments, religious services, scheduled entertainment and general news about the war.

By noon the ship was fully loaded but remained dockside. Tugboats began to pull the vessel away from its moorings at 16:00 hours that afternoon, Thursday, December 23. The day was clear, cold and windy in New York City and a lot of these young troops were quite nervous, not knowing it would be another six months before they would be going into combat. As the great liner got underway, the ship's Captain, Sir James G.P. Bisset, got on the P.A. and informed the soldiers of the rules and regulations regarding ship security. The vessel was divided into three sectors, he told them, designated by the colors red, white and blue. Each army outfit or unit was assigned to a certain section of the ship and was not allowed out of that area. As they boarded the ship each G.I. had been issued a red, white, or blue lapel button, he continued. These were to be worn at all times. Troops assigned to the red sector had to stay in the areas of the ship marked with the color red, and so on. These regulations, he further informed them, would be strictly enforced by the M.P.s or security details on board. He also advised them that *Queen Mary* Voyage WW#30E (Worldwide, number thirty eastbound) carried a total of 11,990 Army troops, including officers and nurses, and a crew of 1,087 on this trip. Commodore Bisset went on to advise his passengers the ship's speed would be 27 to 30 knots (about 30 to 35 miles per hour) and that they would maintain a zig-zag course all the way to their final destination to prevent the enemy's submarines from "sighting up" on the ship. Total passage time, they were finally told, was estimated at five days, ten hours and thirty minutes.[12]

As the ship was tugged down the Hudson River, past the Holland Tunnel and out into the open of New York Harbor, the captain gave the all-clear and the troops were allowed to move about within their assigned areas. "I wanted to see the Statue of Liberty," recalled Glen, "so [Wayne and I] ran up the stairs and at the top there was an M.P. there who told us we couldn't use these stairs—to go back and use this one or that one—so by the time we got to the Promenade Deck, the Statue of Liberty was almost out of sight. That was a big disappointment."[13]

Similarly, a number of G.I.s were disappointed because many of them also missed the chance to see New York's famous statue. In addition to the various troops being restricted to certain areas of the ship, many of the passageways were also designated one-way. Starboard passageways were supposed to be used only for forward movement while port-side passageways were for moving aft. At the same time, the M.P.s seemed to take great delight in sternly warning G.I.s about being out of their assigned areas or wandering any deck without a life preserver—and they had plenty of opportunity to confront them. Below the Sports Deck, Sun Deck, Promenade and Main decks, each level was designated by a letter—A-Deck through H-Deck—having a total of twelve decks in all. Troops were constantly getting lost in the unbelievable maze of decks, corridors, and stairs and were forever confused with what direction aft, port-side or starboard should move. B-Battery's Harvey Edds and his best friend, Billie Colliver, however, had better luck. They happened to be standing on the upper deck as the ship passed the Liberty statue. "I asked Billie if he had bought a round-trip ticket to Europe," recalled Edds, who was kidding around as they both stood along the railing looking out at the statue. However, Billie's serious answer haunted Edds for some time afterwards. "I don't know, Harvey," he responded. "We'll see."[14]

The *Queen Mary*, converted to a troop carrier, leaving New York. (National Archives)

Although all of the carpet and furnishings had been taken out in the ship's conversion to troop transport, it hadn't been feasible to remove all of the paneling and fixtures. Some of the ship's most ornate decor and various other decorations remained while some changes and modifications had been made. The First Class Smoking Lounge had been transformed into the ship's hospital, the tourist-class cocktail bar on the main deck was converted into a pharmacy, the tourist and third-class restaurants were filled with mess tables and benches, and the ship's tailor shop became the ship's military police headquarters and detention center. In addition, nine troop canteens had been established throughout the ship that were well-stocked with soft drinks, candy, cigarettes, razor blades, shaving cream, soap, shampoo, toiletries, and other necessities. Chewing gum, however, was no longer available and not allowed anywhere on board. On the ship's first voyage as a U.S. troop carrier it teakwood decks were nearly covered with discarded wads of gum that took cleaning crews, using caustic soda and scrapers, nearly two weeks to remove.[15]

In addition to the teakwood deck flooring, the marquetry or decorative wood veneers of the ship's cabins, public rooms, and Grand Staircase remained one of the most memorable aspects about the ship for many of these young G.I.s. "The wood around the stairways and around the pillars was some of the most beautiful wood I had ever seen," agreed Speer. Originally built and launched in the mid-1930s, the liner's interior had a very contemporary appearance for that period. Its intrinsic design was of the Art Deco style so popular then and some 56 varieties of rare woods had been used throughout the ship. In addition, the first class bathrooms all featured Formica paneling, a new and fashionable innovation at the time.[16]

The ship galleys labored under the obligation of feeding the overwhelming number of passengers. There were a number of restaurants converted to mess halls throughout the ship. The liner's main restaurant, which originally seated 800 people, was located on C-Deck. Converted to a cafeteria-style mess hall with narrow tables and all eating being done in shifts standing at tables with mess kits, 2,000 soldiers were served at a time. Meals were served in 45-minute shifts starting at 06:30. Thirty thousand eggs were boiled every morning. Orange marmalade, oatmeal, rice and beans were also served. As each soldier left the dining room he was handed sandwiches to use for lunch. Because the ship's crew was British, to the dismay and disliking of many of these American troops, the meals on board were also British. The evening meal often consisted of kidney stew or corned beef served with brown bread but many of these soldiers were raised in rural America and had no experience nor any taste for British fare. "It is still a big question as to whether anyone ate," noted one D-Battery G.I. Lester Cohen of B-Battery claimed he never did eat in the ship's galley during the entire trip. "We were served kidney stew all the way over," complained Wayne Edmondson, "so needless to say, we mostly stayed in our room and ate K-rations on the trip." Sgt. L. James Theriault of D-Battery agreed. "We [also] got by with food from the canteens," he added, "but, of course, we had to pay for that."[17]

The first full day out on the Atlantic, Friday, December 24, Christmas Eve day, they had a practice drill. "This drill was held so that in case the ship was hit by a torpedo or ran into a mine everyone would know just what to do," reported one G.I. "[T]hat is, what stairway to use and what raft to take." These drills were scheduled for each day out but because of the rough sea and the crowded conditions, only the first day's drill was held. By nightfall of the first night seasickness was common. For most, Christmas passed as just another day or with limited observance. The holiday meal served by the British crew that evening included pork chops and that morning chocolate-covered ice cream bars were passed out as a special Christmas treat. "On Christmas morning I was seasick," recalled Glen. "I was so seasick that when they brought around ice cream on a stick, I didn't even take one." According to many G.I.s seasickness was almost epidemic on the voyage. "Stanley Stevensky [of D-Battery] stayed in the latrine nearly the whole time," Speer recalled. "I got over mine," he continued, "but the way I did, I took my sleeping bag up on the top deck and walked around until I found a place I could lay down. If I looked at the horizon I was alright." Glen spent the rest of the trip sleeping on the top deck. He found an area near a vent that was venting out warm air. Cramped as they were below deck, a number of G.I.s abandoned their standee bunks after the first night or so and sought space on the upper decks to sleep. Although many sought the change to help alleviate their seasickness, many also believed they would have a better chance of escaping the ship in the event it was ever torpedoed.[18]

Although the *Queen Mary* had a top speed of nearly thirty-three knots—and the passengers were told it would be running at twenty-seven to thirty—it actually maintained a cruising speed of twenty knots (23 mph) in its zig-zag course across the Atlantic. To ensure the ship's safety from marauding German U-boats, the *Queen Mary* would suddenly alter course in a zig-zag pattern at ten-minute intervals. To prevent its stabilizing gyros from operating against the inertial shifts, the instruments were turned off, thereby making the trip a choppy, uncomfortable, experience for many. Another major problem as a result was the ship's unpleasant potential for going into a violent rolling motion as it fell into the rhythm of the seas.

"When you went into the mess hall, there were no chairs," explained Franklin Johnson of B-Battery. "You ate standing up. There was just these big long troughs. You'd take your mess kit and put it on the trough. You'd start to eat but then the ship would roll and your mess kit would slide about four guys down. You'd have to wait for the ship to right itself to get your mess kit back. In the meantime someone would "upchuck" down there and that would start the whole area [upchucking and] everybody would get sick."[19]

"[Some mornings] that floor was so slick," recalled Speer, "the only way you could get through there was to hang onto each table as you [slowly maneuvered toward] the doors. Needless to say, you just went on through the mess hall and on out the other side with nothing to eat those mornings. It was mighty gross."[20]

Each day the troops were required to police and clean their own living quarters and to assist with the daily duties around the ship. "Our battalion was appointed gun-guard [duty] for the ship," advised Jack Forman of A-Battery. "The ship was equipped with all sorts of anti-aircraft weapons to avoid being bombed and strafed. And as best we could, we were appointed to man the guns." The boys of all four gun batteries were assigned to the detail. "I was very proud," advised Sergeant Wisniewski of Battery-B, "[but] we [all] got a little shook up when we saw the gun positions sitting way out over the rails." These perches extended about twelve feet out nearly one-hundred feet above the water and could be accessed only by a narrow steel walkway or catwalk traversed beyond the rail. A wide variety of armament was mounted on the top decks of the ship including more that 40 antiaircraft and anti-submarine guns. These included such weapons as twenty-four 20mm Oerlikon antiaircraft cannon, ten 40mm guns in five twin mounts, six 3-inch guns in high-angle/low-angle mounts, one 6-inch anti-sub popgun, twelve rocket launchers, a number of range finders, and a central gun-control house. In addition, the ship's hull was wrapped in wire to help neutralize any magnetic mines. "[A]s soon as we left port we went on watch," added Wisniewski."[F]our-hour tricks with two dogwatches of two hours each [around] sunup and sundown." [21]

"Some of us had to take a watch on the *Queen Mary* at night," advised Glen. "I stood watch one night. It was very, very cold in the north Atlantic at night in December!"[22]

"I was assigned the bow gun to help the Irish crew," recalled Pfc. Daniel H. Ciaburri of Battery-B, "[but] they pulled us off the job because the water got too rough."[23]

"Waves were coming up over the deck," agreed Dick Woolson of Battery-B, assigned to another AA gun, "and the water was freezing. We had to pull ourselves with rope attached to the gun. Then tied ourselves to it so we wouldn't slide off."[24]

Once taken off the duty, the men of the 110th AAA became some of the most fortunate G.I.s confined on the vessel. For the other troops, in addition to the areas of their sleeping and eating assignments, they could walk around and explore the Promenade and Main decks but the Bow, Stern Fan Tail, Sun Deck and all other areas where the British crews were performing the ship's duties were off-limits. "We [had been] issued "G" buttons which meant gunners," advised Ciaburri, "[which gave *us* complete] freedom of the ship."[25]

Many of the other G.I.s occupied their spare time napping, playing cards, deeply involved in high stake poker games, and shooting dice. In one dining room there was a bridge game and several poker games that went on continuously and several 24-hour poker games were in constant operation in individual rooms on each deck. There was also repeated showings of several films such as *Pride and Prejudice* and there was organized calisthenics, inspections, and other military routines including numerous lectures about various combat equipment. It was also a daily routine for the crews manning the antiaircraft guns to fire a few rounds for practice, adding to the noise and pandemonium on board.

On every wartime voyage of the *Queen Mary* there were rumors spread among the troops on board of enemy submarine sightings and news reports both in the United States and in Great Britain of the ship's sinking. It was a fact that German Chancellor Adolf Hitler had offered a one-million-reichs-mark reward to any U-boat commander who sank the ship and a number of enemy news reports that it had been sank was generally initiated by German propaganda in the hope that the ship would break radio silence in order to report otherwise and, as a result, pinpoint its location for the enemy but the ship always remained silent during its transatlantic voyage. For security reasons, the ship's departure and arrival dates and times were also kept secret. Due to its immense size there was only one port in the United States that could handle it—New York— and only one in Great Britain—originally two but because Southampton, England was within range of German forces it only left a port northwest of Glasgow, in Scotland—so the ship was most vulnerable as it left or arrived in port. As a result, a ship and plane escort led the *Queen Mary* in and out of those areas. During all of its trips as a troop carrier across the Atlantic, the ship maintained complete radio silence. On this trip, there was one news report that the great ship had been sunk and two occasions when rumors circulated among the troops on board that German subs had been seen in the area.[26]

Perhaps the worst part of this trip, however, was the storm that blew up on Christmas Day. Sometime during the early morning hours the wind picked up and the seas became choppy. By the first light of morning it was misting and the size of the waves and swells had increased dramatically. "As I understand it," advised Speer, "the Promenade Deck was seventy feet above the water line and we had waves coming in on [that] deck! It was very, very, very scary." According to the ship's crew it was the roughest crossing they had ever experienced up to that time. For the American passengers it was the roughest and scariest part of the entire trip. Nearly all of the journals, diaries and letters of those on board provide various details of the storm that developed that day and continued throughout the next. In addition to the 110th AAA, some of the other military units on board included the 118th AAA Gun Battalion, the 225th AAA Searchlight Battalion, the 1st Infantry Division, the 5th Engineer Special Brigade, the 6th Naval Beach Battalion, doctors and nurses of the 28th General Hospital Unit, and the 150th Engineers Combat Battalion, among many others.

The storm had subsided by the evening of Sunday, December 26. That night the announcement over the ship's public address system that the German battleship *Scharnhorst* had been sunk off the coast of Norway with a loss of 1,864 lives by the Royal Navy's *Duke of York* brought cheers from all those on board. On December 27 the announcement that Ortona, Italy had fallen to the Allies after two weeks of heavy house-to-house fighting brought more cheers.

December 28 brought calm seas and smooth sailing for the remainder of the trip. Ships and planes came out to escort the *Queen Mary* later that night. At 06:00 on Wednesday, December 29, the ship dropped anchor about two miles inside the harbor—about a quarter mile off shore—at a place called Firth of Clyde, Gourock, Scotland. Debarkation did not begin until the following day during which Battery-D drew the detail of taking the nurses' baggage ashore. "Most of us enjoyed that job," admitted Eckenrode. Throughout the day other units left the ship and were trained out to various locations all across southern England. After unloading the nursing corps' gear, the batteries of the 110th AAA returned to the ship. By nightfall only a portion of the vessel had been emptied because of the limited number of trains available. Debarkation was halted and began at day-light the following morning. Finally, at 14:00 hours that afternoon—Friday, New Year's Eve, December 31—Battery-D began to disembark. "We were loaded onto a ferry, which landed us at Gourock at four o'clock in the afternoon," reported one of the boys. Long lines of trucks waited dockside to transport the troops out of the area. Once loaded, the convoy slowly moved westbound out of Gourock and through Greenock. Arriving in nearby Glasgow, the trucks proceeded into the center of town and came to a halt at Glasgow Central Station at Hope and Gordon Streets. "We were immediately put aboard a train," reported Sergeant Eckenrode, "and at five o'clock we left the little Scottish town."[27]

Their train took them through the Scottish villages of Airdrie and Bathgate and on into Edinburgh. As midnight—and the celebration of New Years's—approached, the members of D-Battery found themselves standing at a little train depot in Newcastle, England. "Singing was our only means of celebrating," recalled one G.I., "and what a racket we made!" The boys of Battery-B had already boarded a southbound train. "[Our] New Year was rung in with the same old American spirit," advised Sergeant Wisniewski. "[A] noisy display of banging on mess kits, shouting, singing and pounding on [the train] doors." [28]

The rest of the 110th AAA was put on the next train out. By daylight they were rolling south through the English countryside passing the cities and towns of Darlington, Doncaster, Nottingham, Leicester, Northampton, and Watford. "That was a scary thing, too," advised Glen. "Three times on the way down through England from Scotland, [German] airplanes were bombing and the train would stop and wait for an 'all clear.'" At noon that day, New Year's, January 1, 1944, the train pulled into the small village of Henley, along the Thames River, about thirty-eight miles west of London. "We were just in awe of everything," advised Speer. "None of us had ever had experiences like this." At Henley, they boarded buses and headed northwest down the road five miles further to the small community of Nettlebed where a former British military base was located on the outskirts of town. The base consisted of a group of Nissen—or Quonset—huts which were arched-topped or tunnel-shaped prefabricated corrugated metal shelters having concrete floors and enclosed at each end with wood. "They didn't even have cots yet," advised Speer. Straw had been spread down on the floor for the troops. "So we just laid down on the straw just like my dad's cattle."[29]

That night, as many of these boys laid in the straw at Nettlebed and thought about home, Harvey Edds laid there and thought about the conversation he'd had with his good friend Billie Colliver during the trip over. "We were just kidding around," he recalled years later, "but his answer about not knowing if he had a round trip ticket to Europe really bothered me."[30]

CHAPTER 4

Arrival on the Big Isle:
Training and Preparation in England

The village of Nettlebed was about ten miles from Reading, England, twenty-four miles from Oxford, and about forty-two miles from London. Located in the Chiltern Hills area—a region of rolling chalk hills covered with immense old-growth beechwood forests—the community was known for its brick making and the production of various wood products. The hamlet, itself, was thinly strung out along the main road and consisted mostly of modest little homes, pubs, coaching inns, and small shops. Various military camps, both British and American, were located throughout the vicinity—within the forests as well as along either side of the road to Reading. The Nettlebed military complex, in the hills southeast of town, was a small compound divided into two sections called North Camp and South Camp. The 110th AAA was housed in South Camp. Ten days later the 118th AAA Battalion was moved into North Camp. Both units were then attached to the U.S. First Army under the tactical control of the 49th AAA Brigade as part of the 18th AAA Group.

This particular camp had been built sometime in mid-1942 by the 343rd U.S. Army Engineer Battalion. Two small "engineer castles" constructed of locally-made brick were situated on either side of the main entrance.

On numerous occasions, including the 110th AAA Battalion's first day's arrival at the camp, planes could be seen bombing London and the surrounding countryside forty-some miles away.

"We could see bombs landing in the city and see the British firing on the German planes," recalled Harvey Edds. "Often they would hit one [of the planes] and we could see it go down in flames." As the anti-aircraft fire intensified, the planes began to circle out away from the city to dispose of their bomb loads before heading back. "Many of them were falling in our area," marveled Speer. "Close! Scared us! Many of us were running and diving into nearby ditches. It had been raining and they were full of water and muddy so that day I told Wayne Edmondson:'Well, if I'm gonna die tonight I'm gonna die in a clean place. I'm not gonna died in one of these ditches.'" With that, Speer and Edmondson both jumped up and bolted toward their Quonset hut, got inside, and waited out the bombing there. "At least we were [comfortable] and in a clean place," insisted Glen, "[and] that's the attitude I had from there on out: If I'm gonna die, I'm gonna die in a clean place. Not some mud-hole in a far-off land."[1]

After several days, cots were finally delivered for the troops but the 110th still had no vehicles or AA guns. Training here consisted mostly of hikes to keep the boys in shape and extensive training in aircraft recognition. "[W]e had an average of three hikes a week," declared one of the G.I.s. Training in aircraft identification was done with the aid of photographs, drawings, movies, models and flash cards. Decks of "Spotter Cards," manufactured by the U.S. Playing Card Company, were also passed out to the boys. These were regulation playing cards that could be used for bridge, poker, and other games which displayed silhouettes of the various Allied and enemy aircraft to help the boys become more familiar with the different characteristics of all the planes. Officials from the 49th AAA Brigade later sent an Aircraft Recognition Inspection Team to test the 110th after several weeks training and Battery-D set an all-time record for having the highest average in the Brigade.[2]

A week's orientation about England and the British people and their customs was required at the camp before any passes were issued. After that, evening passes were given out to Henley, Oxford and Reading, while 48-hour passes were issued for London.

"On our first leave to London," advised Speer, "Wayne Edmondson and I saw everything in London that tourists go there to see. Since we didn't drink we used our money differently. We got a room in the Hotel Strand, one of the top three best in London and took a horse and carriage taxi around the city. We told the driver to take us to everything the tourists come here to see. So he took us to Westminister Abby and we went through there, the London Tower, Buckingham Palace, saw the Changing of the Guard, the Big Bend tower—we did it all!"[3]

The Strand Palace Hotel was indeed one of the best in London. It was a landmark, itself, located in the heart of the city within easy walking distance of Trafalgar Square, Piccadilly Circus, and the Houses of Parliament. Originally built in 1909, the hotel was completely refurbished in the 1930s to reflect the Art Deco style of that period. It boasted of having three formal restaurants, two cafes, and luxurious individual rooms. During the war, food ration vouches could be exchanged for meals in the restaurants and air raid shelters were provided in the basement for all the guests. The hotel became quite popular with the newly arriving American servicemen and the greatest percentage of its guests during the war were American troops on leave.

On February 23 the battalion's equipment finally arrived at Nettlebed and the various drills and practice began again. "My most vivid memory here," declared Glen, "was that most everyone here had the dysentery bad, real bad. There was a centrally located outhouse at the camp and you would see guys running up the path, trying to get there in time. But sometimes you would see them just stop or slow down and start walking because it was too late."[4]

On February 25 the battalion was ordered to pack up and ready their equipment for transfer. They spent the rest of the day getting ready and at 07:50 the following morning, they left South Camp. After covering a total distance of 177 miles, the motor convoy arrived in Exmouth, a small harbor town along the English Channel in southwest England, at around 16:00 hours that afternoon.

Exmouth was formerly a quiet seaside resort town with beautiful beaches spread out below reddish, grass-topped cliffs. In recent months all of its hotels and nearly all of it large buildings had been taken over for housing various American military units. Because no other lodging was now available, the 110th AAA became the first American unit to be billeted in private homes. "Some people would take as many as six soldiers into their homes," declared Edds. "All of Britain was involved in the war—doing whatever they could to help out." Members of Battery-D were placed in homes in Littleham Cross, a residential section on the east side of Exmouth, while the other batteries were housed in homes within the city itself as well as in the neighborhoods of Littleham and Withy Combe. "Littleham Cross was a beautiful little community," declared one of the G.I.s. "The homes were built of stone or brick [with little] flower gardens [that] bloomed the whole time we were there." The battalion also had the use of the nearby Cranford Hotel as their day-room or recreation facility. "Me and [Lt.] Dick Sisson [of A-Battery] were assigned to [the home of] Mrs. Cawley," noted Lieutenant Forman of A-Battery. Her husband was a Lieutenant Colonel in the Royal Marines in Ceylon . . . . Turns out, too, that her father was a Field Marshal of England, Lord [William] Birdwood." B-Battery's Sgt. Frank Wisniewski and Sgt. Sam Pettinato was billeted in the home of the Clapp family, owners of a restaurant in Exmouth and the entire gun crew of Sgt. Jesse L. James was billeted in one house. Such arrangements in housing provided advantages to both the English and the Americans. "[She had] a pen full of chickens out in the back—in other words, fresh eggs," declared Forman about his private quarters. "I'd get oranges and candy and soap and stuff like that out of battalion supply and trade 'em to her for [the] eggs." Others made similar exchanges or helped in other ways. "In return for [their] wonderful hospitality," noted Wisniewski, "you could always find our men doing odd jobs around the homes, cutting and trimming lawns, hauling coal, repairing anything that wouldn't work and hundreds of other odd jobs."[5]

A typical home in Exmouth that billeted troops of the 110th AAA
(From "What I Remember of WWII," by Frank T. Wisniewski)

On February 28 one-fourth of the battalion, including Speer and some of the other drivers and mechanics, were sent back to Oxford, England, to attend a water-proofing school operated by the Ordnance Corps. It was to be the mechanics' and drivers' responsibility, they learned, to waterproof the various vehicles for the invasion. "Bucky Worboys had the additional responsibility of waterproofing the captain's jeep," recalled Glen, laughing.[6]

The Oxford camp was a huge tent city just outside of town. A large U.S.O. tent stood in the center of the compound and most of the American troops spent all of their free time there instead of in the borough. According to many G.I.s, Oxford was quite different than most other British towns they had been to. The community, as a whole, was less friendly. Perhaps it was because the people, here, were quite busy. Oxford was a big college town with a number of different private schools and a major military hospital was located there. "I got to Oxford as often as I could," noted Lieutenant Forman, who disagreed with that appraisal and spent many of his leaves there when the battalion was stationed at nearby Nettlebed. "It's a fascinating place [with its] antiquity, the colleges, [and] the martyrs' monuments." Oxford's nickname was the "City of Spires" because so many Gothic towers and steeples dominated it's skyline. Practically all of them belonged to the main university, the oldest in England, whose majority of buildings were built in the 15th, 16th, and 17th centuries. In addition, many of these buildings were constructed in salmon or ocher-colored sandstone, a marked contrast from the drab-green tent-city outside of town. "The tents at that water-proofing school had a potbelly stove," advised Speer. "One morning it was cold and the fire was about out [so] I took an open gallon can of gas and tossed some of it into the stove." With a loud 'poof!' an eruption from the stove sent a flame to the opening of the can. "Now if I would of kept my head I could have carried that [can] out, with my thumb over the opening, set it on the ground and nothing would have happened," explained Glen. "I could have even set it down by the stove and nothing would have happened," he continued. "But I panicked and I threw that [container] and it went twirling across the room throwing gas up all over the tent and everything. Well, that tent burnt like a paper sack and all the duffle bags, rifles, and equipment inside [were going up]. One guy had just come in from somewhere and hadn't even unpacked his duffle bag yet."[7]

Speer quickly realized the enormity of his problem because all the troops had been specifically warned against using gas with the stoves. "I grabbed that can and ran down the road probably a half mile," admitted Glen, "and threw that can in a ditch and tromped it flat and [threw dirt over it]."[8]

When Speer returned to the camp he saw a crowd standing around looking at the charred remains of the tent and all of its contents. "The First Lieutenant was there searching through the debris," worried Glen, "so [as I approached] I acted shocked and amazed that our tent had burnt [while] Lieutenant Klein kept walking around saying that he smelled gas." Perhaps Speer's act was persuasive. No one was ever accused or punished for the damage. "Had I been caught," admitted Glen, "I'd been court-martialed and [would have] had to pay for all of that equipment." But Glen was never convinced Lieutenant Klein didn't have his suspicions. One night he caught Speer hitch-hiking to town from the waterproofing school, picked him up and transported him back to the tent telling him to never leave that camp again as long as they were assigned there.[9]

The school lasted one week. Special waterproofing kits were provided for the various vehicles. These G.I.s were taught how to seal all openings in the units and how to install sheet metal vents and extenders on all the exhausts and air intake vents. Officially called "fording stacks," these vents not only provided air flow to the engine but they were also sealed to prevent water from seeping into the engine compartments. They were also designed to quickly detach once the vehicle was up on shore. The crew and driver would simply jump out, pull the attachment pins and the vents would fall off, away from the vehicle so it could be easily driven away. They also learned the proper procedures for attaching air intake tubes on various parts of the engine and how to extend them up alongside the windshield above the water level and how to seal the engine with water-proofing compound. This was mainly Cosmoline, a brand name for petrolatum, a thick black grease normally used by the military as a protection against corrosion of metal items in long-term storage. It was a solid until heated and then it could be sprayed on, gobbed on, brushed on, or parts dipped into it for a protective coating. Cosmoline came in two 25-pound square tin-can containers packed into an olive-green wood box or crate. Truckloads of these were arriving daily and being stockpiled in tents throughout the Oxford camp. Also in general use was a waterproof compound made of asbestos paste that was used in sealing spark plugs, wiring and various other components.

The G.I.s returned to Exmouth on Wednesday, March 8. "Coming back from that waterproofing school we were in a convoy [and the rule was] no English trucks or vehicles were supposed to cut into the military convoy," explained Glen. "They were supposed to yield and let it go by. So we were coming through one town, seems like we were going west and we turned south and started going up a hill, and an Englishman driving a truck cut in front of us—in between some of our military trucks—and of course we were driving on the left side of the road. So going up the hill I cut to the right and pulled up alongside of this civilian truck and as my cab passed by his cab I wheeled to the left. In my rearview mirrors I watched the civilian truck run up onto the cement sidewalk, hit a large plate glass window, and come to a stop in the front half of a store and I thought, 'oops,' maybe I carried that a little too far."[10]

The Corbitt trucks the battalion was driving were "open cab"—with a canvas top and canvas doors—and Glen was wearing his field jacket. As soon as he could, Speer took his jacket off and laid it in the seat and removed the canvas doors. "I always drove near the back of the convoy near the wrecker," he declared. "As the convoy got south of town M.P.s stopped the procession and began walking up and down the line examining the trucks and drivers. The M.P.s were overheard by some of the others saying they were looking for a 6X6 with doors, maybe damage, and a driver with T-5 stripes. But a lot of the drivers in this convoy had Tech-5 stripes. As the M.P.s walked back toward the front of the convoy, Lieutenant Klein, following several yards behind them, slowed alongside Glen's truck and quietly said "Damn it Speer, why do you keep doing things like this?"[11]

"That's all I ever heard about it," advised Glen.

When the group returned to Exmouth, they were reassigned to their original quarters. "We [again] stayed in private homes," recalled Speer. "We stayed in an upstairs room and we were treated very nice. All we had to do here [is] we took care of our guns and equipment, ate lots and lots of good food, and attended lots and lots of classes." Owen Davies, a machine-gunner assigned to Battery-B, was one of a large group from the battalion who regularly went into town to have a fish and chips dinner with a pint of beer at the village pub. Dick Woolson of B-Battery struck up a good friendship with a local baker and often got gallon cans of jelly from the battalion quartermaster and took them into town. "The baker would make us jelly donuts," Woolson proudly declared. Army officials didn't seem to mind at all. "They fed us real good here," said Glen in amazement. "A lot of us farmboys were going around saying they're fattening us up for the kill 'cause we knew there was going to be an invasion sometime soon."[12]

On March 6, new equipment arrived for the battalion. This included the M-9 Directors, an instrument most members of antiaircraft battalions had never seen before, and other computer, radar, and 90mm firing equipment. "The SCR-584 Radar and M-9 Director had been developed by Bell Labs about 7 or 8 months before," advised Captain Julius Reiver. "We were just leaving Camp Edwards to go to England when they gave my battery the job of test firing the system with the Bell Lab engineers. We loved the system."[13]

Minor changes and more adjustments were necessary before the units were finally ready for delivery to the troops stationed in England. The setup was quite advanced for its day. A complete weapons systems consisted of a M-7 Power Generator, the SCR-584 radar, an M-9 computer, and a tracker unit for the M-9. The "584" was used to find, identify, and then track azimuth and range to the [airplane] target while the M-9 computer commanded all four guns of the battery and would compute the lead angle for the weapons—firing fused shells using proximity fuses—at a rate of 22 rounds per minute. The transformation was done in the radar, which was also connected to an IFF antenna—Identification-Friend-or-Foe—but all the calculating and data processing was done in the computer. Training began on these units at once.[14]

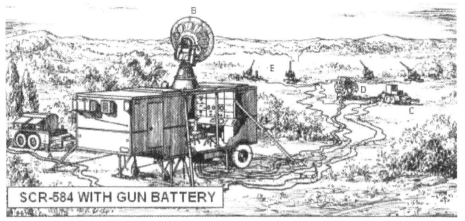

SCR-584 WITH GUN BATTERY

A: POWER GENERATOR M7   B: RADAR SET SCR-584
C: DIRECTOR M9   D: TRACKER FOR M-9
E: 90 MM GUN BATTERY

Simplified illustration of an AAA weapons system set up
(National Archives)

The battalion went on to participate in "Exercise Fox" at Slapton Sands, about 45 miles south of Exmouth, on March 9 and 10. It was the largest of a number of military exercises prior to the actual rehearsals of D-Day. This area consisted of a beach with course gravel, fronting a shallow lagoon that was backed by a line of bluffs. Although the troops didn't know it at the time, the Slapton Sands area greatly resembled the region that Allied troops would eventually invade. Less than two weeks later, on March 19 and 20, the battalion returned to the area to take part in "Exercise Crimson II" at the Merrival Range at Slapton Sands. This training exercise involved all anti-aircraft artillery units that would be assigned to V Corps.

By the end of March Battery-D had only three working Corbitt prime movers. One day Captain Reiver summoned Speer to his office and informed him they had to get four guns to the western tip of Wales for a training exercise at the firing range by April 6 and wanted to know how he planned to do it. "I said I didn't know," recalled Glen, "and he said 'I know! You're gonna shuttle two up there while the rest of us are on the way. You'll take one as far as you can go, unhitch it and come back for the other one.'" Momentarily stunned, Speer recalled hearing Reiver further mention, "You can pick any driver you want." [15]

"I picked my good friend Bucky Worboys," professed Glen. "He was from Maine and used to drive logging trucks. He was a short fella but boy he was a lot of fun."

Earl M. "Bucky" Worboys was from the same area of Maine as Clyde Libby. Like Clyde, who drove a Corbitt prime mover to tow Gun #1, Worboys was assigned to the battery's motor pool and drove a prime mover for Gun #2. Bucky was quite experienced at driving and backing big equipment and had become a good friend of Speer's. Captain Reiver assured Speer that Worboys could be the other part of the team. "As you know," the Captain began as he opened the center drawer of his desk, "Sergeant Pettyjohn doesn't want the engines of those trucks revved up too high." Speer agreed and said he understood. Captain Reiver then smiled and continued, "Well, here's a tachometer key to turn it back just in case that might happen."[16]

The Corbitt military trucks were equipped with tachometers having a redline. One hand on the tachometer would register revolutions per minute (rpms) and another hand would stop at the highest point the engine had been revved that day, allowing the sergeant to check and verify the highest speed the truck might have been going. With the "tac" key the driver could reset the tachometer hands back to zero at the end of the day, preventing his sergeant from determining just how fast or how rough the vehicle had been operated.

After preparing and mapping out the trip, Speer and Worboys began their shuttle of the two guns on Monday morning, April 3. The various other elements of the battalion left Exmouth in a convoy at 09:30 the following Wednesday. Like many other American soldiers in Europe at the time, Glen and Earl were young. And like many others, they tried to make all of their jobs or assignments fun and interesting. As a result, many tried to make a game out of everything they had to do. Glen and Earl were no different. "I guess we didn't know no better," admitted Speer. "I'm not saying everything we did was right, but what I'm saying is it often kept us sane. One time we were going along the road and I was driving. A farmer was in a field with a team of horses harrowing. He had apparently stopped to have his tea and his horses were turned toward the open field with their backs to the road. As we went by, I cut the ignition off and on which made the truck backfire—[This vehicle] had an exhaust on it that was pretty big and it would sound 'bout like a cannon—and then Bucky [leaned out of the window] and beat on the side of the truck as we went by. 'Course it scared the horse team and it took off running and we saw the farmer throw his cup up in the air and start running after the horses shakin' his fist at us. Of course we thought that was pretty funny."[17]

As Glen and Bucky continued their trip, the battalion's main convoy, towing the other two guns and additional equipment, stopped at 19:00 that first night after covering a total distance of 77 miles. They bivouacked eight miles south of Bristol at Brockley Coombe in a large open field. Nearby was a large military installation consisting of a number of Nissen Huts that housed medical personnel and also served as temporary housing for small groups. A one-thousand bed American military hospital had been established here at Frenchay Park. At 08:00 the next morning, April 6, the convoy pulled out and covered another eighty miles before coming to a halt to bivouac at Kington at 20:00 hours. "Once again," declared one of the G.I.s, "we had driven under cloudy skies but the roads had been in good shape." The following morning, Good Friday, the 110th pulled out on the last leg of its trip and, after covering another eighty miles, arrived at the Tonfanau Firing Point, north of Tywyn, Merrioneth, Wales at about 14:00 hours. "We had gotten the two guns to the [west-central] tip of Wales by the time the rest of the outfit got there," declared Glen.[18]

The Tonfanau Firing Point was a British Ack-Ack training center established on the rugged beaches of the coast overlooking Cardigan Bay. "There we learned the British methods of firing," admitted Sergeant Eckenrode, "and how much different those methods were from ours." Here also the battalion received extensive hands-on training with its new computer, radar and tracking equipment. In addition to the British soldiers stationed at the facility, the base housed a division of ATS girls—the Auxiliary Territorial Service, the women's branch of the British Army primarily responsible for antiaircraft duty—and the training center had a number of clubs to provide recreation. "There was the Sergeant's Club, the Corporal's and the P.F.C.'s Club," noted one G.I. "There were always movies and dances going on every evening and some of the fellows evaded the guards and even visited some of the pubs in Tywyn."[19]

At the range, the guns were towed to their positions. The gun, itself, was mounted on a steel cruciform platform that folded up for travel. Two sets of duel wheels, having 22-inch rubber truck tires, were mounted on a single axle at the back of the frame, on each side, in order to transport it. The frame had a ten-foot long, six inch diameter tow bar at the front that was coupled to the back of a prime mover when being moved from one place to another. Once they arrived at their destination, the gun would be backed into position and the crew would then pull the outriggers out to the sides, remove the safety pins, lower the gun onto four pads 90-degrees apart, and then level the gun with hand cranks that were mounted at the ends of the outriggers. This set up could be accomplished by the crew in seven minutes. While this was being done, others in the gun crew would hook up all four battery guns to the computer by a 225-foot cable, set up the radar unit, set up the antennas, and make all connections while the generator and tracker units were set up.

The battalion spent the entire day of Saturday and all day Easter Sunday on the range. "Most of us would have liked to have spent that Sunday back in our cozy little homes in Exmouth," complained one of the G.I.s. "They just don't do things like that in the American Army." The intensity of their training here never slackened. Every bit of the daylight and much of the darkness was used every day over the following week. "Our firing at the range was excellent," one of the battalion historians was later able to brag. "[And] our machine gunners set a firing record by shooting down eleven sleeves during their course of training."[20]

The battalion left Tonfanau at 08:00, Saturday morning, April 15. A repaired Corbitt truck had arrived during the week so a repeat of the boy's shuttle detail was unnecessary. The 110th AAA battalion's convoy normally consisted of 16 prime movers pulling guns, 16 cargo trucks pulling machine-gun units, 20 trucks for headquarters, and 8 jeeps for the officers and high-ranking non-coms, for a total of about 60 vehicles. They stretched out for several miles moving along the hilly, curvy and narrow Welsh and English roads at about 15 to 20 miles per hour. "It was [also] raining during the whole drive," complained Sergeant Eckenrode, "so we bivouacked at a staging area at [Cirencester] at eight o'clock that evening."[21]

The Cirencester bivouac was actually on the wooded limestone hills of the Cotswolds southwest of town. The return trip to Exmouth was divided into only two stages instead of three so they had covered a grueling 150 miles during this first leg. "As we jumped out of our trucks," one of the crew later admitted, "we were slightly damp, hungry, and wishing we were [already] back in our sacks at Exmouth."[22]

After striking camp they headed out early the next morning. A number of the boys still complained of being wet and having no chance to dry their clothes. The last leg of the trip covered 125 miles and brought the battalion into Exmouth at 20:00 hours Sunday night, April 16.

The following morning, as the boys reported for duty, more of their battalion's old equipment was replaced. "We were issued M-4 highspeed Artillery Tractors," recalled Glen, rather proudly. "It was kind of a high-speed Caterpillar."[23]

Sergeant Pettyjohn, left, and Speer with one of the new M-4 High Speed
Artillery tractors that replaced the Corbitt trucks.
(Courtesy of Wayne and Maxine Edmondson)

The machine, made by the Allis-Chalmers tractor company, was
powered by a 210-horsepower Waukesha 6-cylinder gasoline engine. It
could tow a 90mm gun up to 35 miles per hour and could climb grades of
up to 60-percent. The tractor came equipped with a front mounted high-
powered winch, a ring-mount .50-caliber machine gun on its roof, and a
special swing crane for hoisting ammo boxes and shells. Its cab, enclosed
with canvas doors, was divided into two compartments, with seating for
the driver and two men in the front compartment and double seating for
eight men in the rear compartment. Back cushions were leather covered
and canvas zipper bags padded with blankets served as seat cushions.
The 18-ton vehicle could tow the gun and transport the entire gun crew,
along with their dufflebags and other belongs and accessories, their rations,
and up to 500 rounds of .50-caliber ammunition for the machine gun and
shell racks that could accommodate up to 54 rounds of 90mm ammo. "They
were self-sufficient [towing] units," agreed Speer.[24]

The tractor was 16 feet 11 inches long, 8 feet 3 inches high, and 8
feet wide. Its average range was 125 miles on 155 gallons of gas. Sixteen
of these tractors were delivered in exchange for the battalion's Corbitt
trucks.

"They [were originally issued] with steel tracks," advised Glen.
"[Sometime] later Ordnance came around and asked if anybody wanted
rubber treads for their tractor and I chose rubber because the steel tracks
slid real bad on blacktop." Kermit Hart in A-Battery, one of Speer's friends
and a fellow Wayne-Countian, decided to keep steel tracks on his prime-

mover. "He stayed with steel," advised Glen, "so we were always comparing who made the better decision and which [type] gave the best traction." The arguing and good natured kidding continued over the next several says. Finally one day, as others looked on, Kermit and Speer backed their tractors up opposite one another, hitched them together with huge log chains and, as Wayne Edmondson stood off to one side holding a white hanky aloft and then dropped it to signal the beginning of the competition, the two boys shifted through the gears to try and out-pull the other. "I know on the gravel parking lot my rubber tracks just pulled his steel tracks all around," advised Glen. "But when we got over into the blue-grass sod one tractor would pull about a foot, the other would recover and pull back about a foot, until we just dug down into the ground and neither one would out-pull the other. At one point Kermit got out of his cab and I got out of mine as they were both runnin' and spinnin' their tracks and we stood there and watched them dig down to their [undercarriages]."[25]

Speer and Hart staged a number of these races and pulling contests to compare the advantages of the two types of track and to entertain the troops a number of times over the next couple of days until their commander brought it to a halt. Although they were having fun researching the advantages of each type of track on their own, the U.S. Army had completed extensive research into both types long before they had been made available to the troops. Both the steel block and the rubber bushed tracks were just over 16-inches wide. According to the Ordnance Department, Item Number T54E1 was steel track and Item Number T48 was track that had rubber shoes. Neither, though, was all steel or all rubber. The reference is to the cleating across the track's surface. Rubber proved to have more control on blacktop roads, gravel lanes, and cobblestone streets and in turning corners. It also rode more smoothly and reduced wear on the vehicle by cushioning shock and absorbing vibrations and added more miles to the life of the bogie wheels, support rollers, and other suspension components. On the other hand, steel tracks provided more traction in loose dirt or mud but caused more vibration adding to difficulties in steering and increased resistance to movement on more solid surfaces. Steel tracks were also less desirable in terms of weight, being about 25-percent heavier than rubber tracks, but during operation on mountainous roads they handled much better and did not suffer gouging as badly as rubber tread, adding to its milage life. The development of rubber chevron tracks and detachable steel grousers for the rubber track increased its efficiency in dealing with the muddy areas which caused the U.S. Ordnance Department to begin recommending the use of rubber tracks by the early part of 1943. Still,

both continued to have its avid supporters and both continued to compete for favor among the operators.[26]
Other new and updated equipment was issued to the 110th AAA as well. The battalion's old water-cooled machine guns were replaced with new "quad-50" units. Glen's buddy, Wayne Edmondson, had been assigned to drive one of the battery's 2.5 ton GMC 6X6's—destined to become one of the most popular cargo trucks of the war—having a hinged windshield, a front- mounted heavy-duty winch, and fitted out with a ring-mounted AA .50-caliber machine gun up over the cab. Once on location Wayne was responsible for operating one of the battery's new "quad-50s"—or four-barrel, machine guns. Other battalion members assigned to drive 6X6s and tow their own quad-50s included Leo Kania of A-Battery, Harvey Edds, Jim Prescott, Owen Davies, Art Hubbard and Dick Woolson of B-Battery, Henry Thake of C-Battery and Ray Brassard and Leo Cheney of D-Battery, among others.

The trailer-mounted "Quad-50" machine gun replaced the
battalion's old water-cooled MGs. (National Archives)

The quad-50 was an extraordinary unit. It was a trailer-mounted truck-drawn machine gun unit having a quadruple set of barrels that could fire 400 to 550 rounds per minute in selective, semiautomatic or fully automatic fire. Like the 90s, this gun unit was backed into place, usually into a pit dug deep enough to accommodate the 8-foot square trailer but to keep the gun unit itself level with the ground, and was used primarily as an AA gun to defend the 90mm battery from low level strafing. Each battery had four of these quad-50s, one assigned to each gun. Technically called the "M-51 Mount," the gunner sat in the middle of the unit between two large steel plates with two .50-caliber machine guns mounted one above the other on each side. The turret operated on electric power furnished by batteries. The gunner controlled both the horizontal and vertical movements of the gun unit by a center-mounted joy-stick that had a trigger attachment to fire the weapons. He sighted his target through elevated cross-hairs. Using sustained rapid fire the quad-50 could chew a brick wall to pieces or could saw the wings off a low level aircraft.

In addition, that same day two of the battalion's 6X6 weapons carriers and one of its eight jeeps were replaced with newer units. "Section training really began in earnest," recalled a battalion historian, "and everyone got back into the swing of things."[27]

"The task of organizing the final training of the Anti-aircraft Units which were to participate with the Brigade in the invasion of Europe into a [competent] assault combat team was immense," noted Major Michael G. Kelakos, Headquarters, 49th AAA Brigade. "[We] were given little time to do this job, and yet it had to be done and it had to be done quickly and well."[28]

On April 18 the remaining three-fourths of the battalion attended a waterproofing school at Broadsands, outside the town of Paignton, along the English Channel thirty miles south of Exmouth. Here the gunnery crews learned how to seal and waterproof the various guns and gun carriages. The detail returned the following week, on April 24. Two days later, the radar techs attended a training session on the SCR-584 at Blandford Camp near Blandford, Dorset, east of Exmouth while the gun and computer technicians attended classes at North Molton, about fifty miles north of Exmouth. Again, all 16 guns and the computer equipment were transported to the site for the exercise. They all returned on April 28.

The streets of many of these small British towns that the battalion passed through were narrow. Very narrow. "Sometimes going around a corner pulling a gun with a Cat we'd have to put part of the Cat up on the sidewalk," admitted Speer. "Also the streetlights [in these English towns] were just the height of my Caterpillar. The exhaust pipe come up out of that Waukesha engine across the top and some days when we went through some of those towns, and I and Bucky Worboys felt kind of ornery, we would backfire that exhaust just as we passed under a streetlight and we would have a contest to see who could blow [out] the most streetlights—the globes—and women and kids would run off in all directions scared and screaming. The Caterpillars also had a siren mounted on them so after we'd get three globes in a row we'd blow that siren [to celebrate and to let the other Cat drivers know]."[29]

As of May 1, unbeknown to many of the soldiers stationed overseas, all troop mail from England to the United States was stopped and would remain stopped until further notice. But the soldiers and sailors in England were already beginning to realize that D-Day was coming soon. Some were saying they could feel it. Some were saying the weather was right for it. All agreed the training had been intense for it. And the authorities wanted no word to get out about it. "Newspapers aren't even allowed to comment on the weather," complained one English citizen. "[A]t least until the information is too dated to help the enemy."[30]

On May 11 the battalion attended embarkation training at Fowey, on the southwest tip of the British Isle in Cornwall, about 83 miles southwest of Exmouth. The battalion returned to Exmouth the following day but on Monday, May 15, they were ordered to return to the Cornwall district and to proceeded immediately to marshaling area K-7 at Liskeard. Within hours the section leaders, drivers and assistants were all briefed, the batteries had packed up their equipment, turned in what they wouldn't need, and had lined up in convoy, to move out. By daylight they were on the move.

The highway was blacktop but many sections of streets and roads within the villages and towns they passed through were brick or cobblestone. "Those steel tracks on the cobblestone streets were like driving on ice," worried Terry Bye of C-Battery. "Those tracks couldn't grip the roadway in some areas and we would just slowly slide toward the edge of the street as we moved along."[31]

There were additional problems when these vehicles headed down steep inclines on these paved roads. "[T]he combination of the M-4 steering, its brakes and the minimal brakes on the wheels of the towed 90mm gun were only marginally adequate for downhill control," complained Captain James E. Chase of B-Battery.[32]

During the long arduous trip there were several close calls. A number of accidents were barely averted. After many hours of crawling up and down and around the many steep hills and tight curves along the English countryside, the convoy was moving through the darkness twenty miles north of Plymouth. "We were creeping along on a nighttime convoy on a very steep rolling section of a winding narrow roadway observing total blackout status," recalled Captain Chase. On a steep incline somewhere southwest of Tavistock, one tractor and gun began an uncontrollable slide down a hill and went over an embankment. "Battery-A had a track break down so we [had] hooked onto their gun," reported Delwin D. Soll of B-

Battery. "It wasn't very long after this when we started down a hill that we found out we didn't have any gun brakes."[33]

"The tractor and gun from B-Battery [slid] off the road and rolled down the hill turning over and over," reported Harold Mueller, operating a C-Battery tractor further back in the convoy. "All the gun crew got out except one fellow in the gun turret."[34]

"About one in the morning the dark of night in front of the convoy lit up with flames," agreed Sergeant Frank Wisniewski of B-Battery. "The convoy stopped, closed up, and we all went forward to see what was going on."[35]

According to later testimony, Tech-5 Paul Davis had just relieved Dell Soll after many long hours of driving. They were both assigned to B-Battery's Gun #3. With them in the tractor was A-Battery's Sgt. Stan Mirfield and one of his corporals after hitching up to an A-Battery gun. Also in the Cat was Frank Mielczarski of B-Battery Gun #2, Art Farris and Roy Willis from Gun #3, Leo Goldstein from the communications section, and Orin Holstead, Paul Massey and Cpl. John Curran from Gun #4.

As the tractor crested a hill, it began to slowly slide uncontrollably on the old cobblestone pavement. "Low gear didn't do any good," advised Soll. "Davis tried to put it in engine-break but the cat's speed was too great.... He then tried hand brakes and gun brakes ... we kept going down that hill picking up speed every foot of the way [and] sliding toward the side." The eighteen-ton tractor continued its uncontrollable slide until it made full impact against a stone wall bordering the roadway and went over a twelve-foot embankment, rolling side over side. The unit turned over and over and burst into flames as it hit the bottom of the embankment. "[I]t lit up the sky," advised Chase.[36]

"[It] made three complete turns and stopped, bottom side up," reported Soll. "When we came to our senses, Sergeant Mirfield noticed a fire in the back seat and yelled for us to get out." Davis crawled out through the windshield, Mirfield followed Soll pushing him out of the door opening but became stuck and had to be pulled out, in turn, by Dell. Apparently Willis and Holsted had jumped or had been thrown clear of the wreckage as it first began rolling. Massey got out some way and went limping up the embankment toward the road accompanied by Mielczarski who was yelling for someone to help them. As a number of the boys arrived at the bottom of the ravine to assist, Farris crawled out of the wreckage with his clothes on fire. Walt Evanuska, Keith Baker and Al Couturier ran to him, knocked him down and smothered the flames. Then took him up to the road, near the wall, where he was given first aid by battalion medic Henry Schade until a British nurse and several other medical techs came up and took command of the situation. Meanwhile Baker and Couturier ran back down to help Mielczarski and Massey who were still wandering around aimlessly, somewhat dazed, yelling for help.

Four of the crew, including Farris, Massey, Mielczarski, and Del Soll, were hurt badly enough to be transported to a nearby hospital for treatment. In addition to Willis and Holsted, Goldstein had also gotten clear of the wreckage and was unhurt. Corporal John Curran was apparently in the M-4's roof-top machine gun turret at the time and had been unable to get out or jump clear. He had remained pinned in the pulpit as the vehicle rolled down the embankment. Tragically, he was already dead by the time the others were able to get down to him. "[T]hey found him under the [tractor] after the fire," reported Del.[37]

As more medical personnel, M.P.s and other military authorities arrived on the scene to help out and investigate the accident, the remaining units of the convoy proceeded to their destination. All of the artillery tractors in this convoy were carrying 54 rounds of 90-mm ammo, 10 boxes of 50-cal. ammo, and 30 five-gallon cans of gasoline. The fuel continued to feed the flaming wreckage and began setting off the 50-cal. ammunition and then the 90s. Corporal Norm Brown was left in charge of the scene with Philip Brown, Frank Johnson, Jairus Chafee, and Angelo DiMauro to stand guard as the convoy moved on. "I sent my jeep and driver back to B-Battery to notify my 2nd in command to take over command of B-Battery [at the accident scene] and I assumed command [of the remainder] to continue the convoy," advised Captain Chase. "It was a tragic, tragic affair," added Sergeant Wisniewski remorsefully, "but such tragedies are a product of war and little attention can be paid to them . . . we had to move on."[38]

Finally, after twenty-seven hours on the road making the 83-mile trip, the long convoy began to stream into the K-7 staging area. There was army personnel and equipment as far as the eye could see. By dawn the five batteries of the 110th AAA Battalion had all been assigned to their particular sites within the crowded complex and had began to settle in. "[It was] a barbed-wire enclosed area where we were just like prisoners," noted Lieutenant Jack Forman of A-Battery. "We were not allowed mailing privileges. We couldn't mail out anything or receive anything [and] they clipped our hair." These assembly areas were referred to as "Sausage Camps" by many of the commanders because they were shown on their maps as dark sausage-shaped blobs. The G.I.s, however, thought the reference might be to the fact that the wire-enclosed camps resembled pens that animals were kept in before the slaughter. In either case, like the other sausage camps throughout southern England, K-7 had been established in a wooded area outside of town to provide concealment from aerial surveillance. And like them, shelters for the troops consisted of large pyramid tents with tarmacadam roads laid out through the compound for vehicular traffic.

The battalion remained sealed-in here. No one was allowed to leave the camp and, except for certain officials, no one was allowed in. Military Police kept the "sausage" surrounded and sealed off. Vehicles and other equipment were kept parked up against the hedges and under trees and everything remained hidden under camouflaged netting.

During the third week of May many of the G.I.s also noticed an increase in the number and length of worship services in the camp and quietly talked about it among themselves. "Almost every night we [went] to religious services," noted Lt. Clinton C. Gardner of B-Battery, "and we Protestants often [went] to both Protestant and Catholic services—just in case."[39]

During some of the nervous waiting and anticipation, many of the boys began painting names and phrases on their vehicles much like the more familiar "nose art" later seen on various aircraft. Realizing they would be going into battle soon, these young teen drivers began to feel dependent upon their war machines for their safety and security and had already began to develop a kind of camaraderie with their equipment. Since all of these vehicles looked alike, they wanted to individualize it. Make it special. Make it unique to each one of them.

Not all commanders, of course, allowed the practice. "We had a fairly strict 2nd Lieutenant," noted Harvey Edds of B-Battery, "[who] would not allow the machine gunners to paint their guns or any 'sayings' on the trucks."[40]

Likewise, a number of officers in other units would not allow the troops to personalize their vehicles or severely limited what could be done. It was true that personally decorating the equipment displayed a certain amount of individuality and independence—something the Army normally frowned upon—but it also greatly added to the esprit de corps of the group as a whole. As they began to transform these machines of war into personal status symbols, the entire camp saw an explosion of the humorous, the garish, and the often irrelevant art forms take hold as the G.I.s began to personally decorate their vehicle, machine gun units, artillery pieces, and other equipment to take with them into battle.

In Battery-D, Clyde Libby, who towed Gun #1, named his M-4 artillery tractor "Hell's Kitchen" and painted the name across the top of the cab over the divided hinged windshield. Donald Hunter, who towed Gun #2, named his "The Luthwaffe's Nightmare" and painted that above his tractor's windshield. Speer, calling his M-4 "Hitler's Crawlin' Coffin," painted that phrase on the #3 unit, while Bucky Worboys, who towed Gun #4 named and painted "Little Charlie" on his prime mover. At the same time, Ray Brassard painted the phrase "The French Tickler" across the front of his quad-50 machine-gun unit that accompanied Gun #3, and a number of the boys, with Lt. Ernest Eddy's permission, applied running figures of the Bumstead's gray dogs—Daisy and her sisters—from the comic strip "Blondie" along the side of the battery's M-9 computer trailer. In addition, Speer and a number of other drivers applied cut-out figures of pin-up girls to the front of their vehicles. Although Battery-B wasn't allowed to get into the act, a number in Headquarters Battery, including James Brennan who painted "Bucky" on his jeep and another who painted "GI Jive" on his, and those of A-Battery did get in on the action, as well as several of those in C-Battery. Harold Mueller of Battery-C, towing Gun #2, painted "Ruth" on his unit while another driver painted "Priscilla" across the top of his cab.

On May 18 each of the battery commanders met with their executive officers to inform them of the duties and responsibilities they would have as advanced scouts on the day of the invasion. They were further informed that "Deployment Day" was scheduled for the first week of June. After being shown a scaled-down model of the French seashore they were told their landing target would be a section along the west end of the beach. After being provided code names for these areas, they studied the placement of all the German pillboxes, machine gun posts, concrete barricades, beach obstacles, and the terrain, roads and towns beyond it on the model. The officers then went over intelligence information and aerial photographs of the region. The 110th's four gun batteries, they were informed, was to serve as the main defense for the beach against high-altitude bombing and each battery would be positioned near the town of Vierville, about half-a-mile inland. Each lieutenant was then provided a detailed map of his sector to study and was further informed that they would have to be kept isolated from the others in the battalion until those troops could be briefed. "We were bigoted," complained Lieutenant Gardner. "We few thousand who know the time, the place, even much of the strategy and tactics of the greatest invasion in history . . . and our American guards have orders to shoot us if we approach the gate out."[41]

The rest of the 110th AAA was briefed on May 26. "We were all marched into a tent one day," recalled one of the boys. "Four guards were standing around it." The temporary structure had been erected in the middle of a large field and heavily guarded since the day it was put up." In the tent we crouched around a covered table," declared another. "It was a table covered with a tarp," advised Speer. "We were directed to sit on the ground around it." Just then several command staff walked into the tent. "It was General Eisenhower," declared Glen, "and a Major or two and, I think, a lieutenant. You could have heard a pin drop." One of the Majors began lecturing the troops on various types of warfare. Eisenhower and the others stood off to one side. When the cover was lifted off the table it revealed a hard-sand sculpture of a slightly crescent-shaped beach, a scaled-down version of the 7,000-meter-long seashore along the Cotentin Peninsula of France where, they were told, the invasion was to take place. For the purposes of the assault, they learned, Allied commanders had divided the French coast of Normandy into designated code-named areas. British and Canadian troops would come in on the eastern beaches code-named Sword, Juno, and Gold. American troops would land west of them at beaches code-named Utah and Omaha. The area referred to as Omaha beach was further subdivided into four sections referred to from west to east by the code names Charlie, Dog, Easy, and Fox. Each of these were then further subdivided into smaller areas. The portion of beach known as Dog sector was divided down into three smaller areas known, from west to east, by the code names Dog Green, Dog White, and Dog Red. The exits from the beach were code named from west to east as D-1 for the road leading from the beach to the French village of Vierville-sur-Mer, D-3 leading to Les Moulins, E-1 leading to St. Laurent-sur-Mer, and E-3 leading to Colleville-sur-Mer. The U.S. 29th "Blue and Gray" Infantry Division would come in on the beach sectors of Charlie, Dog Green, Dog White, Dog Red, and Easy Green—between the villages of Vierville and St. Laurent—and were to secure and take control of the west exits D-1 and D-3. The 110th AAA was to come in on Dog Green Omaha beach as heavy support for the 29th, move up exit D-1 and set up in a field on top of the plateau to provide continued support.[42]

"It was a simple plan," explained Major Kelakos of the 49th AAA Brigade. "Principally it was based on the initial use of anti-aircraft assigned to the Army, on the beachhead proper, requiring the Corps and Divisional anti-aircraft units to arrive at a much later hour and continue forward with their respective Corps and Divisions. Three AAA assault groups were to land early on D-Day. A Provisional Machine Gun Battalion, followed by Self-propelled units, would be the first to land on each beach. The 40mm AW Battalions would then follow, displacing the Self-Propelled Battalions [moving] forward, then with the Barrage Balloons [Battalions] the 90mm Gun Battalions were to land on the afternoon of the invasion in time to be ready to fire against enemy aircraft expected over the beach on D-Night. This was [to be] the greatest AA force ever to be used in any one undertaking in the history of the U.S. Army."[43]

As explained to these boys, the entire plan sounded quite easy. Two armada, one for the three British beaches in the east and one for the American beaches in the west, would head out of port a day before the attack (D-1) and gather during the night. Slower craft would head out first and the faster ships would join in later. They would be the vanguard of nearly 7,000 vessels making the invasion. Soon after midnight, with the armada approaching the coast, two aerial forces, one British and one American, would begin parachute and glider drops. By daybreak the flanks of the 59-mile front would be secure. Then, shortly after dawn, the air and navel bombardment would begin, followed by the landing of 170,000 troops in eight divisions. It would take a day to secure the beaches. The following day (D+1), forces would link up and create an ever-expanding band of conquered territory.

According to a number of the G.I.s present, one of the other majors then went over vast amounts of intelligence, explaining what was waiting for them on the other side of the Channel. He pointed out exact locations on the model, gave breakdowns of what German units were entrenched at each location, told them how experienced or inexperienced each of those units were, the names of their commanders, and the percentages of what ethnic groups were present in each of those enemy outfits. In addition, they were given further details about their sector of beach code-named Dog Green Omaha and given descriptions of enemy armor there and told what air support was in place above and behind that area. They were warned of various mines and deadly hedge-hogs along the beach, of "Rommel's spaghetti," Belgian gates, tetrahedrons, lethal pointed posts with mines attached, sloped ramps, and other obstacles. He then informed them that for the first time in the history of U.S. warfare, the anti-aircraft guns would be used in direct support of the infantry as anti-tank weapons. "That really knocked us for a loop," admitted Speer. "We never planned on that. We all thought we were gonna be way behind the lines." The boys were further assured that concentrated air bombardment, the most devastating in this nation's history—consisting of nearly 3,000 tons of explosives—would pulverize the concrete barriers the Germans had erected to block the exit from the beach as well as the two large pillboxes and machine gun dens covering that area but admitted that the beach would probably be defended well. "One of the last things I can remember him saying to all of us," recalled Harvey Edds, "was that they were expecting casualties of fifty-percent or more." With that, the major told the troops to look at the soldier to their left and say "Its you or me." According to Edds, "We all *sort of* laughed about that."[44]

At the conclusion of the briefing they were all given French money, invasion money, printed in America, "We had to exchange our legitimate dollar bills and pound notes for invasion francs printed on flimsy paper," complained one soldier. They were each given 200 Francs—about $4 U.S. or 1 Pound Sterling. "In addition, we received a little booklet telling us how to treat and address the natives there," said another. Along with the pocket guide of France and a French phrase book, the boys were also provided a number of German phrases to memorize which promised enemy soldiers cigarettes, hot baths, and all sorts of comforts in exchange for their surrender.[45]

"Afterwards," recalled Glen," many of us lingered outside the tent, too excited to go about our daily duties, and talked about these new developments [with each other]." Although they didn't know the details of how big this operation really was, these boys generally understood the importance of what they were about to do. They had been impressed by the visit of General Eisenhower, himself. Their roll, they now realized, was important. It wouldn't be until after the war that many of them would learn Eisenhower had made it a point to go around and talk briefly to nearly all of the combat units that would take part in the great invasion. "We didn't know it by any of the code names known today," said Speer. "We heard the reference to H-hour and D-day but the terms H-hour and D-day had been used in planning invasions of all areas of Italy and all the islands of the Pacific. We had never heard of Operation Overlord or Neptune but we knew from our [briefing] of the code names Omaha Beach and Dog Green."[46]

Little did Speer or the others realize, however, the importance those names were destined to take in this nation's history, the history of this war, or in the history of warfare in general.

By the end of the week the troops were issued new fatigue uniforms which had been treated with CC-2, a product for neutralizing the effects of blister or poison gas. The Allies were concerned that the Germans might try to avert the invasion with a chemical response. The thick anti-gas paste was designed to stop gas from penetrating the clothing but it made the garments foul smelling and unpleasantly greasy and stiff. They were also issued an inflatable life belt that could be inflated with a CO2 cartridge or, if that failed, inflated by mouth through two air tubes on the front of the belt.

During the last week of May troops were ordered to waterproof their vehicles again. High-speed tractors, trucks, jeeps, and weapons carriers all underwent the procedure. As each vehicle's waterproofing was completed, a U.S. flag sticker was attached to the lower left of the windshield which displayed a check-list along the bottom, beneath the flag, for the inspectors to initial. Instructions for de-waterproofing could be read through the windshield on the back of the sticker. Artillery was waterproofed and flotation belts were attached as an extra precaution. In addition, rifles were wrapped in cellophane bags to keep them dry during the landing, duffle bags were packed and readied, and flotation belts and specially treated M-41 field jackets were laid out. "Every piece of our clothing had to be gas-proofed, waterproofed, and camouflaged in the many various colors of our future landscape," added one G.I. In addition, all vehicles were filled up with the water, gasoline, rations, and other supplies that would be necessary for the invasion.[47]

Another day or two passed. "England has become one vast ordnance dump and field park," declared BBC news correspondent Frank Gillard, in describing the countryside. "I've driven through it today for the best part of one hundred miles, the roads crammed with military traffic and lined, often enough on both sides, with vehicles of all kinds, just pulled off and parked on the verges. There is plenty of cover to be had this time of the year, and for all its concentration this stuff is well hidden from observation from above. In every wood and copse, in leafy dead-end lanes and side roads, often in private gardens, under quarries and embankments, there it all was—trucks, ambulances, tanks, armored cars, carriers, jeeps, bulldozers, ducks, vehicles of all kinds, vast, really vast numbers of them. And great mountains of stores, weapons and ammunition, rations, bridging equipment, tires, timber, millions of tons . . . [a]nd everywhere today, we have met the columns of men in battle dress. Men marching, men running, men deploying on exercises, men being transported here and there by the thousand in trucks and lorries. Men testing their equipment, tuning up their engines [and] waterproofing their vehicles . . . . Certainly, in the whole history of the world, there never had been such a vast concentration of all the paraphernalia of war in so small a space."[48]

Indeed, back in that first week of January when the 110th AAA Gun Battalion first arrived in England, it was part of nearly 750,000 total American troops in Britain at the time. Now, five months later, it was part of over 1,500,000 U.S. troops that was being provided with over 750,000 tons of supplies a month. According to *Yank* magazine, by this last week of May, American troops now outnumbered British civilians 20 to 1 and security all over the country had been intensified. Troops packed their barracks bags and kept them packed. Slowly, soldiers began to disappear from the area. Those who had received recent briefings on their particular assignments were now restricted to their camp areas, in complete isolation, and strictly forbidden to speak to civilians or to any G.I.s not in their unit—or in other words, to anyone who had not been briefed. This regulation was strictly enforced at all levels. In one incident Maj. Gen. Henry J. F. Miller, commander of the Ninth Air Force Service Command, was busted down to a lieutenant colonel by General Eisenhower and sent back to the States because he had told someone at a London cocktail party that D-Day would probably come before June 15.[49]

All of the military vehicles and equipment were covered with camouflaged netting and well hidden from observation from above. (Author's Collection)

Quietly, throughout the next several nights, units all over southern England broke camp in the dead of night and slowly pulled out. At about 04:00 hours on the morning of June 1, 1944, the officers and men of the individual batteries of the 110th AAA were awakened and ordered to entruck. "[S]o we hooked everything up," advised Lt. Jack Forman of Battery-A, "guns to the tractors, radar trailers to the trucks, and machine gun mounts to the trucks." Within a short time their convoy of sixty waterproofed vehicles slowly crept out of the K-7 camp under "cat-eye" headlamp security precautions and headed south along the road toward the harbor quay at Torpoint, on the Plymouth Hard. They arrived at Harbor 31 at Torpoint, on the west side of the bay opposite Plymouth, at dawn. [50]

At Harbor 31 each battery was loaded onto a separate landing craft—designated by the U.S. Navy as an LST [Landing Ship, Tank]. It was as big as a light cruiser—327-feet long—but flat-bottomed and capable of being beached to unload its cargo of tanks, trucks, guns and other heavy equipment, from two large doors that opened at it nose. "[The LST] could handle each battery's 400-ton weight nicely," advised Captain Reiver. Thus, Battery-A was loaded onto USS LST 498, Battery-B onto USS LST 510, Battery-C onto USS LST 291, and Battery-D onto USS LST 506. "They had paved areas down on the beach where these LSTs could come in, drop their ramp, and you could drive right on to 'em," advised Lieutenant Forman.[51]

Each battery loaded its four 90mm guns and artillery tractors, its "584" computer and four gun trackers, its electronic fire control unit, seven 6X6s, four jeeps, two three-quarter ton weapons carriers, tow ammo trailers, twenty-five .50 caliber machine guns, ammo, tarps, nets, and other supporting equipment. "[The boys] spent most of the [day] drivin' onto these LSTs," admitted Forman. The batteries left their supply and kitchen units behind. If all went well, these would join up with them in about a week.[52]

The LST's two huge bow doors opened to its sides and the vehicles were backed into the craft to provide quick unloading later. The tractors, guns, and large trucks were parked and securely chained in the ship's hold while the smaller vehicles, including trailers and jeeps, where chained down on its deck. A number of quad-50 units were chained down on the deck to provide for anti-aircraft protection. The loading of the 110th's vehicles and equipment was finally completed by 17:00 hours. Once accomplished, the officers and men crowded aboard the craft and at 18:45 the LSTs slowly backed off the landing and sailed out to lay offshore in Plymouth Harbor until the following day. Then, various practice sessions and trips were made. "We started practicing amphibious landings and loadings," complained one G.I. "[You] were already going on these LSTs and you didn't know if it was the real thing [or not]. You had to have everything ready and you'd cruise up and down the Atlantic for a day and then you'd land [somewhere] in England again."[53]

"[I]t seems as though everyone is existing merely from one ordinary day to the next, waiting for that great, extraordinary one," complained one newspaper columnist. "Until the invasion begins, even the most momentous domestic happenings are bound to fall flat."[54]

Another day or two passed. The batteries remained on their various LSTs about two miles out into Plymouth Sound making a number of practice

---

93

runs and attending training sessions throughout the remainder of June 1 and on through June 2 and 3. On June 4, still on LST 506, Glen and Wayne Edmondson celebrated Wayne's twentieth birthday. Their days were becoming monotonous, though, and they were losing track of time. Finally, after all the tedious, endless dry runs and all of the practice landings, the waiting was about to end.

CHAPTER 5

D-Day:
My First Visit to France

"From the beginning it had been clear that the choice of D-Day depended on the weather," admitted Brig. Gen. Walter Bedell Smith, Chief of Staff to the Supreme Commander, Dwight D. Eisenhower. "First, we wanted low tide so that the underwater and half-hidden beach obstacles could be seen and destroyed by our demolition crews. The low tide must be late enough in the morning for an hour's good daylight to permit the saturation bombing of defenses which would precede the landings themselves. But it must come early enough in the morning so that a second low tide would occur before darkness set in. Without the second low tide we could not land the follow-up divisions. For the airborne landings . . . we needed a late-rising full moon so the pilots could approach their objectives in darkness but have moonlight to pick out the drop zones. For the naval craft and transports, we must have a reasonable sea and good visibility to reduce the perils of navigation . . . [and] finally, we hoped for a fair wind blowing inshore to drive the smoke and dust of battle toward the enemy." Each and every one of these requirements were taken into consideration by the planners. According to meteorologists there would be only four days in early June, barring any storms, that would meet these exact conditions—the 4th, 5th, 6th, and 7th—with the 5th being ideal.[1]

Intending to get the best possible advantage, the Allied Supreme Command had chosen Monday, June 5. During the late-night hours of the previous day a convoy of ships began to assemble within the Channel all along the British southern coast and, forming a huge line two columns abreast with hundreds of ships before and aft, set out on a course for Calais, France, the closest point in the Channel to Great Britain—exactly where the Germans expected the attack to occur. The procession maintained that heading with no intentions of turning south toward Normandy's Cotentin Peninsula until the very last minute. According to Charles C. Wertenbaker, a *Life* correspondent assigned to one of the LSTs, the AA and machine-gun crews on board were briefed [again] about their assignment sometime after midnight as the ships had sailed along the Channel gathering others into the armada. Later, there was a general-quarters drill. Meanwhile, all the ship's officers were busy collecting signatures on brand-new 100-franc "invasion notes" which they planned to keep as mementos of the occasion. But, later that morning the ship's public address system announced, "Stand by for important message!" and then the troops were informed that the invasion had been postponed. The convoy was instructed to turn back and return to their ports immediately, because of tide and weather conditions.

"A terrible storm hit," advised Speer. "My Cat and gun were chained down in the hold of the LST but I know a lot of the vehicles on deck broke loose before we got back [and caused] a lot of damage."[2]

Actually, it had been storming since June 4. By the 5th a strong gale had blown up, churning the water into large waves. By that evening it was pouring rain, driven by the wind into a pelting force. "I don't remember my mood or attitude," advised another member of the 110th AAA, thinking back about the postponement. "I was entirely focused on the landing." Others, such as Wayne Edmondson, who had celebrated his birthday on ship the day before, and Owen Davies, who was celebrating his 21st birthday on ship that day, recalled that the day was memorable, but uneventful. Like every one else, they were anxious to get the whole thing started and get it over. They spent the remainder of the evening aboard the ships in the various harbors. Then, as the weather began to clear later that night, the ships began to slowly move out again. Rumors circulated that the command ships were gone. By 23:00 the destroyers were nowhere to be seen. Slowly, one by one the others began to gather as they headed out into the Channel. By thirty minutes past midnight, Tuesday, June 6, a great armada was on its way eastward once more, repeating their feint toward Calais.

"You are about to embark upon the Great Crusade," announced General Eisenhower's message to the troops, read over all the P.A. systems once the ships had cleared port. "The eyes of the world are upon you. The hopes and prayers of liberty-loving people everywhere march with you . . . . Your task will not be an easy one. Your enemy is well trained, well equipped and battle-hardened. He will fight savagely . . . . [but] I have full confidence in your courage, devotion to duty and skill in battle. We will accept nothing less than full Victory! Good Luck! And let us all beseech the blessing of Almighty God upon this great and noble undertaking."[3]

The ships pulled out and set sail individually from ports all around the eastern and southern coast of England. Gradually they all came together in one great eastbound fleet to cross the Channel. Overhead, tethered barrage balloons floated above the ships to create numerous obstacles for any attacking enemy aircraft. Sailing under blackout conditions, most of the troops would not see the number of ships in this vast movement across the sea until dawn. For those who would get a glimpse, the scene was an unforgettable spectacle.

"[W]e could see we were joining a lot of other warships after we got out," reported Pfc. Joseph S. Blaylock of Battery-B, 20th Field Artillery, 4th Motorized Division. "There were big battleships and cruisers and destroyers that were escorting us, and that was a sight to see. Just as far as you could see there were ships. After we set sail we went back down below and [a short time later] had a church service."[4]

The total number of naval craft involved was later determined to be more than 7,000 vessels including 6 battleships, 23 cruisers, 122 destroyers, 360 PT boats, hundreds of frigates, sloops, and other small combat craft, and 6,480 transports, landing craft, and special-purpose vessels. The vast armada spread out for thirty miles across the Channel. Command ships, destroyers, heavy cruisers, nine-sweepers, hospital ships, every kind of landing craft including LSTs. LCIs, LCFs, LCAs, LCVPs, and DUKWs, and armed Channel steamers, merchant ships, coasters, trawlers, and tugs.

It was Great Britain's Prime Minister Winston Churchill who had conceived of the idea that amphibious craft would be necessary for a successful invasion of the European continent and it was American ingenuity that had created the series of specialized vessels that could carry the necessary number of troops and equipment onto the enemy's beaches.

The largest of these landing ships were the LSTs, long, flat-bottomed, awkward-looking, gray vessels nearly 330 feet long and 50 feet wide. Smaller landing crafts, the LCVPs, were carried on davits on each side of this vessel to eventually be lowered into the water to await the soldiers to scramble down cargo nets into the boats for transport to a beach landing. The main function of the LST, however, was to transport tanks, artillery, trucks, jeeps, half-tracks, food, ammunition, hospital units, and additional troops onto the enemy beach once it was secured. Hour after hour these unsightly LSTs would plow through the water onto the beach and open their great bow doors from which would drive out all types of equipment to defend, arm, equip, feed, and in various ways supplement the advancing army. The auspicious invasion of Europe would become possible because of these ugly, awkward ships. There was 236 LSTs moving toward the Normandy beach in this convoy. After several back and forth missions to Omaha Beach on these things, though, the Coast Guard personnel operating them would swear that the initials LST apparently stood for Large Slow Targets.

For the invasion the 110th AAA Gun Battalion and Medical Detachment were attached to the 29th Infantry Division, which in turn was attached to the V Corps of the First Army. The 110th AAA was scheduled to go onto the beach as part of the 18th AAA Group, 49th AAA Brigade, in late-morning of D-Day as part of the "Force B" build-up. Slowly the U.S. Coast Guard-manned LSTs took them toward their destination. In all of the ships and LSTs the young soldiers were met below deck by their commanding officers and, after prayer with the chaplain, given a fatherly pep talk. "When I call the roll [tonight]," many of them ended by saying, "I want everyone to say, 'Here!' ... Now, Good luck!" Afterwards, most of the troops returned to the upper deck to wait out the trip.

Although it was still dark, back up on deck above the din of the LSTs diesel engines and blowers and the creaks and groans of the vessel in the sea, Speer and the others could hear the unmistakable hum of aircraft engines overhead—bombers and troop carriers bound for France. "I went down in the hold and sat in the cab of my Cat," advised Glen. "That was a no-no. We weren't supposed to do that but I felt safe in my Cat and with my Thompson sub-machine gun."[5]

While many of the others laid under the vehicles for protection up on deck, Glen sat in his M-4 prime mover and tried to sleep. In fact, even though it was against the rules, many preferred to be off by themselves below deck or in the hold. Few felt like sitting and talking on this trip. Most preferred to be alone to think.

"An invasion ship is a lonely ship," confessed one soldier. "Downstairs in an LST you sit and sweat and nobody says anything because there is nothing to say. You look around and you wonder who will be dead soon.... Then the thought comes, swelling up inside of you ... maybe it's me. Maybe I'll be dead soon."[6]

"You don't talk much," agreed another. "I didn't say a damn word. And don't ask me what I was thinking, because I don't remember. I guess I was thinking a little about everything. And don't ask me what I saw [on the way over], because I don't remember that either. But I remember *everything* once I hit that [damn beach]."[7]

As the great armada continued, the faint light of dawn revealed an outline of the French coast through the fog ahead. "The steeple of the

Vierville-sur-Mer Church could now be seen on the huge bluff that towered at least 100 feet above our beach," reported Harold Baumgarten of Company-B, 116th Infantry Regiment, 29th Infantry Division, heading in for a 06:40 landing on Dog Green Omaha. As his landing craft passed a nearby barge, the air erupted with the frightening sounds of thousands of five-inch rockets being fired toward the shore. "The explosions could be seen [landing] on the beach in front of us," worried Baumgarten. In another landing craft nearby, John J. Barnes of Company-A of the 116th Infantry Regiment, also heading into Dog Green Omaha, was mesmerized by all the sights and sounds around him. "Someone shouted, 'Take a good look! This is something you will tell your grandchildren!'" recalled Barnes. "No one [asked] the question 'What if we don't live?'"[8]

Holding position six miles offshore, the mighty battleships *Texas* and *Arkansas*, and the cruisers *Glasgow*, *Montcalm*, and *Georges Leygues*, opened up and began pounding the French shore and the German coastal batteries. Closer in, rocket-firing landing craft opened up with their rapidly successive barrages of over a thousand 5-inch missiles that went screaming toward the beach. Hearing the big battleships' main battery of twelve 12-inch and ten 14-inch guns over all of the noise, one soldier remarked that it sounded as though they had began pumping freight-train cars through the sky toward the beach. The sound was deafening and the concussions were astonishing. In fact the concussions were so great from the big battleships, according to some sources, they sprung the heavy metal plating on a number of nearby landing craft. One war correspondent on a nearby LCVP noted that those not suffering from seasickness were watching the overwhelming spectacle with "looks of surprise and happiness."

"Under their steel helmets," he noted, while observing their faces being illuminated by the orange-colored flashes of the nearby guns, "they looked like pikemen of the Middle Ages" to whose rescue had come some "strange and unbelievable monster."[9]

But, in the dark and low cloud cover, other forms of intended protection had failed. The great force of 480 Lancasters, Fortresses, and Liberators that Glen and the others had heard passing overhead during their trip across the Channel, had overshot their intended targets and had dropped all of their 1,285 tons of bombs nearly three miles inland, having no affect on the German gun emplacements along the beach. As H-Hour approached, the noise became overwhelming as the fear and excitement became devastating. Additional rocket-equipped assault craft joined in with the nearby battleships and destroyers to fire off more fast-paced salvos at the German defenses. German guns on the coast responded with astounding accuracy and destruction.

The first troops came into Dog Green Omaha at 06:35. Consisting of Company-A, 1st Battalion, 116th Infantry Division, they landed in six LCAs from the British transport *Empire Javelin*. One LCA, the one containing Pfc. John J. Barnes, hit a submerged obstacle 100 to 150 yards off shore and sank, losing most of her troops. Barnes survived. Another landing craft coming in on the right side of Company-A, carrying a company of Rangers, took four direct hits of enemy artillery and disintegrated with all aboard.[10]

As additional landing craft came in and dropped their ramps, the troops floundered out into three to four feet of water and immediately came under intense shelling and gunfire. "We were loaded down like a Missouri mule," complained Theodore L. Lamb, 2nd Lieutenant, Co. F, 116th Infantry Regiment, "[Besides the heavy backpack] we had these assault jackets on and they were all loaded. All the pockets had something in 'em."[11]

Struggling under the heavy load—when simply tripping or stumbling might cause their death by drowning—they were expected to go through 50 to 100 yards of water dodging gunfire and obstacles, cross 200 to 300 yards of beach and get to the limited protection of a concrete seawall. Beyond that lay an artificial seawall protected by tangles of barbed wire, a grassy area of about 100 more yards, then a line of bluffs that, except for a few ravines, defied scaling by man or vehicle. Many never made it. The whole area offered hardly any cover and remained well defended by two regiments of excellent, battle-seasoned, German troops.

"Many men never reached the beach," advised one young soldier, "their dead or dying bodies were held afloat by their inflated life jackets [and] behind a low sand bar just past the water's edge were more dead, the wounded, and the remaining dazed survivors."[12]

"I remember so distinctly seeing some of the living holding some of the wounded and the expression of pain and fear on their faces," recalled Fletcher Harris, 115th Infantry Regiment, 29th Infantry Division, who came in a few minutes later. "I waded ashore [and] dropped down for just a few seconds with a row of battered men from the 116th to let some of the water drain from my clothes. The survivors and I looked at each other but we did not speak." Withering machine-gun and artillery fire from the vicinity of the Vierville exit pinned down all the troops who did make it to shore. Machine-gun fire skittered across the beach throwing up a patchwork of sand. Rifle fire rapidly cross-stitched other portions and an occasional "zing" was heard as shots ricocheted off nearby obstacles. "You could hear the artillery pieces [too]," noted one of the others. "You would hear 'Tonk, Tonk' [and] you'd lean into [the sand] to duck until they hit on the beach . . . . [you'd raise your head] and then you'd hear 'Tonk, Tonk' again and you'd lean in and wait for those to come over."[13]

"Even to land was a miracle," agreed news correspondent Ernie Pyle. "Men were killed as they stepped out of the landing craft. An officer whom I knew got a bullet right through the head just as the door of his landing craft was let down . . . . The Germans were dug into positions they had been working on for months. A one-hundred-foot bluff a couple of hundred yards back from the beach had great concrete gun emplacements built right into the hilltops. They opened to the sides instead of the front, thus making it hard for our naval fire from the sea to have much effect on them [while] they could shoot parallel with the beach and cover every foot of it for miles with their artillery fire. Then they had hidden machine-gun nests on the forward slopes with cross-fire covering every inch of the beach. These nests were connected by networks of trenches so that German gunners could move about without exposing themselves."[14]

"[M]en were falling like flies during a fly tox raid," fretted Lt. Evermonte Huffman, Co. E, 116th Infantry Regiment. "In thirty minutes we had lost 10 of our 31 men and couldn't locate but seven of those . . . . We had a mortar man with no mortar, a flame thrower with no flame thrower man, and a bazooka man with no bazooka."[15]

Robert Capa, war correspondent and photographer for *Life* magazine, remained pinned down on the beach for some time. At one point an Army Lieutenant crawled up beside him and remarked, "Ya know what I can see? I can see my ma on the front porch, waving my insurance policy." Capa understood and had to agree. He had participated in the previous D-Day invasions of Sicily and Salerno, Italy. But by the furious hell and carnage he was witnessing here, he could see this landing was destined to become "the father and mother of *all* D-Days." After six hours of being pinned down on the beach, he lost his nerve. Capa broke for the surf behind him and boarded a Red Cross LCI for safety. Others, of course, never had that option.[16]

"It was a battle of survival with little or no chance to fight, and every man for himself," complained one soldier. "[A] shell fragment hit me in the hip and set off two chemical smoke grenades I was carrying in my pocket."[17]

According to another officer, enemy fire on the beach was horrific. "They used it all," reported Lt. W. L. Wade, USNR, commanding LCI Group 28. "They were using 105mm, 88mm, 40mm, mortars, machine guns, mines—everything."[18]

"From time immemorial," observed the *Des Moines Register & Tribune* in agreement, "it has been a recognized fact that an attack on a fortified coast is about the toughest phase of warfare.

. . . The West or 'Atlantic' wall, as the Germans call it, was not a wall in the literal sense of the word. Rather it was a devilishly ingenious series of obstacles—obstacles fashioned from steel and reinforced concrete—obstacles that consisted of mines, interlocking fire, flooded areas, and every type of land and sea blockade conceivable to the military mind. Machine-guns, artillery emplacements, observation posts, pillboxes, and shelters embedded in concrete all were elements that comprised the 'wall.'"[19]

As the second wave of landing craft approached the beach at 07:00 they, too, were met by heavy and accurate artillery bombardment and equally intense gunfire. This second wave remained pinned down along the surf, behind beach obstacles, and crowded along the seawall. "The cover you think is there, isn't when you get there," observed one worried soldier. "You feel like you're out in the open when you finally get to what looked like good cover."[20]

The following troop waves continued to jam up along the beach behind the first, second, third, fourth, and fifth waves. The eighth wave brought the first vehicles to shore. Then, one wave of landing craft after another became pinned down on the beach or just off shore. German gunners seemed to concentrate on each vehicle as it came up onto the beach and quickly disabled, exploded, or set many of them on fire before they could provide the infantrymen any support. Tanks were especially vulnerable but so were all other types of armored vehicles. It became as difficult to get support vehicles onto the beach as it did troops. Many vehicles never landed under the concentrated artillery, mortar, and small arms fire.

"I had the misfortune of my LCT hitting a large marine mine, blowing up and sinking all 4 tanks with my crews," advised Sgt. Glen E. Gibson, Co. A, 4th Platoon, 70th Tank Battalion. "Out of 37 Army men on the LCT, I am the only survivor."[21]

Not only were there heavy loses of tank support for the Omaha landing but disaster met the attempts to ferry much of the supporting artillery ashore too. In many cases artillery pieces were off-loaded onto small DUKWS causing the craft to founder before reaching shore. The 11th Field Artillery Battalion lost all of its 105mm howitzers except one in this way. The 16th Infantry Cannon Company suffered the same fate and the 7th Field Artillery fared little better. Then the 62nd Armored Field Artillery Battalion came in and experienced a similar conclusion. "Our motors were revved up, [I signaled the driver], and off we went," declared Sgt. Jerry W. Eades, commanding the No. 4 Gun Section of B-Battery. "I vaguely remember seeing the 3rd Section gun fall off the front of the boat and into the water and then I heard a kind of glubb-glubb-glubbing sound." All of the vehicles and the guns they were pulling were lost. In addition, Capt. Bernard J. Sabatino and a number of others with the 111th Field Artillery Battalion were killed coming ashore with their unit. By 08:00, an hour and a half after H-Hour, not a man nor a vehicle had moved off the beach in the western sector. Conditions were so bad there that General Omar Bradley, in command of the First Army and watching with binoculars twelve and a half miles offshore from the *Augusta*, decided by 09:00 that the American troops "had suffered an irreversible catastrophe" and sent a message to headquarters asking permission to transfer the rest of his force to the British beaches and abandon those already pinned down on Omaha. Fortunately for those troops, headquarters didn't receive that message until late in the afternoon while consumed with directing logistical support to the other areas.[22]

By then some order had been created out of the chaos at four of the five invasion sites. Footholds had been established on the beaches code-named Utah, Gold, Juno, and Sword. Allied lines were slowly moving inland there as reinforcements and supplies were steadily pouring in. On Omaha Beach, however, thousands of troops were still pinned down and unable to move. The beach was littered with disabled vehicles and discarded equipment. The dead and wounded laid about and most of the formidable beach obstacles remained in place, unable to be destroyed under the heavy enemy defensive fire. By 08:30 the Navy Beachmaster for Omaha had signaled all control vessels to suspend any further landings of vehicles and equipment. At that time there were more than 50 LSTs, LCTs, and LCIs off shore searching for gaps in which to land. During the next several hours beaching and landing craft milled around back and forth off shore stalling for time.

Between 12:23 and 12:30 the *Texas* put six 14-inch shells into the German stronghold along the Vierville exit. In all, by late afternoon the great ship would pump 190 rounds into the German strong points positioned on either side of the road and onto an antitank wall built along that area. At the same time the *McCook* and the *Carmick* continued to pound the area above the beach and along the cliffs concentrating on the Vierville exit. The *McCook* would fire 975 rounds at this area by the afternoon while the *Carmick* would use 1,127 rounds between there and the village of Colleville-sur-Mer, concentrating most heavily on the Vierville area.[23]

The earliest components of Assault Force "B" (Backup) arrived off Omaha Beach right on schedule. Consisting of additional elements of the 1st and 29th Divisions, the initial convoys were ordered to delay all landing and to stall around off shore, instead. Finally, at 16:30, beaching began for the first group. By late in the day Army artillery had began to come ashore in strength. Only one battery, however, would be able to get set up and get into action on this day.

As part of the initial units assigned to Assault Force B, the batteries of the 110th AAA were scheduled to land with their vehicles and equipment at H-hour plus 210 (10:00 hours) June 6 and each had a designated position they were to take up around the outskirts of Vierville. Engineers were supposed to have landed between 05:30 and 06:00 to begin blowing up the obstacles to help clear a safe landing path. They were to then erect a large canvas banner with a big green "D" displayed on it to help direct the arriving men and equipment. The 110th's scouts were to come in with elements of the 116th Infantry on the 13th wave at 08:20 (H-hour + 110). They were to locate the banner, move up the D-1 draw and establish and mark out the various artillery positions. Due to the hell and confusion on the beach, however, all landings were delayed and seriously backed up as early as 07:30. At some locations pandemonium reigned and by 08:00 disabled tanks, trucks, landing craft and other debris were beginning to collect along the landing sites, adding to the congestion and chaos of the area. The dead, the dying, and body parts were strewn all across the area as well. When the beachmaster suspended all further landings at Omaha at 08:30, four of the fifty LSTs circling off shore contained the various elements of the 110th AAA Gun Battalion. "There was a lot of commotion," agreed one young G.I. "There were a lot of dead bodies floating in the water. Everything was in turmoil. They halted bringing in the supplies [and everything] because they were still overburdened on the beach with the fighting."[24]

"The problem turned out to be the large gun the Germans had dug into the cliff [above Exit D-1 off the beach]," noted Capt. Julius Reiver. That gun, a 75mm artillery piece concealed in a concrete bunker to the right of the exit, was hidden form the view of the Allied ships off-shore but it had a completely unobstructed view of the entire length of Omaha Beach. "The Germans just picked off each vehicle and tank as it landed and nothing left that beach on D-Day."[25]

"I saw three tanks coming along the beach, barely moving, they were advancing so slowly," observed *Collier's* correspondent Ernest Hemingway, from his landing craft circling off shore. "The Germans let them cross the open space where the valley opened onto the beach, and it was absolutely flat, with a perfect field of fire." With that the German gun opened up on the tanks and destroyed them in rapid succession. "[N]one of our ships could hit [that gun] from the water," advised Reiver. "One destroyer backed into the beach until it [nearly grounded] but its stern gun could not [get to] the German piece."[26]

"[It was] the cruiser *Augusta*, I believe," advised Dick Brammann, B-Battery, 110th AAA, watching the devastation and destruction from an LST off-shore, "going in close and firing at the positions on the cliffs with her big guns." At the same time there was a number of active machine-gun pits along the exit and dug into the cliffs overlooking the beach in addition to mortar emplacements located throughout the area. The Beach Master later signaled to all circling craft to stand offshore during the night and not to attempt landings on Omaha until the various guns and the cluttered beach could be cleared out.[27]

On LST 506 Capt. Julius Reiver looked toward the beach, visibly irritated. "We didn't come over here to ride around in a boat," one of his young recruits overheard him saying. "Those guys in there need our help or they won't make it."[28]

"I met with two of our officers," recalled Reivers, "[and] the three of us decided to get off this LST the next morning, orders or no. We sent [Lt. Ernest A.] Eddy out in one of the LST's LCVPs and he went from rhino ferry to rhino ferry trying to talk one of them into taking us ashore .... Eddy finally talked one rhino Captain into taking us, having told him something about 'the General said it was OK.'"[29]

After Lieutenant Eddy's return to the LST and a short consultation, Captain Reiver then turned to his troops. "Now you guys back us up," he said. "We didn't get no orders."[30]

"Everyone agreed," recalled Speer. "There was nothin' we wouldn't do for that guy."[31]

Over on LST 291 there was another turn of events. "I somehow got in with the forward recon of the 29th," complained Elmer J. Potzmann, who went through Basic Training with Battery-C of the 110th AAA but was later assigned to the Medical detachment of its Headquarters Battery. "I told the officer in charge I was a medic with the 110th and he told me it was OK; not to worry about it—Just take care of myself because if they lost a medic, many more men would be lost." In the landing craft next to Potzmann was another young soldier of the 29th who appeared to be about his age. "He was barely 18," advised Elmer. "His only job was to carry a 50-foot pole—it was, I believe, a 2X2—with eight one-quarter pound blocks of TNT fastened to the end, and to shove it into the opening of a German pillbox once we got to shore. I asked him 'What if the Germans shove it back out at you?' and he said, 'Well I don't know. Guess I'll shove it back in—and with its five-second fuse, if I wait one second before I do, maybe they won't have time to shove it back out' . . . [We] hit the beach at about H-hour plus 360 [12:30 hours]. I never did see him [again]."[32]

Goin' In! Dog-Green beach and the Vierville Draw (D-1) under fire. Note the village's church steeple, the aiming point for all the landing craft assigned to this area. (National Archives)

Medics Wayne Kuchar (L) and Elmer Potzmann (R). Elmer somehow got assigned to go in with the forward recon of the 29th Infantry Division. (Courtesy of Elmer Potzmann)

Lt. Clint Gardner of Battery-B, on LST 510, was one of the battalion's scouts sent in on a forward recon with an infantry unit to help locate the area for the assigned beach exit and to help direct his battery's arrival. Nothing went as planned. The first truck off his assigned LCT rolled off into deep water and sank. Confronted by a hail of gunfire, individuals began to jump off the landing craft to fend for their lives. Gardner scrambled off the boat and trudged through deep water toward the beach. The 29th, which by this time was supposed to be off the beach working its way toward the interior, was only fifty feet ahead. The giant markers that were supposed to be posted to help direct the units to their initial staging areas were nowhere to be seen. Reaching the beach, Lieutenant Gardner assisted others moving some of the dead bodies so vehicular traffic could make its way through. German mortar and machine-gun fire raked and pelted the area. Noise and chaos was all around. Suddenly, Gardner was knocked off his feet as mortar fragments tore through his helmet. Dazed, he laid there on the beach as the battle continued around him. Intense pressure built up at his forehead and blood streamed down over his face. Slowly, he was able to reach up. He thought he could feel his brains. In what he believed was slow-motion, he used his fingers to wipe blood from his eyes. After what seemed like an hour others ran up to him and he heard a British-sounding officer order some men to move him out of the way. After dragging him a short distance through the sand, they ran off. Gardner, drifting in and out of consciousness and unable to move or speak, remained at the foot of the cliffs of Omaha Beach, left for dead. "Our Captain, Jim Chase, was on the radio awaiting word from [him]," reported Harvey Edds. "[Then we] got word that the infantry company that had just gotten off our LST had been slaughtered—They had suffered 94-percent casualties." The first report Captain Chase got was that Lieutenant Gardner had been killed.[33]

At the same time, Lt. Henry J. (Hank) Klein of Battery-D was sent in on forward recon to help direct D-Battery to its initial staging area but the LCT he rode in on was subjected to heavy German artillery fire. After a number of near misses, the craft capsized during which Klein also received a head wound and all contact with him was lost. Battery-A, on LST 498, sent Lt. Jack Forman and Cpl. Ronald G. Lambert ahead to reconnoiter for their landing. "People were falling on my left, falling on my right, falling in front of me [and] fallin' in back of me from machine gun fire from machine gun nests that were up on the cliffs," recalled Forman. "So we loaded about ten wounded into the boat and took 'em back to the LST where a doctor from San Antonio had set up an operating room in the Mess Hall (or dining hall or whatever the Navy called those things) and I was damned glad to get back to the ship."[34]

Casualties were reportedly running high all along the beach. Unable to make any contact with Lieutenant Gardner, Captain Chase sent Tech-5 Arthur J. Hubbard, Sgt. Jesse James, Sgt. Robert Pritchard, and Sgt. Frank Wisniewski with 2nd Lt. Robert A. Wilson into the beach on reconnaissance. "[We] spent the [entire] time looking for our position and Lieutenant Gardner," declared Hubbard. "Didn't find either but it certainly was an experience I'll not forget!"[35]

During this time wounded from the initial assault on the continent were already arriving back at many of the LSTs for evacuation. "Each LST had been rigged out as a floating hospital, equipped with an operating room and a ward," advised Joseph Eckenrode. "The plan had been for the LSTs to unload immediately upon reaching their destination, load wounded from the beach, and take them back to England." The problem was the "ward" that was supposed to be capable of holding more than one thousand stretcher patients was to be the entire tank deck of the LST where all of the vehicles and equipment were still chained down due to the delays in landing on Omaha Beach. Crowded as conditions were, there was hardly enough space to accommodate more than fifteen stretcher cases. "It was not long until the first load of wounded, both American and German, were brought to the side of the LSTs," added Eckenrode. Ross F. DiMarco, also a member of the Medical Detachment of the 110th AAA was on board LST 291 as these casualties arrived. Immediately, DiMarco "eagerly and aggressively" assisted in their care and, according to the 110th battalion's commanding officer, Lt. Col. William F. Curren, in at least two instances initiated measures that saved lives.[36]

A young German wounded and captured near Exit D-1 was brought aboard LST 510 where B-Battery was still waiting their turn to beach. "I can still picture him laying there on a litter and the frightened look on his face," recalled Sgt. John F. Kreckler. "One of our comrades walked over to him, pointed his rifle at him and said 'Shoot the bastard.' At that, a medical officer or corpsman quickly moved in, pushed our fellow aside and said: 'Put that gun away and save your energy [for the beach]! The war's over for him; Its just beginning for you!'" In another instance a wounded American soldier was laying on a litter next to a wounded German. "All of a sudden I could see [the American] beginning to move his right arm," declared Edds of Battery-B. "He still had his bayonet on him and he was going to pull it out of his scabbard and kill the German soldier laying next to him . . . . I hollered at one of the fellows standing [nearby] and he took the bayonet away from him."[37]

German artillery and automatic weapons fire continued to riddle the beach throughout the morning and afternoon. Everyone became anxious to get in there to do their part. General Edward W. Timberlake of the 49th AAA Brigade was no exception. He insisted on going ashore and when others tried to convince him it was still too dangerous, he finally ordered it. Traveling parallel to the beach in search of a less active spot, Timberlake was landed at 15:00 on D-Day afternoon accompanied by Major Chase C. Coffey and Major Michael G. Kelakos of the Brigade and Lt. Col. William F. Curren, Commanding Officer of the 110th AAA Gun Battalion and a few other members of that organization. "The beaches were strewn with the dead," reported Major Kelakos. Infantrymen and engineers were hugging the shelter of the cliff side and yelled at General Timberlake to take cover. The General, undaunted, urged them to get up and 'Go get the bastards.' A command post was set up in a nearby beach house but the structure was taking so many hits from the enemy's artillery that they finally moved their operation to open field. The thunder and steady pounding of heavy naval guns firing onto the beach and beyond continued. From shore, orange flame could be seen bellowing from their muzzles. "At two places where landing parties found exits from the beaches," wrote one news correspondent who came onto the beach at about the same time, "destroyers standing in close to the shore were pouring fire into the valleys beyond the exits [while] enemy guns were firing into the valley themselves." The air trembled as both sides fired their heavy guns. The enemy's shelling continued on into the evening but, by then, with less intensity. Their main emphasis seemed to be on the landing craft circling and maneuvering off shore. Whenever the opportunity arose, a craft would come in and unload its troops and equipment and move out of the area beyond the range of the enemy guns. "I spent the evening with the Captain of the LST in the crow's nest," advised Capt. Julius Reiver of D-Battery. "It was almost getting dark when an airplane flew parallel along the beach and then turned and headed out over the invasion fleet. I told the Captain to order his men to shoot, that it was a German JU-88. He insisted it was one of ours. It circled and came in right over us. Directly over us it dropped a large bomb [but its] forward motion carried it in front of us. It burst on contact, with some of the shrapnel coming in our open bow doors."[38]

Fortunately this plane had remained fairly high in order to clear the barrage balloons tethered to the LSTs but still, several enemy planes did come in along the beach and circled out to strafe and bomb the American ships. According to *Life* correspondent Charles C. Wertenbaker, at least one ship was hit that evening. He saw its deck flare up brilliantly for a few minutes before it was extinguished just as quickly. "Those JU-88s could come in there and tip up on their side," marveled Speer, "and slide through there [among the barrage balloons], drop bombs and be gone before you could ever shoot at 'em." Those on the other landing craft found the delay off the coast just as unnerving. "When a couple of German fighter planes swooped out of the sky, looked us all over and swooped back up into the sky," recalled Lester Cohen over on LST 510, "I said to Captain Chase at the time, 'I hope they weren't looking for us.' He smiled and gave me his binoculars and said 'Here, take a look.'" What Cohen saw were ships loaded down with troops and equipment as far as he could see in any direction. He then realized the odds against LST 510 being picked out over any other for attack was probably in his favor.[39]

By nightfall several units of the 115th and 116th Infantry Regiments had slowly etched their way up to and then past the blacktop road that ran along the coast linking the three villages above and beyond Omaha. A patchwork of American-held territory was scattered over an area six miles long and two miles deep. Units were spread out in such a way that there was no discernible front line and, therefore, no chance of needed support. At best, American forces had a precarious hold on the French sector. Working on double daylight savings time, complete darkness fell over the region at 23:30. By then 3,000 Americans lay dead or wounded along the three-mile stretch of sand. As the tide went out that night it took a lot of bodies with it and revealed an immense field of disabled vehicles and other equipment. Slowly throughout the night reinforcements came ashore under sporadic enemy gunfire and continued to land as the hours passed. According to one artillery officer the Luftwaffe then came over and attempted to knock out some of the vast armada as these landings took place. The only protection against air attack that night was the ships' guns and the various artillery units mounted on the decks of the thousands of ships anchored in or roving the Channel. These consisted mostly of .50-caliber quad-50s. There was no antiaircraft batteries on shore to defend the American fleet. "The sun had just set and it was dark enough that the light from the tank deck shining through the opening in the bow of the ships sent a beam of light across the water," noted one young G.I. "Then came the roar of low flying planes."[40]

When one plane swooped in and dropped six floating "chandelier" flares to light up the area everyone in the fleet then realized they were German aircraft. Immediately millions of traces rose up from the ships and flared into the skies in sharp defiance. "[E]very ship in the bay that had a gun on it, every machine gun, and every antiaircraft gun was firing at the flares," noted 1st Lieutenant Forman over on LST 498, in amazement. "The flak from that business was more dangerous than being on the beach for the landing!"[41]

"The planes were so low their bombs could be seen hanging to the external bomb racks on their wings," noted Sgt. Joseph Eckenrode of D-Battery on LST 506. "Then three of the bombs were released [and] everyone dove under the nearest vehicle.... The bombs dropped into the Channel about ten feet in front of the bow! The boat rocked and shook [and] everyone thought it was falling apart."[42]

By then the sky was filled with acres and acres of tracers from the pom-pom guns and quad-50s on the thousands of ships throughout the Channel, lighting the sky like daylight. The attack lasted nearly 45 minutes. Before the action had ended, several German planes had been knocked into the Channel. "Shortly after midnight," reported a *Life* correspondent on one of the landing ships, "three raiders fell slowly flaming into the sea."[43]

For many of these boys, those 45 minutes was the most awesome spectacle they had ever seen. "How an airplane could fly around in that spectacular display of ack-ack was a big question on everyone's mind," recalled one. "[T]hat first night was the greatest fireworks I ever expect to see," noted another, "with all our forces firing tracers at the German Air Force overhead."[44]

"Many of the barrage balloons moored to the LSTs to prevent low level bombing," reported Eckenrode, "were shot down [by our own gunners] during the excitement."[45]

Dawn of D+1, June 7, broke bright and clear. The new day, however, revealed an unbelievably shocking sight to all of those approaching Omaha Beach. It was completely littered with wreckage and bodies from the previous day's heavy resistance. "It looked like a junk yard," exclaimed *Life*'s Charles Wertenbaker. "From the water's edge at low tide to the high-water mark were landing craft, some impaled on obstacles, blown by mines, shattered by shellfire and stranded by the ebbing tide." Equally devastating was the number of American bodies scattered all over the beach and floating in the water. "There was a bulldozer with its guts spattered over the sand," wrote Wertenbaker, "and another with its occupants spattered, an arm here, a leg there, a piece of pulp over yonder [and] there were discarded things all over the beach: life belts, cartridge clips, canteens, pistol belts, bayonets, K-rations." German artillery and mortar fire continued intermittently. "There were still many snipers holed up in the cliffs behind the beach," advised a member of D-Battery, 110th AAA, "and every now and then there'd be a brief exchange of shots." The big gun at the Vierville exit was still active and various machine-gun pits remained in operation. "We were just about 300 yards off shore," complained Cpl. Leo Kania of A-Battery on LST 498. "There was shelling coming in and all ... and they were [still] bringing back the injured, the casualties."[46]

For hours the landing crafts cruised back and forth off shore waiting for more landing areas to be cleared out and seeking permission to beach. In the meantime, American casualties continued to be brought aboard the LSTs. "There were two or three that I thought were pretty bad," recalled Harvey Edds over on LST 510. "One took a direct hit from a mortar. You couldn't tell the front of his face from the back of his head . . . . Another fellow had his legs blown off at the knees . . . . A German machine gun had hit the grenades he was carrying in his knee pockets."[47]

When backing destroyers and cruisers up onto the beach failed to take out the big German gun at Vierville, other ideas were tried. "You could actually see the shells [from the ships] blasting away parts of the cliffs," marveled one G.I. Various troops sent to the gun emplacement from different directions with pole charges were killed before they could even get close. Finally, during the early hours of D+1 a brave group of frustrated American G.I.s took matters into their own hands. "An anti-aircraft half-track landed on the beach," advised Reiver, "headed the wrong way and backed up toward the German gun with its four .50 caliber machine guns blazing. Some of the bullets entered the casemate . . . and killed the gun crew."[48]

"The outfit had landed behind [a] wave of infantry," explained correspondent Ernie Pyle. "Driver Bill Hendrix, from Shreveport, Louisiana, turned their half-track around and drove the front end back into the water so the [vehicle-mounted] gun would be pointed in the right direction. Then the boys poured twenty-three rounds into the pillbox. Some of their shells hit the small gun slits and went inside. At the end of their firing, what Germans were left came out with their hands up."[49]

Although machine-gun, mortar, and sniper fire continued, the silencing of the big gun at the Vierville exit allowed the pinned-down troops in this region to defend themselves more effectively and to move their equipment more rapidly. Traffic on the beach slowly increased as more men and equipment began to move forward and engineer and Ranger units began opening the exits. Finally, late in the morning Captain Reiver was notified that the rhino ferry Lieutenant Eddy had previously reserved was available.

At noon Battery-D received orders to get to the trucks and prepare to go ashore," recalled Eckenrode. Slowly, LST 506 adjusted its aimless course and headed for a line of approach. As the craft entered the queue line, Speer went down into the hold and examined his M-4 artillery tractor and all of its equipment and then climbed up into the cab to prepare for departure. Within a few minutes his gun crew arrived and got into the rear cabin compartment as the machine-gunner, Grayson Tackitt, got up into the pulpit behind the heavy machine gun, checked it out and got it ready for action. "We were anxious to get in there and do our job, do our part," advised one young G.I. assigned to the 110th. "And not only did we feel vulnerable out on the ship, we also felt a little guilty that we weren't [already] in there doing our share."[50]

LST 506 maneuvered into position to approach the beach as close as possible. "Our LST hit [bottom] quite a ways out from the shore at twelve noon," recalled Speer. "So we unloaded onto what was called a Rhino Ferry—a large flat barge-type thing." This craft was apparently available only because it had been heavily damaged the previous evening. It was moving very slowly. "[This rhino] had been hit by the Germans several times," complained Reiver, "and some of the water-tight steel cubes had been punctured." As a result of the damage the ferry rode low in the water and only had one working engine. Being the only one available, however, it was quickly lashed to the bow of the LST, the big bow doors were opened, and the vehicles rumbled aboard the floating platform. After two hours loading the battery's vehicles, guns, and equipment onto the craft, it slowly made its way toward the beach, laboring heavily under its load and crippling damage. "So we went along the beach at one mile per hour to each landing point," confessed Captain Reiver. "These points had been cleared of mines and were the only safe places to land [but] nobody would accept us. So we decided to make our own exit and we instructed the crew of the rhino to go into the beach at the full speed of one mile per hour."[51]

The U.S. Army engineers in charge of the cleared landing points were simply following the Beachmaster's orders allowing no landings. Meanwhile, the slow nerve-racking trip was being made under heavy artillery and mortar attack. German machine-gunners along the hillside continued raking the area but apparently failed to notice the meandering rhino ferry running parallel with the beach. Finally, the craft dropped the units off into about five to six feet of water about a quarter-mile off shore. "Floating the rhino up to the beach was a hazardous job," remembered Eckenrode, "because the least drift of the raft to the left or the right would have tripped one of [the numerous] mines."[52]

As Glen drove his tractor, which was eight feet high, off the ramp and toward the beach, water slapped in through the partially open front windows and seeped in around the canvass doors soaking him from his chest down to his feet. He remembers that he felt fear as he headed off toward the beach but also knew he had a job to do and everyone—including he, himself—fully expected him to get it done. "You realized you were scared," admitted Speer, "but you really didn't know what you were scared of." At the same time, Glen also realized a certain amount of fear was healthy and kept him alert. "You had no time to think," he added, "except of what all you were supposed to do." Occasionally he would hear a ricochet off the side of the tractor or see a mortar round hit and explode in the water nearby as he concentrated on maintaining his course toward the beach and tried to miss all the shell holes and dead bodies along his route. At the same time, as chauffeur for the gun crew, Speer felt responsible for them and the equipment and took his job very seriously—a fact they appreciated. The gun crew sat in the compartment behind the cab. Behind the crew was the ammunition compartment. Each prime mover carried 63 rounds in its ammo compartment for the gun it pulled onto the Normandy beach. It was just enough to get them started, three to four minutes of continuous firing at the most, but it would be more than enough to destroy the entire unit and its crew if it got hit by the enemy now. That was on Speer's mind as he headed toward the beach and he operated accordingly.[53]

The western end of Normandy beach in the area the Allies had code-named "Dog Green" Omaha was just below the village of Vierville-sur-Mer. As Speer drove up out of the surf he found a long expanse of wet and then dry sand thickly planted with a variety of mined obstacles until the beach turned to a rock—and pebble-covered shelf. Just beyond that was a four-foot high concrete seawall draped by a ruff of concertina barbed wire and a wide level grassy area of about 100 to 150 yards above that running back to 100-foot high cliffs that overlooked the beach. To his right was the ravine that contained the narrow unsurfaced road—more like a wagon track—that exited the beach and linked with the village on the plateau. This exit, the one code-named "D-1" by the Allies, was his main objective. "It was a steep and not a very wide road," noted Glen. He recalled no one in the gun crew saying a word as they crossed the beach and began their ascent toward the exit. Heading up the incline and toward the draw, Speer and the crew were startled when the gunner over the cab opened fire with the .50-caliber machine gun as other shots ricocheted off the cab. At once Glen saw a German sniper in a nearby trench pitch off to one side, apparently hit by Tackitt, his roof-top gunner. "My machine gunner got our first German right there," advised Speer. "Right near the entrance to the exit off the beach."[54]

The column of trucks, guns, and other vehicles drove off the beach and into the ravine and traveled about fifty yards up the exit before coming to a complete halt. A traffic jam of jeeps, trucks, tanks, prime movers and artillery pieces completely blocked the roadway as the cry of "sniper" was passed down the line. "The battery was forced to wait almost half an hour until a patrol cleared a nest of snipers holed out in a church about four hundred yards up the road," explained Sergeant Eckenrode. As they sat there an occasional mortar round whistled in and impacted with a thud and a geyser of dirt and sand.[55]

Once traffic began moving again, Speer and the others passed by the steel-reinforced concrete pillbox with its silenced 75mm gun-barrel protruding out over the draw that had caused so much of the damage and destruction on Dog Green Omaha. It sat just behind the beach, across a wide, deep tank ditch half full of water. Dead German soldiers were scattered around the area. As they continued they also saw a number of knocked-out machine-gun posts—originally equipped with Spandaus—that were located on both sides of the ravine and along the hillside. "The [machine-gun pits] were also made of concrete," noted Eckenrode, "but unlike the pillbox they had been painted green and brown to blend with the tough grass which covered the terrain." All along the route dead German soldiers were sprawled out around these sites but bodies in American uniforms were seen as well. "The dead lay in the most grotesque of postures," noted Cleaves Jones, Headquarters Battery, 29th Infantry Division. "What seemed to have been two bodies [lay mangled] across the road in tank tracks. One 'thing,' which seemed to have been killed by a mine, lay at the roads' edge completely stripped of uniform and shoes by the blast, [with] no head [and] legs reversed and blown into jelly-like lumps under the shoulder blades." Maj. Stanley Bach, Headquarters, First Army, attached to the advancing headquarters battery of the 29th Infantry Division, agreed. "[We] came upon a soldier about 500 yards from the top of the plateau who was on his knees," he recalled. "We thought he was praying or scared." But when Major Bach and the others got up to the young soldier and placed a hand upon his shoulder, the body tumbled over dead. "[He had apparently] died on his knees praying after being severely wounded," explained Bach.[56]

The German Pillbox above the Vierville draw that had wreaked havoc with U.S. forces until the a.m. of June 7. (National Archives)

As the convoy containing D-Battery neared the top of Exit D-1, to the right covering or guarding this ravine, they saw another knocked out pillbox. Rumor spread among the troops that U.S. Rangers had taken this one in hand to hand combat. Within a short distance, Speer's attention became focused on a Frenchman up on the plateau. "There I saw a sight that I will never ever forget," recalled Glen. "Among all of this that was going on there was a man standing there with one arm blown off and he had a horse and a two-wheeled cart—the stump of his arm appeared wrapped and covered with dried blood—and he was picking up dead Americans and [hoisting them up] into his cart. I don't know where he might have been taking them [but] it was a terrible thing. A pitiful sight. He must have been in shock or something."[57]

Leading into and out of the village of Vierville-sur-Mer were quaint little groupings of farm buildings, each constructed of thick stone walls in a hollow square design. Between the edge of the bluffs above the beach and the village were rich green pastures. Beyond the ribbon of black-top that connected the various communities were small little fields the French called *bocage*—small pastures or fields often no more than an acre or two bordered by heavy earthen walls topped by a thick growth of hedges and trees. These unique pastures were of interest to the American farm boys passing by. As the battery entered the small village, it turned right at the main intersection in the center of town and proceeded west along the blacktop St. Pierre Highway. "This would've been nothing more than a country road in the United States," reported one G.I. "[but] it was a main highway in France." Orders were received to set up in a transit area about 200 yards up this road. Battery-D was originally supposed to take a position in a field about three kilometers further up the highway in a small community called St. Pierre-du-Mont but fighting was still going on there and the area had not been secured. Then they found that this area hadn't been secured either. "After turning right we were to go into the first field (or grassy pasture) on our left," recalled Glen, "but there was a house between where we turned right and where we were to turn into that first field and machine-gun fire was coming out of there [real] bad—coming out of a bay window." Glen and the other tractors had began their turn toward the field when they were halted by U.S. Army Rangers. Intermittent machine-gun fire was coming from the bay window on the south side of the house. According to Speer there was a wrought-iron fence along the top of a stone wall that surrounded the dwelling. Rangers crawled up along the wall and rushed the house eventually killing or capturing all of those who were inside. "As it turned out," advised Speer, "it was a woman in that window who had us all pinned down with machine-gun fire." According to additional sources, this female sniper, know only as Myra, was captured in civilian clothing and became the first woman prisoner of war captured by the Allies.[58]

As soon as this incident ended the battery, led by Captain Julius Reiver and James W. Lamoreaux, his jeep driver, proceeded past the house to the pasture. At its entrance Captain Reiver jumped out and opened the gate. As the first tractor and gun drove in, operated by Bucky Worboys, Captain Reiver yelled out, "You drive around all over that pasture and see if there's any land mines!"[59]

"Ya know," said Glen, "everyone's kinda scared. We're green and all. It never occurred to any of us to ever disobey an order. But when Bucky heard that, he jumped down out of that Cat and yelled out 'Screw you Sir! If you wanna find out if there's mines in there you drive it around in there yourself!'"[60]

The Captain assured him he didn't mean it that way and told Bucky to get back up into his vehicle and they would all go in there and take up positions to search it out. So D-Battery's guns and equipment were pulled into this pasture and set up. "The guns and range equipment were set up on top of the ground," advised one of the officers. "The guns, computer, and radar were oriented and ready to fire by 17:00. Then the digging of the revetments began." A tank battalion pulled into the next pasture over and set it up as a refueling station and ammunition dump.[61]

By the afternoon hours of June 7 the situation in Omaha's western sector had greatly improved. Although the landing of troops and equipment was still hours behind schedule, many beach landings were still unorganized, and some of the beach obstacles were still intact, some organization was beginning to emerge. The beachmaster ordered the landings to resume and more LSTs moved into position to begin their final runs toward the beach. Those shipping the other elements of the 110th AAA drifted into position on the extreme right of the first line of craft to head in for a landing.

"I remember looking over the side of the LST," said Lester Cohen of B-Battery, "and seeing poor G.I.s floating around and rolling up onto the shore with the waves, and rolling back with the receding waves."[62]

"There were a lot of bodies in the water by the time we went ashore," agreed Owen Davies.[63]

It was a sobering sight to many of these young teenagers. As they continued their trip toward the beach many of the boys began to notice that all the American bodies floated in the water with their heads submerged. "[Then it was announced over] the loud speaker on the LST to put your life preservers up under you arms," recalled Cohen, "[instead of] around your waist because the dead G.I.s floating in the water all had their fannies sticking up" instead of their heads.[64]

"We had the Mae West life preservers," explained another G.I. "So with the men loaded down with their heavy field packs and whatever else they had, it was all carried above the waist and made them top heavy. The life preservers were not very effective because, being around the waist, it turned everyone upside down in the water [when they fell]."[65]

"[T]here were so many dead American soldiers in the water," advised Harvey Edds, "they were impeding the supply boats from bringing in the much needed men and supplies . . . . One Navy officer got the idea of lowering four men in two small boats. They would stick a knife into the floating Mae West jackets causing the dead bodies to sink."[66]

"[I] cried over plowing through the bodies in the water," recalled Sgt. Frank Wisniewski of Battery-B, who would find conditions just as bad up on the beach. "You tried real hard to miss the American bodies," remembered Speer. "You try real hard to drive in without running over any of them," he repeated, breaking down at the thought of it years later, "but it was [simply impossible]."[67]

With the renewed opening of the beach, Battery-A unloaded onto a rhino ferry and headed in. "Drove right off and went up towards Vierville Draw," reported 1st Lieutenant Jack Forman, "turned left about a mile and went in about half a mile [to] an old field and we just set up our guns in there." This put A-Battery—referred to on the field radios as Able-Battery—east of town and D-Battery—referred to as Dog-Battery—west of town. "This little village," noted one G.I., "had once been a summer resort [but] it was now [nothing but] a mass of debris." The other two batteries had a more trying time. "Our position wasn't even taken yet," complained Franklin Johnson of B-Battery. "So we had to wait [in the Channel] with shells dropping in all around us and ships exploding."[68]

Enemy artillery fire had continued to fall upon Omaha beach intermittently and a number of fortified positions outside the troop perimeters came to life from time to time. "When we landed," continued Johnson, "our biggest threat was artillery, enemy artillery coming in [and] heavy strafing."[69]

"I was saying Hail Marys all the way in," admitted Ed Kosicki, also of B-Battery. "The LST next to us took a direct hit from artillery and then

[our] C.O. yelled, 'Let's get the hell out of here.'" Battery-B also found it necessary to transfer their equipment from their LST onto a rhino ferry before going in. "[T]his barge looked like a bunch of fifty-gallon drums laced together with a little outboard motor [attached]," complained Franklin Johnson. "[W]e had to help pull it with one of our M-4 Cats into a water depth our [other] waterproofed vehicles could handle," admitted Captain Chase. As the M-4 tractor crawled up onto the beach and the barge grated to a halt into the sand behind it, another rhino ferry came in just to their right. "As my wheels hit the sand," recalled Kenneth Lang of B-Battery, driving the first B-Battery vehicle off the ferry, "another truck unloading to my right, perhaps 50 feet away, hit a land mine. It was a ball of fire and the explosion threw the men onto the beach and into the water."[70]

"[A] G.I. standing on the tongue of the trailer the truck was pulling was [set] on fire," recalled Dick Brammann, "[and he was] waving his arms and dancing around [before] eventually falling or jumping into the sea."[71]

"The truck lifted off the beach about five feet in the air and came down on all four wheels exploding," remembered Dan Ciaburri. "The driver and [passenger] were killed instantly." The secondary explosion the men saw was a result of the 3/4-ton truck hauling ammo. Shrapnel flew in all directions and other debris rained down onto the beach and into the water as everyone hunkered down. "A Caterpillar came down to the beach to make a track which made it safe to unload," advised Edds. "The driver used a bull horn to let everyone know that they should not get out of the track."[72]

Once B—Baker—Battery got up the draw and into position near Vierville they began setting up their guns. Gun #4 had just about settled in when the cry of "gas!" was relayed down the line. "Thankful for our training and our new combat gas masks," recalled Frank Johnson, "we put them on, checked each other out, and began cursing the war more so than before." The boys soon realized it was a false alarm when they noticed that Pfc. Richard D. (Dick) Wherry had no canister on his mask but seemed OK. "We tried to tell him but he didn't understand," Johnson continued. "When he [finally] did, he went flying over the gun pit to the supply truck. Of course, if this had been a real gas attack he would have died ten times over."[73]

"As it turned out," declared Harvey Edds, "some screwball had run out of gas in his 3/4-ton weapons carrier and he was yelling for someone to bring him some 'GAS!'"[74]

Harvey Edds of B-Battery at one of the first positions established on
French soil by the 110th AAA (Courtesy of Harvey Edds)

Over in C—Charlie—Battery, twins Henry F. and Walter R. Thake
had been separated for the D-Day landing. Due to Army regulations that
prevented members of the same immediate family from performing
dangerous duty together, Henry was sent in on LST 291 and landed with
the battery while Walter was held back in England during the invasion
and was scheduled to rejoin the battery on D+3 if all went well. As Charlie-
Battery began its ascent up the Vierville draw, it started drawing fire.
Renewed enemy action had erupted sporadically all along exit D-1
throughout the day. As enemy snipers, mortar squads and machine gun
units were being cleared by Engineers and Rangers of the 29th Infantry
Division, they were joined by volunteers detached from various other
units. With this renewed action, Pfc. Halton W. Foster of Battery C was
one of those volunteers. He, along with Sgt. Wallace B. McDonell, T4
Elmer W. Guggenheim, T5 George W. Robinson, Cpl. Lawrence E. Scott
Jr., and Pfc Roland S. Cole, charged through barbed wire entanglements
and an enemy mine field that afternoon to engage the enemy which resulted
in clearing a section of the road and the capture of seven German soldiers.
In another incident shortly before this, Chaplain Leo J. Picher of
Headquarters Battery, 110th AAA, came into the crossroads region of
Vierville and found casualties from some of the advance fighting units

lying about unattended while other troops were busy clearing the vicinity of snipers and fighting in intermittent engagements. While under occasional small arms and mortar fire, Father Picher immediately went to work looking after the wounded, assisting them, getting some evacuated for medical attention and administering last rites to a number of others.[75]

Once Charlie-Battery arrived at its assigned location, the problems continued. "We were getting a lot of small arms fire while setting up our gun," reported Harold Mueller, helping set up Gun #2. "Captain [Lester K.] Born rounded up some Rangers and they flushed the Germans out from the next field."[76]

Dog-Battery was experiencing similar problems at their position. "Our field was adjacent to the road along which the 29th Infantry Division traveled to get to their positions," advised Captain Reiver. "One of our gunners, [George P.] Tobery, kept an eye out for his cousin, who was one of them." Eventually his cousin passed by and Tobery ran out into the road to greet him. "[T]hey were having a happy reunion," related Reiver, "when suddenly there was a rifle shot and his cousin fell dead, shot by a sniper in the trees in the hedge row. We sent out a squad to spray the trees with gun fire . . . and out came a white handkerchief on the end of a rifle and the German (actually a Pole) surrendered. Some of the guys wanted to kill him but he was a tired old guy who was just doing what he had been told to do, so we sent him back to our LST as a prisoner."[77]

By that time Charlie-Battery was experiencing loses of a different sort. "We had one man from Battery-C who committed suicide that night," advised medic Elmer Potzmann. "We also had another one who went berserk. It was awful. It was just too much for these two young fellows." Also that night Pfc. Robert Potter of St. Louis was sitting on the ground along a hedgerow cleaning dirt out of the barrel of his Thompson submachine gun. "I was about 30 to 50 feet from Potter just on the other side of the hedgerow," recalled Potzmann. "I heard the gun rapid fire. I wasn't sure what had happened and then some of the men began calling for a medic! I was close and the first [through the hedgerow] there but there was really nothing I could do. I gave him two shots of Morphine; the bullets had entered his forehead just above his eyes and the back of his skull had been completely opened up . . . There was a clip of several rounds in the gun—[we're] not too sure if he knew it or not." By all appearances, however, the incident appeared to have been accidental. After bandaging up the head wound the best he could, Potzmann and the others put Potter on a stretcher and jeeped him out of the area toward a medical aid station at the rear. They later learned that he had died along the way.[78]

Although the village of Vierville had been taken and surrounded by Allied forces by that afternoon, by evening German artillery had began concentrating on the main intersection of the town where American trucks were still passing through hauling ammo. That night one ammo truck suffered a direct hit. "The truck was lifted high above the house-tops," related one witness, "and came down with a crash amid burning and exploding ammunition."[79]

Throughout the region German snipers, machine gunners, and small groups of combat teams operated against the Americans from the hedgerows, roadsides, and sunken lanes. At the same time heavy artillery and mortar rounds were lobbed into the area from a distance and by 19:00 hours, German planes were sent into the vicinity to bomb and strafe.

"The radar picked up the planes as they neared the beachhead," advised one of the tech operators of Battery-D, 110th AAA, "and the Battery fired at the first plane to fly over."[80]

That plane, a JU-88, became the first German airplane to be shot down by an American 90mm anti-aircraft artillery unit on French soil. Thus, Dog-Battery of the 110th AAA became the first battery of the unit to land on Omaha Beach, the first battery of the unit to get set up, and the first 90mm battery unit overall to shoot down an enemy aircraft. What's more, the pilot bailed out and came down in the Channel where he was captured and sent back to England as a POW on LST 506—the same LST that brought the battery to Omaha Beach.[81]

The first German Aircraft shot down by American AA, Battery-D 110th AAA Gun Bn., verified and photographed by officials of the 49th AAA Brigade.
(National Archives)

According to a number of those from D-Battery, there was so much going on during that first night they never did get the gun pits dug. In fact, they didn't even take time to boogy down all four guns. They put only one down. "We fired that gun all night long," reported Speer. "We got that barrel red hot and by morning we had to change barrels because we had warped and ruined that barrel." And it was no wonder. The battery had fired a total of 438 rounds—just over sixteen courses of fire at twenty-seven rounds per course—from that one gun by dawn of the next day.[82]

By then, the greater part of five regiments of the 1st and 29th Infantry Divisions was ashore and, although pockets of resistance still existed between the beach and the American forces, the troops had formed an almost continuous front line a mile to a mile-and-a-half inland that extended from southwest of Vierville to a point east of Colleville.

It was during this time that a burial detail clearing the beach of dead bodies found Lieutenant Gardner of Battery-B—still alive. He was taken to a nearby field hospital where he was given morphine. To clean his wounds, three men were required to gently remove his helmet which was partially embedded into his skull. By all appearances Gardner had received a direct hit from a 50mm German mortar round which had deeply furrowed through the crown of his helmet and shattered the liner. After initial treatment, he was shipped off to a hospital in England for further recovery.[83]

CHAPTER 6

St. Lo and Battling Across the Countryside: Our Tour of France

The province of Normandy was named for the Vikings, known then as Nordmanni or Northmen, who originally settled the region. What eventually became known as the Norman kingdom was ruled over for many years by Duke William of Normandy. In fact, exactly 878 years before Allied troops landed on the beaches to drive out the Nazis, William—in 1066—had taken his knights across the Channel in the other direction to invade and take control of England and to forever afterwards become known as William the Conqueror. Numerous sites all across the French province are historically connected with him. Coincidently, as Allied troops fought across this region, the stone castle that William the Conqueror was born in outside Falaise, was being used as an observation post by the German Nazi troops.

This region is best known for its apples, its seafood—more specifically its lobsters, shrimp, mussels and oysters—and its Camembert cheese. Its countryside is quaint and picturesque. Medieval stone-walled farms and manors and small villages of half-timbered houses are situated throughout its gently rolling landscape.

During the first week of June 1944, the Germans had 58 divisions in place in Western Europe and 10 of those were the dreaded Panzer divisions. Moreover, the German 352nd Division, a top—notch well-trained experienced unit, had been at Omaha Beach during the initial invasion. Its rating was in the German army's highest combat-value category and it, too, took many lives. American army casualties during the first eleven days of fighting in Normandy eventually came to 3,283 dead and 12,600 wounded. According to *Yank* magazine, "[T]hrough-out D-plus-one and D-plus-two, General Eisenhower continued to pour men and supplies into the Bay of the Seine beachheads and nowhere else. Rommel's intelligence, which reported 12 Allied divisions in Normandy the day after the first landings, said two days afterward there were 20."[1]

For the most part, U.S. forces had been surprised upon finding the hedgerow-bordered fields beyond the beaches. The quilting pattern of these crazily shaped pastures had appeared in aerial photographs but their physical makeup was a complete shock. They had hardly been mentioned in the briefings and no appropriate training had ever been conducted for them. These fields, averaging an acre or two each, were tightly enclosed by earthen mounds four to five feet high and three to four feet thick topped by a thick growth of hedges, trees, and underbrush. What had appeared on the reconnaissance photos as narrow stands of timber boarding these fields were, in fact, solid earthen walls covered with thick, tangled vegetation anchored by extensively knotted root systems. Digging into them or through them was virtually impossible.

From the air the hedgerows don't look that steep. (National Archives)

On the ground it's an entirely different matter. (National Archives)

125

The French referred to this unique Norman terrain as the "Bocage" (or grove) region and combat in the bocage proved similar to fighting in a maze. The view beyond any one field was usually blocked in all directions by thick walls of vegetation. In some areas, dirt roads or farm lanes through the region were sunken below the bordering walls of earth from centuries of use and the trees and shrubbery arched out over the roadway to create a tunnel. Such terrain created perfect defensive positions for both sides but terrible offensive situations. Each hedgerow was like a fortress. Troops entrenched in them were practically invisible while their positions were nearly impregnable. Fighting in this region eventually became quite vicious and any gains proved to be slow, often advancing only one hedgerow at a time.

That first evening, after getting dug-in and set up within their small pasture, 21-year old Owen Davies of Hoquiam, Washington, was staring at a dead German soldier laying near one of the bordering hedgerows. "On the right of the entrance to this field," reported Lt. John A. "Jack" Forman, "were two or three [dead] Germans."[2]

"I saw what a guy looks like [after] he gets hit by a machine gun," confessed Davies. As a machine-gunner on a quad-50 for B-Battery, Davies couldn't help but be curious. "All of a sudden all hell broke loose," he recalled. A German machine gun somewhere close by had opened up on Davies and the rest of the group. As they dove to the ground they could hear the leaves in the shrubbery above them being ripped to shreds. "We dropped back a hedgerow," advised Davies, "and I was thinking about what that [dead German] guy looked like and I figured I was going to be like that any millisecond . . . the bullets were flying [and] I thought I was next. I truly did."[3]

When the shooting stopped, Davies remained on the ground, laying as flat as possible, still thinking of the condition of that dead German soldier's body. "I can honestly say I have never been so scared in my life," admitted Davies. After a short time Owen noticed a pair of boots next to his head and someone towering over him. Davies then realized it was his sergeant. "What's sa matter sojer? Ya scared?" he goaded. "I looked up at the sergeant and I said, "Damn right I'm scared,'" recalled Davies. Just then, as Davies stood up, the German machine gun opened up again from the hedgerows and the sergeant dove for cover right along beside Davies. They both laid there hugging the ground until other units moved in and took out the enemy gunner hiding in the brush. "After a long time, we stood up," recalled Davies, "and stared at each other. Then we moved on. [He] didn't say [another] word.[4]"

Later that first night, an anti-tank battery moved into the same field with Battery-D and by the next morning a group of Army Air Corps engineers had moved into an adjacent field. It was this outfit that began to build the first permanent landing strip on the Normandy beachhead. Referred to as Airstrip ARL-9, the battery guns of the 110th AAA were moved into position and assigned to cover and protect the airfield.[5]

"A day after the infantry had cleared our area and we set down our 90mm and quad-50-caliber machine guns," reported B-Battery's Harvey Edds, "the engineers came in and completed a fighter-plane base."[6]

"As the ground was being graded for the runway they were laying interlocking sections called Marston Matting," reported C-Battery's Elmer Potzmann. "It was a solid flooring [necessary] because of all the rainy weather. It was all put into operation by D-Day + two or three."[7]

The emergency airstrip consisted of a 3500-foot runway capable of taking transport planes. After the quick completion of this airfield, General Eisenhower and his staff was brought in on a C-46 recalled Edds. A number of the battalion watched him emerge from the craft and never realized until much later that they had witnessed Eisenhower's first steps onto French soil.[8]

It took some time for the various beachheads to link up. By the evening of June 7 the forces that had landed on the Gold and Juno Normandy beaches during the early morning hours of the previous day had finally met up and joined together to form what was by then being referred to as the Allied Western Front. By June 8 Allied forces who had come in on the Gold and Omaha beaches had eventually linked up. Sometime during the afternoon of June 8, Brig. Gen. Edward W. Timberlake, 49th Brigade Commander, came by to visit the battalion and congratulated the boys in Battery-D on getting the first plane.[9] That night the battalion was in action again. They engaged a number of enemy aircraft and D-Battery shot down another JU-88.

"There was a constant German plane that flew over the area every night about 11:00 pm," advised Elmer Potzmann. "They called him "Bed-Check Charlie."[10]

On June 9 Battery-D moved out of the Vierville area and proceeded four miles west along the coastal highway to St. Pierre du Mont, its originally scheduled position for D-day evening that had been delayed in being secured. The previous day, V Corps had issued warning orders down the lines that the second phase of the beachhead operation *had* to begin. Delays in reaching the initial objectives had made the situation desperate. The beachhead was still far short of its intended depth and landing sites remained within range of German artillery. At the same time, the 110th AAA, within a mile of Point du Hoc at this location, was to provide artillery support to elements of the 5th and 2nd Rangers who were meeting heavy resistance from units of the German 914th Infantry Regiment.

According to the gun crews, it took eight to twelve hours to completely dig the guns into position whenever they moved to a new location. Upon arrival they would begin to dig a circular pit about four feet deep and twenty feet across and fill sandbags with much of the dirt to stack around the rim of the excavation to create a parapet. Thus, while standing on the pit floor loading and operating the gun, the crew remained below the surrounding terrain at eye level with the top of the pit, safe from nearly anything except a direct hit. The battery's four guns were usually dug in about fifty yards apart. During the daytime, the gun and pits remained covered by a large camouflage net to protect against any aerial surveillance. "We'd [also sometimes] stretch a tarp over the pit and make a doorway and have our [living quarters] down under there, protected from the weather," added Speer.

A typical gun crew consisted of thirteen to fifteen men. Some operated dials and levers on the gun, others loaded and fired it, and still others carried the big twenty-three-pound shells from a storage area or "ammo dump" established several yards away. There was also a lot of overlapping of duties. For instance, after towing the gun and crew to its destination, placing it in position and helping set it up, Speer often assumed duties in the ammo line, manning the 50-cal. rooftop gun on his tractor, or temporarily taking a seat and helping out on a M-51 quad-50 machine gun.

Normally a gun crew worked all night firing at targets and slept in the daytime but these guns required a great deal of daytime maintenance as well to keep them in good condition. Therefore, after a night's work, half the crew would sleep while the other half continued to work doing gun maintenance and upkeep. By afternoon, this half went to sleep while the others got up and completed the maintenance and other duties. They all slept in pup tents, the covered gun pit or under half-tracks or other heavy vehicles which were always parked under trees and covered by camouflage netting. Generally, even as the work was being done, two men would constantly sit in the tracker seats behind the gun and another in the seat of a quad-50 keeping a watch on the sky.

Their big 90mm weapon could be aimed manually or mechanically. Manually, the gun was aimed by sighting through cross-hairs mounted on each side of the weapon. There were seats behind the cross-hairs for the "trackers." Large handles extended out toward each seat. The left side cranked the gun horizontally and the right side cranked the gun vertically. One man, called the "loader," stood on the platform and loaded the shells into the breach. The gun cocked automatically by the recoil. After firing, the "loader" would shove the next round into the firing chamber. He fired the gun by stepping on a lever located on the platform. A "gunner" stood on the ground off to one side and directed the fire. Because it was so noisy during firing, the "gunner" sometimes had a rope that was tied to the leg of the "loader." If it became necessary, the "gunner" would jerk on the rope to get the "loader's" attention. The gun could also be aimed mechanically by a director that consisted of a steel box, approximately four feet square full of gears, that was connected to the gun by electrical cable. The director sat on a tripod and it, too, had a leveling mechanism. A scope located on each side of the director allowed the "trackers" to stand here on the ground at each side instead of sitting in the gun seats. The director was set up about 15 feet from the gun. It had to be coordinated with the gun by sighting both of them on some distant object and then locking them together. The trackers had a six-inch diameter wheel located next to the scopes that they moved to keep on a moving target. The gears in the box were supposed to build a lead on a target so that when they were tracking a plane, the projectile would be fired out ahead of it, allowing for the time it took the projectile to reach the plane.

The electrical power needed when using the director with the gun came from a small gasoline-driven power plant or generator. The gun, director, and power plant were all inter-connected with electrical cables laid out on the ground. During the daytime or day-light hours the gun was usually aimed manually for antiaircraft fire. During nighttime firing, the gun was usually set up for automatic or mechanical aim using radar to locate and sight-in on the planes in the dark. When used to support infantry or at specific targets, manual was used in both daylight and dark.

Those first few nights at St. Pierre du Mont, sporadic sniper-fire and small-arms or machine-gun fire continued. During the daytime, when the boys weren't sleeping or assigned to duties, they completed personal details such as shaving, washing or repairing their clothes, or simply sitting around drinking coffee, eating, talking, writing letters home, or wandering about "fishing bodies."

"We never ever fished American bodies, always German," remarked Speer. "Some of the guys talked to 'em or cursed 'em as they did it."[11]

"Fishing bodies" was the practice of searching corpses or going through the dead men's pockets to salvage anything usable. Some G.I.s looked for helmets, patches, Lugers, daggers, and other collectable Nazi items, some searched for money, jewelry, or other valuables, some searched for useful items to help defend themselves, and some, like Glen, just searched out of curiosity. "I never really felt bad about it," admitted Speer, "until [I] happened upon a wallet or single photos of a nice looking women or nice looking children. That got ya to thinkin'. When you realized they, too, had family, wives, or children, that put the body you were searching in a whole different perspective."[12]

129

Examples of "fished" photos from dead German bodies. Realizing they, too, had family, wives, and children often troubled the G.I.s. (Author's Collection)

Most of these boys simply searched the front pockets of the bodies if the corpse was laying on its back or went through the back pockets if it was laying face down on its stomach. Very few rolled the bodies over to search them completely. It was common knowledge that German soldiers fished American bodies as well. "One day," advised Glen, "out of curiosity I picked up a German Mauser laying next to a body and wondered how good it compared with our M-1. Without thinking I fired off a couple rounds. I was pinned down behind that body for over an hour. German rifles sound different than our M-1s and we had all been there long enough to know the difference. Once everybody heard that rifle discharge, EVERY American soldier within hearing distance, including those of my own battalion, opened up on that direction!"[13]

"On another occasion," confessed Speer, "I was cleaning the winch on the front of my [prime mover], had the cable all strung out a good distance from any cover when gunfire erupted from a nearby hedgerow. I began shooting in that direction as I ran for cover and Wayne Edmondson, sitting on his quad-50 dug in several yards away, opened up on the hedgerow. Scared as all get- out, I began running toward Wayne's position. As I dove in near him, he reached out over the sandbags and quickly pulled me into his pit. There's no doubt in my mind he saved my life that day."[14]

Glen Speer, left, and his best friend Wayne Edmondson.
(Courtesy of Wayne and Maxine Edmondson)

It was during these first few days in Normandy that the boys learned to forage off the land. "We had been eatin' K-rations for some time," advised Glen, "and there was a number of Holstein and Guernsey milk cows roaming the orchards. One day our Captain mentioned that we hadn't had good meat for quite awhile and since 'there are several cows in the orchard' he said, 'if one turned up missing and we had steak to eat, he was sure nothing would be said.' Well, no sooner than he had said that, us farm boys had one of those cows shot, butchered, and hanging in a tree ready to cook and several others milked. We ate good that evening. I don't know if other gun crews did stuff like that but I know we did."[15]

On Friday, June 9, Speer celebrated his 20th birthday. "While I was on that LST ship I stole a gallon can of peaches," admitted Glen. "I put it in the tool box on the top of my Cat while down there in the hold. On the evening of June 9th, at about four o'clock in the evening, I decided I would eat those peaches—they were peach halves—to celebrate my birthday. I crawled up on my [tractor] in a hurry because a sniper shot hit my duffle bag next to me and threw the can of peaches down on the ground in front of the vehicle and dove down off there like a swan! I grabbed that gallon can, tucked it under my arm and crawled back under the front of my Cat. I opened that can and I ate that entire can of peaches except for maybe two-inches at the bottom, 'cause I figured if I was gonna die tonight I was gonna die with a full stomach 'cause it was my birthday. I don't remember getting sick from eating all of that but I do remember falling sleeping under the Cat that night."[16]

The Omaha and Utah beaches remained littered with wreckage for several days as German artillery and mortar fire continued intermittently, further delaying build-up, supply, and support of the First Army. At Omaha casualties and loss of equipment delayed the complete clearing of the beach until the late afternoon of June 10. On that day A-Battery, still protecting airfield ARL-9, boogied-up and was moved further southwest toward Louvieres to hold off elements of the German 916th Infantry at that location. Battery-C and B of the 110th AAA remained as cover for the Normandy beachhead airfield. During that time Captain Lester Born, a 52-year-old college professor commanding Battery-C, was transferred out to another unit—promoted to the position of Historian—and Lt. Allen D. Philips was promoted to the rank of Captain and placed in command of the battery.

By June 12, American forces from the Omaha and Utah beaches finally joined together to create a continuous advancing Allied front from the eastern-most beach of Sword to the western-most beach of Utah. The V Corps was advancing slowly against heavy resistance but the U.S. 4th Division of the VII Corps had already begun their planned advance toward Cherbourg. The V Corps zone was suffering the most. Only about 100 tons of the planned 2,400 tons of supplies had been able to be brought ashore and the lack of ammunition was the most severe. Various regiments of the Omaha assault were badly decimated and remained disorganized from the hard fighting and the remnants of the 16th and 116th Infantry Regiments were exhausted. Troops and supplies continued to slowly come in on the various beaches, however, to supplement the slowly advancing front. By June 12 the Allies had landed 326,000 troops on the Cotentin peninsula.

Significant gains were made between June 10 and June 18. In the V Corps sector, German troops had continued to hold out at Trevieres until the night of June 9-10 when the 352nd withdrew to the river, three-and-a-half miles from St. Lo, to form a new defensive line.[17]

"Prisoners were being marched down the road continually," remarked Sergeant Eckenrode. "The strange thing was there were a good many French women being taken. They had been spotting artillery fire for the German field artillery."[18]

That evening Captain Reiver informed Speer and Bucky Worboys that they would be detached from the unit for several days on a special assignment. They were told to report to Utah beach early the following morning along with their tractors to help clear the surf and shore areas of the remaining debris. They set out at daybreak and were shocked at the scenery all along the way back toward the beaches. The destruction of this entire area was spectacular. Gaping shell holes dotted the countryside and all along the approaches to the beach. Towns and villages were decimated—literally reduced to rubble—and various size craters, too deep to be completely filled by the tides, remained in the surf and along the shore.

"Devastation was everywhere," agreed another G.I. "The roads, pastures, and orchards were pocked with artillery craters. Scarcely a tree remained. Horse carcasses rotted under the sun. Burned-out German Tiger and Panther tanks and American Shermans were everywhere."[19]

Some of the remaining inhabitants of this region were devastated as well and, apparently, no longer thankful for liberation. According to Pvt. Roscoe C. Blunt Jr., a demolitions specialist assigned to the 84th Infantry Division, as the newly arriving troops came up off the beach and hiked along the road through the area, heading for the front, the French farmers toiling in their barren orchards pelted them with stones and rotted apples, blaming the American troops for the Allied bomb damage to their land.[20]

Speer and Worboys spent 3 days on the special detail before returning to their unit. In the meantime, steady advances were being made by U.S. troops in spite of the increasing resistance of the Germans who had began to receive reinforcements. The V Corps launched a new attack on June 12th and continued with limited attacks toward St. Lo through June 15.

Late on the night of June 17, two jeeps occupied by a number of men pulled up to the pit of D-Battery's Gun #1 and a small, thin man in army fatigues got out of the passenger side of the first jeep, simply saying "Howdy boys." Everyone immediately recognized him as newspaper columnist Ernie Pyle. "He was a little bitty scrawny fella" noted Captain Jack Forman of A Battery.[21]

"Ernie came late in the evening," noted Sergeant Eckenrode of D-Battery. "He visited all the gun positions that same night and it was well after midnight when he picked his place to stay. He lived with gun number one."[22]

Captain Reiver had great influence with Brigadier General Timberlake and was instrumental in getting Pyle to visit his battery for publicity purposes. Being the first AAA unit to shoot down an enemy aircraft, Reiver was able to talk Timberlake into getting other commanders to arrange the visit.

By 1944 Ernie Pyle had become one of America's most well-known and widely respected war correspondents. His column ran six days a week in 310 different newspapers all across the nation. Pyle interviewed all the boys of the #1 gun crew as well their captain.[23]

"The battery commander was Captain Julius Reiver, of Wilmington, Delaware," wrote Pyle. "He stayed up all night, too, directing their firing from his dugout, where information was phoned in to him."[24]

"We had a command post dug into the perimeter of the field in which First Sergeant [Leo] Lamparty and I slept," noted Reiver, "and we added a bed for Ernie." They rested during the day and remained up most of the night directing the firing.[25]

Although Pyle was scheduled to stay only one night, there was little action that first evening so Captain Reiver and his boys boldly persuaded Pyle and his entourage to stay an additional twenty-four hours.

"When we had finished the night's firing, the boys felt very low," offered Reiver. "This was the first night since we landed on D+1 that we had not shot down a German plane." Luckily, that second night became much busier. "He was with us when we shot down seven planes in one night," bragged Reiver, "which probably is [another] record for an anti-aircraft battery."[26]

"When we were firing," noted Sgt. Arthur W. (Bill) Nelson, "he [remained] in the pit with us. He was a great guy."[27]

"My crew was a swell bunch of boys," wrote Ernie. "There wasn't a smart aleck or gold-bricker in the crew." Pyle went on to explain that on his second day with the unit the boys' commanding officers had granted them permission to write family and friends back home about meeting him. "[S]o the boys all got out paper, and since it had turned warm for a change we sat and [laid] around on the grass while they wrote short letters home, using ammunition and ration boxes for writing boards. When they got through all of them had me sign their letters."[28]

"Ernie was a nice little guy," recalled Reiver. "He wanted to spend time with the gun crew, with the radar, the director, and the battery in general. So I told him 'fine.' Do whatever you want."[29]

"The boys are very proud of their first night on the soil of France," Pyle later informed his readers. "The snipers were still thick in the surrounding hedges, and bullets were singing around them all night. The boys liked to tell over and over how the infantry all around them were crouching and crawling along while they had to stand straight up and dig their guns in."[30]

Ernie Pyle left the following morning. Several weeks later his picture appeared on the cover of *Time* magazine back home, normally an honor extended only to government leaders and generals. In the cover story United Press correspondent Chris Cunningham, who was with Pyle when he visited the 110th AAA, noted that all the soldiers easily identified with Ernie Pyle and everyone felt as if they knew him. The common soldiers, he said, considered Pyle one of them and his readers often prayed for him, wrote to him, and called their hometown newspapers to ask about his health and safety. "He was truly a remarkable man," recalled Clyde Libby. "It was a great honor and privilege to be able to actually meet him, talk with him, and get to spend time with him."[31]

By the 18th, the V Corps line was two-and-a-half miles north of St. Lo, running east from the Vire River. These positions were maintained over the next two weeks. For one thing, landings were still running about two days behind schedule. Then, a big storm hit the area on June 19 further delaying the Allies.[32]

It had been raining or drizzling nearly every day since D-Day but from June 19 to June 22 a massive storm hit the area. "Most of that June the weather fought on the side of the Axis," insisted one Allied officer, "[but] the cruelest blow fell on June 19 when a hurricane struck . . . there had not been such a storm in the Channel for forty years." The raging seas swamped many small craft and damaged the temporary Mulberry ports constructed at the beaches, completely destroying the one at Omaha. "It stopped nearly all landing activity on the beaches for a period of four days," declared a G.I. "The Mulberry at Omaha Beach in the American sector suffered damage beyond repair and great numbers of ships and small vessels were grounded or hurled onto the beach."[33]

"On the day of the storm's ending I flew from one end of our beach line to the other," another noted, "and counted more than 300 wrecked vessels above small-boat size, some so badly damaged they could not be salvaged."[34]

The 110th AAA, however, made the best of the disruption and confusion that resulted. "After the Mulberry pier was destroyed by the storm," confessed Captain Reiver, "supplies [had to be] loaded onto DUKWs, nets and all. On shore the nets full of supplies were lifted by cranes, the DUKW pulled away, and the nets full of supplies were loaded onto regular 2 ½ ton trucks. To make sure only authorized trucks received the supplies, secret markings in white were painted on their front bumpers. Our guys found that they could be duplicated using white adhesive tape and fixed up one of our trucks. It entered the line and was the recipient of half a load of chili con carne and the other half load was pineapple juice. I don't know if these items were ever missed or not but we enjoyed them!"[35]

With improvement in the weather, the Allied build-up begin to increase. By the end of June, 875,000 troops had landed along with 150,000 vehicles. The British had suffered 24,698 casualties and the Americans 37,034. The Germans had lost nearly 26,000 men while their strength in the area had been successfully whittled down by air and artillery bombardment. Still, difficult Bocage fighting limited American advancement. General Bradley tried to maneuver his forces south along the west coast of the Cotentin Peninsula with a push then eastward toward St. Lo in an attempt to break out of the area but progress became stalled.[36]

Early in the morning of June 22, Harvey Edds of B-Battery was out of his foxhole building a campfire. His unit was still bivouacked at the end of air strip ARL-9. "I was squatting down to brew my coffee," recalled Edds, "when all of a sudden I was knocked backwards with a loud explosion." Pfc. Gaylon Webb poked his head out of a nearby foxhole wondering what was going on. Edds' face was covered in blood. Others came running to assist, loaded him into a jeep, and took him to a medic dug out. It was later determined Edds had unknowing built his fire over an embedded German 20mm shell. "I had a piece of shrapnel go through my lower jaw," advised Edds, "another in my left arm, and one in my forehead." The shrapnel was removed, the wounds treated, and Edds stayed with the unit. A night or two afterwards, Jim Oliver hit a German booby-trap trip-wire and was brought down with a shrapnel wound of the foot. "The Germans had driven a stake in the ground on top of the [nearby] bluff and hung some high explosives over the edge," reported Edds. "The intent was for the trip-wire to set off the explosives, causing the bluff to collapse and drop off." Oliver was also treated and remained with the battery.[37]

Around June 23 Battery-D received word that Lt. Henry Klein, who had been evacuated from the beach after receiving a head wound on D-Day, was safe in an English hospital, had recovered and would be rejoining the unit in a few days. This was the first time that they had learned what had actually happened to him. Many thought he might have been killed. B-Battery learned Lt. Gardner was still in the hospital there but doing well. He would be reassigned, they were told, to A-Battery once he made a full recovery. On June 25 Lt. Klein and a number of others originally assigned to the 110th AAA, including Del Sol and others hurt in the accident in England, Thake and others who had brothers sent in on D-Day, the batteries kitchen units, and other equipment and personnel, all arrived and rejoined the unit. They arrived in Normandy on the SS *Sam Colt*.

On June 29 Battery-D of the 110th AAA had boogied-up and moved six miles southwest of St. Pierre du Mont and set up in a pasture near St. Clement la Calvados, three miles northeast of Isigny to assist elements of the 175th Infantry.

"All the installations were dug in by hand as there were no engineer outfits in the vicinity," complained one of the G.I.s. "The radar crew had the hardest job. They had to dig a hole twelve feet wide and twenty feet long with picks and shovels; no easy feat, especially when the ground is all clay."[38]

By the time the battery had been transferred out of the St. Pierre du Mont position it had earned the nickname, "Best AAA Battery in the ETO," having established a record of 19 shoot-downs. "Army photographers [came out and] took pictures of the different installations," bragged Sergeant Eckenrode, "and sent the photos to the War Department."[39]

D-Battery, #3 units, L-R: Dwight Kleinbecker in background, Speer, and Grayson "Bull Durham" Tackitt. (Courtesy of Glen and Betty Speer)

That night the battery was in action again after dark but no planes were shot down. From June 29 to July 3 the battery saw no other action.

On July 3 the First Army launched a major offensive in an attempt to expand and deepen the western end of the Normandy American beachhead. Eventually known as the "Battle of the Hedgerows," its purpose was to break out of the bocage country and reach Countances, twenty miles beyond the current front line. The overall offensive involved 12 infantry divisions in 4 corps attacking along a twenty-five to thirty mile front with heavy artillery, armored and air support. It opened at dawn with an artillery barrage after a night of aerial bombing. The 110th AAA was assigned as ground support temporarily attached to the U.S. 30th Division to aid the 119th Infantry.

"We didn't know what was taking place or what was going on," advised Glen. "We didn't know the overall situation or why we were ordered certain places and doing certain things. We just did what we were told to do."[40]

At 12 o'clock noon on July 4, all 1,100 big guns assigned to the First Army simultaneously fired a one-shot Fourth of July salute in one enormously ear-splitting thunderclap. The event became an ultimate morale-booster for the American artillerymen in Normandy. "The Germans were over after dark and the Battery went into action," declared Sergeant Eckenrode. Those planes mostly stayed over the beach area making a run at the ships, completely out of the range of the battery's guns. However, the attack was close enough to be watched by the men of the 110th. "The sky was filled with tracers from the pom-pom guns on the ships anchored off the beach and the fifty caliber and forty millimeter half-tracks dug in along the coast," advised Eckenrode. "This sight surpassed any fireworks display that was ever put on."[41]

Earlier in the day the Battle of the Hedgerows had expanded to include the southern Cherbourg peninsula as other American Infantry units joined in on the attack. Over the next two days, however, the American First Army's offensive made little headway against the strong hold of the German Seventh Army. A few days later a load of odd-looking ammo was distributed among the U.S. artillery units all along the front. The shells, Ordnance explained, were set with time fuses so they would detonate high above the German lines and scatter leaflets contained in them over the German troops. These leaflets, printed in German, were meant to demoralize the enemy instead of kill.

The following day U.S. artillery opened with a heavy thirty-minute barrage. As the shells exploded over the German soldiers taking cover, thousands of pieces of paper fluttered to the ground. As the troops later emerged from their foxholes and picked up the papers, they read:

YOUR LEADERS HAVE PROMISED YOU:

That the Atlantic Wall is closed without gaps. WE HAVE BROKEN THROUGH

That the Allied troops would not stay for even nine hours on French soil WE'VE BEEN HERE FOUR WEEKS

That the coastal harbors have been transformed into unbreakable fortresses WE HAVE CONQUERED CHERBOURG

That the German Luftwaffe is invincible. IT HAS DESERTED YOU

That your weapons are the best in the world. YOU HAVE FELT THE SUPERIORITY OF OUR ARTILLERY

That victory marches everywhere with the German banners. AND RUSSIA? AND AFRICA? AND ITALY? AND NOW THE WESTERN FRONT?

We, however, promise you:
That through the broken Atlantic Wall, new war materiel and fresh troops will Stream into France hourly

That Cherbourg is only the beginning of coming victories

That your sacrifice in the sector of St. Lo is as senseless as that of your comrades On the Cotentin Peninsula

That you can save yourselves, for yourselves and Germany, if you will see in time—WHO LIES? WHO SPEAKS THE TRUTH?[42]

By July 7, the U.S. 29th and 30th Infantry divisions had slowly extended American gains as the 30th crossed the Vier River near St. Lo and punched a hole in the German defenses. Throughout the day U.S. artillery reluctantly zeroed-in on church steeples in this vicinity because they were being used by the Germans as observation posts. "It was something we hated doing," admitted Speer, "but we had no choice." Once the use of a church spire was confirmed, the artillery would open up with a fusillade leaving any such structure raising above the city in ruins. Even under these circumstances, however, the gunners frequently made every effort to spare the main church building or cathedral from total destruction.[43]

The French town of St. Lo was twenty miles southeast of the coast and served as the provincial seat of government for the Normandy province. It had a total population of nearly 11,000 and was its largest town. St. Lo became the essential objective of the First Army's offensive to break out of the Normandy beachhead region because the area's eight major roads spread out in all different directions from there and on the east and west side of the city its high ground overlooked the Vier valley.

The hedgerow-bordered roads leading from the coast on into the town had become another major obstacle. Any mass movement across this region was restricted to being funneled into these narrow levee-lined routes. This severe disadvantage restricted all cross-country travel. Tanks could offer only limited support to the infantry units crossing the region because of the armored vehicles' inability to get over or through the hedgerows. "[O]ur Shermans bellied up over the tops of those mounds instead of crashing through them," complained General Bradley. "There they exposed their soft undersides to the enemy while their own guns pointed helplessly toward the sky."[44] What's more, since all advances toward the town was restricted to the narrow roads, tanks were easy prey for the enemy's armored vehicles or their close-range antitank weapons, one or both of which was usually waiting around the next bend. In addition, German 88-mm guns were usually positioned around farmhouses and in the hedgerows at road intersections to help halt U.S. tanks advancing through the area. The normal procedure was for infantry units attached to the Armored Divisions to move in, pin down the German gunners with machine-gun fire from close range so the tanks could come up and knock out the position with their guns. All of this was very time consuming and costly to the U.S. forces, both in equipment and lives, as it could only advance a mere average of just 2,000 yards a day. "Much of the success of [these operations] was due to the hairline cooperation between infantry and tanks," reported *Life* magazine. "When tanks came to a strong [German] antitank nest, they often took cover and let infantry units with them move in to take out the position by hand." Thus making the tanks ineffective until the big fight was over.[45]

Noting this problem, Sgt. Curtis G. Culin of the 2nd Armored Division, hit upon the idea of an "anti-hedgerow device" that could push through the earthen dikes. His idea involved welding a crossbar to the front of the tank. "Four tusk-like prongs protruded from it,"advised Bradley, who was given a demonstration of how it worked. "The tank backed off and ran head-on toward a hedgerow at ten miles an hour. Its tusks bored into the wall, pinned down the belly, and the tank broke through under a canopy of dirt." A tank equipped with such a device could easily rip huge holes in the 1000 year old hedgerows allowing other tanks and the infantry to follow through it. "So absurdly simple that it had baffled an army for more than five weeks," General Bradley remarked in amazement. Demonstrated on July 11, 1944, Bradley ordered more than 200 Shermans to be equipped with Culin's "tusks" with the steel for the devices being salvaged from the nearby German beach obstacles.[46]

Historians have frequently pointed out that Americans have often become innovative in order to successfully compete against far superior forces. It occurred in the Revolutionary War as well as the Civil War. The Second World War was no different. The difficulty American soldiers found in fighting in this arduous terrain brought about spells of American ingenuity. Young American G.I.s often improvised to overcome problems in the field and quickly learned to temporally repair their equipment under the stress of heavy gunfire while the Germans, under similar circumstances, simply abandoned their equipment. And it was the inventive common American soldiers—not commanders who failed to initially recognize the severe obstacles in the first place—who came up with ideas of installing devices to overcome the problems found on the battlefield.

Sergeant Culin's battering rams or "hedge-busting" prongs attached to the front of the tanks in order to fight more effectively in the hedgerows was just one of the more well-known devices. In a similar vain, Speer suggested having a ball-hitch attached to the front of the M-4 artillery tractors for easier gun maneuverability. Upon recognizing a problem he and other tractor drivers were having in backing artillery into position in extremely muddy and difficult terrain under heavy enemy fire, Speer went to his commander and suggested that a ball-hitch be mounted on the front of the machine, pointing out that the artillery could then be moved into position more quickly, even under adverse conditions. Given the go-ahead, Glen obtained a large ball-hitch from an Army supply clerk and installed it on the front of "Hitler's Crawlin' Coffin." Once the other drivers saw the advantage, they put in requests as well. Within days, Ordnance came around and distributed ball-hitches to all artillery units. Speer helped some of the other drivers install them. Afterwards it became a quick and simple matter to pull the artillery unit to the desired location, unhitch it, hitch it the front of the tractor, and then push it into position.

Over the following days different units trained using these new devices. "The battalions were rotated between the front and a reserve area where, in company with engineers and tanks, the tactics for attacking hedgerows were practiced," reported one G.I. Once the attack date was set and all the units seemed ready, the XIX Corps designated the 29th Infantry Division to make the main drive. The 29th decided to lead with its 116th Regiment.[47]

"We were to strike astride the Couvains road to the crest of Martinville Ridge," recalled Charles R. Cawthon of the 2nd Battalion, 116th Regiment,"then wheel right, or west, down a farm road that ran along its crest toward St. Lo. Simultaneously, on our left, the 2nd Infantry Division was to go for Hill 192."[48]

The 2nd Battalion of the 116th Regiment was deployed along an east-west rise just above the Bayeux-St. Lo Road. This position was dominated by a parallel ridge line about fifteen hundred yards to the north. This higher ridge was called the Martinville Ridge after the farm hamlet on its crest. The west end of this ridge sloped off into the outskirts of St. Lo. Just northeast of their position the 1st Battalion of the 116th Regiment was set up just east of Martinville and the 3rd Battalion of the 116th was located on a smaller ridge northeast of them. Martinville Ridge also culminated in a hill on its German-held right called "192" after its meter elevation. German defenses were also set up north of St. Lo on Hill 122. Hill 122 was on the German right flank.

The V Corps was assigned the task of taking Hill 192. All units of the 110th AAA were moved up to Sainte Jean de Daye, 8 miles north of St. Lo, to assume a ground role in support.

Promptly at 05:00 on July 11 all the guns of American artillery opened up throughout the valley.

"Three rounds! Commence firing!" the various gun commanders would yell out as the four guns of each battery erupted with a frighteningly-powerful ground-shaking blast, sending a brief sheet of flame squalling out from the muzzles. Stifling, acrid smoke circulated throughout the gun pit, gradually dissipating, as the crewmen moved quickly and methodically passing another big round down the line toward the gun. An empty shell casing clanked to the ground as another round was loaded into the breach. The crew took one step back, some putting their fingers into their ears, as all sixteen big guns of the battalion fired off another salvo.

For fifty minutes the 90-millimeters fired on German batteries, command posts, reserve areas and the enemy's field kitchens that were serving breakfast while the field guns bombarded all known mortar and machine-gun posts in the first three hedgerows. From 05:50 until 06:00

all the artillery and all infantry support weapons throughout the area hit the first hedgerow. The 90mm guns fired shells with impact fuses to collapse dugouts while the 105mm guns fired air bursts to catch personnel in the open. At 06:00 the field guns then commenced a rolling barrage, advancing 100 yards every four minutes. Meanwhile the 90s dealt with the German artillery, as spotted by air observation. American infantry units then advanced behind the screen of this artillery barrage at about noon.

Similar actions continued every day through the 17th. On July 18 U.S. troops of the XIX Corps continued to advance and captured the town of St. Lo, ending what had become known as the "Battle of the Hedgerows." In its three weeks existence, there had been over 40,000 American casualties and over one-thousand French citizens had been killed before the town could be evacuated. Within hours of its ending, a buildup of American troops began in anticipation of a breakout from this area. Over the following 24- to 48-hours, various units were moved to different positions, realigned, or reinforced.[49]

It was during this time that a controversy erupted between U.S. Air Command and Artillery. "Comet" was the radio transmission terminology meaning that all Allied patrol planes were out of the sky. It was the official signal that all artillery units could shoot at anything in the air. One night, at around 22:30 hours, just after "Comet" had been given, a lone P-38 flew in over the area as the surrounding artillery units immediately opened up on it. According to all the units, their battery radars picked up the American-made plane but discovered that it was not giving an IFF signal. "[Our] Battery received orders to hold fire until the plane could be properly identified by the IFF signal," reported a D-Battery gunnery sergeant. "There was no doubt that it was an American P-38, the question was whether there was an American pilot [at the controls]." The plane flew in low over the gun emplacements, banked and circled back over. After nervously waiting some time and receiving no friendly signal, Captain Reiver gave orders to fire. Other artillery battalions and Automatic Weapons batteries throughout the vicinity had continued firing at the plane during the entire time but had failed to hit it. "D's guns opened fire with each gun firing three rounds," noted Eckenrode. "All the shell bursts were near [but] the final burst hit the plane and sent it into a spin. It crashed about six miles from the Battery area."[50]

Many artillery crews throughout the region claimed they saw the pilot bail out. Several members of the 110th AAA, in fact, swear they saw a chute. But no American pilot was ever picked up near the wreckage or out in the Channel and no German pilot was captured in the area. "When the cracked up plane was examined, there was no pilot to be found," exclaimed Eckenrode, "so it was a mystery as to whether the plane was piloted by a German or an American." Still, Air Command reprimanded the gun crew for shooting down an American plane and chastised other units throughout the area for shooting at it.[51]

On July 20, as A-Battery and B-Battery remained at St. Jean de Daye, C- and D-Batteries were ordered to boogy-up and move about five miles west to set up outside Tribehou, about ten miles northwest of St. Lo. This new assignment was to aid elements of the U.S. 83rd Infantry Division against elements of the German 17th S.S. Panzer Grenadier and the 5th Parachute Division of the 13th Regiment in that region as Operation Cobra, the U.S. First Army's planned "breakout" from St. Lo, began. The objective of the 83rd was to take the high ground in the vicinity of Periers, Normandy. However, heavy rains that day delayed the opening of any large scale military action. Meanwhile, during a break in the rain, as the gun crews were digging emplacement pits in the mud, a lone German Messerschmitt ME-109 fighter plane came in strafing the area as Cpl. Leo Cheney, said to be the best machine-gunner in the outfit, opened up with his quad-50, swinging his mount from side to side to follow the plane across the sky with sustained fire. Cheney's gun sawed the right wing off the Messerschmitt, causing it to crash and burn in the adjacent field.[52]

On July 24, rain again postponed the opening of Operation Cobra amid other disasters. Shortly before dawn, as the operation was to begin, 335 American planes of the US Eight Air force that had failed to get the cancellation, came over St. Lo and, in poor visibility, mistakenly bombed the U.S. 30th "Old Hickory" Infantry Division, positioned just outside the city, killing or wounding more than 100 of the troops. At dawn the next morning, Operation Cobra opened in earnest as 3,500 American planes began carpet bombing four miles of the German Seventh Army's front lines west of St. Lo. Brilliantly laid down, the elite Panzer Lehr division lost nearly every tank, gun and vehicle and a substantial number of troops. In the drifting dust and smoke, however, more bombs were dropped short, killing or wounding 700 more American troops of the 30th and 9th Infantry divisions.

"We had called for close support of 800 yards," reported Elmer Potzmann of C-Battery. "The markers were dropped and the smoke markers were right on target for the bombing run. The first wave did fine but the bombers then lost sight of the 800 yards because of the dust and smoke. We had causalities [and] had to call the air force off because they were bombing our own troops."[53]

"Prior to the bombers were 'Pathfinders' that dropped smoke bombs," explained Lieutenant Forman of Battery-A. "When the bombers came in, that was their bomb line. That worked fine for a couple of hours [but] then the wind came up and kept blowing the smoke toward us. Finally, by God, it got behind us and they were all bombing in behind us. They just kept coming in streams for hours—bomber after bomber after bomber."[54]

Among those killed was Lt. Gen Lesley J. McNair, Chief of U.S. Ground Forces, who had recently joined a battalion in the front lines to personally witness the initial attack. McNair suffered a direct hit on his foxhole. "General McNair was killed about a quarter of a mile from us," reported Edds. According to a number of witnesses, the ground began to violently shake with the first wave of bombers as they dropped their loads and continued to shake for some time. "[A]ll the waves and waves and waves of bombers that came over," marveled Lester Cohen of B-Battery, "one after another, at different heights, and bombed the little village of St. Lo and the artillery that was going on at the same time." It was an unbelievable and frightening experience.[55]

Although devastating to our own forces, the bombing overwhelmed the enemy. The initial plan was for a ground attack to be made by VII Corps with the 4th, 9th and 30th Divisions advancing, supported by over 1,000 guns. Once the infantry had seized the roads leading south and had cleared corridors along them, the 2nd and 3rd Armored Divisions and the 1st Mechanized Infantry Division was to pass through to exploit. Having passed through the enemy positions, 3rd Armored would then swing west toward Brittany, the 2nd Armored would move southeast to Canisy and beyond, and the 1st Mechanized would work toward Coutances. Although delayed, once the VII Corps was able to recover from the initial shock of the flawed bombing and take care of their casualties, they moved out with a vengeance. On the first day, American forces advanced 4,000 yards. On the second day, 8000 yards. On the third day the 2nd Armored Division, "Hell on Wheels," broke through into open country and the following day Coutances was captured, opening the door to the west. Two days later, on July 30, the VIII Corps, under the command of General George S. Patton, seized Avranches, at the base of the Cotentin Peninsula leaving nothing but open country in front of his forces. The Third Army became officially operational two days later and on August 2 Patton pushed three divisions through the five-mile gap his forces had made in the German lines at Avranches. By then, all American troops were poised for a break across the countryside.[56]

About this time, the 110th AAA received orders that they would lead the break-through out of St. Lo as soon as feasible. "Actually, what was received," recalled Capt. James Chase, "was a highly classified written order from a much higher Headquarters than the 110th and directed to 'Btry B 110th AAA Gun Bn.' Obviously it was in error and obviously intended for an armored unit, not a 90mm AAA unit." Captain Chase and Edward C. Kosicki, his driver, drove around for the next several nights until they found a First Army officer with the authority to determine that the order was a mistake and intended for a different unit.[57]

"By August 2, however, it was obvious that a breakout and forward movement was indeed imminent," declared Lt. James E. Chase of B-Battery. Myself and two of my officers [1st Lt. Barrett Coates and 1st Lt. Robert Wilson], my jeep driver [T/5 Archie J. Weller], and another driver [Pvt. Donald G. Bridges], and I were out on jeep reconnaissance checking for possible locations to cross the Vire River so that the five of us [could] lead our convoy out whenever the order should come." Weller was in the driver's seat with Lieutenant Chase in the passenger seat. Private Bridges sat behind Weller, with Lt. Coates sitting in the middle of the back seat area and Lt. Wilson next to him, behind Chase.[58]

Fifteen minutes later, driving cautiously along a beaten path parallel to the river, a terrific explosion erupted as they ran over a German ratchet anti-tank mine. Weller and Bridges, on the left side of the jeep, were killed instantly. Lieutenent Coates was blown out of the vehicle and over a nearby hedge. Several soldiers who had heard the explosion stumbled over him as they ran toward the scene. Captain Chase, lying near the overturned jeep, suffered severe wounds, including fractured vertebrae.[59]

The 110th AAA Gun Battalion had been temporally attached to the VII Corps back on July 25 and had began a ground role closely supporting the attack of the 1st Infantry Division, the "Big Red One," in its push toward Marigny. The battalion shelled Marigny, France for the 1st Infantry Division, destroying the town and the German-held MSR Bridge there as well as an ammunition dump at nearby Feugeres. This action eventually helped open the German lines there allowing Patton's heavily armored and motorized Third Army to pull through the breach. The Battalion was relieved of this role on July 28. It was sometime during this period, outside St. Lo, that Glen was crawling along on all fours in a dry ditch during some incoming enemy shelling when he met General Omar Bradley crawling along all fours going in the opposite direction. Both were on their way to locations they needed to be. "I didn't know what to do," admitted Speer. "Before I realized who he was we were face to face. I started to stand up to salute him and he said 'Don't be a fool corporal, stay down.' With that, I saluted and he smiled in amusement as he crawled past me on down the ditch."[60]

It had taken eight enormously costly days to take St. Lo. Initially the Germans had tried to form up and regroup in the woods and ravines south and southwest of the town in an effort to retake it but they were held off by U.S. artillery. "The town was being held by the artillery, really, as the infantrymen were little more than guards for the observation posts," declared Major Glover S. Johns Jr., 1st Battalion, 115th Infantry, 29th Division. "Most of the tanks and tank destroyers were placed to protect possible avenues of approach, . . . in the event any sort of armored attack tried to come in over a road." One day soon afterwards, a bewildered Frenchman came into the divisional headquarters and asked for a pass to go visit, on foot, another nearby town recently captured by American forces. "I explained that he didn't need any papers to travel in France now," reported Captain Donald Wilder, "that this was his own country, not ours. He walked off looking happier than anyone I have seen since I left home." But others saw another side. "The first towns through which we drove had suffered much from our heavy raids," reported one correspondent. "Our tactical air force had bombed them to shambles. In those towns the French were only half happy and complained that if we had dropped as many arms to the French underground as bombs on the innocent French towns, we would have killed more Germans and fewer Frenchmen." One local was able to sum it all up. "Too many explosions everywhere," she remarked after telling of her farm animals being killed or running off terror-stricken, her house and out buildings being destroyed, and all of her belongings being strewn about. "I'm tired and sad. Deliverance?? Perhaps death and ruin instead. Then what should one wish for? [It's] chaos! We don't know what to wish for, what to hope for."[61]

Many members of the 110th AAA sympathized with the locals after what they saw. "[In three or four days] there were 15,000 French people killed by the Eight and Ninth air force," estimated Harvey Edds of B-Company. "They were bombing villages, towns, rail yards and canals to keep the Germans from supplying their forces. There were more French people killed than Americans during that time." In addition, as the 110th rolled through St. Lo many of the boys were struck by the total devastation of the city. "I remember when we finally went through St. Lo," recalled Lester Cohen of B-Battery, "there was nothing standing but chimney stacks."[62]

One of the main roads into St. Lo. (Author's Collection)

"St. Lo was reduced to rubble," agreed Cpl. William A Gushurst of C-Battery. "As we passed through, an old woman with all her worldly possessions on a donkey cart made eye contact with me. I can still see her. I can still see her face. I can still see that look. It was sadness. 'My town, my house. They are all gone, [she seemed to be saying]. Everything that I own is now on this cart.'" She didn't look a bit happy to be "liberated" as Gushurst recalled.[63]

"One of the war's most touching scenes to me," recalled Lou Azrael, correspondent for the Baltimore *News-Post*, who saw just the opposite, "came several days later when, as we traveled through the rubble on the way to the next battleground, I saw an old woman and a child, standing amid the ruins, throwing flowers to the troops who had wrecked their home and town—and [had] liberated it from the Germans."[64]

CHAPTER 7

Arriving Too Early:
Our Own Liberation of Paris

After the liberation of St. Lo, torrential rains halted any further American advances for several days. D-Battery of the 110th AAA was moved to Cricqueville en Bessin, C-Battery remained near Tribehou, and A and B batteries remained in positions at St. Jean de Daye for another week.

While in those positions, A and B batteries engaged several more aircraft, mostly Focke-Wulf FW-190s, nearly every evening. They were also assigned to conduct a field artillery mission to destroy the main bridge on the road to La Neslier. Succeeding, they remained dug in until they received orders to move out toward Pont Hebert.

"I caught a bullet in my left hand when we were getting our camouflage netting down getting ready to move up," reported Delbert Soll, who had returned to duty with B-Battery. Del was immediately rushed behind the lines to a field hospital where he was treated and then shipped back to England for additional surgery and treatment.[1]

In only three days, tanks and infantry commanded by Patton and Maj. Gen. J. Lawton "Lightning Joe" Collins nearly doubled the depth of the Normandy beachhead. The fast moving U.S. 4th Armored division took the key highway junction at Countances and overran Avranches to open the way into Brittany. Spurred on by Patton, the 4th Armored had thundered 25 miles in 36 hours while Collins' 2nd Armored rumbled south, 15 miles out of St. Lo, creating a fast-paced mobile war in open county for the American forces.

This quick pace kept the batteries of the 110th AAA moving from one location to another nearly every other day. "March orders were expected at any moment," explained one member of Battery-D, "so the equipment wasn't dug in for a long stay."[2]

Several days after the propaganda shells had been fired off by U.S. artillery units over the German troops, a retaliatory barrage of leaflets rained down on American forces. They depicted scantily-clad women in the arms of smiling male civilians and asked the soldiers if they wouldn't prefer to be back home with their wives and girlfriends instead of in the army. Others told about the German soldiers and how accurately and expertly they fought and ended by asking "Did you write home already? Do it at once! A few hours from now it may be too late!" The G.I. troops found the pamphlets and illustrations comical and rather ludicrous that the Germans even thought such threats or drawings might have some affect.[3]

As soon as the Germans realized they had lost the "Battle of the Beaches" and were losing the "Battle of the Hedgerows," they had began to concentrate their forces at Caen, the high ground that would control the roads leading into Paris. British troops had planned to capture Caen on D-Day but the Germans had committed their reserve forces to that location to make their strongest stand against the Allied invasion. They continued to reinforce that region to block the road to Paris. On August 1 U.S. forces entered Brittany from Normandy. The gently rolling open countryside was a great relief to the U.S. troops who had endured the fighting in the hedgerows. This was ideal tank country that offered a direct route to the French capitol.

On August 3 Lt. Clinton Gardner had recovered enough from his D-Day wound and resulting skin grafts to his scalp to return to duty. Shipped out from the military hospital in Salisbury, England, he arrived at a personnel replacement depot, referred to by the soldiers as a "repo- depo," or "repple-deppple," set up about twenty miles inland from Omaha Beach. "I had to go AWOL to locate the 110th," declared Gardner, "since repple-depple people don't give a damn about sending you back to your old outfit." Locating Headquarters battery, he was reassigned to Battery-A.[4]

During that first week of August the Germans began to assemble the Fifth Panzer Army—consisting of the 1st, 2[nd,] and 9th SS Panzers and the 2nd and 116th Panzer Divisions—in an area east of Mortain. Upon this discovery, General Bradley moved five infantry divisions between Vire and Mortain, supported by two armored combat commands and three more divisions positioned around St. Hilaire. The Fifth Panzer Army attacked the U.S. forces on August 7. The 116th Panzer Division was held on the northern flanks by the VII Corps advancing south from Vire and St. Sever. The 2nd Panzer Division advanced from Sourdeval and Mortain before it was stopped by elements of the 3rd Armored Division. The 1st and 2nd SS Panzer Divisions were held by the 30th Division, which held the high-ground around Mortain The infantry of the SS Panzer divisions made repeated attacks to seize the hilltops, but the 30th Division held fast and did not budge.[5]

The Mortain attack was known to the Germans as Operation Luttich and was the German Army's attempt to break out toward the west using the Fifth Panzer group to re-take Avranches and to sever the narrow corridor which connected the U.S. First and Third Armies.[6]

For a short time the Germans did manage to take the village of Mortain and briefly hold the high ground to the east of town but forty of the seventy German tanks leading the attack were destroyed.[7]

By August 6 nearly all of the Brittany Peninsula had been overrun by American forces and the ports of St. Malo, Brest, Lorient and St. Nazaire were under siege.

On August 8 A-Battery of the 110th was positioned on Hill 192, east of St. Lo, to hold it for the Allies as C-Battery was moved into St. Lo, itself. Both remained in those locations for several days. D-Battery, recently moved to Le Mesnil-Rouxelin, a small village on the north side of St. Lo, moved through the battered city to take up a position on the other side.

"In St. Lo I didn't see a single building with four walls let alone a roof," advised Glen. "It was unbelievable. Piles of rubble were still smoldering and the city was a total loss."[8]

"There wasn't a single house standing," agreed Sergeant Eckenrode. "The river had flooded the low part of the city so that only the rooftops of the houses located there could be seen [and] the high sections of the city had either been leveled by bombing or shell fire."[9]

"Hitler's Crawlin' Coffin" Comin' through St. Lo.
(Courtesy of Wayne and Maxine Edmondson)

Every night German planes ventured over the area to bomb and strafe in an effort to drive the American forces out of what was left of St. Lo. One evening, as C-Battery personnel were lining up outside of their mess-hall tent, a lone American-built P-47 "Thunderbolt" fighter came lazily flying over the area. Some of the men looked up, even after recognizing the sound as a friendly aircraft, and immediately began to scatter when they realized the plane was going to crash right where they stood. "I was sitting on an ammo box next to the mess tent when the plane crashed about 50 yards away," exclaimed Henry Thake. "The engine flew over me and sprayed flaming fuel and debris all around setting my gas mask [attached to my belt] and my right pant leg on fire."[10]

Parts of the plane tore a hole in the calf of Thake's right leg that later required four stitches to close. "The engine landed about 50 feet from where my machine gun was dug in," added Thake, "scaring the hell out of Maurice Gagnon [who was] manning the gun [at the time]."[11]

Walter Carroll, Thake, and another soldier rushed to the crash site and pulled off sections of the plane's debris to see if the pilot was still inside. "We got singed eyebrows and hair from our attempt," noted Henry.[12]

The remains of the American P-47 Thunderbolt that crashed near C-Battery's mess-tent. (Courtesy of Henry Thake)

Upon finding no pilot, everyone then noticed that he was floating down by parachute about a mile away. Some of the men were angry at being placed in danger by the American pilot. "One of the guys started firing at the pilot coming down," advised Thake. "Carroll and I rushed over and pushed him down."[13]

During the following nights all of the gun batteries were in action after dark as German planes continued to concentrate on the area to drive the American forces out.

After a couple days at these positions, all five batteries of the battalion were then transferred about 50 miles further south to Saint Hilaire du Harcouet, about 7 miles southwest of Mortain. Their new assignment was to take up a field artillery and anti-tank defensive role in the Mortain region as support of the 30th Infantry Division.

"It took twelve hours to travel fifty-five miles," complained one of the men from Battery-D. "The trucks, with only blackout lights burning, followed the lead jeep [but] what the lead jeep followed was a question to everyone."[14]

The convoy, consisting of a long line of artillery tractors, trucks, jeeps, trailers and other equipment, moved out after dark in the fog and it began raining around midnight. The night became so dark that at one point the battalion convoy passed another parked convoy along the roadside without even knowing it. Before long all the men were sleepy, soaked to the skin, and miserable. "Drivers were changed frequently," added Sergeant Eckenrode, "to prevent anyone from falling asleep at the wheel."[15]

The village of St. Hilaire had suffered nearly the same fate as St. Lo. The center of town was virtually destroyed with only the walls of a cathedral left standing. The various batteries took up positions in and around the area. Battery-D took up a position on a hill about three miles north of town that was bordered by the main highway to Mortain, an orchard, and a wooded area. "A tank-dozer was acquired and used to dig the radar and director emplacements," reported Sergeant Eckenrode. "The gun crews dug in their equipment by hand [and] the kitchen and supply trailers were placed in the orchard." Two days and nights passed with no action. On the third night a couple of German planes flew over the area and were immediately engaged by each battery as they passed. The guns of Battery-D fired a total of 24 rounds with no results. The others fired similar action. After two more days with no sightings, rumors began to circulate that the Luftwaffe was suffering from a fuel shortage. "To get away from the routine battery duty," advised one of the boys, "a sports program was organized." The various gun sections of the batteries competed in a baseball tournament over the following few days. On the evening of the

18th, however, a severe thunder storm hit the area. In a matter of minutes everything was flooded, including all the pup tents, gun pits, and foxholes. According to a number of men in all the batteries it was the worst storm they had been in since the destructive storm of June 19. They all ran to the various supply tents, truck and Cat cabs, and director and radar trailers to take cover as lightening strikes hit all around. "Lightening struck our telephone switchboard and the unfortunate men who were manning the telephone headsets felt the shock," noted Sergeant Eckenrode, "[but] the machine gun section took the most punishment for the men in the quad-mounts sitting in the steel turrets and soaked to the skin were wide open."[16]

Fortunately no one was killed by the numerous lightening strikes throughout the area. "The most serious casualty," declared one man, "was that one of the machine gunners, lifted by the shock [of a nearby lighting strike], banged his head on the quad-mount cross-bar and knocked himself out."[17]

The batteries of the 110th were actually positioned southwest of the bulge of what would later become known as the "Mortain Pocket." The village of Mortain was about eighteen miles west of the Argentan-Falaise pocket created when the U.S. Third Army and the Canadian First Army began to surround the German forces there. The original plan was for Allied forces to break through west of St. Lo and to capture Marigny, then to swing west to Coutances, cutting off the nearly 100,000 German troops in the pocket that resulted, and open a route south down the Cotentin Peninsula to Brittany. Events began to happen too quickly, however, even for the Allied troops. General Patton, having reached the Loire Valley, began a sweep with his Army to the northeast. Forward elements of the U.S. Third Army began to approach Argentan from the south as the Canadian First Army pushed down from Caen toward Falaise. German Army Group B, consisting of the Fifth Panzer and the Seventh Army, all under the leadership of Field Marshall Gunther von Kluge, fought fiercely to prevent being surrounded while evacuation of their troops took place. General Bradley, by then in charge of the 12th Army Group including the First and Third American armies, and General Sir Bernard L. Montgomery, commanding the newly formed British 21st Army Group that included the British Second and Canadian First Armies, feared the American Third and Canadian First might end up attacking each other by mistake since they were closing the gap between the two armies so quickly. Immediately both advances were ordered to halt as a new plan of action was created to avoid any confusion.[18]

At this position the 110th AAA saw only limited action, occasionally being directed to fire volleys on forward elements of the German Seventh Army. Relieved of their Mortain assignment with the 30th Infantry, all five batteries were transferred out of St. Hilaire on August 21 to be redeployed 138 miles east to La Loupe, a city about ninety miles southwest of Paris. The 110th AAA was to be attached to a task force of the 4th Infantry Division as direct support. Their officially assigned mission was to destroy any or all German road blocks along the route to Paris, assist in ridding the city of any snipers, provide harassing fire on any enemy troops returning to the city, and to protect the city against enemy aircraft. The batteries moved out at 20:00 hours and, instead of traveling all night, bivouacked around 02:00 in a cow pasture near Alencon. "Some of the men erected pup tents, others slept in their blankets beneath the summer sky," reported one of the boys, "and still others curled up in the cabs of the trucks and tractors."[19]

After a K-ration breakfast at dawn they headed out and finally reached their destination around 16:00 hours. Moving across the countryside, the boys passed many smoldering damaged and destroyed German tanks, motor vehicles, wagons, and artillery pieces abandoned along the route. None of the batteries saw any action during their 3-day stay at this position. "Having nothing better to do," advised Captain Reiver, "we went into the town bar and started drinking." A crowd of French gathered around the Americans giving them food and drink. "A jeep drove up and Ernest Hemingway and another reporter whom we did not recognize came in," advised Reiver. "They didn't speak so we did not make any attempt at conversation" While there, other American soldiers, mostly of the 4th Division, which was also concentrating its units in the city, came and went. "When we were ready to leave," complained Captain Reiver, "our jeep was gone." Reiver and his group hitched a ride to the nearest telephone and called the battery who sent someone to pick them up. We strongly suspected that the jeep was taken by members of the 4th Signal Battalion of the 4th Division," claimed Reiver. "I visited them and accused them but they would not admit it. For all we know, Hemingway might have taken it."[20]

According to Captain Reiver, the unit replaced their battery's stolen vehicle with an abandoned jeep that the boys later took apart, rebuilt, fixed and reconditioned. "We painted the same serial number on it that one of our jeeps had," admitted Reiver," which worked well [until] we sent two jeeps to Battalion Headquarters one day and they both had the same serial number on their hoods." Soon after, Captain Reiver received a call from Lt. Col. William F. Curren, Jr. "[He] *suggested*," noted Reiver, "that we never again send two jeeps with the same number to the same place."[21]

While in the bar the Theriaults, Gunnery Sergeant of Battery D's Gun #4, L. James "Buster" Theriault, and Donald, a fuse-cutter assigned to the same gun, began to develop a routine they would eventually use all across Europe to get free drinks for the group. "We were from the same town," advised Jim, "Lincoln, Maine, but we were cousins, not brothers." In fact, everyone in the battery, except Clyde Libby who was from Lincoln and knew better, thought they were brothers for a long time and referred to them as the Theriault brothers long after they had learned otherwise. "We didn't look a thing alike," admitted Jim. "I was tall and Don was short; so short he could stand under my outstretched arm. But we won a lot of bar bets when we claimed to be brothers and pulled out our IDs. When they saw our same last names and same hometowns, they reluctantly paid up their bets."[22]

On Wednesday, August 23, the battalion was notified to be ready to move out at any time. "This meant that the fall of Paris was expected at any moment," speculated one of the boys. Finally, at 04:00 hours the following morning, the battalion received march orders to move out promptly at 13:00 hours later that day. At about 10:00 that morning a recon. party left La Loupe bound for Paris. The group consisted of five jeeps and five trucks, one each from each battery. One truck pulled a trailer with its M-51 quad-50. "The quad-mount was taken along to furnish more fire power in case the reconnaissance party was confronted by a German road block," explained Sergeant Eckenrode. With only ten vehicles in the convoy, the recon party covered the ninety miles from La Loupe to Paris in four hours. Arriving in the outskirts of town, they found all the roads leading into the city impassable. Roads had been barricaded, as pockets of German resistance had resurfaced within the district, and were now jammed with parked military trucks, tanks and field artillery pieces delayed from moving in as the turbulence intensified. By late afternoon there had been no change in the status of the situation so Lieutenant Colonel Curren ordered that each battery recon. find its own bivouac area for use until the city was cleared and the traffic started moving again. He was worried the main portion of the battalion, having left at 13:00 hours, was due to arrive sometime after dark and would need a cantonment somewhere in the outskirts instead of adding to the traffic congestion.[23]

While out scouting for possible camp sites, Battery-C's Captain Allen Philips and his driver hit a land mine and were severely wounded. This led to them being evacuated for hospitalization and Lt. Richard D. "Dick"

Sisson of Able-Battery being promoted to Captain and placed in command of Charlie-Battery.

Meanwhile, when the batteries arrived sometime around 20:00 hours they were all directed to their bivouac areas. The quad-50s were the only pieces of equipment set up and readied for action. The 90mm guns and range equipment were all kept in march order because, as one GI explained, "[our] next assignment was Paris and nowhere else."[24]

A-Battery and B-Battery stayed in a little town called Nogent Le Rotrou, just south of Paris. "While we were there," advised Forman, "General Timberlake came up and [American singer-actress] Dinah Shore was with him." The troops were gathered into a nearby field where Dinah Shore put on a singing performance. "She started singing," recalled Forman "and the guns were booming [off in the distance] and she kept on singing and then it started raining." The General suggested she postpone the performance but she told him that as long as the troops stood there listening she would sing to them. "She was bare-headed and her hair [was] hanging down her back and rain [was] running down her face," remembered Forman, "and ever since then I've had a very great regard for Dinah Shore."[25]

Battery-C and Battery-D were bivouacked at Lamours, a small village about two miles outside Paris.

That night, August 24, Captain Raymond Dronne of the Regiment of Chad, 2nd French Armored Division, under orders of Maj. Gen. Jacques Philippe Leclerc, led an advance party, including members of the U.S. 4th Infantry Division and the 110th AAA Gun Battalion, to probe into the city of Paris. "I don't care what the history books say," insisted Speer, "we went into Paris for a little while on the night of August 24. The first Americans went into that city *before* the 25th!"[26]

At 21:22 hours on the 24th six half-tracks, three tanks, a number of trucks and several jeeps arrived at the Hotel de Ville, the huge Renaissance-style Paris city hall building at rue de Rivoli and rue du Temple Streets near the center of town. To get there the small convoy approached from the south, driving quickly down the avenue d'Italie avoiding German roadblocks, check-points and barricades by using side streets in and around the area. As they sped past the Gare d' Austerlitz, German troops fired on the group. They ducked down and continued without returning fire. As they approached the square, the tracked vehicles slide to a stop in front of the massive building, creating a shower of sparks. Their presence was announced by the ringing of church bells from the areas from which they had just passed. While being surrounded by a welcoming crowd, sniper and machine-gun fire opened up on the crowd from some of the nearby buildings.[27]

Civilian victims of sniper fire in Paris. (Author's Collection)

"There was sixteen of us [from Battery D, 110th AAA] who went into Paris that night," insisted Glen, "in a 6X6 following our captain's jeep. Wayne Edmondson was driving, I was riding 'shotgun,' and the others were in the back of the truck." According to Speer, as the Parisians crowded around the convoy, many of the boys jumped out mingling with the crowd or running into nearby department stores. When the gunfire broke out, Captain Reiver ran around and regrouped his command as they, and all the others in the convoy, jumped back into their vehicles and fled the city. "I don't care what they say," Glen repeated, "that was on the night of August 24. The first Americans entered Paris August 24!"[28]

The following day Major General Leclerc, given the official honor of taking Paris, even though US divisions encircled it, returned this time accompanied by the full complement of heavy weapons of the French 2nd Armored Division, the U.S. 4th Infantry and the 110th AAA. "As a scout in our reconnaissance jeep," reported Lt. Gardner, "I was among the first Americans in Paris. I got that assignment because I was designated as our battalion's interpreter."According to a number of official sources, the 110th AAA became the first American outfit to enter the city from the south because they were temporarily attached to the French division under General Leclerc, who had no antiaircraft guns and it was feared the Germans would send in planes to level the city. "Civilians gave us exuberant greetings, sparkling champagne, and equally sparkling kisses," declared Gardner. "My French at Exeter and German at Dartmouth certainly paid off."[29]

The 110th officially entered Paris that day from the south by way of Porte d'Orleans with elements of the 2nd French Armored under Col. Pierre Billotte, and elements of the 4th Division. They arrived in the city at about noon. "I was riding on a quad-50 machine gun as we drove into Paris," recalled Harvey Edds of B-Battery. "People lined the streets . . . shouting, crying, and throwing us kisses [and] flowers."[30]

The 2nd French Armored Division had been divided up into three columns, some arriving with Major General Leclerc and Lt. Col. Paul de Langlade from the west and two others coming in from the south with the U.S. units.

According to a number of G.I.s, the French they had come into contact with in the Normandy and Brittany regions had never seemed very enthused with the American presence. In Paris, however, it went to the other extreme. Men, women, and children of all ages lined the streets cheering, clapping, calling out to wish them well, and rushing out into the street to greet them. The Parisians were grateful for their presence and liberation and showed it. "Everyone wanted kissed," exclaimed Sergeant Eckenrode. "Mothers wanted kissed, mothers wanted their babies kissed, the gals wanted kissed. Girls climbed up on the truck, into the Captain's jeep, and onto the M-51 trailers. One girl even climbed up and rode on the hood of the Captain's jeep."[31]

"As our jeep eased through the crowds," noted one news correspondent, "thousands of people crowded up, leaving only a narrow corridor, and frantic men, women and children grabbed us and kissed us and shook our hands and beat on our shoulders and slapped our backs and shouted their joy as we passed."[32]

"As we slowly made our way down the street I could hear the crowd chanting 'Viva la Ruth!,' 'Viva la Mary!' and any other names they saw painted on our vehicles," added Lt. Ted Noel of D-Battery, 110th AAA. "I didn't have any names or sayings painted on my jeep but I did have a Prestone antifreeze decal that I had found somewhere. As I drove through the crowd I began hearing them yell 'Viva la Press-stone!' 'Viva la Press-stone!"[33]

"Parisians pelted gladioli, asters, carnations and dahlias into every passing vehicle," noted William Walton, a *Life* magazine correspondent who was in another jeep farther down the line in the American armored column. "Every few yards the crowd surged in. Conservatively, I estimate I kissed a thousand females from 2 to 90 [years old] that afternoon." Off in the distance, however, the sound of explosions could be heard over the commotion. It was the Germans trying to destroy the bridges over the Seine.[34]

Members of 110th AAA in Paris on August 25. The jeep "GI Jive" was a 110th AAA Headquarters-Battery vehicle. (Courtesy I. Glen Speer)

Trailed by exuberant children and followed along side by celebrating adults, all of whom where calling out "Les Americains! Les Americains!," and all along the way presenting the soldiers with bottles of wine and bouquets of flowers, elements of the 110th penetrated as far into the city as the Luxembourg Gardens outside the Senate Building on Boulevard Saint Michel, before being fired upon.

"As we crossed the Seine River, near the Cathedral of Notre Dame," one of the 110th noted, "the crowds disappeared and the streets were deserted." The men of the battery quickly learned that German snipers remained in many of the buildings on this side of the river as machine-guns, rifles, and mortars opened up. "[The German mortars] were particularly dreaded," reported one American G.I., "because the shells approached with a whisper in contrast to the warning banshee scream of incoming artillery fire."[35]

"Our column moved to a point one block from the Luxembourg," reported Don Whitehead, an Associated Press news correspondent accompanying the 4th Infantry Division. "Then, from all sides burst machine-gun fire. From housetops and windows, guns rattled. Machine guns of [our] tanks opened up in reply. We leaped from the jeep and took cover behind a tank." As American G.I.s sought cover in order to return fire, F.F.I. resistance leaders crouched and ran from door to door, pointing out positions of the snipers in windows and roof-tops. "Ahead of us," Whitehead continued, "the patriots crouched along the buildings and answered the enemy fire. Lying there, I felt lonely and lost in the city which all of us had dreamed of entering as a joyous occasion."[36]

The bulk of the occupying German force had withdrawn into strongholds in the heart of the city including, it was later learned, 2,600 in the Bois de Boulogne and an untold number holed-up in the Place de la Concorde, Quai d'Orsay, Tuileries, Gardens of the Louvre, the Madeleine, the Chambre des Deputes, the Palais du Luxembourg [Senate] building, and the Hotel Crillon, leaving only sparse patrols of tanks and infantry in the outlying urban areas to engage the Allied units as they entered the city.

It was later estimated by U.S. military authorities that as many as 5,000, and probably more, German soldiers remained hidden throughout Paris after Allied troops had entered. Skirmishes broke out in various sections of the city during that first day but sniper fire continued to be a major problem long after Allied units had established positions throughout the metropolitan area. "We were constantly shot at," reported Edds in agreement, "early in the morning and late at night."[37]

"We were fired on from a building and we could tell which one because of the tracers," added Harry Pasku, also of B-Battery, in describing one such incident. "I dove into a slit trench and told someone to go up there and get them. They came back with wigs. They were women who were bald from being with the Germans."[38]

After Paris was liberated, French women known to have collaborated or associated in any way with German soldiers were often taken into custody by the local citizenry and, after being ridiculed and chastised for aiding the enemy, was forced to have their head shaved. "[T]hey whip her, strip her, and shave all the hair off her head," declared Nelvin M. Tyree, Btry D, 441st AAA Bn., "I have seen [several] who got these haircuts! Then they run her through town for all to see." Quite often the formality took place in the town square where the girls were later driven down the streets in various states of undress, barefoot, with swastikas painted onto their faces and bodies ahead of a jeering crowd shouting "Salaud!"[39]

After a few more similar incidents such as Pasku and others experienced, it wasn't long before rumors began to circulate among the various Allied units that the snipers were actually the girlfriends left behind by the evacuating German soldiers.

By noon of the 25th, the French flag was flying over the Eiffel Tower and later that afternoon, over Napoleon's Arc. To accomplish the liberation, nearly 10,000 German soldiers and more than thirty tanks had been captured while nearly a thousand freedom fighters had been killed with another 1,500 wounded.

As Maj. Gen. Raymond O. Barton's 4th Infantry Division had entered from the south with orders to clear the eastern part of the city, the batteries of the 110th AAA had split off from the long columns of armor, assault guns, half-tracks, and supply trains that had fanned out onto the many different streets. The 110th had orders to set up in locations that would help protect the city against aerial attack.

"We went on into Porte d'Orleans and turned right, past the University of Paris on sort of a hill out there called Fort Mont Rouge," advised Lt. Forman of A-Battery. Battery-B moved in and set up in the city park further down the street. "The Germans had a lot of their anti-aircraft guns set up in this big park," noted Franklin Johnson. "We had to move in and pull their guns out and put our own in." According to him, however, the Parisians were so happy to be liberated and to see American troops that they became nearly as dangerous as the enemy. "[W]e had set up barbed wire around to keep people away," advised Johnson, "[and] they knocked the barbed wire down. The young women were coming up and being so nice. Well, for a 19 year old guy it was overwhelming." Battery-D had the same problem on the other side of town. "The battery had no sooner moved into the area then the people started to congregate in the gun park," complained one of the gunnery sergeants. "In half an hour it was estimated that there were 2,000 people gathered around our equipment. Wire was placed around each piece of equipment to keep the people from touching it. This made the gun park look like a fair ground."[40]

According to Edds, Baker-Battery's position in the city park was about two or three blocks north of Orly airfield. "Later that day," reported Edds, "a large crowd was dragging a man down the street. He had been in German uniform and had been caught in civilian clothes. They brought him down to our corner and threw a rope up over a tree and hanged him. They left him there until the next afternoon when someone came and cut him down."[41]

"Headquarters battery of the 110th was billeted in the American building on the university campus," added Corporal Gushurst, "and C-Battery was positioned further east, in the rail yard."[42]

The rail yard was a sort of ammo dump abandoned by the retreating Germans. A number of rail cars containing German ordnance was discovered so Charlie Battery was shifted to the rail yard and placed at that location. The yard was in the Ivry-sur-Seine district, southeast of the city.

The following day, August 26, the Free French leader, Brig. Gen. Charles de Gaulle, entered Paris amid hysterical crowds and occasional sniping to proclaim his government without Allied sponsorship. That night German bombers came over to destroy the city.

Hitler had originally ordered that Paris be held at all costs or reduced to rubble if completely impossible. When told Paris had been captured by the Allied forces, his only response was a simplistic, "Is Paris burning?" Finding out the "City of Lights" had been spared, he insisted that his bombers burn it to the ground.

The gun crews never had time to boogy-down before the German bombers came in, many of which targeted the abandoned ordnance so, according to Gushurst "they just ducked." Their quad-50s, however, did get into the action. "They escaped injury," offered Gushurst, "but their equipment didn't."[43]

"[T]he Germans sent over 65 planes to bomb the bridges along the Seine [river] there," advised Lieutenant Forman. "We shot down 16 of them and they didn't bomb [any of] the bridges."[44]

"[We] fired up four cases of .50-caliber machine-gun ammo [on my gun]," advised Edds. "About 800 rounds. Then we could hear the lead dropping down through the trees—it sounded like hail. We got under our machine gun as best we could."[45]

D-Battery set up at Bois de Boulogne, on the west side of Paris, west of the Seine, in a horse racing track out there named de L'Haye les Roses. Overlooking five major bridges into the city, including the Pont d'Iena at the Eiffel Tower, they had also withstood the bombing as they engaged the enemy that night. "The bombers were concentrating their attack on the 4th Division bivouac area on the opposite side of Paris from us," noted Eckenrode. "The ground shook from the explosions and in a little while the sky became cherry-red as the buildings in that area began to burn." The rail yard where Charlie Battery was positioned was about eight or nine miles to the east of their position. Able and Baker Batteries faired better, being a safer distance just southeast of C-Battery. By the time it was over, nearly 600 buildings in the eastern vicinity had been destroyed leaving 213 civilian dead and another 914 injured.[46]

The following day, A-Battery was ordered out to the race track area and transferred to the Bagneux district of Paris, where they would remain for several days. D-Battery was moved from the race track to the other side of the city about seven miles. "Lieutenant Colonel Curren had us move to the city dump," complained Captain Reiver. "I think just to be mean."[47]

Battery-D, it seemed, had run afoul with the higher command, again. They had originally come into Paris, even on the 25th, a short time before everyone else. "We followed the 4th [Division] and were making good time," offered Captain Reiver. "When we were very close to Paris we started out with our recon party only, so that we could pick positions and direct the rest of the Batteries to them." The battalion was to go all the way into Paris and then break off into four directions with each battery heading toward their assigned positions to locate good spots to set up. "As we started down the main road," claimed Reiver, "we ran into a heavy road block formed by tremendous trees which had been cut down. They might have been booby trapped so we by-passed them and continued." It soon became obvious to the group that the battery had somehow passed the 4th Infantry Division "Not knowing where they were or how to contact them," maintained Reiver, "we continued on the road to Paris." Battery-D arrived at the large open square of Porte d'Orleans and found it deserted. In a short time a crowd began to gather, talking with D-Battery members, thanking them, and wishing them well. Finally, the French 2nd Armored and the U.S. 4th Division arrived, drawing a much bigger crowd. "We later found out that the 4th Division had been told to pull off the road and let the French in first," noted Captain Reiver. "I don't think they were happy to see us there."[48]

While still at the race track, a group of children from the orphanage down the street came to the American position and sang songs to them in English. "They gave me some paper American flags they had made," recalled Reiver.[49]

It was also during that first day in Paris, at the race track, that Captain Reiver was approached by a Frenchmen identifying himself as the city's Chief of Police. After introducing himself, he requested that Captain Reiver accompany him down to a former Gestapo headquarters building. "He showed me bodies which were still unmoved," reported Reiver. The captain then learned that before the Germans fled from the city they had machine-gunned a number of captured French Resistance collaborators being held there. "We did take pictures of them," advised Reiver, "[but] I told him that I wasn't high enough, that we had to get a General." The proper authorities were then contacted and began an investigation.[50]

Several days after entering Paris the gun crew saw Ernie Pyle go by in a jeep. "He didn't have a chance to stop and talk," noted one of the men, "but he gave a yell as he rode by."[51]

Another incident in Paris involved Speer helping two French girls who were trying to move to another apartment. Speer saw them along the side of the road struggling with all of their belongings and stopped to offer help. He was operating his prime mover at the time and since it was empty he saw nothing wrong with helping out. He loaded their clothing and small furniture items into the tractor and headed off down the Paris street with the girls sitting in the cab with him. "As luck would have it," recalled Captain Reiver, "Col. [Thomas W.] Munford, commanding officer of the AAA Group Headquarters to which the 110th was attached, saw him."[52]

Munford immediately called Reiver, telling him of the incident and demanded that Speer be Court-Martialed. "He was a good man," professed Reiver, "[and] I didn't feel right in doing it." After chastising Speer upon his return to the Battery area, Reiver then went to First Army Headquarters and spoke with the Inspector General who later informed Colonel Munford that the incident would be dropped.[53]

Speer was worried about the incident at the time but later recalled, "On the front lines we often did stuff—or were allowed to do stuff—that wouldn't be tolerated by commanders in the back lines," advised Glen. "Many of us committed minor violations that didn't seem to us to be a big deal but apparently was to the some commanders. Another thing we did, we often painted white stripes or racing stripes on our trucks, put decals and straight pipes on 'em, and ran our vehicles with mud flaps. Maybe the commanders in the back lines just had more time to worry about [discipline] or to prevent such stuff. The ones up front had other things to worry about besides who we were giving rides to or what we were all doing to soup-up or customize our vehicles."[54]

Battery-Dog's position in the Bagnolet dump was actually a strategic location. It was about the highest point around Paris and over-looked the city, giving a good wide range and clearance. Because a lot of brick and stone rubble from bombed out city buildings had been dumped there, the guns and equipment could not be dug in so additional layers of sandbags had to be used.

"The civilian population of Bagnolet treated the members of the Battery as life-long friends," noted one of the battery. "In fact, they became so friendly that after a couple of days the F.F.I. placed a guard around the area at the request of the Group Commander."[55]

Colonel Munford wanted the civilian population kept out of the battery's area entirely. He did not want the French entering the U.S. compound. Part of the reason both adults and children were entering the gun park was to retrieve food scraps and donations from the G.I.s. "It was really a pitiful sight to watch these hungry people fight over the food which we couldn't eat,"remarked Sergeant Eckenrode. "These people were so hungry that they would scour the garbage cans which the cooks had set out. [They] would fill their pails and take them home."[56]

Captain Reiver and his boys quietly ignored Col. Munford's order and the captain made arrangements with the F.F.I. sentry. "Without the Group

Commander knowing it," admitted Eckenrode, "the people were allowed to enter after every meal so that they could get the leftover food."[57]

During this same time, Battery-C was moved out of the rail yard area and repositioned in the southeastern suburb of Vincennes. After four days there the battery was then transferred north to the Pantin district. Battery-B followed a similar route and A-Battery was moved to the St. Quen district. The batteries remained in these positions throughout the first week of September while U.S. forces continued to consolidate and bring up more troops, material, and ammunition.

On Tuesday, August 29, the U.S. 28th Infantry Division paraded triumphantly down the wide straight stretch of Champs-Elysees from Napoleon's Arc de Triomphe to the Place de la Concorde to help alive the fears of the French people and to show them that there was an overwhelming Allied force in the region.

Meanwhile, many of the boys of the 110th AAA were getting passes to go into the city for sightseeing and shopping while others volunteered for a special assignment.

CHAPTER 8

Going Through the Siegfried Line: The Only Road Home

As the freeing of Paris became history, Allied troops continued their advance toward Germany. "The plight of the German army in France seems as bad as it had been in late 1918," reported *Life* magazine on September 4. "Southeast of Paris, in a vast continuous series of flanking movements, U.S. tank forces move toward the Belfort Gap and Germany. West of the city the Germans are being squeezed to extinction against the Seine. From the south, U.S. and French troops speed northward for the great junction which will free three-fourths of all France." Between Paris and the sea the Canadian First Army and the British Second Army broke across the Seine and swept toward Belgium. Northeast of Paris the U.S. First Army fought through Sedan, itself a renowned battlefield of WWI, and moved on into Belgium. During this time, elements of the First and Third Armies were engaged in rapid pursuit of the enemy across France and Belgium simultaneously consuming an average of over 800,000 gallons of fuel per day. The First Army, in fact, used 782,000 gallons in one day alone.[1]

The decision to cross the Seine and immediately pursue the German Army without waiting to fully develop the Allied supply lines was a major revision of the original Operation Overlord plan. The quick annihilation and withdraw of German forces was completely unexpected. Orders to pursue was a gamble the commanders were willing to risk. "The armies will go as far as practicable," noted General Bradley, "and then wait until the supply system in the rear will permit further advance." By D+87, in just over a month, the First Army had moved more than 300 miles inland. The Third Army had done comparatively well. Before long, the fast-moving forward divisions were outrunning their supply lines as they fanned out and extended the front. The system, at first strained, was reduced to a trickle. The French rail system had been destroyed west of Paris and the Germans still held most of the French ports. In an effort to bridge the gap between the front lines and the mounting stockpiles at the Normandy coast, a long distance, one-way "loop-run" roadway system of delivery was developed using the Army's workhorse, the 2.5-ton 6X6 trucks already out in the field. These vehicles had wooden slats arched across the back bed or body with a canvas tarpaulin stretched over that. The trucks were normally used to tow the M-51 quad-mount machine-guns, the power plants, the directors, to haul ammunition, tents, cots, rifles, gas masks, basic cooking gear, duffle bags with the troops' clothes, the sand bags to construct gun pits, and any other equipment or gear for the regiments or battalions. Simply put, it was an all-purpose vehicle. Trucks and drivers from every available unit were pressed into service, including newly arrived infantry divisions awaiting transfer to the front, engineer companies, artillery units, and antiaircraft battalions. "They came to our outfit and asked if anybody wanted to go on detached service to drive cargo," advised Speer. Between August 29 to September 15 a number of boys from all four batteries of the 110th AAA Gun Battalion volunteered to drive for what would become known as the "Red Ball Express." Glen Speer and Wayne Edmondson immediately volunteered. "Being a 'Red Ball' trucker meant that you were charged with driving battalion trucks to the Red Ball depots to pick up supplies, especially gasoline and ammo" advised Glen, "and then ferrying it to your battalion's position or to somewhere else along the front." Lieutenant Clinton Gardner of A-Battery was placed in command of the battalion's detail. "I was [assigned command] of six trucks from the 110th," advised Gardner. Sometimes the Red Ball Express consisted of a convoy of trucks led and followed by a jeep, occupied by a Lieutenant, and other times just two or three trucks traveled together. Drivers picked up freight at St. Lo near the Normandy beaches and drove as fast as they could to Chartres to supply the U.S. First Army or to Dreux to supply the U. S. Third Army. Either route was a 700-mile round trip. Their cargo was artillery shells, other ammo and gasoline. "We hauled truck-load after truck-load of 5-gallon Jerricans full of gas," remarked Edmondson, "and loads of ammunition, too."[2]

The trucks rolled 24-hours a day. "At night we would sometimes pull off to the side of the road and nap," added Glen. "I would always get way off the road and try to park under hedge trees but I'd sleep right there among the ammunition. I'd lay my bed roll out and sleep right there."[3]

One night others began to see the wisdom of Speer's preference to park under the canopy of the trees. A German Messerschmitt came in low and began strafing the area. Fortunately no one was hurt and no trucks were destroyed. "He strafed the blacktop road," advised Glen, "[but] that's enough to make you sit up and pay attention to what's going on!"[4]

During the big 10 to 100 truck convoys, designated rest or bivouac areas were established along the route. Engineer battalions erected road signs with large red balls centered on white placards to designate the Red Ball Highway and made thousands of "one-way" signs and "keep off" and other signs warning French drivers and unauthorized military vehicles to stay off the road. M.P.s were stationed along the route at major intersections to direct traffic to prevent the cutting in or splitting up of convoys by other traffic. The Red Ball Express had the right-of-way through all intersections over any other traffic.

The truckers were supplied with a sticker in the shape of a red ball to affix to the left side of the front bumper to identify the vehicle as being used in the Red Ball Express. This sticker gave the truck official right-of-way through any intersection and permission to speed if necessary. The twenty-four hour movement of traffic required a set of strict rules. All vehicles that traveled in convoys had to maintain sixty-yard intervals between them. They could not normally exceed the maximum speed of 25 mph and no passing was allowed. After dark, additional MPs were positioned at major intersection check points not only to assist in traffic control but to record pertinent information. Colorful, and quite often comical, signs and markers were erected along the routes to prevent drivers from getting lost. And any disabled vehicles were to be immediately moved to the side of the road and either repaired on the spot by roving Ordnance units or towed to the rear.

Of course, few drivers observed the 25-mph speed limit set by the Army. Most did 40-mph or more. It is said that the British soldiers and French civilians recognized the red-ball symbol and would run at the sight, knowing they had better get out of the way of the "crazy" American drivers. Wrecked trucks off the side of curves or at the bottom of steep hills was a common sight along the established routes of Red Ball Express. A popular expression among the drivers was that "Red Ball trucks broke but they didn't brake."[5]

"If you wrecked your truck, or something happened to it, and they couldn't fix it in 24-hours," advised Glen, "they would give you another one. So one day one of my buddies, J. D. Pittman, was looking at some women walking down the street as we were passing through one town and when he looked back the convoy had stopped. He plowed right into the back of the truck in front of him. Well, he claimed the brakes must have failed and in twenty-four hours he had another truck and was goin' again."[6]

One Red Ball trucker remembered one occasion driving down a narrow street through a town where the road turned sharply to the right. He found himself having to drive up onto the sidewalk to make the curve, causing a French bicyclist to ride into the nearest open doorway to prevent getting run over. Another remembered the loud exhausts on most of the trucks. The young drivers would often poke holes in the mufflers to make the trucks sound louder and more impressive. "I had a straight pipe on that 6X6 I drove," admitted Glen. "In fact, we ran straight pipes on about everything we had. Goin' down a hill, I could rev that engine 'bout to its peak, drop 'er in gear, let off the gas, and it would sound just like I was sawin' the tailgate off the back of that truck!"[7]

Other drivers remembered bridges that had been blown up or destroyed that often had to be bypassed through fields where cattle lay dead and decaying in the heat of day.[8]

"That [Red Ball Express] was quite a detail. We had a lot of fun," recalled Speer. "Sometimes when we came back empty we would get to goin' fast, playing around. Sometimes we would come to a little bombed out bridge and we would try to crowd each other off the road to see who could get there first and drive down through the ditch around the bridge or to block it so the others couldn't get through."[9]

Basically, there were three models of the 6X6 GMC trucks—affectionately referred to as "Jimmys" by the G.I.s—in use on the Red Ball Express. Speer and Edmondson both used the short wheelbase GMC 6X6 which had the long hood. There was also the standard version of the 6X6 Jimmy with the short hood which the G.I.s referred to as the "snub nose GMC" and the COE Jimmy, or cab over engine, model. The drivers pushed themselves hard on this detail, maintained a high morale and were very dedicated. At its peak the Red Ball Express consisted of 5,958 vehicles that hauled 12,342 tons of supplies to the front. In its 81 day existence, a total of over 412,000 tons of supplies were transported. Although the detail continued until mid-November, Glen and the others returned to their regular battery assignments after September 15, when the majority of the hauling had ended.[10]

Takin' a short cut! Another Red Ball Express detail.
(Courtesy Wayne and Maxine Edmondson)

In their absence Battery-D had gone into action only once, on September 3, when three enemy aircraft was fired upon, with one "confirmed kill." They received march orders to move out of Paris to St. Laurent, France, a distance of 178 miles to the northeast, a few days later and headed out on September 8. Headquarters and A-Battery were moved out of Paris that same day to the same area. They set up at the larger city of Meziers while B and C Batteries took positions around nearby Charlesville. All three locations were on the west bank of the Meuse River within ten miles of the Belgium border. "Being railroad towns," advised one of the boys, "they had received quite a bit of bombing and shelling. The railroad yards in both places were completely destroyed." The battalion spent nearly three uneventful weeks at these locations during which those who had been on detached service with the Red Ball Express rejoined their batteries. [11]

On September 29 all of the 110th AAA battalion batteries were transferred out to recently liberated Liege, Belgium. On the trip east, many of the boys saw little groups of small wooden crosses crowned with helmets in the ditches and along the hillsides. They realized they were American helmets and these were temporary graves of G.I.s, hastily buried where they fell in battle. Honored by the French, many of these crude stake or tree-branch stick crosses had flower bouquets lying at their base." "As a final act of defiance,"observed Private Edds, "the French people would very often pull up the stakes and throw away the helmets on the German graves to remove all knowledge of their whereabouts."[12]

As a final act of defiance, the French people would often pull up the markers
and throw away the helmets on the temporary German graves.
(Courtesy Harvey Edds)

By mid-afternoon the battalion had crossed the border. "Many of the towns and cities," warned the military guide book for Belgium provided to the troops, "have been bombed and shelled by us as we approached and shelled by the enemy as he retreated." The boys were told there would be a strict non-fraternization rule in effect and no issuing of passes once inside German occupied Belgium. "It was not known whether the people in this area were pro-German and no chances were to be taken," advised Sergeant Eckenrode, "as there were many people in Belgium of German decent [and] it was expected there would be some German sympathizers in the country."[13]

By 1800 hours of that date, all the batteries had set up around the vicinity of Liege and were shooting trial fire to check the orientation and synchronization of their guns. Liege was located behind the First Army's left flank. Huge supply dumps were located there, strategically positioned by General Bradley's 12th Army Group to supply the eventual drive into Germany. The various batteries set up at different locations in and around the city. Battery B set up at Jemeppe, a suburb of Liege.[14]

"When we arrived," recalled Harvey Edds of B-Battery, "people came running up to us, hugging and kissing us—they were so glad to see us after being under German occupation for over four years."[15]

Before they could dig-in their quad-50, Harvey Edds and Jim Prescott were invited to a nearby studio by a Belgium photographer who offered to take their picture. Edds and Prescott went to the man's house where his wife fed them a hot meal, heated water so they could bathe and offered to wash their clothes if they returned to camp for clean ones. "Both of us were filthy dirty," admitted Edds. "[W]e both washed our hair and face to look more presentable and [they] cut our hair as we had not had a haircut for several months." The photographer provided the two with laundered clothes and their photographs the following day and gladly offered to develop some film Edds had at no charge. "They just wanted to show us that they were truly grateful for what the Americans had done for them," advised Edds who had continued to offer payment for the various services. "They treated us like royalty."[16]

The following morning a little twelve year old girl came up to the area of B-Battery's Gun #1. "She could speak fairly good English," advised Harvey Edds, whose quad-50 was dug-in nearby. "It was good enough that we could converse with one another quite easily." After not talking with a lot of civilians about fun things and nonsense for over four months the boys of the battery got a kick out of talking with her and learned that her name was Josee Scevenels. Soon Josee began daily visits to the battery, being treated by all the boys like the little sister many had left back home. "I think the entire company adopted her," advised Edds. "She had a personality that matched her beauty." Among other things, Josee would tell them about the difficulty of living under German occupation and how hard it was to get food. Hearing such stories, the boys would try to help out, even though it was against Army regulations. "[T]here was very often young boys and girls standing near the three garbage cans that we washed our mess kits in," advised Edds. "The kids were not much more than 7, 8 or 9 years old." Holding pails or other containers, the kids would fill them with the G.I.'s garbage or leftovers whenever possible and run home with it, apparently assigned to the task by their family. "I'm sure we fed many families," recalled Edds. "Many guys who were at the tail end of the chow line would take extra helpings and give it to the kids."[17]

Headquarters and Battery-A set up just outside of the city too. "[It] was the country home of the Ford dealer [of] Liege," advised Lieutenant Forman. "We took that over and made it our battery headquarters and set up [A-Battery's] guns on the grounds."[18]

On or about the evening of October 1 a formation of Lancaster British Bombers flew over Liege. American antiaircraft units in the area immediately opened up on them. "We were not at fault," offered one of the boys of Battery-B, 110th AAA. "Their briefing office had [apparently] failed to give them the proper altitude which was 10,000 feet over Liege. They were flying at 5,000 feet. Also [they] had failed to give them the proper code so that our I.F.F would know they were friendly planes." In the confusion, a number of British bombers were shot down. "There were at least 14 men on a Lancaster plane," fretted Harvey Edds. "We shot down 5 British Lancaster planes."[19]

On October 6 the batteries went into action again, this time against confirmed enemy aircraft but there was still many problems.

"As Liege was located in the Meuse River Valley with the river running right through the center of the Belgium city, it was surrounded by comparatively high hills," offered Sergeant Eckenrode, All of the 110th's batteries were set up on one of these hills overlooking the city. The German Army had destroyed all the bridges of Liege that spanned the Meuse as they had retreated. After the city was liberated, U.S. engineer battalions had erected pontoon bridges over the river. The assignment of the 110th AAA Battalion was to protect those temporary structures and, of course, they were the target of the approaching enemy aircraft.[20]

"When the German planes flew in low, the surrounding hills often interfered with the radar's ability to pick up and remain locked onto the target while the batteries were firing," worried Eckenrode. "Consequently, the data entering the computers was erratic." Battery-D fired 17 rounds with no confirmed hits that night. The other batteries experienced similar action.[21]

It was also during this time that the Germans were launching the V-1 flying bombs and the V-2 rockets against civilian and military targets in Great Britain, northern France and Belgium. Two principal targets of the V-1 and V-2s were the vast American depots at Antwerp and Liege. "The Germans sent these rockets into Liege, Belgium, by the hundreds," agreed Harvey Edds.

The V in the V-1 stood for Vergeltung swaffe or revenge weapon. Officially, it was known by German military authorities as the Fieseler FZG-76. It was literally a winged, robotic flying bomb. Packed with 1,870 pounds of high explosives, it was about 25 feet long with a wingspan of nearly 18 feet and cruised along at 360mph with a jet-pulse engine. Its range was 150 miles and they had been in use since the previous June 13th when the first ones were shot off toward London, a week after D-Day. By July 22 nearly 5,000 V-1s had been launched. They became known to American G.I.s as "Buzz Bombs" as Allied advances continued across Europe and more and more of them were being seen. Generally, G.I.s on the front had not seen them unless they had been back to Britain for any reason after June 13 but this particular region of Belgium was quickly becoming known as "Buzz Bomb Alley" as American forces continued to gather in the area.[22]

"They were cigar-shaped," advised Glen, describing the first one he saw, "with a small little jet rocket attached to the top."[23]

The V-1 sputtered through the sky sounding like a passing motorboat or small motorcycle and drew a barrage of fire from the antiaircraft guns all along its path. It was actually an antiaircraft gunners dream target. It flew straight, level and at a constant speed. Once the boys realized what it was they could lead it like a clay pigeon and blast it from the sky. Nearly 3,000 were eventually launched toward Liege and Antwerp, and over 6,500 were fired at other targets in Belgium. Nearly 2,500 of those were brought down by AAA fire.[24]

"The first one we ever saw, we couldn't figure out what it was," admitted Speer. "We kept shooting and we could tell we were continually hittin' behind it. Finally some of the gunners who were duck hunters started yelling to give it a bigger lead so they kicked off the computers and started firing manually. That's when we brought the first one down."[25]

The V-2 was a ballistic missile. Officially known by the Germans as the Peenemudne A-4, it had a liquid-oxygen and ethyl-alcohol fueled liquid propellant rocket engine that carried a 2,150-pound high-explosive warhead. It had a speed of 3,440 mph and a range of 185 miles. The V-2 was nearly 47 feet high and 5.5 feet in diameter with a tail-fin span of about 12 feet. "The Buzz Bomb, you could hear it coming," exclaimed Lieutenant Forman who, with others of A and Headquarters Batteries, experienced their first V-2 outside Huy, France, on the way to Liege, "but the rocket went up about thirty or forty miles and came back down and it got there before the sound did. So all you heard was the [sudden] explosion and it was one hell-uv-an explosion."[26]

The first offensive use of the V-2 came on September 8 when two rockets were fired off from the Hague toward London. Witnesses in the city said they heard what sound like two loud claps of thunder, the ground shook, and several houses disintegrated with the appearance of a huge crater in the ground. In another incident, six members of the 3597th Quartermaster Truck Company were killed in northern France when a V-2 made a direct hit on an ammunition dump. "Every hour or so one of those new German V-2 rockets came streaming down [and] exploded in Liege, sometimes quite near us," reported Lt. Clinton Gardner. "[They] seem to have about a ton of explosives and dig a hole about 50' in diameter and 20' deep . . . . We can see them coming in on us, leaving a white vapor trail . . . . The less exotic V-1 buzz bombs, around since June, cruise over us regularly, chugging along at 200 m.p.h. only 500' up [and] spitting fire out of their tails."[27]

Needless to say, duty in "Buzz Bomb Alley" remained nerve racking and kept the boys alert. By this time Allied forces had liberated most of the German-occupied areas of western Europe except the Netherlands and some scattered regions of France. The front now extended from the North Sea near Ostend, Belgium, eastward to include the crucial port at Antwerp and then generally southward to include most of Luxembourg following the flow of the Moselle River through eastern France to the border of Switzerland.

On October 7 the battalion was unexpectedly ordered to move out to a "secret" position later found to be three miles south of Verviers, Belgium, at a little village of Pepinster, a distance of about 15 miles southeast of Liege. This location became known as "Position X" because it was a "Top Secret—Classified" position that was not recorded in the Battery morning reports. Their assignment was to set up on the hills at different locations around this area to provide anti-aircraft protection for a meeting of high ranking generals who would gather here. Of course, the boys were never told anything more than it being a "high-level meeting" and never knew exactly what was taking place at a nearby Chateau in the hills outside Pepinster. "[W]e assembled the U.S. senior command," revealed Lt. Gen. Omar Bradley, "to greet the King of England then touring the Allied front." In addition to King George VI, his entourage and Bradley, others present included General Eisenhower, Gen. George S. Patton Jr., Lt. Gen William H. Simpson and Brig. Gen. Charles E. Hart. "During the ten day stay at "X" the Battery did not fire a single round," reported Sergeant Eckenrode. "This was fortunate for the guns, sitting in mud a foot deep, would have been thrown out of orientation the moment they were fired."[28]

One of the B-Battery gun positions over-looking the valley.
(Courtesy Harvey Edds)

It had rained heavily since the second day of their arrival. After a couple days of continuous rainfall the gun parks of all the batteries was flooded and muddy. "The gun pits were kept at six inches only by constant bailing of the gun crews," reported Eckenrode. "This kept the water below the platforms of the guns." The radar pit was also filled with mud and water but the trailer kept the unit from being damaged. However, the command post and computer had been placed in the same excavation and constant bailing was necessary to prevent damage to the low-sitting computer trailer. Eventually the command post was lost. No amount of bailing could save it so Captain Reiver moved the CP and its electronic equipment to a truck parked nearby and kept it there the remainder of the mission. Before long, the nearly continuous rains began to create problems with the roads as well. "I remember one evening," remarked Edds, "the vehicles were deep in the mud. The mud was like mush. We had to hook a 'cat' to a jeep [that had] chains on and winch [it] out."[29]

Heavy fall rains and cold weather continued to dominate the battalion's first few weeks in Belgium. "Darkness has settled around us shutting the tent off from the outside world with the shroud of night," wrote one G.I. in mid-October, "somewhere" in Belgium. "Today we had four heavy rain storms and one mixed with hail. It sounded strange on our canvas [enclosures]. We are situated in a field covering a considerable portion of a hill. Our portion of the hill is now chewed up into a sea of mud anywhere from one-half to six inches deep. You put on clean dry clothes early in the AM and before breakfast is over your feet are wet and you have sloped mud all over your legs up to your knees. The uniform of most of us is O.D. pants and shirt, field jacket, mackinaw or overcoat, wool underwear and socks, shoes, leggings, helmet with liner and perhaps a wool knit cap which fits under the helmet.[30]

As the weather turned colder, men in the ETO were issued winter uniforms around the end of September through the first part of October. "We were lucky to get combat jackets instead of field jackets," noted one G.I. "These new jackets, supposedly designed by [General] Ike, are much more comfortable and warmer [and] look very snappy; dark green about [6] inches below the waist, concealed button holes and four roomy pockets." He went on to provide further details in another letter to assure his family he was OK. "Yes, we have plenty of winter clothing. Two sets of O.D.s, 4 of long johns, 7 of wool socks, gloves, cap, overcoats, field jacket and a nice sweater but arctics were in short supply for a long time."[31]

While at Liege the 110th AAA Gun Battalion had been assigned to the Ninth United States Army as part of the 30th Infantry Division. The Ninth was under British command at the time and drew British rations, which included a quart of Scotch and a quart of Gin. As with the cigarettes in Army rations, the boys who didn't drink or smoke—such as Speer and Edmondson—sold theirs off. The "X" detail ended on October 17 and the battalion received orders to move on in and set up around Verviers. Battery-D took up a position on a hill northeast of town. Meanwhile, the U.S. First Army, now under Lt. Gen. Courtney H. Hodges, who assumed command on August 1 when General Bradley was placed in charge of the newly formed 12th Army group, had been reducing the perimeter around nearby Aachen for several days and finally gave the German troops occupying the town 24-hours to surrender. When they refused, the town was put under air and artillery attack on October 12 to pound them into submission. Finally, American troops entered the desolated city and after eight days of fighting from house to house took it on October 21. The fall of Aachen was the first successful Allied penetration of the Siegfried Line.

The Siegfried Line presented one of the most formidable defensive border barriers ever constructed. A type of defense born in medieval times, this modern-day version contained minefields, tank traps and obstacles, pillboxes, concrete emplacements and fortresses of various sizes. Some of the fortifications, which extended 35 miles deep in some places, actually dated back to1917 and World War I. Reinforcement of those areas and others had been on-going since 1938. The French had constructed a similar line of defenses along their east border with Germany during the 1930s, called the Maginot Line, but it proved to be easily breeched.

After rapidly advancing across France, Belgium, and Luxembourg, Allied forces came up against this fortified line of defenses called the Siegfried Line all along the German border. Known to the German people as the "West Wall," this fortified line ran from east of Basel, Switzerland, to Karlsruhe, Germany, following along the borders of France, Luxembourg, Belgium, and the Netherlands. One branch paralleled the Rhine River and its southern end faced the French Maginot Line. The Allied attack on the Line was actually a series of battles that had began in September and continued through October and on into November. The 30th Infantry Division had been busy attacking the Siegfried line between Aachen and Geilenkirchen ever since October 2. All along a front that stretched from the North Sea to the Swiss border bitter fighting continued. The U.S. First and Ninth Armies came up against heavy resistance not only at Aachen but also in the Hurtgen Forest, while the Third Army pushed through and defeated a powerful counter-attack by German armor and infantry near Metz. On November 23, the U.S. Seventh Army in the Vosges seized the vital Saverne Gap and took Strasbourg.

Meanwhile, on October 25 the 110th AAA Battalion had moved about 14 miles from Verviers to the area of Spa, Belgium. Positioned on the surrounding hills that overlook Spa, their mission was to protect First Army Headquarters that had been set up at a large hotel there. "MASTER," the official military code name given to First Army Headquarters, had just moved their command to the fashionable baths of the city, only 12 miles from the German border, and set up at the stately Hotel Britannique. According to General Bradley, First Army signs were erected on the street corners, its trucks and troops crowded along the boulevards, field desks were moved into the hotel's casino under huge crystal chandeliers, its cocktail lounge and bar was outfitted with the First Army's dispensary, and a war room was created in the conference rooms with maps mounted on the walls and laid out on the tables.[32]

When the battalion originally transferred out of Liege back on October 7, the boys of Battery—B had been in the process of packing up when they saw Josee come running up the hill. Sad they were leaving, she told Harvey she had something for him and handed him a photograph she had taken by the town's photographer. On the back she had written "To my friend Harvey" and signed her name. Edds promised Josee he would write when he got back home to Topeka, Kansas and gave her a copy of the print of him and Prescott, taken by the same photographer. After being transferred to Spa, the boys learned that Josse had been killed by a buzz bomb when one had hit her family's home a few days after the battery had transferred out. All the boys of the battery were devastated by the news. Harvey Edds was deeply affected.[33]

All the batteries were billeted in large country estates surrounding Spa. By this time they were again under American command, attached to the 18th AAA Group under the 49th Brigade of the First Army. Battery-D was billeted in a large three-story Chateau two miles outside Spa in the small farming community of Creppe. Each battery section was assigned a room in the upper floors of the house while Captain Reiver's office, Command Post and the battery's mess hall were all located on the first floor. There was also a room on the first floor set aside as a day room where the men could spend their leisure time. "It had enough rooms," advised Reiver, "that all of the 165 men in the battery could sleep inside."[34]

"My room was on the top-most floor," advised Speer. "It was a very fancy big old house. Instead of wall paper it had tapestry on all the walls. And boy we ate good while we were there. I got up to 180 pounds; the most I've ever weighed and I didn't like that. I was so big I could hardly breath when I walked up the stairs."[35]

German officers had occupied the estate prior to evacuating the area but had left the buildings intact. The owner lived in Liege but a caretaker and his family lived in a small house at the side of the Chateau. "We called them Mom and Dad," recalled Glen. "They had a boy named Robert and a girl named Margarette, and a another [very young] little boy."[36]

Glen and the others also recalled how "Mom" often made them many apple pies while they were there and how on cold evenings when any of the G.I.s fell asleep in the easy-chairs sitting in front of the fireplace, "Mom" or "Dad" would walk by and spread a blanket over them to keep them warm. "Some nights when some of us would fall asleep there," advised Glen, "they would walk quietly and whisper so as not to wake us up. They were so nice."[37]

The big old house was surrounded by a huge lawn with elaborate flower beds and large evergreens. Located across the narrow highway from the Chateau was a large pasture where the battery's four guns were dug in. The revetments were sodded over to help blend in with the surrounding terrain.

The situation for the 110th AAA in the Spa area remained relatively quiet and stable. "We sat there as 'Palace Guards' for the First Army Headquarters," remarked Lieutenant Forman. "We were the envy of all the other battalions in the 49th Brigade," professed Sergeant Eckenrode, "because we had such a nice setup." The gun crews performed their daily maintenance of cleaning their guns, vehicles, and other equipment, making minor repairs, and keeping gasoline and water tanks and cans filled. After a week had passed at this location, passes were issued.[38]

Thirty-percent of each battery was allowed out at one time to visit Verviers or Spa. Since First Army Headquarters were located in Spa, there was always some form of entertainment going on in that town. There were new showings of American-made movies each week and a stage attraction with big-names at least once a week. "Marlene Dietrich and Mickey Rooney were among the stars whom we were able to see," recalled Sgt. Joseph Eckenrode.[39]

"We'd leave the house with a load of boys in the back of the truck and go down into Spa for the movies," advised Glen Speer. "I remember one night going down the hill and I revved that engine and dropped 'er into gear to 'saw that tailgate off' creating a heck of a racket through the valley and I forgot Sergeant Pettyjohn was in the back of the truck goin' to town with us that night. When we got there he just chewed me out somethin' terrible for doin' that. He couldn't believe I did stuff like that."[40]

During this time there was still a lot of rain. While stationed in Creppe, Glen and Bucky Worboys were sent out one day with their Prime Movers to a field artillery position to help move their guns. "It was so muddy," advised Glen, "we had to hook up two cats to each gun just to get them out to the road." The roads, however, were often just as soft and muddy.[41]

Many units became hopelessly bogged down in the mud.
(Courtesy I. Glen Speer)

As the heavy rains began to slack off in mid-November, cold weather moved in permanently. One day Battery-D's Captain called Speer into his office at the Chateau. "Captain Reiver said he could always count on me to get things done," recalled Glen, "that whatever he told me to do he knew I would be [persistent] until I got it done. As I walked into his office that day he said: 'It's getting colder isn't it?' and I answered 'Yes sir' and he then asked 'Do you see any coal around here?' and I responded 'No sir' and then he said 'Then you take a driver and leave and don't come back until you have a load of coal."[42]

So Glen went out, told his friend Wayne Edmondson, and they left in Wayne's 6X6. "We took off, heading out toward the main road," advised Speer, "out through a muddy orchard slinging mud everywhere."[43]

After driving around Spa and Verviers without finding a coal yard that wasn't under guard by U.S. troops, the boys headed for Liege, about 39 miles from the Chateau. There, on the north side of town, they located several large piles of coal in a railroad yard being watched over by a Belgium caretaker. By this time Glen was driving so he cautiously pulled up to the front gate and started in just as the Belgium guard waved him off and approached the truck, telling him he could not go in there. As they were talking, Wayne casually got out of the passenger side of the truck and walked around to the guard, putting a Tommy gun to the man's stomach. "If I was you," ordered Edmondson, "I wouldn't talk no more except to welcome us to get a load of coal and to say no more about it." The guard agreed that was probably a good idea and stood off to the side as the two drove in, quickly shoveled a load of coal into the back of the truck, and left.[44]

Back at their military installation, the Germans had been sending buzz bombs over the area more and more frequently as the days passed. "[By] late November," professed one of the 110th, "there were days when they would be less than a minute apart." The boys watched helplessly as the mechanical devices sputtered through the sky and passed over their positions. Just beyond the location of the 110th the motor would stop and the bomb would silently drift or glide into Liege. When the battalion first took up positions in this area, the 90mm gun crews and boys on the quad-50s fired at will on the robotic explosives. But orders came down soon afterwards that anti-aircraft batteries were not to fire on these guided missiles for fear that anything other than a direct hit would only alter their course and endanger surrounding encampments, emplacements, or Headquarters, itself.[45]

While stationed in the First Army Headquarters area, the 110th AAA Battalion was inspected by high-ranking military officials and political figures on numerous occasions. Because of the constant possibility of these inspections, continual maintenance, upkeep and attention to detail was always necessary. The men of the battalion soon tired of such scrutiny and became restless. The battery had not seen any real action since their positions at Liege. Passes had been the only reprieve during their assignment in the Spa area. Captain Reiver and the other battery commanders pleaded with Lieutenant-Colonel Curren to be reassigned. It was out of his hands but he appealed to the Brigade commander, Brig. Gen. Edward W. Timberlake, to take the Battalion off the assignment. Timberlake denied the request.

As a result, in an effort to increase moral in his battery Captain Reiver organized weekly dances at the Chateau. "Twenty-five or thirty girls from Spa were invited," recalled Sergeant Eckenrode, "and the dances were a huge success." Reiver had contacted an organization of women in Spa and persuaded them to bring their daughters and daughter's friends to the estate and to act as chaperons. The Captain then warned and threatened his troops to be on their good behavior. The first dance was such a great success that it became a weekly Saturday night event complete with refreshments of sandwiches, coffee, lemonade and cake, for the remainder of the "Palace Guard" assignment.[46]

Throughout the period of November and the first part of December, all seemed calm. No enemy planes had been in the sky over the area for nearly six weeks. Only the buzz bombs remained as a menace but, for the most part, after plotting their paths and impact sites, troops, equipment, and installations were moved and they were allowed to go unmolested. Although a First Army drive into the Hurtgen Forest toward Cologne was still in a bitter struggle, General Patton's Third Army had gotten beyond Metz and had reached the border of Germany both north and east of there while General Jacob Devers'6th Army Group was making good progress in Alsace. At the same time the American Seventh Army had reached the German frontier along the Rhine River, capturing Strasbourg on the southern France-German border and holding that city despite intense German counterattacks. Farther south the First French Army had liberated Belfort and entrapped sizable German forces in the Colmar pocket. In fact, despite heavy losses, Allied troops all along the front were steadily moving forward. For the most part, the war was going good. The German Army was being defeated or pushed back nearly everywhere. There was even talk that the war would probably all be over by Christmas. Many of the boys of the 110th AAA Battalion were already making plans for the future and looking forward to going home.

CHAPTER 9

The Battle of the Bulge:
Our Belgium Tour

Once the West Wall had been breached, the American First, Third, Seventh, and Ninth Armies continued to fight their way deeper into Germany. The boys of the 110th learned that the British and Canadians were making slow but steady progress, too, and the Russians were battering their way into the eastern side of the country. Since mid-September nearly one million Allied troops had been committed in the fighting to penetrate the German Wall. From Geilenkirchen, opposite Holland, in the British sector in the north, to Aachen in the American sector in the middle and Saar, opposite France, in the south, the Wall had been penetrated in about six different locations.

What the boys of the 110th AAA Battalion did not know was just how shallow the penetration had been and the total cost in human life and suffering thus far.

The U.S. First Army reported a total loss of 7,024 killed in action, 35,155 wounded and missing in action, and some 4,860 captured. The Ninth Army had reported 1,133 KIA, 6,864 WIA and MIA, and another 2,059 taken prisoner. There was another 11,000 American casualties suffered by outfits serving under the British and Canadians. In addition, the First Army reported another 50,867 non-battle casualties and the Ninth Army reported 20,787 while Patton's Third Army reported 64,956 total battle and non-battle casualties in their West Wall and Saar fighting. The German Army had suffered just as badly but had succeeded in holding the Allied forces to a penetration of a mere twenty miles or less into their homeland—the deepest being near Juelich—and not more than thirty miles in length—between the Huertgen and Aachen—hardly wide enough or

---

deep enough for a powerful thrust into the interior after suffering the loss of nearly 200,000 troops in 96 days of fighting.[1]

It had taken the Allies six and a half months to get to these positions. The front now extended nearly 600 miles from the North Sea south to the Swiss border. It was a long front that could not be held strongly everywhere. Because the Ardennes region was such a rugged, semi-mountainous, and heavily forested area containing a limited network of roads through it, the area was left lightly defended. The Allies were concentrating the bulk of the Twelfth Army's forces north and south of that region for planned offensive actions and left the eighty-mile length of the Ardennes sector, possessing its own formidable natural barriers, thinly protected by three divisions of the VIII Corps. It was believed that the German Army was on the verge of collapse, anyway, and that they were stretched just as thinly as the Allies along this area. "In those first weeks of December," agreed Terry Bye of C-Battery, "all the talk was not if, but when the war would end. Many of us hoped and believed that Christmas might be spent at home with our families."[2]

The truth was, the German Army *had* been spread thinly in this area but had quietly began to concentrate their forces here since November. At 02:00 on Saturday morning, December 16, the 110th battalion's radar units began to pick up a large formation of unidentified aircraft approaching the area. The planes plotted on the boards as being over Aachen, just out of range of the battery's guns. For the first time in two months the gun crews were alerted to "stand by at the ready." Everyone scrambled to their positions, checked their equipment, and prepared for combat. "I was on duty [that] night at the radar," noted Lieutenant Forman, "and it started picking up planes just in bunches about twenty or twenty-five miles northeast of us. I called [battalion headquarters] and told the duty officer there to report to First Army that there was something going on." Meanwhile, the planes began to circle and came just within range of the 110th's big guns. Everyone waited intently. Moments later all of the Gun Sergeants yelled out the order, "Commence Firing!" The heavy guns roared into action bellowing shot, orange flames and smoke from their muzzles. The crews passed another 23-pound shell down the line as a big empty brass shell-casing ejected and clanked to the ground and was replaced by another live round. Seventeen rounds were fired by D-Battery before the planes were out of range and the "Cease Fire" order was given. Battery-A and the others reported similar action. There were no confirmed hits. The radars stayed on target but the planes remained too far out. As bombs dropped beyond the 110th's range, other AAA batteries throughout the region were heard going into action. Within a short time, the situation quieted and most of the boys returned to quarters. Finally, just a few hours later, southeast of their position, the Germans launched a massive attack along a forty-mile front within the Ardennes Forest of Belgium and Luxembourg. At 05:30 hours a horrendous barrage of 1,900 big German artillery guns opened up against the American positions all along the front, lasting exactly 90 minutes. Startled awake, many American soldiers thought the noise was friendly fire from their own guns toward the German lines. Others, on duty at the time, thought the tremendous firing was simply a demonstration by the enemy. Before long, however, nearly all the G.I.s realized the fire was definitely incoming and that the weight and severity of it meant it was something major. Then, brilliant search lights came on, bouncing their powerful beams off the low-hanging clouds and penetrating the dense fog to eerily light the area with a strange artificial moon-light glow that illuminated the American positions. At the same time, three powerful German Armies, the Sixth Panzer Army, the Fifth Panzer Army, and the Fifteenth Army, totaling nearly 200,000 troops and 600 tanks, emerged from the West Wall under the cover of darkness and the early-morning fog, guided by the big searchlight beams overhead. A total of nine German divisions struck at various points along the line of the VIII Corps and the southern sector of the V Corps front. Behind them was another 300,000 troops and 400 more tanks ready to follow their advancing breakthrough. The Germans successfully created complete confusion and shock. Many U.S. troops later said that as the artillery died away and the lights came on, shadows of approaching enemy troops could be seen advancing through the forest in "swarms." The U.S. First Army's front line divisions initially held most of their positions until they were completely overwhelmed by superior numbers. "They came at us four to one," insisted one G.I. "That's how they drove us back fifty miles in ten days and created the bulge." As the morning progressed, columns of German tanks and troops continued to break through the American front lines.[3]

The German Army was easily moving through the Ardennes. Although it was originally believed this dense forest terrain made the area unsuitable for any offensive action, the Germans had used it once before—in 1940 when the French had also ignored the area and had reinforced their defenses along the Maginot Line. The main German objective was to take the crucial port of Antwerp and at the same time drive a wedge to separate the British and Canadian forces from the American. Simultaneously, the German Army would isolate the U.S. First and Ninth Armies from the Third and Seventh to halt any further progress into Germany. The plan was to launch an attack along the front from Monschau, southeast of Aachen, to Echternach in the south. The Sixth Panzer Army was to attack between Monschau and the Losheim Gap, pass south of Liege, cross the Meuse River, and head northwest fighting their way toward Antwerp. On their left, the Fifth Panzer Army was to attack through St. Vith, cross the so-called "Skyline Drive" and then head for the Meuse, crossing just east of Namur, and then turn toward Antwerp in the northwest, covering the Sixth Panzer Army's southern flank. Two days later, the German Fifteenth Army, north of all of them, would attack around Aachen to pin down any American units that might attempt to go reinforce those in the Ardennes, and then work their way south to reach the Meuse at Liege, thus trapping all the American elements around Aachen in the process. Although moving through the Ardennes on the offensive could be done—creating an element of surprise in the process—control of the roads through the area *was* of the upmost importance.

South of St. Vith, the First Elite Guard of the Adolf Hitler Armored Division moved westward as the Twelfth Elite Guard Hitler Youth Armored Division struck north of town. Meanwhile, additional attacks were being carried out all along the whole line from Monschau to Trier. Throughout the day the rumble and clanking of German armored vehicles and tanks could be heard throughout the region as the German Army continued their counter-offensive. In all, twenty German divisions had attacked four American divisions. Once able to swing to the north, the German force would eventually join ten more divisions to become a total of thirty.

Known to the Germans as the Eifel Counteroffensive, the whole plan of Hitler's Ardennes attack was referred to as the "Watch on the Rhine," with a code-name for the offensive itself being "Autumn Mist." Hitler had given his priority in providing men, equipment, and supplies to the Sixth SS Panzer Army, which was assigned to be the main armored spear-head of the attack. It was under the leadership of Lt. Col. Joachim Peiper, himself a ruthless individual who had an intense hatred for Americans.[4]

Peiper's 4,000 troops—reinforced later with another 1,800—and immense force of heavy tanks—72 medium and 20 Tiger—tore into the American lines at the boundary between V and VIII Corps east of Malmedy, Belgium, southeast of Spa, and was in the V Corps' rear area by daybreak. East of the village of Honsfeld, Peiper's column came upon some U.S. vehicles in retreat and calmly pulled in behind them. The German force, initially consisting of two Panther tanks and three half-tracks, followed them into town, completely surprising the American troops. Rousing eight sleepy G.I.s from their quarters in a private house, barefoot and in their underwear, they were pushed and prodded to the center of town at gunpoint where they were executed with a burp gun for all to see. From another house five Americans reluctantly emerged under a white flag, whereupon German soldiers opened fire, killing four and severely wounding the fifth. As this fifth soldier rolled around on the ground in agony, a German tank drove over him and crushed him to death. Another group of nearly 100 from the U.S. 612th Tank Destroyer Battalion offered to surrender and were immediately cut down. Peiper and his column moved on to Bullingen, a major support center for the 2nd and 99th Infantry Divisions. There, the German force ran into some strong resistance.[5]

Meanwhile, furious battles of attack and counterattack raged throughout the region all day long. Many small units fought off some of the forward elements of the 1st SS Panzers as they moved up the roads leading toward Liege, apparently feeling out the resistance in between the two American Armies. "At some points the German tanks ran up against the delaying positions manned mostly by the so-called 'Palace Guard' of Gen. Hodges' headquarters," reported the *Army and Navy Journal*. "These consisted of the 23rd Chemical Battalion, the 80th Smoke Generating Company, Troop B of the 125th Cavalry, a detachment of six-footers from the 509th Military Police Battalion, the 110th Anti-aircraft Artillery Battalion, and the 99th Infantry Battalion of the Army Security Force."[6]

In addition, Cub planes of the 153rd Liaison Squadron flew reconnaissance missions to help direct artillery fire of the 110th AAA—some of which was called in by Lieutenant-Colonel Curren, himself—and to report the progress of the approaching tanks. At the same time, Buzz-bombs that used to chug past the Spa area were now dropping all around. Liege, and all of its supply activities, had apparently become second choice. The range of the flying bombs had been noticeably shortened and they were now dropping on the Liege-Spa road and on Spa itself.

Later in the initial attack, German planes came in low and strafed and bombed the area all around Spa. "It was during the noon hour," recalled Harvey Edds. "We were in a small box-car-like building. They started their strafing run and everybody hit the deck." When it had started, one of the B-Battery boys, Jim McGorray, had been writing a letter home as a shell whisked past his ear and hit the paper he was writing on before he could react. Another, sitting on a gun outside, had a shell pop past his ear and hit the azimuth clock that he was facing. A radar unit was also hit. As everyone scrambled for cover they heard a child screaming and crying hysterically. As Edds and several of the boys ran out of the building they saw that it was a young girl of about 8 or 9. "I grabbed her and headed for the radar hole," advised Edds. "It had about three-and-a-half feet of water in it. I could see the bullets from the [plane's] guns hitting the dirt as [I ran]." Harvey took cover in the flooded pit with the little girl until the planes passed out of the area. "After the planes left," recalled Edds, walking back to the building, "[William J.] Boksanski stood up and I noticed a two-inch hole in his jacket. I said 'Bo, what happened to you?' He looked at it and I thought he was going to pass out. A bullet had gone through his jacket pocket and hit a tube of tooth paste [he was carrying] and it had exploded!"[7]

Shortly before the planes had come in, the battery had gotten march orders and the boys were instructed to take only one change of clothing and their toilet articles. Many, like Bo, had simply put them in the pockets of their field jackets as they got ready to move out. "In the D-Day invasion you were scared but you didn't know of what. You had no idea what could happen to you," advised Speer, understandably. "But by the Battle of the Bulge, you knew what you were scared of—you knew exactly what could happen. You had seen a lot of things by then."[8]

By midnight of the 16th the enemy had advanced as much as three miles in several locations along the V Corps and VIII Corps fronts. Peiper's penetration was aimed at Malmedy, because it was situated along the shortest route to Liege. In addition, to get to Liege they had to cross the Ambleve River and the most favorable crossing of that waterway was at Stavelot because of an excellent bridge at that location and the fact that two main roads to Liege converged at Stavelot. What's more, one of those roads passed through Spa—only 9.5 miles away—where the U.S. First Army Headquarters was located.

The American forces at Bullingen had strongly resisted and delayed Peiper's troops for a day. At 06:00 the following morning, Sunday December 17, however, the German troops broke through, executed another fifty POWs and captured 50,000 gallons of fuel. Peiper then continued toward Ligneuville and Stavelot on his push to the Meuse River and his eventual drive to the north. Ligneuville was headquarters for the 49th Anti-aircraft Brigade. Brig. Gen. Edward Timberlake had established his command in the luxurious Hotel du Moulin there. The German force entered the town and captured eight Americans of the 843rd Tank Division. Marching them out into the street, each of them was executed one after another with a machine pistol aimed at their face. Later that morning Peiper entered the hotel and, by then quite confident and in good spirits, sat down and finished Timberlake's still-warm lunch. The American Brigadier General had successfully fled with his staff just ten minutes before Peiper's arrival. His dress uniform was abandoned in a closet and a Situation Map of the front, with all the positions of Timberlake's AAA units, including those of the 110th AAA, was left hanging on the wall.[9]

At 11:15 hours December 17, the 30th Infantry Division, holding a sector of the Ninth U.S. Army front between Juelich and Altdorf, Germany, farther north, was ordered down to the vicinity of Eupen, Belgium, to assist in the V Corps sector. A short time later the 30th Infantry was requested further south as soon as possible to assist in the Stavelot—Malmedy area. During this time, elements of the 110th AAA were sent out with a combat team commanded by Capt. Alan V. Hooper, Battery D, 639th AAA AW Battalion, with troops of the 143rd AAA Gun Battalion, to occupy a section of road in the vicinity of Butgenbach, between Bullingen and Waimes, with the mission of blocking the route that ran through Malmedy, Francorchamps, and Spa.

By that time the Sixth Panzer Army had already reached the junction known as Baugnez, about five miles southwest of the Butgenbach position and just 2.5 miles southeast of Malmedy and, at around 13:00 hours, had rounded up another group of Americans. A convoy consisting of thirty-some vehicles of Battery-B of the 285th Field Artillery Observation Battalion, three trucks of B-Company of the 86th Engineer Battalion, an ambulance of the 575th Ambulance Company, three ambulances of the 575th Medical Company and one from the 546th Medical Company, were traveling along the Ligneuville-St. Vith road when they came under fire of the 7th SS Panzer Company of Peiper's German Army approaching from the opposite direction. Following closely behind, Peiper reportedly ordered the shooting stopped so the Americans could be captured and their vehicles confiscated. Although some managed to escape, 113 American G.I.s were captured, disarmed and led to an open meadow on the southwest side of the junction, just south of the Café Bodarwe located there. At 14:15 hours German soldiers under Peiper's command, surrounding the group of Americans, opened fire on them. Some fell and pretended to be dead. Moments later, another group of German soldiers entered the field and shot into many of the prone bodies that showed any signs of life. In all, 84 men were killed and another 25 were badly wounded before the Germans moved on toward Stavelot.[10]

The terrain between Malmedy and Stavelot is mountainous with thick pine forests and steep ravines. Creeks and roads traverse the region along the valley floor. Any forward movement through this area is limited to those routes. The surrounding hills are valuable only to the extent that they offer a clear and dominating view of the important roadway system below. Peiper's forces moved quickly through this valley as it continued west. Incidents all along this route occurred at lightening speed.

Throughout this second day, events around Spa continued to evolve just as quickly. At 19:00 hours two 90s and two M-51 quad-50s from Dog-Battery were given "March Orders" to head out to the main road between Spa and Francorchamps on a TD (tank destroyer) mission.

Just to the north of Stavelot, on an old mountain road to Francorchamps, was a major fuel dump—Depot Number 3—containing about a million gallons of gasoline. Smaller dumps of this depot—Number 3—had been established near Mista and Blanchimont, on the road between Malmedy and Francorchamps. Plans were to have it all moved out and established elsewhere by midday on Monday, December 18.

The normal procedure for TD, tank destroyer or anti-tank, missions was for each 90mm gun to be placed on a curve so it could knock out an approaching enemy tank as it's front end came around within sight. Each gun was then backed up by a quad-50 because when there was a tank there was usually infantry in the vicinity. The AAA units carried plenty of armor-piercing ammo for their anti-tank assignments. While the M4 "Sherman" Medium tank was the mainstay of the Allied tank force, it was severely outclassed by the German Tiger and Panther models. The German tanks had much thicker armor and were better armed. According to Lieutenant Forman, when out on these details the men would search for a defilade position—one naturally protected from a frontal or rear assault while allowing them enfilading fire—sitting the guns down behind a rise. "The German tanks had to come around the corner and expose themselves," advised Forman describing their preferred positions, "and [would have to] make a couple switch-backs before they could get around to where we were."[11]

Depending on the terrain, another TD procedure was to position the AAA gun at the bottom of a slope or incline and aim it up to hit an enemy tank as it exposed its underside—and before it could site-up on the gun crew—as it crested the hill. "My [biggest] fear," admitted Frank Wisniewski of Baker-Battery, "was that we would miss the belly of that first tank coming over the hill." Luckily, none of the gun crews of the 110th AAA saw any more action that night. However, it was just a matter of time. Unknown to them, the enemy had, again, passed within five miles of their positions, approaching the village of Stavelot.[12]

A town of 5,000 people, Stavelot is situated in the valley of the Ambleve River, surrounded by high, sparsely-wooded cliffs. Most of the town was built along its northern bank, reaching up toward the top of the ridge. A single row of houses ran along the river's south bank. Although the river, like most of the waterways in this part of the Ardennes, presented no great obstacle to infantry units, the town's bridge was necessary for the heavy German tanks to be able to negotiate around the sharp turns in the steep valley roads over the water. By the night of December 17 the Stevelot crossing was still guarded by only one squad of the 291st Combat Engineer Battalion. As Peiper's first three tanks rounded a sharp curve in their approach to the bridge, there was a muffled roar as a violet sheet of flame erupted from beneath the first tank The armored vehicle shook and rocked from side to side as it became disabled and brought the entire column to a complete halt. The first tank had run over a chain of explosives set out as a roadblock. With that, rifle and machine-gun fire erupted from a row of nearby houses, sending a stream of white and green tracer bullets through the darkness. The Germans took cover and waited for day break.[13]

Peiper allowed his men to rest as he sent a tank company to check the road to Trois Ponts. He knew that if he could get down to that town, about four miles west of Stavelot, and cross the Salm River there, he would be out in the open with better roads and a straight shot to the Meuse.

By 08:00, Monday Dec 18, Peiper launched an attack on Stavelot and quickly overwhelmed the 291st. Crossing the bridge, the German force rumbled southwest along the river-road toward Trois Ponts. About a half mile outside of town Peiper's forces were halted again by a roadblock set up by Company-C of the 51st Engineer Combat Battalion, rushed to the site shortly before midnight with orders to blow the bridges over the Salm at first sight of the enemy. Consisting of only 140 men, 8 bazookas, 10 machine guns, and an antitank gun, the 51st opened fire and halted the lead tanks and then retreated over the river and blew the bridges. Undaunted, Peiper then turned his forces to the north, heading toward the LaGleize-Stoumont area.

As this action closed, First Army Headquarters was informed that a number of enemy columns were moving toward Spa by various roads. Earlier that morning the range equipment of the 413th AAA Battalion was brought into Battalion Headquarters of the 110th. The 413th's position southeast of town had been overrun by the Germans and the range equipment, which had been on the road at the time, was all they had left. Their guns and prime movers had to be abandoned. "Battery-D fed the members of the 413 in the Chateau," advised one of the boys. The two 90s and M-51s that had set up over night on the Spa-Francorchamps Road returned to set up as field artillery but the order was cancelled at the last minute. General Hodges began evacuating all of his non-essential staff. By mid-day nearly all personnel had moved out except for the General, his intelligence units, his operations units, and a few service troops. Then Hodges threw in his "palace guard," consisting of the MPs, the antiaircraft troops, the motorized cavalryman, engineers, chemical unit troops, clerks, cooks, and miscellaneous personnel, to help defend the town of Spa. Even the First Army's censors were sent into the field to battle enemy tanks with their M-1 rifles.[14]

"Things were now happening fast," professed Sergeant Eckenrode. "German tanks were reported seven miles from Spa. [Our own] P-47s had strafed Battery-B and bombed a convoy of American ambulances that were moving the hospital from Spa [and] elements of the First Army Headquarters were moving out toward Liege [while] tank and infantry battalions were moving their headquarters back from Malmedy and Stavelot and into Spa and the surrounding area."[15]

Each battery of the 110th AAA was provided added strength with the addition of men from a Searchlight Battalion and the 639th AW (Automatic Weapons) Battalion. By afternoon, the battalion was attached to the First Army Security Section with the additional order to hold any assignment at "any cost!" With this, the battalion ceased to be in antiaircraft. All range equipment was put into march order and taken to Liege. At noon, two 90s and two M-51s of Dog-Battery were given march orders again and sent to Stoumont, southwest of Spa, and placed on a TD mission. These were Guns #2, under the command of Sgt. Joseph Eckenrode, and Gun #3, under the command of Sgt. Lloyd Noteboom and including Speer, Edmondson, and the others, along with elements of the 639th AW. At the same time, the two other battery guns, #1 and #4, under the command of Sgt. Bill Nelson and Sgt. L. James Theriault, and two of their M-51s along with two M-51s of the 639th AW were sent north of Stoumont on the road to LaReid. Both missions consisted of 25 men from the battery and 25 men from the 639th. Lt. Hank Klein accompanied guns 2 and 3 while Captain Reiver went with guns 1 and 4.

In the meantime, the 117th Infantry Regiment, first of the 30th Division regiments to arrive in the area for deployment, was fed into the lines around Malmedy. Its 1st Battalion was ordered to occupy Stavelot and circled through Francorchamps to approach the town from the north. Finding it occupied by German troops, the 1st Battalion launched an attack that continued throughout the night. When the 119th Infantry Regiment arrived in the area that evening they were ordered to nearby Stoumont and deployed in a hastily established line north, south, and east of the town. The 1st Battalion of the 119th assembled in an area about three miles northwest of Stoumont. Once they were able to establish and report that a large German force was in the area, they were assured they would be reinforced with a tank company by morning. For the remainder of the night, they dug foxholes, planted mines, and reinforced their position waiting for dawn and the arrival of the tanks. The 3rd Battalion of the 119th, deployed all around the outside of Stoumont, was reinforced by light 3-inch towed tank destroyers of the 823rd Tank Destroyer Battalion, two 90mm antiaircraft guns detached from the 143rd AAA Battalion, and three battalion 57mm antitank guns. The 110th AAA was attached to the 3rd Battalion of the 119th Infantry Regiment in their anti-tank role.[16]

"There at Stoumont it was muddy off the roadway," advised Glen, "so the guns were set down without being dug in and started firing. Mortar teams [of the 639th] were set up along behind us lobbin' mortars over our gun toward the enemy." The group was positioned along side the road, on a curve, and remained there throughout the night. "So here come a whole platoon of our infantry [trotting] back along the road," continued Speer, "and a major leading them said 'Get the hell out of here 'cause we're pullin' back; they're slaughterin' us down there!'"[17]

That night Stoumont was lost. By morning the troops were retreating. U.S. loses in the battle were heavy. The 3rd Battalion of the 119th Infantry Regiment, alone, suffered 290 casualties and lost its three 57mm anti-tank guns, while Battery-C of the 143rd AAA lost both its 90mm guns and A-Company of the 823rd TD Battalion lost all eight of its Tank Destroyers, six half-tracks, and suffered casualties of nine men wounded and sixteen others missing. The 110th AAA lost equipment before it could clear out, too. As the boys scrambled to boogy up and tow their equipment out, they discovered their big 90mm was hopelessly stuck in the mud. "[As the 3rd Battalion was retreating] my gun sergeant yelled at the M-4 drivers to get their Cats and trucks turned around and loaded up and to move out," advised Glen."With that he [then] ran over and blowed the breach block up [with a thermite grenade] and we left the gun there."[18]

"[That night] I was ordered with two other men to go up to the top of a hill and set up an observation post," advised Bob Hall, Headquarters Co., 3rd Battalion, 119th Infantry Regiment, 30th Infantry Division. "At daybreak we observed [German] tanks and infantry coming toward us. My buddies took off to the rear [but] I waited a few minutes longer and ran about 300 yards to a house. [Surrounded], I could not go any further and joined about 30 other 30th men in the cellar. Shortly, I looked out the broken window pane and a German soldier was right there—he was less than a foot from me without knowing it. I immediately went to another part of the cellar [but] was captured."[19]

In all, more than 250 G.I.s from the 3rd Battalion, 119th Infantry regiment were captured during the night or later that following morning. The 110th AAA and the 639th AW escaped without any casualties. From there they withdrew to the west and set up just beyond Stoumont Station on the Zabompre Farm, located between the highway and the railroad tracks on the north side of the Ambleve River. With them was a battery from the 143rd AAA Battalion and remnants of the 3rd Battalion. The 1st Battalion of the 119th was already dug in at this location. Sergeant Eckenrode had Gun #2 set up along the highway near Stoumont Station, east of the farm. Gun 3 was set up just beyond the farm, near a lumber yard. Lieutenant Klein stayed with Gun #2 because it would be the first of his two guns to see action. Once they got their guns into position and set up, the boys dug in, helped lay mines, and assisted in preparing stronger defenses. At around noon, a platoon of four Tank Destroyers from A-Company of the 823rd TD Battalion and two Sherman tanks from the 3rd Platoon of Company-C, 743rd Tank Battalion arrived to help reinforce their location. All then remained quiet until about 15:00 hours when a number of enemy tanks were heard approaching the area from a distance. These were later determined to be seven Panthers of SS Lt. Ostuf Christ's 2nd Company probing toward Stoumont station. The U.S. troops patiently waited, growing more anxious as the minutes passed. Finally, as the lead tank came around the bend about 200 yards east of the station, all the American units opened up on them. The 90mm gun crew of the 143rd AAA, Battery-C, set up out front of the others, took credit for knocking out the first tank and blocking the road. A second tank was hit and badly damaged. The remaining five, soon followed around the bend by several SPWs (self-propelled weapons) of the 11th Panzer-Grenadiers, and infantry, continued their advance down the road as the SPWs and accompanying infantry opened up on the Americans. The crew of the 143rd AAA was forced to destroy their own gun as they came under intense machine gun fire from their right flank and had to withdraw to the safety of the other American units. Klein and Eckenrode's piece was in a well-fortified position so the crew remained at their gun and continued firing. The first two of the remaining Panther tanks were knocked out as they rounded a bend across from the Zabompre Farm and a third became disabled as it became mired in mud when it drove off the south side of the road toward the railroad tracks to get around the other two blocking its path. It was then hit several times by the heavy guns. The Americans continued to put up stiff resistance as Peiper's forces advanced west along the main road.[20]

Meanwhile, D-Battery's guns Number 1 and 4 didn't arrive at their assigned destination along the old Spa-LaGleize road until about 02:00. They had been required to travel this steep, treacherous mountain route under strict "cat-eye" blackout conditions. They set up on this road about four to five miles south of Spa, just beyond the turn-off to Andrimont where millions of gallons of gasoline—the First Army's largest supply depot—was being stored. This was referred to as Fuel Dump #2 and consisted of jerricans stacked up in dumps around the vicinity that were being temporally protected by U.S. service troops. "The entire First Army reserve supply of gasoline, three million gallons in all, was stored in cans along the road," advised the battalion's historian. "There was a stack of cans about every fifty yards." It was an unpaved narrow mountain road that was difficult for these vehicles to maneuver. There were deep ditches on each side which was where the jerricans were stacked to a certain height above the roadway. Prior to the convoy of Guns #1 and #4 moving down this road, a U.S. tank battalion had passed through and had run into a number of stacks, crushing enough of the cans that gasoline "flowed like water down the mountainside." A dense fog blanketed the area and gasoline fumes permeated the air. "We were all afraid that a truck or cat would backfire or someone would light a match and set the gasoline on fire," he continued. "The convoy traveled very slowly because every time a stack of cans was passed one of the vehicles would bump the cans and send them tumbling all over the road." Finally a group of G.I.s was assigned to walk along side the convoy to pick up the cans and stack them back along the roadside so the convoy could continue without damaging more. However, the entire process slowed their advance along this road immensely. "It was drizzling, we traveled under blackout conditions on a narrow dirt road, half of which was taken up by five-gallon cans of gasoline [and] we drove right by the spot we were to defend," complained Capt. Julius Reiver. The spot indicated on his map where he was instructed to set up was not a road intersection at all but a firebreak in the forest. "There was no way to turn around," continued the Captain, "so we went on a mile or two until we came to a real road junction where we decided to [set up] our defense."[21]

The narrow mountain road through Fuel Dump #2. (National Archives)

They were attempting to set the two 90mm guns to cover the road from LaGleize when one slid off the roadway into soft forest mud. The crew attempted to winch the gun back up onto the dirt road without taking time to anchor the prime mover to a nearby tree. As soon as power was applied, the M-4 prime mover was pulled back into the deep mud as well. The remaining tractor was pulled up, anchored to a tree, and set to work straining to pull the pair back out onto the road. "To do this we had to rev the engine many times [and] kept breaking shear pins—the safety devices to keep the winches from breaking,"admitted Captain Reiver. "With much digging, replacing shear pins, refilling gas tanks, and hard work, the gun came loose from the mud and we got it into position."[22]

As this was taking place, the others set up three quad-50s between the planned positions of the 90mm guns, and the bazooka and mine teams got into strategic locations along the road to set up roadblocks. Among them were elements of the 639th AW Battalion. By dawn, the M-51s and 90mm guns were all in place and well camouflaged. A platoon of infantry from the 30th Infantry Division was expected to arrive as support sometime around 09:00 but as that hour came and went they never showed up. Reiver sent Sergeant Thomas F. Monahan with a squad down the mountain toward LaGleize on reconnaissance. They later returned to advise that a number of enemy tanks and infantry was moving north toward their location. Nervously they waited. At noon Sergeant Ernest F. Breit, in charge of a machine gun section of Battery-D and sitting on an M-51 belonging to the 639th AW Battalion, reported that he could see an armored column coming up from LaGleize. Breit's gun was positioned along the Andrimont road about 150 yards east of the intersection. From there he could see glimpses of the enemy through a small clearing in the trees down the side of the mountain. "Orders were given to hold fire and let the Germans come on up the road to the bend nearest the intersection," advised the 110th's historian. "At this bend anti-tank mines had been strung across the road." The minutes passed by like hours. At 15:45, as the first vehicles of the German column finally came into view, an excited gunner of the 639th on another nearby quad-50, immediately mashed his trigger button. "Suddenly one of our quad machine guns opened up," advised Captain Reiver. "I had not given the command to fire and all hell broke loose." The Germans opened with everything they had as the Americans returned with everything they could. "We did not fire our 90mm guns," confessed Reiver, "because the Germans were downhill from us and the 90mm gun will not depress below horizontal." The first vehicle coming around the bend immediately responded to the initial fire of the quad-50. German shelling—return fire—pelted the turret, several shell piercing the shield and taking the top of the gunner's head off. "The armored car [at the beginning of the column] quickly returned fire and bullets riddled the M-51 from top to bottom," reported one of the crew. "The gunner was instantly killed and Breit received a [wound] on the chin."[23]

The fight only lasted about 15 minutes. Then, the German column, consisting of one armored car, two half-tracks, a light tank and six personnel carriers, retreated back down the road to LaGleize. "It was presumed that it had been an armored recon party," advised one of the men. The battery's report claims one enemy tank and one half-track heavily damaged and several enemy killed.[24]

That night, fearing a return of the enemy with their tanks, the boys of the 110th employed a number of imaginative measures in the hopes of keeping them away. Several drove their 6X6s out of the area under blackout conditions and then drove them back with headlights blaring to give the impression that reinforcements were arriving while others fitted chains over the tires of their big trucks and drove them back and forth in the dark to give the impression tanks were arriving in support. "Bruce Lyons and Clyde Libby stayed up all night driving around the gas dump area in their prime movers," advised Sgt. Jim Theriault, "hoping to convince the Germans [down at the bottom of the mountain] that there were a lot of American tanks already in the area."[25]

The next morning as a German Messerschitt ME-109 flew in over the area, instinctively, the Battery spun the gun around, quickly elevated the barrel and shot it down, using the tank sights on the gun, with one round of 90mm armor-piercing ammo. It was the first time that an aircraft was ever shot down by an antiaircraft gun equipped with such sights.[26]

In the meantime, Able-Battery of the 110th AAA, which had been set up on a TD mission in the woods about a mile north of Stoumont the previous night, was eventually joined by about 80 troops of Company-L of the 3rd Battalion of the 119th Infantry Regiment as they withdrew from the town toward Monthouet. In the woods with the 110th were two Sherman tanks of the 743rd TB and some armored cars of the 639th AW. At about 14:00 that day, they all watched two German tanks move to within a short distance of their position but they held their fire when the tanks stopped advancing and headed back down the road. At about 15:10, all four 90mm guns of Charlie-Battery, positioned to the northwest, outside the village, opened up from their position on four Panther tanks passing through Stoumont. Lieutenant-Colonel Curren directed the fire himself from a light aircraft overhead, causing the tanks to take cover. These tanks were later determined to be Panthers belonging to Christ's 2nd SS Panzer Company that had been assigned to occupy the village following its capture. By that evening there was no further activity around Stoumont. All the American units had received orders to relocate and were preparing to move out.

Although these small units put together and sent out by First Army Headquarters were unable to completely stop the German advance, they were able to offer up enough resistance to slow their progress and allow time for other divisions to be transferred into the area. In many instances these units were completely overwhelmed by enemy numbers. The units defending the villages all around the Spa vicinity were going up against enemy columns consisting of anywhere from a half dozen to 800 vehicles and hundreds of troops.[27]

"While these divisions moved to new positions," agreed the *Army and Navy Journal*, "small units such as engineer, ordnance companies, and anti-aircraft battalions, fought furiously and often alone to stem the growing attack. There were innumerable instances of bravery and of heroism."[28]

By mid-day of December 19, Able, Baker, and Charlie Batteries of the 110th AAA remained in the vicinities of Stoumont, LaGleize, and Stavelot, respectively. A-Battery was positioned outside Stoumont. B-Battery was north of LaGleize, and C-Battery was north of Stavelot. Lt. Col. William Fiske, commanding officer of the Security Detachment of the First U.S. Army Headquarters, to which the 110th had been attached, had established a number of roadblocks in the form of anti-tank "daisy chains" strung across the road at all of their assigned locations.

A "Daisy chain" was a string of explosive claymore mines connected with demolition cord, commonly used as "roadblocks"to stop enemy armored vehicles. Once strung, the G.I.s would take positions in the ditches or brush along side the road and wait. "If the [tanks] came," explained one G.I., the chains would be pulled into the path of the lead tank at the last possible moment. At the same time, another chain would be pulled [across the road] behind the tank, boxing it in. If the mines didn't damage or destroy the tank, a bazooka team lurking nearby would try. As soon as the bazooka team sprang into action, the daisy chain teams would jump up and scatter for better cover before the tank's machine gunners could zero in on them.[29]

Baker-Battery of the 110th AAA was with a unit of the Security Detachment commanded by Lt. Walter R. Butts Jr., along with two M-8 armored cars from Troop B, 125th Cavalry Reconnaissance Squadron and one halftrack from Headquarters Company, 9th Armored Group, north of LaGleize. Two 90mm guns and four quad-50s of the battery were assigned to cover a mined intersection while the other guns were set up to cover all other approaches. Within a short time they learned that the enemy was probing this secondary road and moving toward their location. It was a small German column of two armored cars, two trucks, and two 88s being pulled by prime movers. Moving north along the road from LaGleize, the column came up over a ridge to a point about one mile north of Cour where these American units were set up. The lead armored car stopped short of the mines and, apparently seeing one of the "daisy chains," two German soldiers started toward it on foot. As they neared the string of mines, all the troops manning the roadblock opened up with every weapon they had. The enemy took cover and returned fire. The fight lasted nearly ten minutes before the enemy column, apparently thinking they had come up against a much larger force than they actually had, pulled out and left the area. The American units let them go unmolested for the lack of fire-power to follow up.

By December 19 it was clear this area of Belgium bounded by the communities of Malmedy, Stavelot, Stoumont, and Spa was going to remain a hot zone of activity for some time as the enemy launched attack after attack against the American positions throughout the vicinity. As U.S. troops continued to frantically load up and haul out all the fuel from Depot #3, situated along the Francorchamps road just north of Stavelot, the bridge over the Ambleve River in the town of Stavelot was increasingly becoming the center of attention of both armies. The Germans wanted to seize the bridge to clear a path through the town. U.S. forces, which had recaptured part of Stavelot the previous afternoon, intended to blow the bridge to prevent the possibility of the enemy from getting across and discovering the fuel dump. The American defenders here consisted of the 1st Battalion of the 117th Infantry Regiment, four M-10 Tank Destroyers of 1st Platoon C-Company 823rd TD Battalion, 3rd Platoon B-Company 743rd Tank Battalion, 3rd Platoon A-Company and Mortar and Assault Gun Platoons of the 526th Armored Infantry, 1st Platoon A-Company 105th Combat Engineer Battalion, the 118th Field Artillery Battalion, and C-Battery of the 110th AAA Battalion. The first German attempt to cross the bridge occurred around daybreak. Five tanks approached the structure but were driven back by heavy American fire from all along the river and from nearby buildings. The complete evacuation of the U.S. fuel dump was finally completed around 13:00 that afternoon, December 19, a day behind schedule. Shortly afterwards a second, much larger, attack began as ten more enemy tanks came into town and tried to force their way through. This attack ended when a Tiger tank was hit by an M-10 of C-Company, 823rd TD Battalion, that blocked the southern approach to the bridge. Again at 15:00, another attempt was made as the 2nd SS Panzer-Grenadier

Company stormed over the bridge and a number of very accurate direct hits were fired by Battery-C of the 110th AAA. Damaging the structure, one shell hit the bridge ramp, decimating the two German squads trying to cross. Those who made it, ran into the first houses north of the bridge for cover. At the same time the town came under attack by additional forces from the west lasting throughout the evening. At 19:30, under cover of an intense artillery barrage from the 110th AAA and 118th FA, a squad from A-Company of the 105th Engineer Battalion carted 1,400 pounds of TNT to the north span of the Stavelot bridge and detonated it, creating a 25-foot gap that put a halt to any further armored traffic through the town.

Later that night, all batteries of the 110th were ordered to the Malmedy area. "We set up beside a barn on a farm east of Stavelot," advised Speer, hauling D-Battery's Gun Number 3, "and fired into Malmedy." The others looked for buildings as well. Battery-A was in a brick farmhouse with its guns positioned all around. "I had my guns out along a road where there was a nice farm house, a stone farmhouse," advised Lt. Jack Forman. "We set up our 90mm gun next to a strongly built commercial building," advised Harold Mueller, Cat driver for Charlie-Battery's Gun Number 2. "It was also a good place to get out of the cold and get some much needed rest when not on duty. We drivers had no sleep for three days and [were taking caffeine] pills to keep awake."[30]

The constant stress and relocating of the batteries was beginning to take a toll. In addition, the Belgium weather was getting colder and creating additional problems for the G.I.s. A light snow laid on the ground in this vicinity and the temperature had hovered for several days in the freezing range. By this time the ground was frozen hard and the troops nowhere near buildings were having to use axes and grenades to excavate foxholes for cover. "Our principal activity was to try and keep warm," recalled Kenneth Lang of B-Battery. Even worse, the cold often stiffened the grease in the guns causing them to lock up late at night or in early morning hours if left unattended. In one typical incident, Wayne Edmundson of D-Battery was on watch, manning his M-51 when a German plane came flying in strafing the area at tree-top level. Wayne tried to fire the guns of his quad-50 but found them locked up. Immediately he jumped off the unit and dove into his nearby fox hole. Glen Speer came running out of the nearby barn and jumped onto another M-51 but found its guns frozen too. Wayne swore the plane was so close he could see the wrinkles in the pilot's face. "If I had had a pitchfork," insisted Glen, "I could of ripped out the belly of that plane." To their amazement, the pilot waved as he passed by but was shot down by another unit a mile or two farther down the line. "In Italy it was rain, rain, and more rain," complained Nelvin

M. Tyree of Battery D, 441th AAA Gun Battalion who had recently arrived in the Belgium area. "Here, its rain, sleet and snow. Right now I am all piled up here in the cab of my gun with the motor running." Later he added, "[W]e can't have any fires at all 'cause ol' Jerrie may see us."[31]

The snow and penetrating cold of the region was hard on the guns as well as the gunners. (Courtesy of Harvey Edds)

Another problem encountered was the use of the buildings for shelter. Such structures often drew enemy fire and it wasn't prudent for the troops to cluster up in such close proximity to one another. In addition, any buildings that might have been abandoned by evacuating German troops were frequently left booby-trapped. Therefore, the G.I.s were often instructed to refrain from using them as shelter. In cases where no other cover was available, however, the G.I.s considered them better than nothing in such cold weather. The proper procedure for their use in these cases was for the first group who entered to search all floors, closets and enclosures, including the cellar and any piles of rubble, to clear the structure of any snipers, booby traps or holdouts so others could safely enter. In the case of barns, the entire structure, including the hayloft, stalls, and hay or straw piles had to be searched and cleared. Once completed, the boys would move in and spread out into different rooms or areas within the building.

"The first night, after my duty on the gun was over," advised Harold Mueller, "I went inside [our building] around midnight with the other G.I.s and fell [asleep]. During the night an 88mm shell hit the building and buried our truck under tons of brick. It was reduced to a pile of rubble." A hot tile from the fireplace flue, approximately twenty inches in diameter, thirty inches long and weighing about 100 pounds, hit the floor between Mueller and his sergeant. "It missed us both by inches," advised Harold. They laid there and used their feet to push the big tile and some of the other rubble toward the center of the room away from them. Since there didn't seem to be any imminent danger from additional shelling, the boys fell back asleep. "In the morning, we found that five guys asleep on the other side of the room had the soles of their shoes ripped off to the instep by the concussion," noted Mueller, "[and] one gun crew member [had] received a slight shrapnel wound."[32]

Harold Mueller of C-Battery. Heavy shelling the previous night nearly brought a building down on him and the others." (Courtesy Harold Mueller)

By December 20, day five of the Eifel Counteroffensive, the German bulge created in the American front line was more than forty miles deep— reaching into Rochefort, Belgium—and sixty miles wide—stretching from Malmedy, Belgium, in the north to Echternach, Luxembourg, in the south. The U.S. 28th Infantry Division's defenses all along the Skyline Drive had virtually collapsed. German troops were again advancing on Stavelot and to other points around Malmedy. Bastogne was under siege in the southwest. U.S. troops were being pressured at St. Vith in the south. And the 106th Infantry Division had withdrawn to Schonberg in the southeast, and was now trapped, having difficulty getting out. "The 106th was gettin' beat up real bad," recalled Harold Mueller, set up with C-Battery about twenty miles from their location. "They were taking a terrible beating," agreed Elmer Potzmann. "We kept runnin' across stragglers from the 106th [while we were in the Malmedy area] who had gotten out and were searching for the American lines." Finally, all Allied offensive actions against the Rhine came to a complete halt as military officials began to divert troops and shift equipment, supplies, and reinforcements toward the threatened areas. The entire length of the Bulge then became a bewildering maze of attack, counterattack, and counter-counterattack. "I only know that in the Siegfried Line fighting we fought for each yard or mile," offered one G.I., "but in the Ardennes, we were clawing for every inch."[33]

All four guns of D-Battery were reunited at Malmedy. Guns Number 1 and 4 were transferred to the area and set up on a hill just above the town while Guns Number 2 and 3 came in and set up about a mile west of them, next to the barn just off the Malmedy-Stavelot road. Captain Reiver's guns were hidden by the thick stand of pines on the crown of the hill they occupied but Captain Klein's guns, in the valley, were constantly being fired upon. "There wasn't a day that went by that the Jerrys didn't throw some shell into the area," confessed one of the crew. "I always slept in that barn,"noted Speer. "Most of us slept in the barn. I slept in the hay loft. Those German 88s were always hittin' around the area. Lieutenant Klein slept in the nearby farmhouse. One morning as he came out and walked down off the [porch] stairs an 88 shell came in and destroyed those steps! I know for a fact that in two steps he was down off those stairs and in three more steps he was clear across the yard layin' in a ditch in front of the house." The experience, they realized, simply proved an old Army saying—artillery fire respects no one. On December 21 a 40mm gun was added to Captain Reiver's force, giving him a total of two 90s, four M-51s, and the one 40mm. Klein's fire power remained at two 90s and two M-51s. Some had been added by other units traveling with the 110th. All other guns had been lost, destroyed or abandoned during the various engagements of the past five days. That day, military officials from the 82nd Airborne Division and other dignitaries came by the camp and issued medals to a number of those in the 110th AAA for their meritorious actions at the gas dump back on the 19th. By then it had become general knowledge that the German Army in this vicinity was in desperate need of petrol and that it was the action of various U.S. units that had prevented the capture of the U.S. gas depots. Several men of the 110th AAA received Silver Stars, including Sgt. Thomas Monahan and Sgt. Ernest Breit. Captain Reiver was awarded a Bronze Star. Accompanying these officials for publicity purposes was a number of young newspaper reporters, one of whom had met Captain Reiver previously when the battalion had been stationed in Spa. "[H]e came up asking for some inside information [about the battle] so he could have a scoop for his paper," advised Reiver, "so I told him that it wasn't much of a battle, just a little fire fight." The reporter went back and wrote up a detailed account of the skirmish, embellishing on all the details and apparently misunderstanding Reiver's "firefight" term. "I was astounded to read his report that we had used fire to fight the Germans—that we had started a fire to defeat [them]," declared Captain Reiver. "The men of Battery D of the 110th [became] instant heros."[34]

On Thursday, December 21 German forces launched an attack in an attempt to take Malmedy and the roads and bridges beyond. Six artillery battalions, including the 110th AAA, fired in support of the town's defense. These six battalions fired nearly 3,000 rounds during this battle. Most of it was general-purpose ammo fitted with instantaneous fuzes and armor-piercing ammo with delayed-action fuzes however, it was also one of the first occasions that these units used a new, highly secret anti-personnel or "Pozit" fuse, which caused a shell to explode above the ground rather than at contact with it, thus showering fragments over a much wider area. It had a devastating effect on the attacking Germans. American losses that day were light while the 150th Panzer Brigade suffered 150 casualties.

The next day, Friday, December 22, a light snow fell over the area while Klein's position was shelled throughout the morning—this time by German 105s. That afternoon the sky cleared and a small formation of U.S. planes came over to bomb the German forces that had been gathering to the east of town. In addition, the 291st Engineer Combat Battalion was assigned to destroy the town's Warche River bridge, a massive railway viaduct nearby and the rue de Falize underpass, all in an effort to seal and protect the south and west flanks of Malmedy.

The following day, at 15:26 hours, a flight of U.S. bombers came over Malmedy and mistakenly dropped eighty-six 500-pound bombs on the town. Their intended target was actually the village of Zulpich, Germany, 33 miles to the northeast. The U.S.120th Infantry Regiment suffered ten casualties, civilian property was badly damaged, and a number of civilians were killed and injured. As if that wasn't bad enough, within a mere 24-hours another group of bombers of the Eighth U.S. Air force came over the area again dropping their loads, causing additional massive damage and more injuries and death to U.S. forces and civilians of the area. There was never any official explanation of that miscalculation. Then, a few days later, on December 30 at about 16:00 hours, eighteen B-24 heavy bombers of the Eighth U.S. Air Force came over the area and made another bombing run. "[They] were quite low," explained Harvey Edds of B-Battery, "and flew in over the American lines and then [circled] around and started back dropping their bombs, continuing through the German lines and on into the American lines." The A-Battery guns were also set up outside Malmedy, to the north. "We had a command post in the city," advised Lieutenant Forman, "and while we were there, damn if the American Air force didn't bomb us again." This time the A-Battery command post of the 110th AAA in Malmedy was hit, and hit hard. "Corporal Cohen, Corporal Stein, Private Reinart, and myself were getting chow ready when we heard bombs dropping," recalled Lieutenant Gardner. "The windows shook and the house rocked [so] we put on our helmets." According to Gardner, Sergeant John Loftus of the 120th Infantry had just entered the room as he was ringing up battalion headquarters to report being bombed. Loftus quickly turned and headed out the door with Reinart to see what was going on. "I had just finished saying "Red 3" [their battery command-post designation] and Loftus and Reinart were out of the room only a second or so when a terrific explosion flattened the house to the ground," reported Gardner. Recovering somewhat, Gardner crawled out of the debris and staggered out of what had once been a room. "From a heap of rubbish, dirt, bricks, and plaster in front of me came groans and cries from Cohen and Stein." he reported. He cleared away the debris and then noticed another soldier of the 120th Infantry getting up out of the debris behind him. "I saw the man standing up, clothes torn, dazed, [and] streaked with blood," recalled Lieutenant Gardner. Clint yelled at the man to help but he didn't reply. "Then I saw that his arm, his right arm, was blown off at the shoulder," recalled Clinton. After getting Cohen and Stein uncovered and they hobbled out of the area they passed a dead body on the ground. "I didn't recognize him at the time," confessed Gardner, "but he was our friend Loftus."[35]

Lt. Clinton Gardner was wounded again along with the two battalion medics, T5 Mark Stein and T5 Stanley B. Cohen, and Pfc. Reinart. "We'll all get purple hearts even though it was our own B-24s that bombed us," complained Gardner. Along with Sergeant Loftus, there was a number of others from the 120th Infantry Regiment, 30th Infantry Division, and the 291st Engineer Combat Battalion in the building at the time who were also killed outright, including Sergeant Clifford Greenwood, 120th Infantry, who had established his office in the room next to Gardner's. In addition, four civilians in the house, a man, a women, and two children, were also killed and a number of others, both civilian and military, were injured. "In just two minutes an American bomber squadron had flattened the town of Malmedy, killing about a thousand of our infantry defending it," bemused the Lieutenant. In fact, the main square and the town's market center were both leveled and many other parts of the town were devastated by the bombs and resulting fires. It was later determined that, in addition to the four injuries in the 110th AAA, the 120th Regiment suffered a total loss of 98 casualties and the 291st Engineers sustained one killed and one badly injured. "Someone back in Paris apparently thought the Germans had captured the town," complained Gardner, "and never bothered phoning up to see if that was the case."[36]

"[T]here was a total lack of communication," agreed Harold Mueller of C-Battery. "We were being shelled by both the Germans and the Americans. We pulled back about 500 yards and set up a new position on top of a hill [but] we continued to be strafed by our own planes until we were able to contact the Air Corps."[37]

"There was a lot of confusion all during the Battle of the Bulge," admitted Speer. "Often you would pull out into an intersection and the signs would indicate that you should turn left to head for a certain town when it seemed you should be turning right." In one well-publicized account, a half-track of B-Company, 526th Armored Infantry Battalion, towing a 57mm anti-tank gun, showed up in the middle of the night in Trois Ponts having intended to arrive in Malmedy, in the opposite direction. The crew had become separated from its convoy and turned off onto the wrong roadway. The unit was immediately commandeered for use in an impending battle. In another case, a trailer-mounted quad-50 of D-Battery, 203rd AAA drove right into the middle of a battle in Stavelot on the Malmedy road while trying to get to St. Vith. The crew detrucked, deployed the gun and opened fire then loaded up and left when they realized they were in the wrong town. There were a number of times when units were getting lost or arriving in the wrong towns at the wrong time. It wasn't until a few days later that Allied forces learned that German troops had infiltrated the lines. Dressed as American G.I.s in stolen or captured uniforms, wearing dog tags taken off dead or captured troops, speaking fluent English, and often driving captured American vehicles, it became difficult to trust any soldier you did not personally know. "It was a strange feeling to be stopped and interrogated by our own MPs everywhere we went," complained one G.I. "They often threw baseball questions at us and I sometimes had difficulty verifying I was an American. I wasn't much of a baseball fan." Eventually U.S. military personnel learned that the German infiltration teams had arrived by a combination of both being parachuted in at night behind the American lines or they had simply walked or drove across the lines in the darkness and had then mingled with the American troops. Their intentions were to capture crucial bridges over the Meuse, hamper communications, disrupt enemy defenses, and to spread confusion, disorder and fear among the Americans. They often turned or removed road signs, changed village directional signs, and generally just caused havoc. The German Army referred to this clandestine program as "Operation Greif" and it was conducted by the 150th Panzer Brigade. "One day I was servicing our equipment along the side of the road [and] glanced up just as two clean shaven young soldiers, their M-1s slung over their shoulders and walkin' along like the war was over, passed by me," recalled Harold Mueller. "As I turned back to what I was doing, I heard one of our gun crew ask them for the password." Because of this newly discovered activity by the enemy, the password was changed several times throughout the day. These two did not know the new password and were immediately halted at gunpoint by a number of boys from C-Battery. "[We] searched them," advised Mueller, "and discovered that they had forgotten to change out of their German underwear!" They were immediately taken into custody and turned over to the military authorities.[38]

Another major problem encountered by the troops during the Battle of the Bulge was the inability of tracked vehicles to operate properly on snow and ice. The very nature of the terrain in this vicinity confined nearly all movement to the roads and during this time of the year they remained generally snow and ice-covered. When the American forces came upon deep snow or ice, the crews of the tanks, half-tracks, prime movers and other tracked vehicles discovered there was no advantage to either smooth-block rubber tracks or steel-block tracks. Idling vehicles simply slid out of control down any snow or ice covered incline and on ice-covered or deep-snow flat surfaces, the vehicles just sat there in one place while their tracks spun without gripping any surface. "Those Cats were as useless as a sled," complained Speer. "I could pull my cat out onto an ice covered blacktop road, set the brake, and it would slide down the hill just like a sled." Again, American ingenuity played a vital role. The crews began to improvise and shared their ideas and methods with other squads. Some added small welded sections of steel bar to the running surface of the track blocks to create ice cleats, some had sharp steel spikes welded to the end-connector wedges, and still others added rubber track blocks to every sixth steel block and attached a steel grouser on the block midway between for better gripping power.[39]

By the 22nd of December, the determined Allied drive to lift the siege of the German Army slowly got underway. The Germans had timed their Eifel Counteroffensive for an expected bad spell of weather that they had hoped would keep the Allied planes grounded. It had, until the 22nd. "I can remember we cheered, we actually stood there waving our arms cheering," admitted Glen, "when those planes first started coming over."[40]

As the 101st and 82nd Airborne struck out from their bases and began to hammer the German positions, Patton's armored columns drove up from the south to add their fire power and the defenders of St. Vith pushed out and started a destruction of the German line in front of them. Bastogne remained surrounded and under pressure to surrender but the American troops there continued to hold out and refused to give up. One foggy night when visibility was less then ten feet, Charlie-Battery of the 110th AAA could hear a tank moving slowly up the road toward their position. "We could hear the clank of the metal track tread as it hit the pavement because he was having trouble staying on the road in the [snowy conditions] and dense fog," advised Harold Mueller. The gun crews ran to their positions and readied their weapons. The quad-50 barrels were cranked into horizontal and the operators nervously steadied their fingers above the trigger buttons as they watched to see what might come at them out of the fog. The gun crew of the 90mm gathered on the platform, anticipating action—an armor-buster already loaded and set for "outgoing." Nervously, they watched and listened. "We held our fire," reported Mueller, "[because] by the sound of the motor we were almost certain it was one of ours. The American [G.M.] motors sounded much smoother than the Germans." Finally, the war machine slowly came out of the fog. "We all breathed a sigh of relief when we saw that white star," confessed Harold. "That tank driver will never know how close he was to our anti-tank gun. Thank God we did not fire."[41]

Over the next several days sporadic shelling of the various Allied positions continued, with incoming hitting the vicinity of Dog-Battery's post every day. "They just kept sending over [those] Christmas gifts," complained one of the gun crew. "At about 20:00 [on December 24] we were alerted by radio that we could expect German paratroopers,"recalled Harvey Edds of Baker-Battery. "Shortly they came over and dropped right in the middle of [a nearby] engineer battalion. They were ready for them and fired up a parachute flare [which lit] up the sky almost like day. We also fired on them with our quad-50s. There was about 200 of them and I'm not sure that any of them hit the ground alive."[42]

December 25, Christmas Day, dawned with the 110th AAA nearly cut off by a combination of the Germans and the weather conditions. "[B]y that time the snow was about three feet deep," complained Lieutenant Forman, "and about ten or fifteen degrees above zero." It was becoming a brutal Belgium winter and the Germans were still dug in on the outskirts of Malmedy, attempting to take control of all routes leading into the town. "We thought we were going to be overrun," worried Jerome Varrato of B-Battery. "Our supplies were held up [and] we did not receive our regular food supply," added C-Battery's Harold Mueller. "We wrapped ourselves in newspapers and dug a hole in the snow," continued Varrato. "[I] ate C-rations for Christmas dinner and was just happy to be alive."[43]

Later that morning planes of the 82nd Airborne came over and began dropping bombs. The roads were soon opened and supplies began arriving. "[And] here came the kitchen 3/4-ton truck with turkey sandwiches," declared Lieutenant Forman. "I'll tell you they tasted good." The boys were grateful. These were hot sandwiches. These men had not had a bath or a hot meal in over a month. Although the kitchen unit couldn't maneuver down around some of the snow-covered damaged roads, they made sure the Christmas dinner got delivered. "Here come a jeep up the road lickety-split," advised Speer. "He delivered kettles of hot food like pork chops, mashed potatoes and gravy, and hot turkey sandwiches."[44]

At 16:00 hours, yet another small formation of planes came over Malmedy. Although the artillery crews looked up and recognized the aircraft as "ours," they still ran for cover. After their experiences at St. Lo and now here, they were beginning to refer to the Eighth U.S. Air Force as the "American Luftwaffe." As the planes came over, despite all the ground to air recognition panels that had been hastily erected on many of the buildings as a result of all the bombings of the past two days, sixty-four more general purpose explosives where dropped on the village. Their intended target was reportedly St. Vith, twelve miles farther south.

"[The] Chaplain was going down the street looking into the burning buildings," noted Edds. "He noticed an American G.I. in one of [them]. He went in and the soldier's leg was pinned under a burning beam." The boy asked the Chaplain to just shoot him and put him out of his misery. Unable to move the beam, the Chaplain took out his knife and amputated the trapped leg at the knee and carried the soldier to safety. "There were a lot of Americans killed that day," advised Harvey.[45]

In addition to all the American losses during these three bombings, there were 178 civilians killed and an unknown number injured. The town of Malmedy was virtually destroyed. Sometime during all these bombings, the German forces quietly withdrew from the town.

On the day after Christmas, American forces finally went from defensive actions to offensive. The First and Ninth Armies on the north and the Third Army on the south opened their own counteroffensives in an effort to close the Bulge. The enemy's failure to capture the great fuel dumps in the Spa region began to take a toll. German tanks of the spearhead columns began to run out of fuel just four miles short of the Muse River. They had gotten as far west as the outskirts of Dinant and Givet, Belgium but were immediately halted by British forces and American armor. German units that had been sent into Luxembourg and other locations began to withdraw to the Siegfried Line. As they continued to falter, American forces pounced on them. American bombers returned to add tactical support to the land troops. Field artillery and antiaircraft battalions were taken off Tank Destroyer missions to fire field support. The 110th AAA and others blazed a trail with their heavy barrages to cover the thrusts of the ground forces. Exhilarated at their own success, American artillery crews raked the German forces unmercifully while the First and Third Armies continued to smash into the Bulge and drive the German forces back.

On New Year's Eve another light snow fell on the area. "The last day of December was a quiet one for the U.S. Army around this sector," advised Sergeant Eckenrode. As a result, some of the batteries were transferred out to other locations. Baker-Battery was transferred back to Stavelot and Charlie-Battery was moved back to LaGleize. A and D batteries remained at Malmedy, although one gun and one M-51 of Dog-Battery was moved west about five miles to help defend Stavelot as skirmishes seemed to be leading up to another battle in that area.

That evening, Lieutenant Wilson ordered B-Battery to clean their guns. Because of the snow and frigid conditions, the gun crews were able to talk him into waiting until first light of the following day. "The following morning," noted Edds, "we had the four guns all torn down when fourteen [JU-88s] came over. They were real low—at tree top level. They were headed for the various American air bases to bomb them."[46]

On New Year's Day, January 1, 1945 Germany launched its last major offensive of the war, Operation Bodenplatte—an all-out assault on the allied airfields in the region by more than 1000 aircraft of the Luftwaffe. "They sure made a haul that day," declared Harvey. "One of [our] worst losses of the entire war."[47]

At about 09:00 hours the gun crew of Battery-D saw nine German Messerschmitt ME-109 fighters pass overhead. "After the first plane had flown over, the element of surprise was over," declared Sergeant Eckenrode, "but still none of our guns were firing! The frost and cold weather had frozen the solenoids—the electrical triggers attached to each gun on the quad-mounts so that the gunners could fire them by pushing a single button." About the same number of fighters with bombers had passed over Lt. Hank Klein's position in the Malmedy valley and over the positions where Baker-Battery was set up outside Stavelot. "[At my position] my gun jammed," declared Art Hubbard of B-Battery. "[O]verloaded, with oil [it] froze that cold morning."[48]

The German operation continued through the following day during which six ME-109s and two ME-262s—the newly developed German turbojet fighter—passed over Battery-B. These latter aircraft streaked across the sky, shocking the gun-crews and taking them by surprise. It was a totally new sound, "not a buzz bomb," recalled one G.I., "but a whistling roar that made us all look up." It took the gunners a day or two to establish the proper lead on these new machines. "We had nothing that would go that fast," worried Edds. "They raised havoc with our air force for awhile."[49]

"I and Ray Brassard watched two American P-38s collide while chasing a ME-262," advised Sergeant James Theriault of D-Battery, giving one example. The two U.S. aircraft were in a dogfight with the German jet trying to shoot it down, when the plane whizzed downward between the two American planes and they collided. "It was the first jet we had ever seen," continued Jim. "Ray [a quad-50 machine gunner assigned to Gun #4 at the time] sawed it's wing off before it got away and we watched the pilot bail out and drift down somewhere over behind the German lines."[50]

In all, about 125 Allied planes were lost during Operation Bodenplatte, caught on the ground in various airfields of France and the Low Countries, but the results were worse for the Germans. The Luftwaffe lost 364 of their own aircraft, along with many experienced pilots.

While this had been going on, Wayne Edmondson and Speer were sent on an assignment into Malmedy, early on New Year's Day, to help haul out the dead and wounded. "Wayne had his truck parked on the north side of the barn," advised Glen. "[Because of the snow] we had chains on all four duels and the front wheels." As they walked out and climbed into the truck, 88mm shells began dropping all around the area again. Wayne sat there in the driver's seat revving the engine, making sure the truck was warmed up good, as Glen sat in the passenger seat watching the explosions. They both knew the old adage that "the Germans were so accurate with their artillery, they could put a shell into your hip pocket whenever they wanted." The general belief was that with a muzzle velocity of 3707 feet per second, you would never hear the 88 that would hit you and if you heard the whistle, it was best to just duck down and stay put. Finally Wayne looked over and said, "Well, we just as well try 'er" and Glen responded with "Yep, we gotta do 'er." With that the two shook hands, not sure if they would make it out of the yard. "We took off around the east side of the barn," advised Speer, "and out onto the road and headed out eastbound as fast as we could. Never did get hit. Nothin' even came close." The two spent the following 36 hours helping haul wounded and dead out of Malmedy. "It wasn't a pleasant thing to do," the two later confessed.[51]

Over the following days sporadic artillery fire continued and short exchanges took place in nearly all of the battalion's positions. At the same time, enemy planes continued coming in low over the area, strafing the sites attempting to drive the Americans out. "[T]he sky was filled with the familiar dots of bursting 40s and the brief red streaks of the 50-caliber tracers," noted Sergeant Eckenrode. In one incident, as the planes came in low, banked and spread out into different directions, the attached gun crews of the 639th AAA AW Battalion on the 40s began to concentrate on one particular ME-109 that was showing signs of engine trouble. At the same time, Leo Chaney swung his M-51 "quad" onto the aircraft. "Both poured lead at the same plane," witnessed Eckenrode. "You could see the forties bursting on the fuselage and the 50s going on through!" All of a sudden one of the 40s hit the plane's fuel tank just as it was going out of range. "[T]here was a puff of smoke and then the plane was a mass of flame," the sergeant continued "and he went into a dive behind the hill hiding Malmedy from us. That was the last we saw of him."[52]

Six inches of snow fell on the area on January 2 and another ten inches on the 4th. Battery-B was trying to dig gun emplacements for their weapons at the time. To begin, they had to "blow the holes" with grenades. "On January 7 we had finished digging in," advised Edds, "[but] the holes drifted over and [we] had to throw the snow out before we could put our gun in it."[53]

It was during this first week of January that Captain Julius Reiver was promoted to Major and transferred to the 134th AAA, where he was assigned as Operations Officer for the battalion. At the same time, Lt. Henry Klein was promoted to Captain and placed in charge of Battery-D.

The American counterattack to decrease the bulge in their front line had began early in the morning on January two. Very slowly, as the days passed, the German Army was driven back. By the 13th the 30th Infantry

Division started their drive which included the 110ᵗʰ AAA backing them by firing field support.

On January 14, the 4ᵗʰ Platoon of 3060ᵗʰ Quartermaster Graves Registration Company was sent out to the east side of Malmedy to recover the contorted, snow-covered frozen bodies laying in the pasture along the south side of the Malmedy-Ligneuville Road at Baugnez. It hadn't been until January 13 that U.S. forces had been able to recapture and get into that area. It had remained a highly contested battle zone since the day of the killings. There had been a handful of survivors who successfully made it back to the American lines and reported the massacre the evening of its occurrence. In fact, around 14:30 that day, the first survivors of the incident had been picked up by a patrol from the 291ˢᵗ Engineer Combat Battalion and by late that night the rumor that the SS were shooting American POWs had already reached the front line divisions. After that, it is said that very few SS survived capture after December 17. The 4ᵗʰ Platoon, under the supervision of an Inspector General and a team of Army physicians from the 44ᵗʰ Evacuation Hospital, began to recover, process, and identify the remains with every effort to preserve evidence for a war-crimes prosecution. It had snowed on the bodies several times since the shooting and temperatures had remained below freezing since then, keeping the bodies remarkably preserved. It was eventually learned that a number of atrocities had been carried out by German troops in this sector during the December battles. In addition to Honsfeld, Bullingen, and Malmedy, the SS had killed prisoners beyond those towns, including civilians. Back on December 20, soldiers of the 117ᵗʰ Infantry Regiment, while clearing the villages of Parfondruy, Renardmont, and Ster, had come across a total of 117 bodies of men, women, and children who had been killed by small arms fire. Allied authorities also learned that a similar atrocity had occurred the day before at Stavelot. There, German soldiers had killed another 130 civilians in and around that town for "harboring American soldiers" in the days preceding the German reoccupation. This execution included 47 women, 23 children, and 60 men.

As the recovery efforts and the gathering of war-crime evidence continued throughout the Ambleve Valley, the remaining elements of the 110ᵗʰ AAA were transferred out to assist the 30ᵗʰ Infantry. Battery-A returned to an antiaircraft role at Mont, Belgium. Battery-B set up in the same area. "We were reassigned to LaGleize from Dec 31 to Jan 18," advised Mueller. All four guns of Battery-D were regrouped on January 15 and positioned alongside the Francorchamps road north of Stavelot. "The battery went back into AA that day," advised Sergeant Eckenrode. "[We were] set up to give Air protection for the advancing army around Stavelot."⁵⁴

By January 18 all batteries of the 110th AAA Gun Battalion had received march orders to return to Spa. "We went back to Spa and set up outside First Army Headquarters, who'd moved back in," complained Lieutenant Forman, "and there we were, palace-guarding again."[55]

As the weather cleared again on January 22, Allied bombers flew in over the area and found the roads east-bound through the valley packed with retreating German vehicles, troops, and armor and began a systematic destruction of the retreating force. At about this same time, G.I.s of the 110th AAA learned that Peiper and his troops had abandoned their equipment and had walked out of the LaGleize area sometime around 03:00 on Christmas Eve, long before Charlie-Battery had been assigned to the area to help cover the town for the 30th Infantry Division.

Skirmishes and short engagements continued in various locations throughout this region but, for the most part, by January 25 the "Battle of the Bulge" had ended. By the 28th the remaining Germans had been eliminated from the Ardennes bulge and the American front lines had been restored to their original December 16 positions. The German offensive had only delayed the Allied push into the Germanic countryside by six weeks but it had inflicted nearly 95,000 casualties—including nearly 20,000 deaths—on 29 U.S. and 4 British divisions. In turn, however, the German Army had suffered more than 100,000 casualties and had lost over 800 tanks and nearly 1,000 planes.[56]

CHAPTER 10

Remagen Bridge and Crossing the Rhine: Heading Home

Once the bulge had been flattened and eliminated, the Allied forces again turned their attention to the final defeat of Germany. The first step was to cross the Roer River, which had been interrupted by the German's Eifel Offensive, and then to drive on to the Rhine River. As they retreated across the border the Germans dug in and set up heavy defenses to defend their homeland.

The Allies made no major advances until February of 1945 when the Canadian First Army reached the Rhine River on the 14th. The U. S. Ninth Army crossed the Roer River on the 23rd and linked with the Canadians at Geldern, Germany, on March 3. Two days later elements of the U. S. First and Third Armies attacked toward the Rhine, taking Coblenz, Bonn, and Cologne on March 7. During that drive toward Cologne, the U. S. First took much of the Rhine plain while the U.S. Third Army breached the Siegfried Line north of the Moselle and the U.S. 6th Army Group attacked and neutralized the German First and Seventh Armies. These offensives eliminated German resistance west of the Rhine River so that, eventually, on March 22 the Americans were able to cross that river at Oppenheim and, again, at Boppard on March 24.

In retreating across the Rhine, the Germans blew every bridge crossing the river in an effort to delay the advance of their enemy. There was a total of 47 bridges—22 road and 25 rail structures—spanning the Rhine inside Germany. One, however, remained at the little resort town of Remagen. Demolition charges, it seemed, failed to go off and destroy the Ludendorff railroad bridge there.

Upon their return to the Spa area that last week of January, each of the four batteries of the 110th AAA had taken up the same hillside positions surrounding the town as they had previously occupied before December 16. It was a great relief for the boys to finally be able to get a good deep sleep after 32 days of nothing but "cat-naps" and to get a good bath. According to Harold Mueller, during 25 of those 32 days the temperature had remained at 24-degrees or below. "It was so cold," he said, "there was no sweat, no body odor." But upon their return to Spa, with its rich mineral baths and palatial bath houses, the boys eagerly looked forward to their first good soaking. The tubs in all of these resorts were large copper affairs having perforated bottoms that allowed hot mineral water to bubble up through. It was their first chance to rest and relax in over a month. "We'd get a big kick out of how white and pale we looked after we got several months' dirt off," admitted Forman.[1]

While guarding the skies over First Army Headquarters, which had also returned and set up at the same casino resort, all remained quiet and no incidents took place. As Allied progress continued against the enemy, though, March Orders were issued to the battalion on February 26 to assist the First Army's drive with antiaircraft defenses. The battalion moved fifty miles into Germany, passing through Aachen and then northeast. Batteries A and D set up on the hills surrounding Eschweiler, just three miles west of Duren, while Batteries B and C set up about a mile northeast of them, near Merken. Their assignment was to defend the First Army's supply route, along the Eschweiler-Duren road, against enemy air attack. The following night, enemy planes passed over Dog-Battery's position and 46 rounds were fired, bringing down two planes.[2]

During this time, Pfc. Franklin Johnson of Battery-B found his way back to his unit after nearly a ten-week absence. Johnson had been transferred back to England just before the Battle of the Bulge had erupted. "I hadn't been feeling well for quite a while," he recalled. During the first week of December of 1944 Johnson had been out on artillery watch feeling worse every night. "The medic in [our] outfit had been giving me what they call an APC (All Purpose Capsule)," noted Johnson. However, the medication didn't seem to have any affect. "Finally I broke out with full-fledged pneumonia. I had trouble breathing, so I was evacuated."[3]

At first Johnson was taken to a field hospital for treatment but doctors there discovered he was also suffering from hepatitis. Eventually he was evacuated all the way back to England for medical care. Once he was well he was transported back to the front and found himself in a "re-po depot" awaiting reassignment. "This was a big outfit where hundreds, maybe even a thousand, other guys that had been wounded or sick or for some reason had been taken away from their outfit," complained Johnson, "[and] were waiting to be sent someplace else with little or no chance of getting back to [their old] outfit."[4]

Franklin, from Naugatuck, Connecticut, found an old friend from Hartford working at the depot. He told him he was from the 110th AAA and asked that they try and get him back to that outfit but was told he couldn't be promised anything. "One day he came back," advised Johnson, "and he said 'Hey Frank, I was sitting out on the wall [and] saw this truck go by that had 110 AAA on it.'" Johnson ran to the depot Chaplain and told him about the sighting, requesting he try and find out if the Battalion was assigned nearby. Within the next day or two the Chaplain got back to Johnson and told him the truck was an A-Battery truck that had picked up supplies and that they were set up about 40 miles away. Later the Chaplain found out where B-Battery had set up but cautioned Johnson that he might have been replaced and the battery might not be able to accept him. However, the Chaplain arranged for his aide to jeep Franklin out to the site and made arrangements to have the proper paperwork completed so Johnson wouldn't be noted as AWOL. "Cause every night you had to check in," explained Johnson. "[A]s it was I got right back to my gun crew. There wasn't any openings on the gun crew but they had moved somebody else in the ammunition line. So I got back to my outfit. Wow! That was unbelievable!"[5]

On March 1, the battalion was ordered out to other positions. Baker and Charlie Batteries moved out to the hillsides east of Duren while Able and Dog passed through the town and set up several miles further east, on the Cologne plains that had just been vacated by the U.S. 116th Infantry Regiment. The nearest town was Birkesdorf, several miles to the northeast. By 17:00, Dog battery was set up and had fired their trial rounds.

That night, between 21:30 and 23:30, German planes came in over the area with the intent to stop the First Army's supply line. Able-Battery and Dog-Battery opened with all they had and continued until the skies had cleared. Interminable flashes of light from the muzzles silhouetted the gun crews as their man-made thunder shook and vibrated the ground around them. Battery-A engaged at least 8 enemy aircraft that night and several were brought down in a combination of artillery and quad-50 fire. "[Dog] Battery fired eleven courses of 27 rounds each at the enemy planes, claiming eight category ones and one category two," exclaimed Sergeant Eckenrode. "It was necessary to borrow more ninety ammunition from the other battery as all but eleven rounds of our ammo had been expended. That [was] the busiest night we had had since the night we fired 438 rounds on the Normandy beachhead."[6]

During all of the excitement, the D-Battery tracker crews had seen three or four of the aircraft burst into flames when they were hit. With the ability to actually watch the planes going down in the darkness and with the plotting boards and radar working in perfect coordination, they and the men in the Command Post were able to plot the courses of the falling planes and come up with the coordinates of where they had hit. The following morning Sgt. Thomas F. Monahan, of Gun Number 4, and several others went out with a map and the coordinates to locate the downed planes but they found the region covered with land mines. Unable to reach any of the wreckage, they returned. "Without [proper verification of] the wreckage as proof of our shooting them down," complained Sergeant Eckenrode, "our claims could not be confirmed but we knew in our minds those babies had crashed and that we had prevented the Luftwaffe from bombing the supply route."[7]

The following day, Battery-C and B got into the action defending the supply route and the nearby Roer River bridge crossings by opening up on 50 more planes and bringing 18 to 21of them down. At about the same time, Battery-D engaged two ME-262 jets that came over their position at 07:30. "The machine guns fired 800 rounds and the 90s fired 13 rounds but the speedy jets eluded our fire," acknowledged one of the D-Battery gun crew.[8]

The battalion eventually dug in and remained at these positions for nearly two weeks. While passing through the area to get to these locations, the boys had been amazed at the destruction they had seen. "We were able to see the ruins of Duren," confessed Eckenrode. "We had all seen the ruins of St. Lo and all of us said bombing and shelling couldn't ruin a city any more. Then we saw Aachen and we changed our minds. Aachen [we decided] couldn't have been worse. Then we came to Duren."[9]

There wasn't a building in the center of the city left standing nor a house within the city limits that hadn't been damaged. Because of the amount of debris scattered all around, the streets were all one-way. Building-stones and bricks were strewn about so deeply that engineer battalions had been sent into the town to clear a one-way lane through the area with bulldozers to provide the First Army's supply convoys a direct route. "Passing through these streets was just like going through a tunnel," professed one of the gun crew, "[because] the debris was piled so high."[10]

Clearing captured buildings and warehouses in Germany was another eye-opener for many of these young G.I.s. "Being a young man straight off an Iowa farm, I often wondered what was going on here? What was this war *really* all about?" asked Glen. "What were we mixed up in?"[11]

He saw evidence of what appeared to be advancements brought to the region under Nazi rule. Road construction, transportation, and many manufacturing plants were much more advanced than what he had previously seen—at least in his home state of Iowa—and upon capturing

German-held factories, crates full of mechanical parts and equipment marked "Detroit, USA" or other American cities and other American companies were frequently found. "Sometimes it was just difficult to put all of this into perspective," he continued. "You'd see that the Germans used a lot of '41 Fords—sedans and trucks. And we would see '40 and '41 GMC and Ford parts crated-up in many warehouses. And the Shell Oil Company had outlets throughout Germany. To someone fresh off the farm and thrown into this confrontation, it made you wonder. The perspective was difficult to grasp sometimes."[12]

By March 4 the U.S. First Army had advanced onto Cologne after crossing the Erft River, entering that city the following day. It too was in ruins and was quickly cleared of any remaining enemy troops. Meanwhile the U.S. Ninth Army succeeded in clearing the area of enemy troops from the Roer River to the Rhine. German demolition teams began blowing all the bridges up and down the Rhine River as the American forces continued to advance. At the little village of Remagen, a forward patrol of the 27th Armored Infantry Battalion of the U.S. 9th Armored Division unexpectedly found a railroad bridge across the river fully intact. By afternoon, the 9th and 78th Infantry Division had moved into position to defend the structure and to exploit the major find. Under intense German small arms, machine-gun, and 20mm anti-aircraft artillery fire, the American units advanced over the bridge on the afternoon of March 7 under cover of tank fire from the 9th Armored's 14th Tank Battalion to establish a bridgehead on the other side.

The Ludendorff Railway Bridge at Remagen, Germany, inadvertently left intact by fleeing German forces. (Courtesy of Elmer Potzmann)

The first Antiaircraft Artillery unit to reach the Ludendorff Railway Bridge was the 482nd Automatic Weapons (Self-Propelled) Battalion. They had arrived in the area at around 03:00 on March 8. At 05:30, their 2nd Platoon of Battery A became the first AAA unit to cross when that unit's lead vehicle became the thirteenth vehicle in the convoy to pass over the structure. German fire, including rifle, machine gun, mortar and artillery, increased at the bridge throughout the day in an effort to stop the crossings and to destroy the bridge. On March 8, alone, over 600 German artillery shells were fired into the area. U.S. commanders knew it was just a matter of time until the Luftwaffe arrived. The 413th AAA was moved into the area and set up along the west bank of the river. The 49th AAA Brigade was asked for reinforcements. General Timberlake alerted the 110th AAA Gun Battalion around Duren and the 639th AW Battalion around Stolberg to anticipate attachment to III Corps. At 16:45 that afternoon, the first enemy planes arrived. Three "Stuka," JU-87 dive bombers and one Messerschmitt ME-109 fighter came in along the river on a low level attack against the bridge. All four got knocked down by a combination of repetitious fire between Battery A and D of the 482nd. Thirty minutes later a column of eight Stukas came up the river from the south at 3,000 feet and passed over the bridge one by one. Despite the heavy AAA fire, they took no evasive action during their approach. Several jettisoned their load before reaching the structure, however, but one bomb did hit near the southwest approach to the bridge. Before they could get out of the area, four were brought down by Battery-B of the 413th AAA set up furthest to the south on the west bank and the other four were brought down by quad-50 machine-gun fire from all over the area. Not long afterwards, the 109th AAA, the 462nd AAA and the 634th AAA arrived and set up. The 109th took up a position between the bridge and where the 413th was dug in while the 462nd split up with part of the Battalion crossing the bridge to set up north of the structure on the east bank and the others setting up just north of the village of Kripp on the west bank. The 634th crossed the bridge, the first entire AAA battalion to do so, and set up just north of where Battery-D of the 482nd AW was located in order to engage the aircraft further up the river—further out before they could reach the bridge. By 19:00, Remagen was designated as an Inner Artillery Zone or IAZ, whereas all AAA units within that zone, during hours of darkness, were authorized to fire at any unknowns in a radius of 15,000 meters of the bridge up to an altitude of 10,000 feet. Two planes came in that night to apparently test the defenses but were quickly driven off. The following morning, the 49th AAA Brigade ordered the 110th AAA Gun Battalion and the 639th AW attached to the 16th AAA Group and again advised them to be ready to move out at any time.[13]

221

By 06:00 on March 9 there were five AAA battalions defending the bridge. German shelling of the site increased. Their artillery units were massing in the hills east of the Rhine River. At the same time, seventeen aircraft came in one at a time, some taking evasive action as AAA fire opened up, some coming in nearly skimming the river, and others approaching at 1200 feet, diving and leveling off around 800 feet to drop their load, and then steeply climbing out of the area. The Germans were sending in everything they had including fast Messerschmitt ME-210 fighter-bombers, ME-109s, Focke-Wulf FW-190 fighters, Heinkel HE-111 bombers, and Junkers JU-87 "Stuka" dive-bombers. Many of the AAA gun crews were mesmerized. After nine months experience, few had ever seen the "Stukas" before, except in photographs. That same day, the Germans sent in their ME-262 and AR-134 jet aircraft which was an equally rare site. However, during the 9th, thirteen of those seventeen enemy planes were downed—although there were no "kills" scored against the jets. But, the increased speed of those machines, luckily, also reduced their bombing accuracy. At the same time, during this day's engagement, one AAA gunner was killed and 19 were wounded.

The request went out for more antiaircraft battalions. Although AAA units were being pulled off of various defenses, including Roer River bridges of the First Army supply route, the bridge at Remagen was now considered high priority. Units were being sent with orders to "hold the bridge at all costs." On the 10th, the 552nd AAA (AW) and the 563rd AAA (AW) arrived in the area. As they came in, Batteries B and C of the 552nd crossed the river and took up positions near the town of Unkel, 2.5 miles north of the bridge, while A and D Batteries crossed the river and set up at Linz, three miles south of the bridge. The 563rd came in and set up north and south of the Ahr River along the west bank of the Rhine, south of the Remagen bridge, to provide additional strength to the other AAA units dug in all around the area.

Battery-D of the 110th AAA, still positioned east of Duren, was up at 03:00 on March 10th. With their new march orders they were packed up and ready to roll by 05:00. Shortly afterwards, the convoy headed out for Merken, the assigned assembly area where they were to join up with the other batteries. "There we waited overnight for further orders from the 16th Group," advised Sergeant Eckenrode. "The men just rolled their bed roles out on top of their trucks or on the streets and slept 'till six the next morning."[14]

At Remagen, dense fog limited visibility throughout the morning of the 10th but once it lifted at around noon, the German Air Force converged upon the site like a bunch of bees. For six and one-half hours a variety of aircraft attacked from varying angles, from varying altitudes and from various directions. The III Corps AAA scored a total of 28 kills, with the 634th credited with 14, the 462nd with three and the 413th with two. The rest were downed by quad-50 fire. The U.S. suffered 9 casualties for the day and some heavy damage to a number of guns and other equipment.

By mid—morning on March 11 the 110th AAA of the 49th Brigade and the 134th AAA of the 115th Brigade arrived at Remagan. Shortly afterwards the 376th AW Battalion came in.

"From Merken to [Remagen] we saw the largest concentration of field artillery guns ever," noted one of the boys. "Guns of all types, and now at Sinzig we are surrounded by 155s and while we were setting up our equipment they were blasting away, darn near breaking our ear drums." The action continued all around them. Without any time to settle in, Dog-Battery immediately got into the fracas "Just after the Battery was set up and in firing order," he continued, "two FW-190s dropped out of the clouds and our machine gunners opened up."[15]

These planes had come in after a pontoon bridge that had just been built across the river at Sinzig. Dog, Baker and Charlie-Batteries of the 110th AAA were all set up west of the Rhine on the north side of the Ahr River across from the village of Sinzig. They were dug in along the railroad tracks, two to three miles south of the Remagan Railroad bridge. Able-Battery was positioned along the railroad tracks northwest of the Remagen bridge, between Batteries D and C of the 109th AAA. The Headquarters Battery of the 110th was set up several miles west of the bridge just north of the village of Ahrweiler while Headquarters, itself, was established in a large white castle nearby. Although the Germans were using every kind of aircraft they had against the Rhine River bridge, the Americans were using every AAA gun they could concentrate in the area to defend it. There were 30-calibers, 50-calibers, 40-millimeter guns, 90-millimeter guns, and 155-millimeter guns. "The Rhine was well protected as far as AA guns were concerned," noted Eckenrode.[16]

"We were on a hill southwest of the bridge," advised Glen. "Shortly after setting up, an ME-262 came streaking over the site. I happened to be standing next to my Cat and climbed up onto it and grabbed ahold of the roof-mounted 50-calibur machine gun and started firing with everyone else. "I was leadin' it like I normally would and saw my tracers falling in behind it." The plane banked and circled around to come back and apparently the enemy pilot wasn't accustomed to the plane's speed either. Just as it approached the bridge it dropped a single bomb that arched upward and then fell into the river on the south side of the bridge, exploding in a geyser of water. "That was my first personal encounter with a jet airplane," Speer admitted.[17]

The Germans had just planked the Ludendorff bridge to allow vehicular traffic across before the Americans had captured it. By March 11, in an effort to fortify their bridgehead and speed reinforcements to the east bank, U.S. Army Combat Engineers, the 51st and 291st, had also constructed Bailey bridges across the Ahr River at Sinzig, across the Rhine River linking the villages of Kripp and Linz north of the Ahr, and a treadway bridge across the Rhine between the villages of Remagen and Erpel along the northwest side of the Ludendoff bridge—in effect, creating even more vital targets for the Luftwaffe.

Raids on both the main and pontoon bridges continued throughout the day. By evening, Dog-battery's machine guns, alone, had fired 5,400 rounds of 50-caliber ammo and had one verified kill on a "Category 1" ME-109 fighter.[18]

Constant patrols along the river banks were necessary to watch for German saboteurs. In addition, booms were laced across the river upstream to guard against submersibles and radio-controlled mines while barrage balloons were cabled to the hills on both sides of the river to discourage low flying enemy aircraft. At the same time, depth charges were occasionally dropped into the river to prevent frogmen from slipping through and the engineer battalions used smoke to camouflage the bridges during the day and powerful 60-inch carbon-arc searchlights at night to aid in the defense of the bridges. During the 11th, the Germans mounted a total of 13 sorties against the bridges between 17:00 and 18:45. The American AAA battalions accounted for a total of five "Category 1" kills and two "Category 2s" during the engagement with no damage or casualties sustained. The following day, March 12, the 639th AAA AW, the 535th AAA AW, and the 203rd AAA AW battalions arrived and began setting up. Just after noon, as the fog burned off, 83 enemy aircraft, primarily FW-190 fast fighter-bombers, but also a few ME-262 jets, several ME-109s, and one JU-87, came over the area. "No formation attacks were attempted," noted one of the reports. "[and] all attacks were made from low level of about 1000-feet."[19]

The enemy planes came in mostly single file, although on several occasions two, three, or four came in together, and dropped bombs in the vicinity. Those dropped near the bridges all fell wide of the target. "Another eight raiders operated over the area between 20:16 and 01:52 at altitudes of 5,000 to 8,000 feet," the report continued, "and were engaged by all the AAA gun battalions." Of the 91 enemy aircraft that came over on the 12th and early morning hours of the 13th, 26 were verified destroyed and another 8 were "probably" destroyed. The high claimant for the day was the 552nd AAA AW with a total of eight "Category 1s" and two "Category 2s."[20]

As if the heavy concentration of German Artillery fire and the daily bombing of the area by aircraft wasn't enough, after March 12 the German's had started firing V-2 rockets at the bridges from an area somewhere northwest of Bellendoorn, Holland. In all, a total of eleven V-2s were eventually sent into the area, some of which landed in the Rhine not too far from the bridge and several others which destroyed homes in and around the village of Remagen. In one incident, a group of American soldiers billeted in a private home about 300 yards from the bridge were killed instantly during one hit.

As busy as every unit was, very few of the guns and equipment had been completely dug in. In addition, most of the gun batteries were situated on low ground along the river valley. "[Y]ou could only dig down about five feet 'till you hit water," complained one of the 110th's D-Battery crew. Engineer battalions were kept busy with their bulldozers trying to help out amid the incoming shelling, bombing, strafing, and the constant arrival of additional units. By March 13 a bulldozer pulled up to D-Battery's position. Their gun and quad-50 trailer had been sandbagged into place but they had not yet dug emplacements for the computer and radar equipment. "Finally the holes were finished [by the bulldozer]," advised Sergeant Eckenrode, "but water forced us to build ramps over to a layer of sandbags and run the computer in on top of them." Unable to dig the guns in deeply, the crew had built sandbag revetments around them. "The bulldozer [pushed] dirt, or I should say mud, up against the bags," explained Eckenrode.[21]

By the following morning, the crew found themselves ankle deep in muck. "[A]nd the cloudy weather kept it that way," complained one of the crew. "Most of the trucks and guns were stuck in the mire and the Cats had to be unhooked from one gun to pull another gun and Cat out."[22]

Mud or not, the battery was in action by 15:00. The 90s fired 11 rounds, driving them deeper into the mire, and the "quads" fired 7,040 rounds in seven courses. At 20:00 they were in action again as the 90s sent 20 rounds out. There were no confirmed kills for the day, however. Part of the problem or confusion the artillery observers experienced in "scoring kills" was the old ploy often used by the flyers. The German planes invariably laid a faint trail of smoke behind them as they dove behind the hills to avoid the antiaircraft fire, often leaving the impression that they had been hit.

By March 15 there were nearly 65 units employed in and around the vicinity of Remagan as far west as the village of Ahrweiler, as far east as the village of Honnef, as far south as the village of Waldorf, and as far north as just above the village of Rheinbreitbach. These consisted of the

11th AAA Group, the 16th AAA Group, the 109th AAA Gun Battalion, the 110th AAA Gun Battalion, the 134th AAA Gun Battalion, the 203rd AAA Automatic Weapons Battalion, the 376th AAA Automatic Weapons Battalion, the 413th AAA Gun Battalion, the 462nd AAA AW, the 482nd AAA AW, the 535th AAA AW, the 552nd AAA AW, the 563rd AAA AW, the 634th AAA AW, the 639th AAA AW, and the 839th AAA AW in what had become the mightiest concentration of anti-aircraft troops and guns of World War II. And even later other units arrived, including the 549th AAA who were seen driving into the area by the 110th AAA. It was the first time since leaving Camp Edwards that the guys of the 110th had seen their old training-barracks neighbors. "It was a big reunion," laughed Terry Bye of C-Battery. "We were so happy to see each other again."[23]

That afternoon the ultimate in anti-aircraft defense of the bridge came as the Luftwaffe sent 21 more fast bombers over the area. "When a German plane (they almost always come singly) shows," explained one news account, "some alert machine gunner spots him and lets lose with a stream of red tracers. Following [his] aim, hundreds of other men standing impatiently behind their guns, spot the Jerry and within five seconds the air over the bridge is filled with neon crosses as thousands of tracers light up the [gray cloudy sky]." At the same time, "black flak-bursts start flowering in the sky as the heavy ack-ack batteries open up."[24]

The American AAA units shot down 16. One was credited to Dog-Battery of the 110th, an ME-109 that crashed in Sinzig. During the engagement, Don Peterson of D-Battery was slightly wounded by shrapnel as he drove a prime-mover down the hill, southwest of the railroad bridge.

Over the next few days, the number of bombing runs over the site continued to decrease. For one thing, during that second week of March a total of 372 German aircraft had come in along the Rhine to attack the various bridges and the Allied antiaircraft units had shot down 80 of them. The general speculation among the American troops was that the Luftwaffe was nearly depleted. By then the U.S. First and Third Armies had firmly established a strong bridgehead on the east bank of the Rhine River here. They had repulsed all attempts by the German Army to drive them back and were firmly dug-in all along the east bank as well as all along the west bank of the river. During this drive nearly 250,000 Germans had been captured and somewhere between 60,000 to 100,000 had been wounded or killed while American casualties amounted to nearly 15,000. Meanwhile, they had overrun more than 3,000 square miles of the enemy's homeland in less than five days and did not hesitate. General Hodges continued to transfer First Army troops and equipment across the Rhine to strengthen and enlarge the bridgehead at Remagen as General Patton's Third Army turned southeast to join the Seventh Army of General Jacob Dever's 6th Army Group in a bold sweep across Germany southeast of the Moselle River.[25]

Shortly after 15:00 on the afternoon of March 17 the Ludendorf bridge collapsed and fell into the river as about 200 men, mostly engineers from the 276th Engineer Combat Battalion and the 1058th Port Construction and Repair detachment, were working on the structure trying to strengthen it. The collapse was not the result of bombs or sabotage but, instead, simply of structure failure. As the bridge collapsed, 28 men were killed and another 63 were injured. Medics from the various units, including Elmer Potzmann of the 110th AAA, all rushed down the river bank to the pile of rubble and twisted metal to help the injured. "It was a terrible situation,"advised Elmer. "A number of them were trapped in the rubble that we had to get out and several others were unconscious in the river."[26]

The bridge at Remagen after the collapse that resulted in more than ninety American casualties. (Courtesy Elmer Potzmann)

By the third week of March, many pontoon bridges had been built across the Rhine all along its route between Cologne and Koblenz and an automatic weapons barrage had been laid out to protect them. According to the boys of Dog-Battery, M-51 quad-mounts had been set up in strategic locations all along both banks of the river. At any given signal or order, each gun could provide a sweeping fire action all across the area assigned to it. Thus creating a deadly zone of fire over the river that would prevent or stop any low flying bomber or fighter from coming near the river. Meanwhile, Allied forces were now rushing deep into the heart of Germany. The battery moved out of their Sanzig position at 07:00 on March 20 and followed the Rhine River north past Remagen for about eleven miles. Just south of Bonn, near the village of Rolandswerth, they set down on a hill overlooking the river. "In years past it was a golf course," advised one of the gun crew. Their assignment was to guard and protect a Piper Cub airfield of the Observation Corps at this position. At the same time, Battery-A received March Orders for Kassel, several miles northeast of Remagen, and B and C were ordered several miles southeast to Bandorf.[27]

For several days, the battalion saw no action at these new positions. One day, while stationed here, Glen, Wayne, and several others of D-Battery drove into nearby Bonn. The city had been one of Germany's most important business and banking centers. The boys found it in ruins. "I could have stood on a kitchen chair and looked all across Bonn," insisted Glen. While pillaging around, the boys found a bombed out hattery. They all took a top hat and often wore it instead of their G.I. helmet throughout the rest of the war.[28]

On April 8 Battery-D saw its only action at Rolandswerth. Around 22:00 the Battery went into action against a couple passing enemy aircraft and fired 22 rounds without any kills. On April 13 the battery was transferred ten miles further east to Leubsdorf. That day, the battalion learned of President Roosevelt's death. "It was a great shock to all of us," noted Eckenrode. "We could hardly believe it was true." For one thing, all of these boys had grown up with him. He had been President ever since many of these young soldiers had been in grade school. For many, it was hard to imagine anyone else in his place. "The President had been the soldiers' friend," Eckenrode continued, "we all realized it and mourned his death."[29]

There was no action for the battery at Leubsdorf. The boys heard that the Luftwaffe was "Kaput" and that, except for a few pockets of resistance, for the most part the German soldiers were surrendering without much of a fight throughout the rest of the countryside. The other batteries of the 110th were all transferred into the same area. "Most of us amused ourselves by playing softball," advised Sergeant Eckenrode. "The battery had a softball team and played the other batteries, losing it's first two games and then winning six straight before dropping to A-Battery in the second game of a double header."[30]

Leubsdorf was their last AA position in the ETO. With no more German aircraft in operation there was no longer a need for antiaircraft units. They were all reassigned to security duties. "The Armies were taking towns and cities so fast and so great in number that we did not have enough MPs," explained one of the men. The Military Police were badly needed to occupy these cities, towns, and villages to help prevent lawlessness, looting, quell riots and keep the peace, and to enforce curfew.[31]

On April 19, the battery personnel packed up all of their AAA equipment and big guns and put it all in march order to be turned in to Ordnance and transported out of the area. The quad-50 crews were allowed to keep their trailer-mounted guns and trucks. They were all then trucked out of town to the north with their M-51s in tow, their rifles and their backpacks, and bivouacked at Kassel. The following day they trucked east to the town of Muhlhausen, their first Security assignment. "We were housed in a German Garrison, or what had been a German Garrison," noted Sergeant Eckenrode. "Each battery had a large three-story building in which to live." After a day, some of the battalion was sent south to the village of Schmalkalden on security details and three days later the battalion was split up and transferred out to separate locations. Headquarters Battery and Battery-B remained on MP duty at Schmalkalden. Battery-A was sent several miles to the southeast to do police duty at the town of Weimar. Battery-C was assigned to Meiningen, several miles south of Schmalkalden, and Battery-D was transferred up to Gotha, located back to the north, about halfway between Muhlhausen and Schmalkalden. "Here we were housed in a bank building," advised one of the D-Battery crew, "and we set up our cots and beds among the desks." In addition to patrolling the streets and maintaining order, part of their MP duties was to maintain road blocks and check points on all of the out-going roads of Gotha. The gun crews set up their quad-50s along with extra personnel on the four exits from the town. These consisted of the Gotha-Erfurt road on the east end of town, the Gotha-Eisenach road on the west side, and the smaller Gotha-Ohrdruf road to the south and the Gotha-Langensalza road to the north. On the night of April 26, a U.S. jeep drove up on the Gotha-Erfurt roadblock and was challenged by the Battery-D guards there. The jeep slowly rolled up to the barricades and shut off its headlights as one of the occupants fired a round from a carbine. Pvt. John Connors had been off duty but had remained with the crew, sleeping in the ditch along side the road where the jeep had stopped. Upon hearing the shot, Connors was startled awake and jumped up to grab his M-1 just as the quad-50 opened up on the other side of the road. Connors was hit ten times and was killed instantly. "Johnny was one of the nicest and best liked kids in the Battery," advised Eckenrode. "He was a quiet kid who was respected by everyone."[32]

Within moments the battery crew was all over the jeep occupants—two men and a woman—and had them disarmed, subdued, and in custody. "[They] were found to be two negroes who had been AWOL for 13 days with [the] Polish women,"advised one of the crew. "[Miraculously] they [had] escaped injury and were brought into Battery Headquarters. Later they were turned over to the MPs for courtsmartial"[33]

While the battery was still grieving over the death of Connors, the following day brought more disturbing news. They learned of correspondent Ernie Pyle's April 18 death on the island of Ie Shima in the Pacific. "He was a friend of all G.I.s," advised Sergeant Bill Nelson, "and particularly a friend of our battery."[34]

The batteries of the battalion continued to be transferred farther and farther east into Germany to perform its mission in protection of the vital army installations and the main supply routes in the various zones and to act as police in the various towns and villages. At the end of April, Headquarters and Battery B, again, remained in place and Battery-C remained at Meiningen while Batteries A and D were transferred to the towns of Suhl and Zella-Mehlis to guard the captured German pistol-manufacturing plants there. "The Germans had moved [the] factories underground, safe from our air attacks," noted Lt. Jack Forman of A-Battery. Forman's unit was assigned to Zella-Mehlis to guard the Walther Factory. Allied forces had found it staffed with Russian slave labor. "We had 'em run off a couple o' thousand pistols before they ran out of parts," admitted Forman. The men then dispersed the weapons, Walther P-38s, among themselves. "We also ran into, of all things, an accordion factory," asserted the Lieutenant. "We got a bunch of [those] and some of the boys could play 'em. We had a lot of fun with that." Meanwhile, Battery-D was assigned to the town of Suhl, five miles further south, where the Sauer pistol factory was located. "The parts of the pistols were all there," noted one of the boys, "[so] in a couple of days Captain Klein and Sgt. [Leo] Lamparty made arrangements to have enough pistols put together so that each man in the Battery would have at least one P-38 and-or one P-32."[35]

The termination of hostilities over the next few days came as no surprise. It had become common knowledge that like the Luftwaffe, the German Army was nearly played-out. Like everyone else, the boys in the 110th AAA Battalion were elated. "The news that the war in Europe had ended reached us about noon [on May 7]," reported Sergeant Eckenrode. "There was quite a bit of celebrating as the Battalion sent over a good bit of Cognac for [us]."[36]

"[W]hen I heard the war was officially over," recalled Lester Cohen of B-Battery, "I ran into the school building we were occupying, ran down stairs to the kitchen [where] Smaha was the cook, [and] I said, 'Buddy, give us a cup of coffee 'cause we're gonna celebrate!'"[37]

Back in March Battery-A had run across a German supply dump that was actually storage for an accumulation of looted items the German Army had confiscated from all over Europe. Most of the items were turned over to Allied military authorities. However some of it was held back. "We wound up loading a truck with French Cognac, several hundred cases of it that the Germans had brought in from France," admitted Lieutenant Forman. "On V-E Day we issued out a bottle per man [throughout the battalion]."[38]

By mid May the batteries were moved out to various SS hospitals to guard German wounded. Battery-A was sent back a few miles northwest of Zella-Mehlis to a little spa village outside Bad Liebenstein "We set up our command post in a small hotel called Haus Helene," noted one of the men from the battery. Battery-D was sent back west 123 miles to Kubach, about three miles southeast of Weilburg. They bivouacked in tents in the forest outside of town while guarding the hospital there. After several days of rain, Captain Klein arranged for the battalion to be billeted in four large houses, or chateaus, in the hills outside nearby Weilmunster. The battery remained on this detail throughout May and June, guarding the hospital and manning roadblocks in and around Kubach and Weilburg. along with personnel of the 563rd AAA AW Battalion. Softball teams were organized and the boys spent their off-duty hours participating in a tournament. "We took over two or three castles as we moved across Germany," recalled Glen. "At this one, Bucky Worboys raced past us and was the first boy up to the house. There was a lot of chickens in cages out in the back yard. Well, he immediately slapped padlocks on all the chicken coops so that anytime that we wanted eggs, we had to pay Bucky for them!"[39]

Speer recalled that the battalion ate good while billeted here. "One day," he recalled, "driving down the road we saw a deer run across the road and as it was scrambling and struggling up the opposite bank, Edmondson leaned out the window and shot it with his submachine gun." That night they had venison, fried potatoes with onions, and milk. The battery was also in this chateau when it came time to celebrate Wayne Edmundson's birthday on June 4 and for Glen's on June 9. "I spent my 21st birthday in a castle on the Rhine River," recalled Glen, proudly. "We had Schnapps that day, fresh eggs, and we dug some potatoes and had fried potatoes." Although the homes were quite opulent, the boys later admitted that because the chateau's former owners were Germans, the boys in the battery didn't concern themselves much with the care of their quarters or the numerous possessions left in it. "The houses were full of very nice things," admitted Glen. "We ate on expensive china but sometimes we didn't bother washing the dishes, we'd just sail them out the window toward the river."[40]

The softball tournament continued through the last week of June. "Eddie Buntemeyer led the League with a batting average of .419," advised Sergeant Eckenrode. "He and Ive Witte, D's star pitcher, were both named for the Battalion All Star team."[41]

By June 25 a big shuffle had began as the Army's "point system" went into effect to determine who got to go home. "It took 75 points to get home," advised Lt. Jack Forman. "Each decoration counted as five points, each month overseas counted as one point, and so on." The 110th AAA lost 25 men immediately as a number were sent to the 127th AAA, the 132nd AAA and the 142nd AAA and replaced by higher-point men from the same outfits. "I was transferred out," advised Forman. "[and] sent to the 132nd Gun Battalion. I stayed with them for two or three weeks and I then got orders to transfer into the 68th AAA. When I got there, the whole original staff of the 110th [was there in command of that unit]."[42]

Back at Schmalkalden, B-Battery's Billie B. Colliver of Hale, Missouri, sadly did not have a "round-trip-ticket"to Europe as he and Harvey Edds had kidded about while passing through New York Harbor back in December of 1943. Sometime during the last week of June 1945, Billy had received a letter from his wife, informing him she would be getting a divorce when he got home as she had met another man some time ago. "[I]n the early morning hours of June 29," recalled Harvey, "I saw him get out of his sleeping bag and get his Tommy-gun off the wall. He climbed back into his sleeping bag and [apparently] put it to his chest and pulled the trigger. He died instantly." Billie had committed suicide. A short time later, a 1st Lieutenant of B-Battery took his own life as well.[43]

The following July 5 all the batteries were transferred out to other towns for MP duty. Battery-C, which had been transferred from Meiningen to Runkel to Aumenau, was sent to Schwab Hall along with Headquarters Battery. Battery-A, Battery-B and Battery-D were all sent to a German SS POW camp, Camp #72, just south of Ludwigsburg, as guards. Colonel Jochen Peiper, the German commander who operated all around the vicinity of Malmedy to Stoumont, was one of the 2,500 SS imprisoned here. "One day a staff sergeant was sent in to get him for an interrogation," offered Harvey Edds. "Peiper demanded to talk with an officer—said he wasn't going to be led around by some sergeant. With that, the sergeant reared back and slugged him up-side his head and knocked him down, telling him he wasn't in a position to be giving orders any more. Peiper got up and said he would go with the sergeant."[44]

"[The prison also held] local big-wigs from the Nazi Party, generals, admirals, and diplomats," advised Lieutenant Forman, "[and] anyone else they were holding for [the] war crimes trials." Able, Baker and Dog batteries of the 110th staffed and operated the prison until they left for home in late November and early December. "I remember we put them on a 1300 calorie per day diet," remarked Forman. "On the average each [prisoner] lost 35 pounds."[45]

According to Edds, they had to be tough with these prisoners. "They were the most ruthless guys on earth," he admitted. "When [we] first went to the camp there was at least one prisoner killed every day."[46]

Eventually, First Army directed a memo to the guards advising them to quit shooting the SS unless they were trying to escape. In all of the investigations being conducted regarding war crimes, they were advised, they might kill someone who could provide the ultimate link or eyewitness account needed for a conviction. One night, not too long after that, Edds was on duty in one of the guard towers, talking to one of his friends, Neal, when they thought they heard something on the back side of the building, near a storage room. Neal headed off in that direction to investigate and as he shined his flashlight around in the building three SS POWs jumped up from behind some mattresses and tried to get out past him to escape. Neal opened up with his M-1 and immediately killed two of them as one got out. That POW was apprehended a short time later, however, and returned to the guardhouse and placed in solitary confinement. During another occasion an SS POW was standing by a window of the prison and took out a handkerchief to wipe the window. A G.I. outside shot and killed him. "He wasn't trying to escape," insisted Edds, "but the [guard] said he might have been signaling to someone."[47]

Northeast of Weimar, Lt. Clinton Gardner, and others of Headquarters Battery had been assigned to the Buchenwald Concentration camp. Gardner had been transferred to a military government unit in late April. Because he had a rudimentary knowledge of the German language he was, at the age of 22, placed in temporary command of the just-liberated concentration camp. Buchenwald had been "liberated" by the U.S. Third Army the previous April 13, about a week before A-Battery was assigned to MP duties at nearby Weimar. According to Gardner, it was not the sort of dramatic liberation one usually imagines. In this case, U.S. Army tanks rolled past the camp on a nearby road on April 11 and many of the prisoners used the occasion to retrieve crude weapons they had been hiding to attack their German SS guards, most of whom had already fled when they saw the American units near the area. In reality, the Americans were unaware of the camp. When a U.S. Jeep carrying intelligence officers drove up to the site two days later, Buchenwald was, in affect, liberated. According to those who first walked into the compound, the odor of the place was overwhelming. Corpses were stacked like cordwood in front of the furnace buildings, where it was later learned bodies were cremated to provide heat to the 55 prisoner barracks of the camp. While talking to a prisoner one of the officers noticed a commotion behind them. When asked what was going on, the prisoner told him one of the former SS guards had apparently committed suicide. As the crowd dispersed, the SS guard was found with his throat cut but no knife anywhere around. Others recalled how the prisoners would chant and encourage the American soldiers to shoot the SS as they were captured around the camp. In some cases, the American soldiers obliged. There were about 20,000 prisoners, mostly men, in the camp when the U.S. troops arrived. "It was a processing center," explained Gardner, "where people were evaluated and sent to other [death camps]." Most of the prisoners here worked in the camp mine or at the binocular-repair factory established on the site. The American military government immediately set up a hospital to help the former inmates slowly recover their health. Still, in the first week, 40 men a day died at the prison before their health and diets could be stabilized. Lieutenant Barrett Coates and Lieutenant Robert Wilson along with six enlisted men of B-Battery were also assigned here. Lieutenant Gardner was relieved by a Captain in the last week of May. By the end of June the Americans had turned the camp over to the Soviets.[48]

Finally a number of those in the 110th AAA got orders to prepare for their trip home. It took them two full days to travel from Ludwigsburg or Weimar, Germany to Marseille, France. There, they checked into the POE—Port of Embarkation—established nearby. It was a big camp outside of Marseille. There was no separation of units, since all units had been officially disbanded, so all the G.I.s arriving here, no matter what unit, regiment, or battalion, were assigned randomly to the barracks. Then they went though the usual military procedure of processing and paperwork for their return home. Jack Forman was processed out at Marseille and assigned to the ship *USS Howard Victory* for his trip back to the States. Harvey Edds was assigned to the victory ship *USS Tuscullum Victory* for his return trip. Henry Thake, who had been transferred to the 494th Armored Field Artillery a month or two before, came back on the *USAT Bardstown Victory*. Like many others, Speer was sent to Heidelberg, first and then to Marseille. "They put us on trains at Heidelberg," he advised. "Then we rode in what they called 'forty-and-eights' from Heidelberg,

Germany to Marseille, France." The reason the railroad cars were called 'forty and eights' is because the wooden boxcars could haul up to forty men or eight mules. "There wasn't anything in the cars," noted Glen, "except maybe a little straw or hay and we just slept on the wooden floor on the hay. After being processed at Marseille, Speer boarded the Liberty Ship *USS Westminister* on November 22. Sailing the following day, he arrived in New York harbor at 08:45 Monday morning, December 5. "As we passed by the Statue of Liberty," recalled Glen, "we all went topside to watch and I don't think there was a dry eye anywhere on that ship." Later, as they all came down off the gang-plank Glen remembers that there was a band on the pier playing "The Victory Polka," "Sentimental Journey" and "The Sidewalks of New York." Like the others, Speer was taken to Camp Kilmer in New Jersey for further processing.[49]

The first thing Glen did after the paperwork was to call home and then run to the PX for a hotdog, a malt, and then a sundae—items he hadn't had in almost a year. "I called my Dad from Camp Kilmer on December 5," advised Glen. "He was helping [brother-in-law] Bill Showalter pick corn [later] that day, using a mechanical corn picker, and that morning [Dad] got his index finger caught in the machine and it was cut off. I've always thought my phone call had something to do with that. The excitement of the call or me coming home took his mind off what he was doing."[50]

After several days at Camp Kilmer, Speer boarded a train for what seemed like a long trip back to the mid-west. He arrived at Camp Grant in Rockford, Illinois on December 10, 1945, where he was officially separated from the Army. From there he proceeded by train to Des Moines, Iowa where Wayne Edmondson and "some guy wearing a hat and a long coat, smoking a cigarette" met him. "Wayne had gotten back before me," advised Glen, "and drove up to Des Moines to pick me up. I still didn't know who he brought with him 'till I greeted Wayne and looked at the other guy real hard. 'Don't you know who I am?' the stranger asked me. 'You must be my brother,' I said as the guy smiled and said 'yes'." Lloyd Rex, his brother, had been 12, going on 13, when Glen had left. "I think he hugged me around the waist when I left," recalled Glen. At 15 he was now much taller and looked a lot older wearing a dress hat and a long suit coat, and puffing on a cigarette. "I almost didn't know him," advised Glen.[51]

On Christmas Day, 1945, the Speer family celebrated Glen's safe return home. "We had a big, big holiday dinner at our place," he recalled proudly. "All of my uncles and aunts were there and all of my cousins—many who had been in the [Service]—were there. And mom fixed a big turkey—the first time that we had ever had turkey. It was a great big feast!"[52]

"But I learned for the first time," continued Glen, "that one of my most favorite cousins, Harold Acheson, had been killed in the war. We had wrote letters back and forth while in France and we had talked about meeting. He had been sent over as a replacement after the invasion, maybe a couple months after, and he [apparently] got killed quite soon after he got there. It was very sad to learn that."[53]

Years later Glen sadly remembered that day which should have been a happy occasion. "I have been very lucky," he said. "I know of so many who were affected by the war in so many different ways. I know of men who broke down on the field or who broke down and could not take it after they got home. And I knew those who didn't make it back at all. It's very sad. I guess I have been blessed. I have had a wonderful life with a loving wife and five great kids."[54]

During the eleven months that it had been at war—from the initial assault of the Normandy Beaches in France to the drive to the Weser River in Germany—the 110th AAA Gun Battalion (Mbl) held the distinction that no objective defended by it had ever been damaged by aerial attack. During the course of the war the personnel and weapons of the 110th AAA Gun Battalion had been used for everything from antiaircraft duty to field artillery duty, anti-tank duty, infantry duty, and as a trucking company. "During this period there were a lot of acts of individual heroism," noted Col. William F. Curren. "This battalion does not claim to have stopped enormous armored drives or gigantic infantry penetrations but in presenting a determined front to the advance columns of the enemy it slowed down the advance columns of the enemy enough to check it until reinforcements in strength could arrive and repel the enemy." During that time the battalion participated in 601 aerial engagements destroying 65 enemy planes and had been in 22 ground engagements, destroying 11 enemy tanks, 80 armored and motor vehicles, and innumerable gun positions, bunkers, ammunition dumps, bridges and supply dumps, while greatly facilitating the advance of front line Infantry. The battalion received five Campaign Streamers: Normandy with arrowhead, Northern France, Rhineland, Ardennes-Alsace, and Central Europe.

The battalion was originally scheduled to be shipped to the South Pacific to finish out the war. However, when the war came to an end with the Japanese on August 15 the various batteries were assigned local duties as they awaited processing for the return to the States.

On October 6, 1945 the battalion was officially inactivated while in Germany. Personnel not already scheduled for the return home were transferred into other units or carried in as the battalion was broken up and its elements were redesignated to become the core of other batteries.

Although Headquarters of the 110th AAA was disbanded—and its personnel assigned to the 68th AAA—the Headquarters Battery was redesignated and used as the core for the 943rd Coast Artillery Battery, Battery-A was redesignated the 944th Coast Artillery Battery, Battery-B became the 945th Coast Artillery Battery, Battery-C the 980th Coast Artillery Battery, and those left in Battery-D became the core of the 981st Coast Artillery Battery.

Appendix A

Rosters
110th AAA Gun Bn. (Mbl)

Headquarters and Headquarters Battery

Curren, William F. Jr.—Lt. Col.
Doten, Robert K.—Major
Rice, William H.—Major
Breck, Donald W.—Capt.
Johnson, Robert J.—Capt.
Kovar, Edward B.—Capt.
Ryan, Joseph P.—Capt.
Schubert, Uriel—Capt.
Amato, Anthony M.—CWO
Maness, Thurman T.—WO JG

Adams, Ervin E.
Angelo, Louis J.
Banas, Stanley J.
Barlow, Harry R.
Bennett, Frederick A.
Brasas, Alexander J.
Brennan, James J.
Cheskin, Joseph
Desmond, Thomas H.
Devlin, Paul A.
Dow, Alfred N.

Elder, Maurice J.
Faulkner, Stephen M.
Faxon, Francis J.
Fox, Carroll N.
Francis, Paul J.
Glancy, Edwin J.
Goldsmith, Milton H.
Grimm, Robert F.
Hanselman, Carl R.
Harmert, Michael
Hope, William J. Jr.

Howard, Newton M.
Johnson, Raymond S.
Kahl, Byron J.
Karlson, Eric P.
Mallard, William J.
Martin, Robert J.
Mlocek, Emil J.
Monda, David T. C.
Moriarty, Frederic J.
Morrison, William J.
Norton, Robert M.

Osborn, I. J.
Rivet, William J.
Rutledge, Bernard V.
Salafia, Joseph T.
Spring, Earl F.
Vonning, Alfred J.
Swecker, Bayard L.
Wolverton, Thomas K.

Medical Detachment
Fegley, Homer B.—Capt.
Weintraub, I. Irving—Capt.
DiMarco, Ross F.—Lt.

Berck, Marvel D.
Cohen, Stanley B.
Edgar, William L.
Gushurst, William A. "Gus"
Hohl, Oliver H.
Kuchar, Wayne R.
Mondahl, Gilman N.
Potzmann, Elmer J.
Sceery, Raymond T.
Schade, Henry J.
Wynkoop, William D.

Battery A

Silverman, Theodore H.—Capt.
Forman, John A. "Jack"—Lt.

Abt, Roman A.
Adamaitis, Joseph M.
Albert, Robert L.
Arel, Joseph L.
Audet, Patrick L.
Beiswenger, Franklin H.
Blackston, Reuben L.
Bousema, John
Buckley, Joseph S.
Butterbaugh, Kenneth W.
Carlson, Henry W.
Coates, Richard K.
Collings, Arthus J.
Collins, Kenneth R.
Comeau, Stanley A.
Conant, Gilbert E.
Corro, Wilbert T.
Crave, James M.
Creeden, Joseph A.
Cretty, Tom J.
Davis, Clifford L.
DaPasquale, Giocondo P.
DeSpencer, Arthur V.
Doherty, Edward J.
Dueles, John L.
Dziuba, Frank J.
Ehle, Ernest H.
Ellis, Frederick W.
Espinosa, Julio C.
Foth, Donald C.
Fouse, Warren H.
Fuller, John H.
Gauthier, Joseph F.
Gaynor, Joseph P.
Gentile, Louis T.
Godbout, Roger V.
Gorchinsky, Walter

Guanci, Samuel E.
Hagen, Joseph J.
Hajj, James J.
Hart, Kermit E.
Heckart, Jean P.
Heims, Elmer W.
Hemmingsen, Arnold
Hickey, William A.
Hogen, Obert J.
Hook, Ralph R.
Houle, Omer
Igel, Clement E.
Kania, Leo C.
Kendrick, Wilber B.
Kinsey, Howard W.
Kramos, Pete J.
Lamb, Dana E.
Lambert, Ronald G.
Lameureux, Maurice R.
Lasky, Joseph
Legere, Joseph
Luppey, Michael
Marine, Ereole W.
McDonald, John A.
Melladew, Herbert G.
Miller, Arthur R.
Miller, Clarence C.
Miller, William E.
Mirfield, Stanley C.
Mochon, Bruno
Norris, Warren O.
O'dell, Donald E.
O'Neal, James C.
Pagnani, Delmo
Pelequin, Mervin L.
Phillips, George J.
Poitras, Roger L.

Roueche, Peter J.
Roy, Stanley M.
Rumsey, Benjamin F. Jr.
Ryznic, Stephen W.
Sanderson, Lawrence
Scalora, Joseph A.
Schatz, Burton
Schroeder, Henry J.
Sciacca, Hugo E.
Sents, Edwin F.
Sestito, Joseph F. J.
Shattuck, Dean E.
Short, Joel W.
Smith, Roy J.
Sperdute, James S.
Spooner, Norman E.
Stachowicz, Cornelius M.
Stein, Mark
Stirler, Walter H.
Storey, William
Swanson, Ralph N.
Tekarz, Frank J.
Thiede, Harold A.
Thompson, Charles A.
Vikander, Vernon J.
Vincent, Robert L.
Waldron, Lee V.
Walker, James J.
Walker, Rolla L. Jr.
Ward, Schnitzer
Watson, Philip P.
Way, Dwight N.
Willard, Thaedore E.
Wolver, Marwood J.
York, Charles W.
Zack, Michael

Battery B

Chase, James E.—Capt., later WIA
Knollman, Anthony B.—Lt., later Capt.
Gardner, Clinton C.—Lt., later WIA twice
Wilson, Robert A.—Lt.
Coates, Barrett N.—Lt.
Ballard, John A.—Lt.

Baker, Keith W.
Batchelder, Simeon
Beaulieu, Arnold
Bellerose, Aurele
Benson, John M.
Bingham, Sebird M.
Boksanski, William J.
Bowley, Charles R. Jr.
Brammann, Richard C.
Brinkert, Robert S.
Bridges, Donald [KIA]
Brown, Everett
Brown, Norman D.
Brown, Philip L.
Brown, Richard
Bryant, Ernest
Burke, John T.
Burke, William F.
Butz, Harry W. Jr.
Carey, Albert
Carlton, Edward
Caron, Melvin
Carter, Clarence D.
Cavanaugh, Earl J.
Chafee, Jairus E.
Choquette, Charles L.P.
Ciaburri, Daniel H.
Cochran, John
Cohen, Lester M.
Conlon, Donald E.
Colliver, Billie B. [DOD 6/29/1945]

Couturier, Albert G.
Crow, Edons
Curran, John [DOD 5/16/1944]
Czesztyicki, Joseph
Daher, James M.
Davies, Owen T.
Davis, Melvin W.
Davis, Paul F.
DiGiantomaso, John J.
DiMauro, Angelo S.
Diserio, Anthony
Doucette, Donald A.
Ebel, Melvin J.
Edds, Harvey W. Jr.
Ertel, Paul
Evans, George T.
Evanuska, Walter
Ewing, Bob M.
Fako, Stephen
Farris, Arthur
Faulkner, Walter J.
Fisher, William B. Jr.
Foster, Roy
Gearin, James
Goldstein, Leo
Gotwalt, Robert W.
Grasso, Pasquale F. "Pat"
Griffith, Wesley W.
Groathouse, John W.
Hadala, Walter
Hadley, Lewis G.
Harris, Maurice F.

Hermort, Michael
Holstead, Orin M.
Holt, David
Hubbard, Arthur J. "Art"
Hunt, Emmett
Hussey, Bruce W.
James, Jesse L.
Johnson, Franklin E.
Kaulman, Barney
Keefe, Thomas
King, Kenneth
Kittleson, Ray
Kosicki, Edward C.
Kott, Edward J.
Kraemer, Jacob
Kreckler, John F.
Kruschke, Dennis B.
Labonte, Armond M.
Lang, Kenneth W.
Lanier, Lavern
LeBlanc, Leo A.
LeBlanc, Peter
Lee, William
Lemire, Hubert
Lennon, Leo
Lien, O'Donnell M.
Litton, Thomas G.
Lowell, Kenneth E.
Loyd, James W.
Lucid, Frank J.
Lyon, Leslie F.
Malone, Leslie E.

Mannon, George
Martin, Raymond J.
Martin, Willie
Massey, Paul
Maxey, Harry
Maxon, Curtis
McClintock, Donald S.
McGorray, James W. Jr.
Merola, Bartholomew
Mielczarski, Frank P.
Miller, Edwin
Mitchell, Richard L.
Morgan, Kenneth L.
Morrison, Clarence
Munsey, John A.
Nishanien, Nishan
Norton, Donald W.
Oliver, James W. "Jim"
Page, John
Pasku, Harry J. Jr.
Pettinato, Sam J.

Preedom, Merle F.
Prescott, James W. "Jim"
Pritchard, Robert J.
Proctor, Charles C. Jr.
Reardon, John R.
Reed, Warren A.
Rogala, Stephen S.
Russo, Lawrence
Seferyn, Stanley A.
Sholomith, Max
Shoultz, Ralph G.
Slachta, Charles D.
Slowik, Albert A.
Smaha, Michael
Smith, Harold E.
Smith, Marvin P.
Soll, Delwin D. "Del"
Spaltro, Lindsey B.
Spodnick, Stephen J.
Sterling, Carl E.
Stulce, Ranie L.

Tassey, Louis A.
Taylor, Daniel L.
Trotter, Walter
VanderTuig, Wilber
Vaughn, Donald E.
Verratto, Jerome "Jimmy"
Wadsworth, Harold
Waters, Alvin T. Jr.
Watson, Frank S.
Way, Norman R.
Wear, Harold L.
Webb, Gaylon
Weller, Archie [KIA]
West, Robert H. "Bob"
Whalen, George
Wherry, Richard D. "Dick"
Willis, Roy D.
Wisniewski, Frank T.
Wiswell, Harold W.
Woolson, Richard "Dick"
Zaia, Albert

Battery C

Born, Lester K.—Capt.; transferred out 6/9/44
Philips, Allen D.—Lt., later Capt.; later WIA
Conner, Richard R.—Lt.
Salidas, Charles L.—Lt.
Sisson, Richard D.—Lt., later Capt.
Sokoloff, Solomon—Lt.

Adams, Jesse
Adkins, Rudolph R.
Allen, Vergial R.
Anderson, Raymond C.
Andrews, Joseph [DOD 7/20/1943]
Annis, Orville J. "Junior"
Aspinall, Francis W. Jr.
Bachman, George W.
Baker, Donald W.
Bartolotta, Angelo L.
Bauer, Harold R.
Benally, Harry
Bennard, Anthony
Blais, Joseph R.
Blodgett, Alan H.
Bostick, Walter L.
Branaman, George J.
Brezny, Charles
Briggs, Henry J. Jr.
Broadbent, John T.
Bunich, Harold S.
Burgess, Edward N.
Burnett, Dean M.
Bye, Terrell W. "Terry"
Cady, Charles W.
Carroll, Walter E.
Casey, Felix A.
Cekala, Joseph T.
Clarke, Harry Jr.
Collard, William E.
Cook, Robert E.

Cooper, Fred J.
Cormack, Francis W.
Creedon, Joseph F.
Criscuolo, Peter J.
Croteau, Napoleon B.
Czajka, Alexander C.
Dalbey, Earl E.
DeMoulin, Howard M.
Dillon, Robert W.
Dionisio, Albert P.
Dixon, Edward T.
Duquet, Charles H.
East, Marvin R. "Curly"
Eastman, Robert S.
Ecker, Donald W.
Fechner, Willis W.
Fleming, Donald W.
Foster, Halton W.
Frank, George J.
Gagnon, Maurice A.
Garfield, Wiliam H.
Gering, Dale M.
Giles, William T.
Gill, John T.
Giltner, Orval D.
Glass, David B.
Haney, Chester L.
Hawkins, Hobart H.
Henry, Carl E.
Hickson, Howard H.
Hospodar, Joseph F.
Huber, Albert J.

Ingram, Douglas F.
Jaeger, Rudolph F.
Jenks, Nelson A.
Jennings, James J.
Johnson, Theodore
Jones, John H.
Kasting, Harold G.
Keck, Ross N.
Kitson, Arloe J.
Kuchar, Wayne R.
Kyc, Bernard P.
Lancey, Donald V.
Lashier, Charles N.
Lemay, Paul A.
Levcowich, Michael V.
Levine, Joe
Lewis, Alvis A.
Lewis, Charles E.
Liska, Willard G.
Littlewood, Donald F.
Lothrop, Arthur D.
Luckner, Edward S.
Ludgewait, John O.
Lynch, William
Lyons, Thomas B.
Malboeuf, Gerald B.
McDonald, Frank P.
McKee, Koa L.
Melladew, Herbert G.
Metaxapolous, Frank
Meyer, Ferdinand E.
Meyers, Forrest K.

Mills, Noah K.
Moffatt, Chester A.
Moore, Wayne
Morang, Herbert F.
Mourousas, Stephen
Mueller, Harold W.
Myers, Logan T.
Nevius, Paul W.
Nielsen, Elmer N.
Noss, Richard R.
Omen, Henry J.
Paoletti, Raymond
Peck, Frederick R. Jr.
Peck, Joseph N.
Pessalano, Arthur E.
Pitler, Simon S.
Porter, Howard
Price, Joseph N.
Prue, Thomas G.
Rietscha, Ferdinand T.
Roberts, Leo E.

Robbie, Frederick
Sagen, Kenneth T.
Sarver, James Jr.
Sawyer, Leonard B.
Saydera, Theodore F.
Schadt, Harold V.
Scieszinski, James D.
Sebastian, Walter J.
Seesock, John
Shevlin, John J.
Simons, Donald R.
Small, Gerald B.
Smart, Melvin L.
Smith, Harold F.
Smuozerowicz, Leonard
Spada, Louis
Starr, Francis X.
Staver, Ralph G.
Stroud, William F. "Bill"
Sullivan, John E.
Swett, Leon E.

Taylor, Floyd H.
Thake, Henry F.
Thake, Walter R.
Thibodeau, Norman J.
Tolzman, LaVern A.
Tomlin, Charles S.
Treadway, Charles H.
Triantifillou, Socrates
Trowbridge, Stuart B.
Turner, Joseph F.
Uliano, Joseph
Walters, Norman G.
Wedberg, Lloyd W.
White, Jack P.
White, Marshall E.
Wilson, Lucian C.
Wilty, Richard G. "Dick"
Wolfe, Charles J. Jr.
Wykert, Charles C. Jr.
Zuehlke, Erwin E.

Battery D

Reiver, Julius "Jules"—Capt., later Major
Klein, Henry J. "Hank"—Lt., later Capt.
Eddy, Ernest A. Jr.—Lt., later WIA
Noel, Theodore N.—Lt.

Abate, Edward P.
Adamowicz, Joseph W.
Alegi, Dominic J.
Arthur, Allen W.
Baldwin, Arthur
Barnes, James L.
Bean, John G.
Bennett, Bryce L. Jr.
Bizup, Joseph W.
Bobotas, Aristides
Brassard, Raymond A.
Breit, Ernest F.
Bresnehan, James W.
Buntemeyer, Edward F. C.
Bush, Thomas E.
Cahman, Reinhart H.
Chamberlain, Philip T.
Cheney, Leo W.
Clear, William A.
Clegg, Leonard Jr.
Cobb, Kenneth L.
Colbert, James E.
Coleman, Joseph E.
Connors, John
Copeland, Arthur E. Jr.
Costa, Francis R. Jr.
Covell, Walter R.
Craver, Claud R.
Crescimanno, Salvatore T.
Crosley, Lionel P.
Davis, Berton
Davis, Daniel F. Jr.
Davis, Robert E.
Diorio, Vincent J.

Duggan, William F.
Dunlap, Harold E.
Dunlevy, Frank J.
Dunshee, Carl A.
Durham, Ernest
Eckenrode, Joseph B.
Edmondson, Wayne W.
Eldridge, William L.
Evans, Edward J.
Failla, Joseph J.
Francis, Clifford L. Jr.
Francisco, Ernest L.
Fredrickson, Virgil H.
Fullington, Gerald A.
Furs, Frank E.
Gacioch, Alexander J.
Gamache, Fernand A. Jr.
Gold, Norman
Gross, Allen E.
Hanson, Nin L.
Heim, George H.
Hennessey, Richard J.
Hills, Robert C.
Hopkins, Clifford M.
Horen, Robert L.
Hoyt, Charles R.
Hunter, Donald C.
Jacques, Felix G.
Jenness, Clarence E.
Jennings, Raymond B.
Kaszynski, Stanley J.
Kelley, James W.
Kimmey, Norman E.
King, Edward M.

Klawiter, Joseph C.
Kleinbecker, Ernie Dwight
Kobbe, Alvin L.
Kramer, William C.
Lamoreaux, James W.
Lamparty, Leopold F.
LaPlante, Louis T.
LeBlanc, Patrick G.
Leftwich, Dick C.
Lewis, Charles E. Jr.
Lewis, Robert J.
Libby, Clyde R.
Lyon, Cary M.
Malatesta, Charles J.
Marshall, Charles F.
McAllister, Charles W.
McElroy, Armond W.
McKinney, Norman J.
Merrill, Vernon I.
Merrithew, Lynwood E.
Metzler, John H.
Militello. Dominick
Millea, William V.
Mitchell, George M.
Mitchell, Kenneth E.
Moose, David T.
Monahan, Thomas F.
Neddermann, Charles E.
Nelson, Arthur William
Nesland, Otto A.
Nevius, Paul W.
Noble, Charles J. Jr.
Noteboom, Lloyd
O'Brien, Patrick J.

O'Leary, Daniel J.
Osgood, Robert D.
Omen, Henry J.
Paige, William E.
Patterson, Gerald L.
Pearce, James R.
Peikett, George A.
Penn, Arthur T.
Petersen, Donald C.
Pettyjohn, Walter R.
Pisarczyk, Charles P.
Picinisco, Bernard J.
Pittman, James D. "J. D."
Price, Henry N.
Provencher, Armand
Pycior, Edwin J.
Pycior, Stanley F.
Randall, Chauncey F.
Rascovsky, Louis F.
Reiser, Walter E.
Renehan, Gordon R.
Rice, Leonard M.
Richey, James F.

Richts, Otto Charles
Riggins, Edmund C.
Robertson, Kingsley
Romano, John
Rosen, Stanley J.
Russo, Sebastian J.
Samuelson, Joseph H. Jr.
Schultz, Clarence
Sczygiel, Roman
Sell, William R.
Shaffer, Otis C.W.
Shepherd, Tevis M.
Sidlick, Albert
Siraguso, Carl
Sites, John William
Slanda, Leon S.
Slaven, George M.
Smith, Virgil W.
Somolik, John Jr.
Speer, Ivan Glen
Sprau, Robert H.
Staton, Elmer G.
Stevens, Clarence G. Jr.

Stevensky, Stanley
Stewart, Allen C.
Stiles, Henry M.
Suman, Albert L.
Taber, Harry J.
Tackitt, Grayson
Theriault, Donald W.
Theriault, Layzime James
Tidlund, August N.
Tobery, George P.
Trombley, Paul T.
Vesledahl, Donald S.
Wagner, Herbert W.
Walker, Edwin
Wartonick, John
Wergin, Deryl H.
Whitman, Leonard W.
Wilson, Russell I.
Witte, Ivan E.W. "Ive"
Wolfe, Abe
Worboys, Earl M. "Bucky"

Appendix B

Cities and Towns Occupied by the 110th AAA

Various induction centers	March 25-31, 1943
Camp Edwards, MA	March 31 to Dec. 6, 1943
Camp Kilmer, NJ	Dec. 6 to Dec. 23, 1943
Queen Mary ship	Dec. 23 to Dec. 31, 1943
Gourock, Scotland	Dec. 31, 1943
Nettlebed, England	Jan. 1, 1944 to Feb. 25, 1944
Exmouth, England	Feb. 25 to May 15
Oxford Waterproofing School	2/28 to 3/8
Tonfanau, Tywyn, Wales,	4/6 to 4/15
Broadsands/Paignton	4/18 to 4/24
K-7 "sausage camp," Liskeard	May 15 to June 1
Torpoint, Harbor 31	June 1
English Channel	June 1 to June 5
Batt. A	LST 498
Batt. B	LST 510
Batt. C	LST 291
Batt. D	LST 506
Normandy coast, France	June 6 to June 7
Verville-sur-Mer	
Batt. A	June 7 to June 10
Batt. B & C	June 7 to July 5
Batt. D	June 7 to June 9
St. Pierre du Mont	
Batt. D	June 9 to June 29

Louvieres
    Batt. A   June 10 to July 10
St. Clement la Calvados
    Batt. D   June 29 to July 10
La Cambe
    Batt. C   July 5 to July 10
St. Jean de Daye
    Batt. A, B, C & D   July 10 July 20
Tribehou
    Batt. C & D   July 20 to July 30
Criegueville en Bessin
    Batt. D   July 30
Cavigny
    Batt. C   July 30 to Aug. 8
St. Lo
    Batt. C   Aug. 8 to Aug. 10
St. Hilaire du Harcouet
    Batt. A, B, C & D   Aug. 10 to Aug. 21
La Loupe
    Batt. A, B, C & D   Aug. 21 to Aug. 24
Nogent Le Rotrou
    Batt. A & B   Aug. 24
Lamours
    Batt. C & D   Aug. 24
Paris
    Batt. A, B, C & D   Aug. 25 to Sept. 8
        various positions around the city
    (Red Ball Express   Aug. 25 to Sept. 15)
        various volunteers from all batteries
St. Laurent
    Batt. D   Sept. 8 to Sept. 29
Mezieres
    Hdq. Batt. & A Batt.   Sept. 8 to Sept. 29
Charlesville
    Batt. B & C   Sept. 8 to Sept. 29

Liege, Belgium
    A, B, C & D   Sept. 29 to Oct. 7
"Position X" (Pepnister)
    A, B, C & D   Oct. 7 to Oct. 17

Verviers	
A, B, C & D	Oct. 17 to Oct. 25
Spa	
A, B, C & D	Oct. 25 to Dec. 16
Francorchamps	
Batt. D	Dec. 16 to 19:
Stoumont	
Batt. A & D	Dec. 16 to 19
LaGleize	
Batt. B	Dec. 16 to 19:
Stavelot	
Batt. C	Dec. 16 to 19
Malmedy	
A, B, C & D	Dec. 19 to Dec. 31
Stavelot	
Batt. A & B	Dec. 31 to Jan. 15, 1945
LaGleize	
Batt. C	Dec. 31 to Jan. 18, 1945
Mont	
Batt. A & B	Jan. 15 to Jan 20
Francorchamps	
Batt. D	Dec. 31 to Jan. 15, 1945
Spa	
A, B, C & D	Jan 20 to Feb. 26
Eschweiler, Germany	
Batt. A & D	Feb. 26 to Mar. 1
Merken	
Batt. B & C	Feb. 26 to Mar. 1
Duren	
A, B, C & D	Mar. 1 to Mar. 10
Remagen	
A, B, C & D	Mar. 10 to Mar. 20
Kassel	
Batt. A	Mar. 20 to April 13
Bandorf	
Batt. B & C	Mar. 20 to April 13
Rolandswerth	
Batt. D	Mar. 20 to April 13
Leubsdorf (last position as AAA)	
A, B, C & D	Apr. 13 to Apr. 19

Muhlhausen	
A, B, C & D	Apr. 19 to Apr. 20
Weimer	
Batt. A	Apr. 20 to Apr. 30
Schmalkalden	
Hdq. Batt. & Batt. B	Apr. 20 to July 5
Meingen	
Batt. C	Apr. 20 to May 12
Gotha	
Batt. D	Apr. 20 to Apr. 30
Zella-Mehlis	
Batt. A	Apr. 30 to May 15
Suhl	
Batt. D	Apr. 30 to May 15
Runkel	
Batt. C	May 12 to May 26
Bad Liebenstein	
Batt. A	May 15 to June 30
Kubach	
Batt. D	May 15 to June 30
Aumenau	
Batt. C	May 26 to July 5
Weimer (Buchenwald Concentration Camp)	
Various from Hdq. Batt.	Apr. 15 to May 30
Schwab Hall	
Hdq. Batt. & Batt. C	July 5 to Oct. 6
Ludwigsburg (SS POW Camp #72)	
Batt. A, B & D	July 5 to Oct. 6

Battalion broken up or disbanded after Oct. 6
Most personnel returning to USA by mid-November

Attachment:

Jan. 1, 1944 to May 17, 1944:	18th AAA Group, 49th AAA Brigade, V Corps, First Army
May 17, 1944-June 7, 1944:	29th Infantry Division, V Corps, First Army
June 7, 1944 to Aug. 10, 1944:	18th AAA Group, 49th AAA Brigade, First Army
Aug. 10, 1944 to Aug. 23, 1944:	11th AAA Group, 49th AAA Brigade, First Army
Aug. 23, 1944 to Aug. 27, 1944:	115th AAA Group, under V Corps, First Army
Aug. 27, 1944 to Aug. 30, 1944:	18th AAA Group, under V Corps, First Army
Aug. 30, 1944 to Sept. 7, 1944:	18th AAA Group, 49th AAA Brigade, First Army
Sept. 7, 1944 to Sept. 14, 1944:	18th AAA Group, under V Corps, First Army

Sept. 14, 1944 to Sept. 29, 1944:	Ninth U.S. Army, 30th Infantry Division, 21st Brit. Army Group
Sept. 29, 1944 to Dec. 7, 1944:	18th AAA Group, 49th AAA Brigade, V Corps, First Army
Dec. 7, 1944 to Dec. 16, 1944:	Attached directly to 49th AAA Brigade, First Army
Dec. 16, 1944 to Dec. 20, 1944:	103rd AAA Group, 49th AAA Brigade, First Army
Dec. 20, 1944 to Dec. 22, 1944:	11th AAA Group, 49th AAA Brigade, 18th Airborne
Dec. 22, 1944 to Dec. 28, 1944:	Ninth U.S. Army, 30th Infantry Division (anti-tank defense)
Dec. 28, 1944 to Jan. 24, 1945:	823rd Tank Destroyer Battalion, 30th Infantry Division
Jan. 24, 1945 to Feb. 7, 1945:	103rd AAA Group, 49th AAA Brigade, First Army
Feb. 7, 1945 to Feb. 14, 1945:	16th AAA Group, 49th AAA Brigade, First Army
Feb. 14, 1945 to Mar. 10, 1945:	49th AAA Brigade, First Army
Mar. 10, 1945 to Mar. 20, 1945	16th AAA Group, III Corps
Mar. 20, 1945 to April 19, 1945	18th AAA Group, 49th AAA Brigade, First Army
April 19, 1945-October 6, 1945	49th AAA Brigade, First Army

Appendix C

The 90mm Anti-aircraft Gun
Basic Operation

Gun Crew and Gun Operation

The 90mm gun was the most successful and widely used heavy AA gun in World War II. It was both compact and well-designed. Typically, the anti-aircraft gun battalion consisted of five batteries, designated A (Able) Battery, B (Baker) Battery, C (Charlie) Battery, D (Dog) Battery, and Headquarters Battery. The four letter-designated batteries were further broken down into four gun sections each—referred to as Gun #1, Gun #2, and so on. Speer was in D-Battery, gun section number three of the 110th AAA Gun Battalion. So, when he referred to his outfit verbally, he would simply say: "110th Triple-A Battalion, Dog Battery, third section" or "third section, Dog Battery, 110th Triple-A." Headquarters Battery consisted of men involved with supply, training, logistics, and paper shuffling. Each battery had its own kitchen and staff. In addition to the main Battalion Headquarters and supply system, each letter-designated battery also had its own facilities in these areas.

The gun, itself, was mounted on a steel cruciform platform that folded up for travel. Two sets of duel wheels, having 22-inch rubber truck tires, were mounted on a single axle at the back of the frame, on each side, in order to transport it. The frame had a ten-foot long, six inch diameter tow bar at the front that was coupled to the back of a prime mover when being moved from one place to another. Once they arrived at their destination, the gun would be backed into position and the crew would then pull the outriggers out to the sides, remove the safety pins, lower the gun onto four pads 90-degrees apart, and then level the gun with hand cranks that were mounted at the ends of the outriggers. This set up could be accomplished by the crew in seven minutes. At the same time, other members of the battery went to work hooking up all four battery guns to the computer by a 225-foot cable, set up the radar unit, set up all the antennas, and made all the connections as the generator and tracker units were set up.

Depending on the terrain, it would generally take about eight to twelve hours to completely dig the guns into position whenever they moved to a new location. Upon arrival they would begin to dig a circular pit about four feet deep and twenty feet across and fill sandbags with much of the dirt to stack around the rim of the excavation to create a parapet. Thus, while standing on the pit floor loading and operating the gun, the crew remained below the surrounding terrain at eye level with the top of the pit, safe from nearly anything except a direct hit. The battery's four guns were usually dug in about fifty yards apart in a diamond pattern in order to "bracket" the target with artillery fire. During the daytime, the gun and pits remained covered by a large camouflage net to protect against any aerial surveillance. Sometimes a tarp was stretched over the pit and, with the addition of a doorway, a command center or living quarters was created around the gun.

A typical gun crew consisted of thirteen to sixteen men. Some operated dials and levers on the gun, others loaded and fired it, and still others carried the big twenty-three-pound shells from a storage area or "ammo dump" established several yards away. There was also a lot of overlapping of duties. For instance, after towing the gun and crew to its destination, placing it in position and helping set it up, the tractor operators often assumed duties in the ammo line, or manned one of the battery's machine guns.

The gun section leader—in charge of Gun #1, Gun #2, and so on in each battery—had the rank of Sergeant, sometimes called Buck Sergeant—having three stripes up and none down on his sleeve—and was often only two or three years older than the rest of the gun crew. A Corporal usually had the title of "gunner" and selected targets and directed the operation of the gun. Another Sergeant was in charge of the machine-gun section and a soldier with the rank of Corporal was also typically in charge of each of the individual M-51 quad-50 machine-gun mounts. All the truck and prime-mover drivers had the rank of T-5—Tech-5, having Corporal's two stripes over a "T" on their sleeves. The others on the crew held the ranks of Private First Class and Private. Generally, a sixteen-man gun crew would be divided into nine men for the 90mm gun and six for the M-51 mount.

Normally a gun crew worked all night firing at targets and slept in the daytime but these guns required a great deal of daytime maintenance as well to keep them in good condition. Therefore, after a night's work, half the crew would sleep while the other half continued to work doing gun maintenance and upkeep. By afternoon, this half went to sleep while the others got up and completed the maintenance and other duties. They all slept in pup tents, the covered gun pit or under half-tracks or other heavy vehicles. The various vehicles were always parked under trees or covered by camouflage netting. Generally, even as the work was being done, two men would constantly sit in the tracker seats behind the gun and another in the seat of a quad-50 keeping a watch on the sky.

Their big 90mm weapon could be aimed manually or mechanically. Manually, the gun was aimed by sighting through elevated cross-hairs mounted on each side of the weapon. There were seats behind the cross-hairs for the "trackers." Large handles extended out toward each seat. The left side cranked the gun horizontally and the right side cranked the gun vertically. One man, called the "loader," stood on the platform and loaded the shells into the breach. After firing, the "loader" also cocked the gun to put the next round into the firing chamber. On later models, the gun cocked automatically during recoil. The gun was fired by stepping on a lever located on the platform. A "gunner" stood on the ground off to one side and directed the fire. Because it was so noisy during firing, the "gunner" sometimes had a rope tied to the leg of the "loader." If it became necessary, the "gunner" would jerk on the rope to get the "loader's" attention.

The gun could also be aimed mechanically by a director that consisted of a steel box, approximately four feet square full of gears, that was connected to the gun by electrical cable. The director sat on a tripod and it, too, had a leveling mechanism. A scope located on each side of the director allowed the "trackers" to stand here on the ground at each side instead of sitting in the gun seats. The director was set up about 15 feet from the gun. It had to be coordinated with the gun by sighting both of them on some distant object and then locking them together. The trackers had a six-inch diameter wheel located next to the scopes that they moved to keep on a moving target. The gears in the box were supposed to build a lead on a target so that when they were tracking a plane, the projectile would be fired out ahead of it, allowing for the time it took the projectile to reach the plane.

The electrical power needed when using the director with the gun came from a small gasoline-driven power plant or generator. The gun, director, and power plant were all inter—connected with electrical cables laid out on the ground. During the daytime or day-light hours the gun was usually aimed manually for antiaircraft fire. During nighttime firing, the gun was usually set up for automatic or mechanical aim using radar to locate and sight-in on the planes in the dark. When used to support infantry or at specific targets, manual was used in both day-light and dark.

During operations, each gun was connected by telephone to the battery command post in a nearby dugout. At all times, one member—usually the gunnery Sergeant—of each gun crew had a telephone to his ear. Once the rangefinder and director station determined a target, the battery commander gave the order to "Stand by." As the gun commander relayed the order to his gun crew, they sprang to action. Part of the crew aimed the weapon in accordance with the electrically-transmitted instructions while the ammo carriers and loader went to work. An ammo relayer at the rear passed a big shell up to the second relayer who inserted it into the fuse setter and hit the trip lever with his left hand. Once set, the shell is then relayed toward the pit. Reserve shells were always kept stored in shelves or pigeon-holes created at different locations all around the inside wall of the gun pit. As the gun crew began firing, ammo carriers passed new shells from an ammunition dump several yards away to the fuse-setter and then to the rim of the pit where an ammo-carrier waited below. His job was to keep the pigeon-holes filled as the gun constantly turned or revolved around inside the pit so there was always a shelf full of ammo available to the loader, no matter what position the gun was in. The 90mm M-1 AA gun weighed about 19,000 pounds and had a barrel about 15 ½ feet long.

The Ammo

The gun elevated 90-degrees, traversed 360-degrees and fired a 23-pound shell with a muzzle velocity of 2,700 feet per second. With an effective ceiling of 33,800 feet, it could shoot 15 rounds per minute (rpm) manually. Loaded by an automatic rammer, the gun could fire 23 to 28 rounds per minute with a maximum range of 40,500 feet (13,500 yards or over 7.5 miles) vertical or 63,000 feet (21,000 yards or nearly 12 miles) horizontal.

Pulled by Tracked Vehicles

The M-4 Artillery Tractor was the most commonly used vehicle for towing these guns. Also referred to as a High Speed Tractor, these vehicles weighed 18 tons and had a top speed of about 40 miles per hour. They were powered by a 210-horsepower 6-cylinder Waukesha side-mounted gasoline engine that could tow a 90mm gun up to 35 miles per hour and climb grades of up to 60-percent. The tractor also came equipped with a front-mounted high-powered winch. The term "Cat"—short for Caterpillar—often used by the G.I.s, was a complete misnomer as the Caterpillar Corporation had no connection with the vehicle whatsoever. It was built by American tractor maker Allis-Chalmers and was armed with a pulpit-mounted 50-caliber Browning heavy machine gun on a skate-ring mount on the back-side of the cab's rooftop.

The cab was divided into two compartments with seating room for the driver and two men in the front compartment and double seats accommodating eight additional men in the rear compartment. Back cushions in this second compartment were leather covered and canvas zipper bags padded with blankets served as seat cushions. Both compartments had canvas doors.

Ammo shell racks for up to 54 rounds were located in a compartment behind the crew and their other gear, extra machine-gun ammo, camouflage netting, and cases of U-rations were also stowed here. A special swing crane was mounted on the back deck for hoisting ammo boxes and shells.

Overall, the M-4 highspeed tractor was 16 feet 11 inches long, 8 feet 3 inches high, and 8 feet wide. It used both steel-block or rubber-bushed tracks and its average range was 125 miles on 155 gallons of gas.

Notes

Prologue

1. Ernie Pyle, *Brave Men* (NY: Henry Holt, 1944), p. 245, hereafter referred to as Pyle, *Brave Men*.
2. Ivan Glen Speer, Author's interview.
3. Pyle, *Brave Men*, p. 246.
4. J. Robert Slaughter papers, Veteran's Survey Project, U.S. Army Military History Institute, Carlisle Barracks, Pennsylvania, hereafter referred to as Slaughter papers, USAMHI.
5. Bob L. Sales papers, Veteran's Survey Project, U.S. Army Military History Institute, Carlisle Barracks, Pennsylvania, hereafter referred to as Sales papers, USAMHI.
6. Ibid.
7. Slaughter papers, USAMHI
8. Warner H. Hamlett papers, From the Peter S. Kalikow World War II Collection, courtesy of The National D-Day Museum Foundation, Inc., New Orleans, Louisiana.
9. Alfred Lang papers, Veteran's Survey Project, U.S. Army Military History Institute, Carlisle Barracks, Pennsylvania, hereafter referred to as Sales papers, USAMHI.
10. Stephen W. Sears, ed. *Eyewitness to World War II* (Boston: Houghton Mifflin, 1991), p. 223-224.
11. Ibid., p. 224.
12. Stephen E. Ambrose, *Citizen Soldiers* (NY: Simon & Schuster, 1997), p. 27; Jon Meacham, "Caught In The Line Of Fire," *Newsweek*, July 13, 1998, p. 54.
13. Don McCombs and Fred L. Worth, *World War II, 4,139 Strange and Fascinating Facts* (NY: Wings Books, 1994), p.339, hereafter referred to as McCombs and Worth, *Facts*; Tracy Sugarman, *My War* (NY: Random House, 2000), p. 77, hereafter referred to as Sugarman, *My War*. Rommel's

famous reference was used as the title of Cornelius Ryan's 1959 book about D-Day as well as for the title of the 1962 movie.

14. Franklin E. Johnson papers, Voices of the Second World War, Thomas J. Dodd Research Center, University of Connecticut, hereafter referred to as Johnson, "Franklin Johnson Papers."

Chapter 1

1. Ross Gregory, *America 1941—A Nation At The Crossroads* (NY: Free Press, 1989), p. 110, 113, 227.
2. Ivan Glen Speer, Author's Interview. The minimum draft age was lowered from 21 to 18 on November 13, 1942.
3. Ronald H. Bailey, *The Homefront: USA* (Alexandria, VA: Time-Life Books, 1977), p. 44.
4. Ivan Glen Speer, Author's Interview.
5. Ibid.
6. Ibid.
7. Ibid.
8. Ibid.
9. Nearly 130,000 Iowans were processed through Camp Dodge before it was closed as an induction center at the end of June 1944. By July 1944, all Iowa inductees were sent to Fort Snelling MN, Jefferson Barracks MO, or Fort Leavenworth KS for processing. *Yank*, Vol. 3, No. 4 (July 14, 1944), p. 18.
10. Ivan Glen Speer, Author's Interview.
11. Ibid.
12. Ibid.
13. Ibid.

Chapter 2

1. James T, Lingg, "WWII Memoirs of James T. Lingg," (pvt pub., 1998), p. 2.
2. John A. "Jack" Forman, "World War II Memories," typed manuscript, 1985, p. 7, hereafter referred to as Forman, "Memories."
3. Shelby L. Stanton, *Order of Battle, U.S. Army, World War II* (Novato, CA: Presidio Press, 1984), p. 599. Camp Edwards, originally north of present-day Otis Air Force Base, was also later used as a prison camp for German POWs.

4. Marion Hargrove, *See Here, Private Hargrove* (NY: Henry Holt, 1942), p. 15, hereafter referred to as Hargrove, *See Here.*

5. Richard T. Gaige, *Me and the Army* (NY: American Artists Group, 1943), p. 15. In 1943 members of Headquarters Battery, 110th CAC became the first troops to be housed in the base's two-story barracks buildings.

6. Forman, "Memories," p. 7.

7. John S. Stradling, *Johnny*, edited by Harriet J. Stradling (Salt Lake: Bookcraft, 1946), p. 27, hereafter referred to as Stradling, *Johnny.* K.P. stood for "Kitchen Police," Army slang referring to being assigned to the food preparation and cleanup detail.

8. Fred E. Brake, "A Soldiers' City Rises From The Dust," *The Quartermaster Review*, (Mar.-Apr. 1941), p. 25-28; *1000 and 1 Questions about Camp Edwards*, (Special Service Branch, Camp Edwards, Mass., 1943), p. 1-24; *The Camp News*, April 5, 1943, p. 1.   Prior to the first of the year, the newspaper's name was *Camp Edwards News* (August 12, 1942).

9. Thus Speer's dog tags appeared as such:

    Ivan G. Speer
    37667197 T 43 0
    Dewey O. Speer
    RFD 2
    Corydon, Ia.

10. *1000 and 1 Questions about Camp Edwards*, p. 7. Two bits is equal to 25-cents.

11. Basic Training programs initially lasted 12 to 13 weeks but immediately after the attack on Pearl Harbor programs were cut to 8 weeks for a short time. By 1943 however, nearly all training programs had been fixed at a 13 week period with another 3 to 4 weeks of specialized training. George Forty, *U.S. Army Handbook 1939-1945* (UK: Alan Sutton Publishing, 1995), p. 13, hereafter referred to as Forty, *U.S. Army Handbook.*

12. Hargrove, *See Here*, p. 2.

13. Ibid.; Michael H. E. Marsden, *Khaki Is More Than A Color* (Garden City, NY: Doubleday, Doran and Company, 1943), p. 62-63, hereafter referred to as Marsden, *Khaki*; Cleveland A. Harrison, *Unsung Valor, A GI's Story of World War II* (Jackson: University Press of Mississippi, 2000), p. 15, hereafter referred to as Harrison, *Unsung Valor*; Ivan Glen Speer, Author's Interview.

14. Harrison, *Unsung Valor*, p. 34; Hargrove, *See Here*, p. 6-7.

15. Ivan Glen Speer, Author's Interview.

---

16. Billie Houseman, *York* (PA) *Daily Record*, June 6, 2001. And Houseman, later assigned to Battery-B, 561st Field Artillery Battalion, had arrived at Basic Training 110 days after his 18th birthday; Interestingly enough, the 110th AAA contained several sets of brothers—even twins—and several sets of cousins. Ironically, Dwight N. Way of A-Battery and Norman R. Way of B-Battery were from the same town in Middlesex County, Mass., the same block, grew up, played, and attended the same school together, were both assigned to Gun #1 of their assigned batteries while Dwight was the youngest in the battalion and Norm was the oldest, YET they were not related in any way!

17. Harrison, *Unsung Valor*, p. 14.

18. Hargrove, *See Here*, p. 115.

19. Joseph H. Scarangella, *Battery "A" History, Battery "A" 137th Gun Bn.* (n.c.: pvt. pub., circa 1944), p. 2, hereafter referred to as Scarangella, *Battery "A" 137th*.

20. Drill Sergeants were more often referred to by the recruits as D.I.s (drill instructors) although they preferred to be called "Cadre."

21. These young recruits had no way of knowing that their "Basic" had two purposes: Technical training and psychological training. The first was to teach every new soldier how to use light infantry weapons under any conditions and under any circumstances. Sometimes it was intense training such as with the M-1 rifle. The second purpose was to turn civilians into useful soldiers. Everything, including discipline, was done to them in squad and platoon formation. Even the arrangement of their equipment on their bed and the clothing in their locker wasn't allowed to be their decision on how to lay it out and hang it up—it was the Army's! The intent was to stop these boys from thinking as individuals and to encourage them to think and act as a team—as members of a combat unit.

22. Gene Gach, *In The Army Now* (NY: Dodd, Mead & Co., 1942), p. 47, hereafter referred to as Gach, *In The Army*.

23. Stradling, *Johnny*, p. 45. "Gigged" was an Army slang term of the period meaning "caught" or "punished."

24. Henry J. Peterson, "Henry Peterson's Life Story," typed manuscript, p. 3.

25. Stradling, *Johnny*, p. 179.

26. Hargrove, *See Here*, p. 116.

27. Stradling, *Johnny*, p. 39.

28. Joseph Eckenrode, "History of D-Battery, 110th AAA," typed manuscript, transcribed from his war diary, p. 72, hereafter referred to as Eckenrode, "D-Battery, 110th AAA."

29. Scarangella, *Battery "A" 137th*, p. 2.
30. Ivan Glen Speer, Author's Interview.
31. *Falmouth* (MA) *Enterprise*, May 14, 1943, p. 5.
32. There was never complete uniformity in the training, even for troops being taught the same specialty at the same base in two different sessions. It often varied from base to base and from instructor to instructor, and sometimes even from date to date at the same base. Therefore, minor variances on some points in soldiers' memoirs is not unusual. Lee Kennett, *G.I., The American Soldier in World War II* (NY: Charles Scribner's Sons, 1987), p. 49 and 52, hereafter referred to as Kennett, *G.I.*
33. Ivan Glen Speer, Author's Interview.
34. Ibid.
35. Stradling, *Johnny*, p. 51. Throwing into the shell holes or trenches during the training helped contain the shrapnel, or metal fragments, from the explosions.
36. Ibid., p. 63.
37. Gach, *In The Army*, p. 56.
38. Ivan Glen Speer, Author's Interview.
39. Kennett, *G.I.*, p. 51.
40. Stradling, *Johnny*, p. 175.
41. Ivan Glen Speer, Author's Interview.
42. Ibid.
43. Clyde R. Libby, Letter to Author.
44. Hargrove, *See Here*, p. 14.
45. Ivan Glen Speer, Author's Interview. Finally, one night Sergeant Sites, Sgt. Henry J. Omen, and Sergeant Hawkins went out drinking and when they returned to Camp Edwards after the bars had closed, they broke into the mess hall and cooked themselves breakfast—frying up a bunch of eggs, bacon, and sausage. Interrupted by the M.P.s, they were all later court-martialed and busted down to Privates as a result. Afterwards, L. James Theriault of C-Battery was promoted to Sergeant and transferred over to Battery-D to take Sites' position as a Gunnery Sergeant. Sites and Omen did, however, stay with the battery and would eventually go in on the Normandy Beach on D-Day +1 as Privates.
46. Eckenrode, "D-Battery, 110th AAA," p. 1; Elmer J. Potzmann, Author's Interview. Officially, the 110th AAA was constituted in the U.S. Army on December 19, 1942 as the 110th CAC and activated at Camp Edwards on January 20, 1943. After being re-designated an AA battalion in February, it was officially re-designated an AAA battalion on June 28, 1943.

---

47. Eckenrode, "D-Battery, 110th AAA," p. 1; Terry W. Bye, Author's Interview; Elmer J. Potzmann, Author's Interview.
48. Marsden, *Khaki*, p. 32.
49. Ivan Glen Speer, Author's Interview.
50. Ibid.
51. Ibid.
52. Ibid.
53. KP included everything from peeling potatoes to assisting the cooks and helping serve meals, cleaning tables, washing dishes, and mopping the mess hall floors. The assignment was normally from sun up to sun down—having to get up one hour before everyone else and getting back to the barracks after everyone else—but it included the benefit of getting extra food as well as the choice pick of what was being offered. Although KP was often assigned as punishment, each recruit was assigned to the detail at least once during Basic Training. Hot water for showers, washing, etc. was provided by coal-fired boilers and heat for the barracks in colder weather was provided by coal furnaces. Recruits were assigned this detail as well. It consisted of keeping a continuous supply of coal burning and the removal of ashes when necessary. The assignment was sometimes referred to as "Fireman" or "Night Brigadier" and often required twenty-four hour duty; Lillian E. Kosicki, "1937—The Beginning—The Trumpet," p. 5, quoted from a letter from Edward Kosicki to his parents dated May 12, 1943.
54. Eckenrode, "D-Battery, 110th AAA," p. 1.
55. Ivan Glen Speer, Author's Interview.
56. Ibid. Grayson Tackitt of Kentucky was better known as "Bull" or "Bull Durham" to everyone in the battery. Years later, like "Peter Rabbit," few recalled his real name.
57. Ibid.
58. Ibid.
59. Ibid.
60. Stradling, *Johnny*, p. 26 and 55.
61. Sean Gonsalves, "A Historic Farewell, Ceremonies, displays and dancing to a big band help folks say goodbye to landmark USO building," *Cape Cod Times*, December 2, 2001; Karen Jeffrey, "Day of dedication, Event honors veterans, USO volunteers who created 'homes away from home,'" *Cape Cod Times*, November 12, 1998; Ivan Glen Speer, Author's Interview; Henry F. Thake, Author's Interview.
62. Ivan Glen Speer, Author's Interview.

63. Johnson, "Franklin Johnson Papers."
64. Scarangella, *Battery "A" 137th*, p. 2.
65. Johnson, "Franklin Johnson Papers."
66. Ivan Glen Speer, Author's Interview.
67. Ibid.
68. Harold W. Mueller, Author's Interview.
69. Ivan Glen Speer, Author's Interview.
70. Scarangella, *Battery "A" 137th*, p. 1.
71. Harold W. Mueller, Author's Interview; Louie Whitlow, "Battery C, 132nd AAA Gun Battalion, 1943-1946" (New Bedford, MA: pvt pub., 2001), p. 2, hereafter referred to as Whitlow, "132nd AAA."
72. Ivan Glen Speer, Author's Interview. According to a number of AAA battery histories, the tail section of several tow planes was nearly shot off on several occasions during these Wellfleet training exercises.
73. Terry W. Bye, Author's Interview; Elmer J. Potzmann, Author's Interview; Harold W. Mueller, Author's Interview; Harvey W. Edds, Author's Interview. Andrews was from Erie, PA. Salidas was from Allston, MA.
74. Eckenrode, "D-Battery, 110th AAA," p. 1; Ivan Glen Speer, Author's Interview.
75. Eckenrode, "D-Battery, 110th AAA," p. 1; Whitlow, "132nd AAA," p. 2; Scarangella, *Battery "A" 137th*, p. 2.
76. Ibid.
77. Ivan Glen Speer, Author's Interview.
78. Marsden, *Khaki*, p. 94-95.
79. Ivan Glen Speer, Author's Interview.
80. Ibid.
81. Ibid.
82. Ibid.
83. Ibid.
84. Ibid.
85. Ibid.
86. Clyde R. Libby, Letter to Author.
87. Ivan Glen Speer, Author's Interview.
88. Capt. Julius Reiver, letter dated September 30, 1943. Speer's Will was witnessed and signed by Pfc. Thomas E. Bush of Abilene, Texas, Pfc. Thomas K. Wolverton of Derby, Iowa, and Sgt. R. H. [Reinhart H.] Cahman of Joplin, Missouri, while his insurance and other papers were witnessed and signed by Pfc. Patrick G. LeBlanc, Pfc. Donald S. Vesledahl, and Pfc. George Prentice Tobery.

Chapter 3

1. Fares quoted are for U.S. Servicemen. Bus and train fare to Philadelphia was $1.50 round-trip.
2. Ivan Glen Speer, Author's Interview.
3. U.S. Dept. of the Army, Special Services Branch, *A Short Guide To Great Britain* (Washington, DC: GPO, 1943), p. 25.
4. *New York Times*, December 19, 1943, December 25, 1943; Ivan Glen Speer, Author's Interview; Harold W. Mueller, Author's Interview; Elmer J. Potzmann, Author's Interview.
5. Eckenrode, "D-Battery, 110th AAA," p. 2.
6. Ivan Glen Speer, Author's Interview; Lester Cohen, "Memories of World War II, Battery B, 110th AAA Gun Bn.," manuscript, p. 1.
7. Ivan Glen Speer, Author's Interview; Harold W. Mueller, USAMHI, Carlisle Barracks, PA, 110th AAA Bn., WWII Survey Collection, Army Service Experiences Questionnaire, p. 5. question 13b; Harold W. Mueller, Author's Interview; Elmer J. Potzmann, Author's Interview.
8. Chester Wardlow, *The Technical Services, The Transportation Corps: Movements, Training, and Supply* (Washington, DC: Office of the Chief of Military History, Department of the Army, 1956), p. 128-29; Thomas Parrish, ed., *The Simon And Schuster Encyclopedia of World War II* (NY: Simon and Schuster, 1978), p. 512, hereafter referred to as Parrish, *Encyclopedia of World War II*.
9. Harrison, *Unsung Valor*, p. 116; Ivan Glen Speer, Author's Interview; Wayne Edmondson, Letter to the Author; Leslie Lyon, "Memories of World War II, Battery B, 110th AAA Gun Bn." manuscript; Frank T. Wisniewski, "What I can Remember of WWII, 1941-1945, 110th AAA Gun Battalion," p. 11, hereafter referred to as Wisniewski, "WWII."
10. C. W. R. Winter, *The Queen Mary* (NY: W. W. Norton & Co., 1986,) p. 21-26, hereafter referred to as Winter, *The Queen Mary*; Melvin Maddocks, *The Great Liners* (Alexandria, VA: Time-Life Books, 1982), p. 154, hereafter referred to as Maddocks, *The Great Liners*; Daniel Allen Butler, *Warrior Queens, The Queen Mary and Queen Elizabeth in World War II* (Mechanicsburg, PA: Stackpole Books, 2002), p. 84 and 124, hereafter referred to as Butler, *Warrior Queens*.
11. Ibid.; Ivan Glen Speer, Author's Interview.
12. Eckenrode, "D-Battery, 110th AAA," p. 2-3; Ivan Glen Speer, Author's Interview; Kennett, *G.I.*, p. 114-16; Winter, *The Queen Mary*, p. 21; Terry Bye, Letter to the Author; Terry Bye, Author's Interview. Copy of ship's schedule and boarding information copies provided by Terry Bye.
13. Ivan Glen Speer, Author's Interview.

14. Harvey Edds, "Memories of World War II, Battery B, 110th AAA Gun Bn., Harvery's Story," p. 1, manuscript, hereafter referred to as Harvey Edds, "Memories." Harvey W. Edds, Author's Interview. Edds and Billie B. Colliver, of Hale, Missouri, had developed a close friendship during basic training. Unfortunately, unknown to both boys, Billie did not have a round-trip ticket. He would die at Schmalkalden, Germany. See Chapter 8, for details.

15. Maddocks, *The Great Liners*, p. 153-54; Winter, *The Queen Mary*, p. 150.

16. Ivan Glen Speer, Author's Interview; Maddocks, *The Great Liners*, p. 150-54; Butler, *Warrior Queens*, p. 84 and 124.

17. Winter, *The Queen Mary*, p. 26; Maddocks, *The Great Liners*, p. 150-54; Butler, *Warrior Queens*, p. 84 and 124; Eckenrode, "D-Battery, 110th AAA," p. 3; Wayne Edmondson, Letter to the Author; L. James Theriault, Author's Interview.

18. Eckenrode, "D-Battery, 110th AAA," p. 2; Ivan Glen Speer, Author's Interview; Maddocks, *The Great Liners*, p. 150-54. Although up to 15,000 troops were carried, the *Queen Mary* never had enough boats, rafts, or other flotation devices for more than 8,000. (Winter, *The Queen Mary*, p. 150).

19. Johnson, "Franklin Johnson Papers." The "troughs" he refers to were long tables with highly raised ridges along the edge to prevent dishes from sliding off during the rolling motions of the ship.

20. Ivan Glen Speer, Author's Interview.

21. Forman, "Memories," p. 11; Winter, *The Queen Mary*, p. 148; Maddocks, *The Great Liners*, p. 150-54; Butler, *Warrior Queens*, p.124; Wisniewski, "WWII," p. 11, 12, 13.

22. Ivan Glen Speer, Author's Interview.

23. Daniel H. Ciaburri, "Memories of World War II, Battery B, 110th AAA Gun Bn., manuscript, p. 1, hereafter referred to as Ciaburri, "Memories."

24. Dick Woolson, "Memories of World War II, Battery B, 110th AAA Gun Bn., manuscript, p. 1, hereafter referred to as Woolson, "Memories."

25. Ciaburri, "Memories," p. 1.

26. Winter, *The Queen Mary*, p. 146-50; Butler, *Warrior Queens*, p. 87-90; Terry Bye, Letter to the Author; Terry Bye, Author's Interview.

27. Eckenrode, "D-Battery, 110th AAA," p. 4; Ivan Glen Speer, Author's Interview.

28. Eckenrode, "D-Battery, 110th AAA," p. 4; Wisniewski, "WWII," p. 19.

29. Ivan Glen Speer, Author's Interview.

30. Harvey Edds, Author's Interview.

Chapter 4

1. Harvey Edds, "Memories," p. 1; Ivan Glen Speer, Author's Interview.
2. From the maker of Bicycle Brand playing cards of Cincinnati, Ohio, it was a 55 card deck, including 2 Jokers along with an "explanation-instruction" card, that displayed the front, top, and side silhouette views of each aircraft in use; Eckenrode, "D-Battery, 110th AAA," p. 4.
3. Ivan Glen Speer, Author's Interview.
4. Ibid.
5. Harvey Edds, "Memories," p. 1; Eckenrode, "D-Battery, 110th AAA," p. 5; Forman, "Memories," p. 12; Wisniewski, "WWII," p. 24.
6. Ivan Glen Speer, Author's Interview.
7. Forman, "Memories," p. 12; Ivan Glen Speer, Author's Interview.
8. Ivan Glen Speer, Author's Interview.
9. Ibid.
10. Ibid. The town is believed to have been Bristol, England.
11. Ibid.
12. Ibid.; Dee Ann Shaw, "At Omaha," Owen Davies interview, *The Daily World* (Aberdeen WA), Nov.11, 2001, p. B1, hereafter referred to as Owen Davies, "At Omaha;" Harvey Edds, "Memories," p. 1; Dick Woolson, "Memories," p. 1.
13. Julius Reiver, "D-Day Recollections," manuscript, p. 3, hereafter referred to as Reiver, "D-Day Recollections."
14. U.S. War Department, *Antiaircraft Artillery Field Manual, Fire Control, Guns, FM4-121* (Washington, DC: GPO, December 22, 1943), p. 3-7, 10-16; *Life*, June 21, 1943.
15. Ivan Glen Speer, Author's Interview.
16. Ibid.
17. Ibid.
18. Eckenrode, "D-Battery, 110th AAA," p. 5; Ivan Glen Speer, Author's Interview. Speer and Worboys had arrived on the day they were told to, April 6.
19. Eckenrode, "D-Battery, 110th AAA," p. 5. Ack-Ack was a military slang term for antiaircraft fire. The term is derived from the British Army's old WWI radio-telephone phonetic alphabet in which "A" was pronounced "Ack" to eliminate any confusion. Thus "A.A." for anti-aircraft came out "Ack-Ack."
20. Eckenrode, "D-Battery, 110th AAA," p. 5-6.
21. Ibid., p. 6.
22. Ibid.
23. Ivan Glen Speer, Author's Interview.

24. Ibid.; Fred W. Crismon, *U.S. Military Tracked Vehicles* (Osceola, WI: Motorbooks International, 1992), p. 284-85; U.S. Department of the Army, Chief of Ordnance, *American Army Vehicles of World War II, Official U.S. Encyclopedia of Tanks, Trucks & Other Military Vehicles* (Andover, NJ: Portrayal Press, n.y. Reprint, originally published as *Catalogue of Standard Ordnance Items, Restricted-Confidential,* March 1, 1944 by GPO, Washington, DC), p. 73.

25. Ivan Glen Speer, Author's Interview.

26. Ibid.; Constance McLaughlin Green, Harry C. Thomson, and Peter C. Roots, *The Ordnance Department: Planning Munitions For War* (Washington, DC: Office of the Chief of Military History, Department of the Army, 1955), p. 306-08.

27. Eckenrode, "D-Battery, 110ᵗʰ AAA," p. 5.

28. Michael G. Kelakos, *"The Forty-Niners," Unit History of the Headquarters And Headquarters Battery, 49ᵗʰ AAA Brigade* (654ᵗʰ Engineer Bn., n.c., 1945), p. 12, hereafter referred to as Kelakos, *"The Forty-Niners."*

29. Ivan Glen Speer, Author's Interview.

30. Mollie Panter-Downes, *London War Notes, 1939-1945*, edited by William Shawn (NY: Farrar, Straus and Giroux, 1971). P. 326, hereafter referred to as Panter-Downes, *London War Notes.*

31. Terry W. Bye, Author's Interview.

32. James E. Chase, Letter to the Author.

33. Ibid.; Del Soll, "Memories of World War II, Battery B, 110th AAA Gun Bn." manuscript p. 1, hereafter referred to as Del Soll, "Memories."

34. Harold W. Mueller, Letter to the Author; Harold W. Mueller, Author's Interview.

35. Wisniewski, "WWII," p. 25.

36. Del Soll, "Memories," p. 1; James E. Chase, Letter to the Author.

37. Dell Soll interview in Wisniewski, "WWII," p.25-26.

38. James E. Chase, Letter to the Author; Wisniewski, "WWII," p.25-26.

39. Clinton C. Gardner, *D-Day And Beyond, A Memoir of War, Russia, and Discovery* (Philadelphia, PA: Xlibris, 2004), p.29 hereafter referred to as Gardner, *D-Day.*

40. Harvey Edds, "Memories," p. 1; Harvey W. Edds, letters to the Author.

41. Gardner, *D-Day,* p. 28-29. The 110ᵗʰ AAA scouting parties where scheduled to go in on the 13ᵗʰ wave at H-hour plus 110—or at 08:20 on D-Day—with members of the 116ᵗʰ Infantry Regiment of the 29ᵗʰ Infantry Division.

42. Ivan Glen Speer, Author's Interview; Johnson, "Franklin Johnson Papers; Harvey Edds, "Memories," p. 1.

43. Kelakos, *"The Forty-Niners,"* p. 14.
44. Ivan Glen Speer, Author's Interview; Johnson, "Franklin Johnson Papers; Harvey Edds, "Memories," p. 1.
45. Ivan Glen Speer, Author's Interview.
46. Ibid.; Terry W. Bye, Author's Interview.
47. Robert Capa, *Slightly Out of Focus* (NY: Henry Holt & Co., 1947), p. 142, hereafter referred to as Capa, *Slightly Out of Focus.*
48. Imperial War Museum, Sound Archives, SR 1604/H/C.
49. *Yank*, June 30, 1944, p. 9.
50. Forman, "Memories," p. 13; The highway was present-day A347 into Torpoint. "Hards" were specially constructed paved slipways at loading points along the harbor.
51. Reiver, "D-Day Recollections," p. 1; Forman, "Memories," p. 13.
52. Forman, "Memories," p. 13.
53. Forman, "Memories," p. 13; Johnson, "Franklin Johnson Papers."
54. Panter-Downes, *London War Notes*, p. 325.

Chapter 5

1. Walter Bedell Smith, *Eisenhower's Six Great Decisions* (NY: Longmans Green, 1956), p. 41-42.
2. Ivan Glen Speer, Author's Interview.
3. Eisenhower Papers, No. 1735, Dwight D. Eisenhower Library, Abilene, KS. Copy on file with the Author.
4. Joseph S. Blaylock Sr., Papers. From the Peter S. Kalikow World War II Collection, courtesy of The National D-Day Museum Foundation, Inc., New Orleans, Louisiana
5. Ivan Glen Speer, Author's Interview.
6. Ralph G. Martin interview, *Yank*, June 30, 1944.
7. Robert Miller interview, *Yank*, June 30, 1944.
8. Harold Baumgarten, *Eyewitness On Omaha Beach* (Jacksonville, FL: pvt. Ptd., 2000), p. 17; John J. Barnes, *Fragments of My Life With Company A, 116th Infantry Regiment* (Holland Patent, NY: Jam Publications, 2000), p. 63.
9. Ernest Hemingway, "Voyage to Victory," *Collier's*, July 22, 1944, p. 12, hereafter referred to as Hemingway, "Voyage to Victory."
10. Samuel Eliot Morison, *The Invasion of France and Germany, 1944-1945* (Boston: Little, Brown and Company, 1959), p. 136, hereafter referred to as Morison, *Invasion.*

11. Theodore L. Lamb papers, Veteran's Survey Project, U.S. Army Military History Institute, Carlisle Barracks, Pennsylvania, hereafter referred to as Theodore L. Lamb papers, USAMHI.
12. Fletcher Harris papers, Veteran's Survey Project, U.S. Army Military History Institute, Carlisle Barracks, Pennsylvania, hereafter referred to as Fletcher Harris papers, USAMHI.
13. Fletcher Harris papers, USAMHI; Theodore L. Lamb papers, USAMHI.
14. Ernie Pyle, "Even to Land Was A Miracle, Pyle Declares," Des Moines (IA) *Register & Tribune*, June 12, 1944.
15. Evermonte Huffman papers, Veteran's Survey Project, U.S. Army Military History Institute, Carlisle Barracks, Pennsylvania, hereafter referred to as Evermonte Huffman papers, USAMHI.
16. Capa, *Slightly Out of Focus*, p. 145, 147, 148-49.
17. Evermonte Huffman papers, USAMHI.
18. W. L. Wade, USNR, Com. LCT (L), Group 28, Action Report, July 25, 1944, as quoted in Morison, *Invasion*, p. 142, 150.
19. Des Moines (IA) *Register & Tribune*, June 10, 1944.
20. Theodore L. Lamb papers, USAMHI.
21. Glenn Edward Gibson papers, Veteran's Survey Project, U.S. Army Military History Institute, Carlisle Barracks, Pennsylvania.
22. Jerry W. Eads papers, Veteran's Survey Project, U.S. Army Military History Institute, Carlisle Barracks, Pennsylvania; Morison, *Invasion*, p. 140; Edmund G. Beacham, "Fortieth Anniversary of D-Day June 6, 1944, A Physician Remembers," *Maryland State Medical Journal*, Vol.33, No. 6, p. 451; John Man, *The D-Day Atlas* (NY: Facts On File, 1994), p. 54, hereafter referred to as Man, *D-Day Atlas*; Omar N. Bradley, *A Soldier's Story* (NY: Henry Holt and Company, 1951), p. 271-72, hereafter referred to as Bradley, *Soldier's Story*.
23. Morison, *Invasion*, p. 121, 144-45, 148.
24. Gardner, *D-Day*, p. 14; Forman, "Memories," p. 14-15; Reiver, "D-Day Recollections," p. 1; Eckenrode, "D-Battery, 110th AAA," p. 8-9; Vance Carter, Erie (PA) *Times-News*, Nov. 11, 1999. Actually, because of the resulting casualties and loss of equipment, Omaha Beach was never sufficiently cleared until the afternoon of June 10. (Morison, *Invasion*, p. 164).
25. Reiver, "D-Day Recollections," p. 1.
26. Hemingway, "Voyage to Victory," p. 57; Reiver, "D-Day Recollections," p. 1.
27. Dick Brammann, "Memories of World War II, Battery B, 110th AAA Gun Bn," manuscript, hereafter referred to as Brammann, "Memories."

According to Naval records, it was actually the light cruiser *H.M.S. Glasgow*, however at least nine destroyers—the *Glasgow, McCook, Carmick, Frankford, Emmons, Doyle, Harding, Thompson* and *Baldwin*—all steered within 900 yards of shore, nearly running aground, that day in an effort to pump thousands of their 5-inch shells at the enemy's fortified positions. In the four miles between Vierville to St. Lauren there were 8 casemated batteries, 35 pillboxes, 4 field artillery positions, 18 anti-tank gun positions, 6 mortar pits, 38 rocket pits and 85 machine-gun posts. (Richard Collier, *D-Day 06-06-44, The Normandy Landings*, London: Cassell, 1992, p.105 and 182)

28. Ivan Glen Speer, Author's Interview.

29. Julius Reiver, "Reiver's Retrievers—Battery D, 110th AAA Gun Bn (MBL)," manuscript, p. 4, hereafter referred to as Reiver, "Retrievers."

30. Ivan Glen Speer, Author's Interview; Reiver, "Retrievers," p. 4.

31. Ivan Glen Speer, Author's Interview.

32. Elmer J. Potzmann, Author's Interview. The contraption referred to is a "pole charge" with a two to four pound demolition pack attached. Some had as much as twelve pounds attached. Twin lines of prima-cord ran down the pole to two M1 fuse igniters. The length of the poles also varied. Most were eight to twelve feet fixed. Longer "pole charges" were hinged in four-foot sections for ease in carrying, after which the hinges locked into place as it was unfolded.

33. Clinton Gardner, "Memories of World War II, Battery B, 110th AAA Gun Bn., unidentified/ undated newspaper (interview) clipping (circa Norwich, VT area, 1994) hereafter referred to as Gardner, "Memories"; Clinton C. Gardner, Letter to Author; Harvey Edds, "Memories," p. 2.

34. Forman, "Memories," p. 15.

35. James Chase, "Memories of World War II, Battery B, 110th AAA Gun Bn., manuscript, hereafter referred to as James Chase, "Memories;" James E. Chase, Letter to Author; Arthur Hubbard, "Memories of World War II," manuscript; Wisniewski, "WWII," p. 34.

36. Eckenrode, "D-Battery, 110th AAA," p. 8-9; *The Evening* (Uniontown, PA) *Standard*, news- paper clipping, no date, circa Nov.1944; Commendations dated November 16, 1944 signed by Lt. Col. William F. Curren, Capt. Milton Goldsmith, Surgeon, and Capt. Wilbert L. Jones, CAC.

37. John Kreckler, "Memories of World War II, Battery B, 110th AAA Gun Bn.," manuscript; Harvey Edds, "Memories," p. 4.

38. Kelakos, *"The Forty-Niners,"* p. 21; Charles C. Wertenbaker, "Beachheads of Normandy, The Big Days" *Life*, June 19, 1944, p. 31, hereafter referred to as Wertenbaker, "Beachheads of Normandy."

39. Wertenbaker, "Beachheads of Normandy" p. 31; Ivan Glen Speer, Author's Interview; Lester Cohen, "Memories of World War II, Battery B, 110th AAA Gun Bn.," manuscript, p, 1, hereafter referred to as Cohen, "Memories."

40. Man, *D-Day Atlas*, p. 57; Robin Neillands and Roderick de Norman, *D-Day, 1944* (London: Weidenfeld and Nicolson, 1993), p. 156, 229; Rad Dedmon, "From Massachusetts to Normandy, Capt. William C. Goodwine and the 18th AAA," *Military History*, January 1998, p. 12; Sugarman, *My War*, p. 78.

41. Forman, "Memories," p. 18.

42. Eckenrode, "D-Battery, 110th AAA," p. 10.

43. Ibid.; Wertenbaker, "Beachheads of Normandy," p. 31.

44. Ibid.; Evermonte Huffman papers, USAMHI

45. Eckenrode, "D-Battery, 110th AAA," p. 11.

46. Ibid.; Wertenbaker, "Beachheads of Normandy," p. 31; Owen Davies, "At Omaha;" Leo C. Kania, Letter to Author.

47. Harvey Edds, "Memories," p. 4-5.

48. Johnson, "Franklin Johnson Papers."

49. Pyle, *Brave Men*, p. 263. The "pillbox" was one of the German Army's main defensive fortifications used along the Atlantic "Wall." They were huge reinforced concrete structures, two to three feet thick, round like an old-fashioned pillbox, with a small hole or horizontal slit from which they could fire their weapons while protected from enemy fire. The other American crew members involved in this incident was Hyman Haas and Frank Furey of Brooklyn, NY, Cpl. John Jourdain and Austin Laurent of New Orleans, LA, Ray Bullock of Coello, IL and Frank Bartolomeo of Ulevi, PA. The name of their half-track, mounted with a 37mm gun, was "Blip," which represented the first letters of each of their home town or states.

50. Eckenrode, "D-Battery, 110th AAA," p. 12; Ivan Glen Speer, Author's Interview; Johnson, "Franklin Johnson Papers.

51. Ivan Glen Speer, Author's Interview; Reiver, "Retrievers," p. 4; Reiver, "D-Day Recollections," p. 2. A Rhino Ferry was an American-designed pontoon barge 42 feet by 176 feet, powered by two large 500 horsepower outboard motors.

52. Eckenrode, "D-Battery, 110th AAA," p. 12.

53. Ivan Glen Speer, Author's Interview.

54. Ibid.

55. Eckenrode, "D-Battery, 110th AAA," p. 123; Ivan Glen Speer, Author's Interview.

56. Eckenrode, "D-Battery, 110th AAA," p. 13; Wertenbaker, "Beachheads of Normandy," p. 31; Cleaves Jones papers, transcript, National Archives; Stanley Bach papers, transcript, National Archives.

57. Eckenrode, "D-Battery, 110th AAA," p. 13; Ivan Glen Speer, Author's Interview.

58. Ibid. She was later sent to an internment camp established on the Isle of Man in the English Channel. (*Yank*, Vol. 3, No. 3—July 7, 1944, p. 4).

59. Ivan Glen Speer, Author's Interview.

60. Ibid.

61. Eckenrode, "D-Battery, 110th AAA," p. 14.

62. Cohen, "Memories," p. 1.

63. Owen Davies, "At Omaha."

64. Cohen, "Memories," p. 2.

65. Elmer J. Potzmann, Author's Interview.

66. Harvey Edds, "Memories," p. 6. Today 1,500 American soldiers are listed as Missing In Action (MIAs) or unaccountable from this battle. "I feel quite sure," added Edds, "that they are some of the men who were left to sink to the bottom of the ocean on D-Day."

67. Frank Wisniewski, "Memories of World War II," typed manuscript; Ivan Glen Speer, Author's Interview.

68. Forman, "Memories," p. 16; Eckenrode, "D-Battery, 110th AAA," p. 14; Johnson, "Franklin Johnson Papers; Reiver, "D-Day Recollections," p. 2.

69. Johnson, "Franklin Johnson Papers; Reiver, "D-Day Recollections," p. 2.

70. Ed Kosicki, "Memories of World War II," typed manuscript; Johnson, "Franklin Johnson Papers; Reiver, "D-Day Recollections," p. 2; James Chase, "Memories, typed manuscript; Kenneth Lang, "Memories of World War II, Battery B, 110th AAA Gun Bn.," manuscript.

71. Dick Brammann, "Memories of World War II, Battery B, 110th AAA Gun Bn.," manuscript.

72. Dan Ciaburri, "Memories of World War II, Battery B, 110th AAA Gun Bn.," manuscript; Harvey Edds, "Memories," p. 7.

73. Johnson, "Franklin Johnson Papers; Harvey Edds, "Memories," p. 7.

74. Harvey Edds, "Memories," p. 6.

75. Henry F. Thake, Letter to Author; Rad Dedmon, "From Massachusetts to Normandy, Capt. William C. Goodwine and the 18th AAA," *Military History*, January 1998, p. 12-13; Elmer J. Potzmann, Author's Interview.

76. Harold Mueller, Letter to Author; Harold W. Mueller, Author's Interview.

77. Reiver, "Retrievers," p. 5; Reiver, "D-Day Recollections," p. 3; Eckenrode, "D-Battery, 110th AAA," p. 14-15. Within 24 hours at this location, three German snipers concealed in the hedgerows surrounding the 110th AAA killed at least twenty U.S. infantrymen before all three could finally be killed or captured. (Eckenrode, "D-Battery, 110th AAA," p. 16)

78. Elmer J. Potzmann, Author's Interview; Harold W. Mueller, Author's Interview; Terry Bye, Author's Interview.

79. Eckenrode, "D-Battery, 110th AAA," p. 14.

80. Ibid., p. 15.

81. Ibid., p. 14-15; Commendation, Headquarters, 49th AAA Brigade, APO 305, U.S. Army, dated June 24, 1944, Signed by Maj. Gen. L. T. Gerow, 1st Endorsement, Lt. Gen. O. N. Bradley, First U.S. Army, Commanding; Commendation on Performance of Duty, Headquarters, 49th AAA Brigade, APO 230, U.S. Army, dated: Germany, May 10, 1945, Signed by Brig. Gen. E. W. Timberlake, 1st Endorsement signed by Hdqs., 18th AAA Group, Col Thomas W. Munford, CAC, 2nd Endorsement signed by Hdqs., 110th AAA, Lt. Col. William F. Curren Jr.; *Stars & Stripes*, October 10, 1944, p. 4.

82. Ivan Glen Speer, Author's Interview; Eckenrode, "D-Battery, 110th AAA," p. 62.

83. Harvey Edds, "Memories," p. 2-4; James Chase, "Memories," p. 1; James E. Chase, Letter to Author; Gardner, *D-Day*, p. 34-35, 36; Clinton Gardner, "Memories;" Clinton C. Gardner, Letter to Author. Gardner remained at the base of the cliffs on west Omaha Beach nearly 30 hours before he was found and received medical treatment. He recovered after hospitalization and will return to the battalion for the advance into Paris.

Chapter 6

1. *Yank*, June 30, 1944, p.10; July 14, 1944, p. 17.
2. Forman, "Memories," p. 17.
3. Owen Davies, "At Omaha."
4. Ibid.
5. Elmer J. Potzmann, Author's Interview; Elmer Potzmann, Letters to Author; Harvey W. Edds, Letters to Author; Located just south of Omaha Beach, southeast of Vierville, near Saint-Laurent-sur-Mer, the actual site of the emergency landing strip is where the U.S. military cemetery is located today. This became the first operational American

airfield in France. The 110th AAA was assigned to guard its approaches on June 7. Both D and A batteries of the unit were transferred to other locations during the following weeks but B and C Batteries would remain to cover ARL-9 through July 15.

6. Harvey W. Edds, Author's Interview

7. Elmer J. Potzmann, Author's Interview; Elmer Potsmann, Letter to Author.

8. Morison, *Invasion*, p.161-62; Harvey W. Edds, Author's Interview.

9. Ivan Glen Speer, Author's Interview; Eckenrode, "D-Battery, 110th AAA," p.16; Reiver, "D-Day Recollections," p. 3; Reiver, "Retrievers," p. 5. At the time it was reported that D-Battery was the first U.S. 90mm unit to down a plane over Omaha Beach but confirmation several months later would determine that the battery was the first to down a German plane over *any* French soil, including Utah beach.

10. Elmer J. Potzmann, Author's Interview; Elmer Potzmann, Letter to Author.

11. Ivan Glen Speer, Author's Interview.

12. Ibid.

13. Ibid.

14. Ibid.

15. Ibid.

16. Ibid.

17. Ibid

18. Joseph Balkoski, *Beyond the Beachhead, The 29th Infantry Division in Normandy* (Stackpole Books, Mechanicsburg, PA, 1989) p. 67, hereafter referred to as Balkoski, *Beyond the Beachhead*.

19. Eckenrode, "D-Battery, 110th AAA," p. 15.

20. Roscoe C. Blunt Jr., *Inside the Battle of the Bulge*, (Westport, CT: Praeger, 1994), p. 5-6, hereafter referred to as Blunt, *Inside the Battle of the Bulge*.

21. Ibid.

22. Foreman, "Memories," p. 17; Pyle, at 40 years old, 5' 8" and 115 pounds, often looked even more diminutive because of his habit of wearing several layers of clothes to prevent getting cold so easily; Col. Reiver and his battery had actually been informed several days in advance that Pyle would be visiting sometime on the 17th.

23. Eckenrode, "D-Battery, 110th AAA," p. 19.

24. Pyle, *Brave Men*, p. 264-65. These boys, along with their names and hometowns, were all noted in a newspaper column that followed and were also mentioned in his book, *Brave Men*, in Chapter 28, about the "American Ack-Ack" boys, in pages 263-270.

25. Ibid.
26. Reiver, "D-Day Recollections," p.1.
27. Ibid.
28. Arthur William "Bill" Nelson, Author's interview.
29. Pyle, *Brave Men*, p. 265.
30. Reiver, "D-Day Recollections," p. 2.
31. Pyle, *Brave Men*, p. 265-66.
32. *Time*, July 17, 1944, p. 65; Clyde Libby, Author's Interview.
33. Morison, *Invasion of France and Germany*, p. 166; Nigel Cawthorne, *Fighting Them on the Beaches* (Edison, NJ: Chartwell Books, 2002), p. 207, hereafter referred to as Cawthorne, *Fighting Them on the Beaches*.
34. Walter Bedell Smith, *Eisenhower's Six Great Decisions*, p. 70; Eckenrode, "D-Battery, 110th AAA," p. 18.
35. Eckenrode, "D-Battery, 110th AAA," p. 19.
36. Reiver, "Reiver's Retrievers," p. 5; DUKWs, often referred to simply as "ducks" by the GIs, were U.S. Army amphibious vehicles that could boat through water and drive onto land.
37. Cawthorne, *Fighting Them on the Beaches*, p. 206-09.
38. Edds, "Memories," p. 9-10.
39. Eckenrode, "D-Battery, 110th AAA," p. 32.
40. Ibid. "ETO" was military parlance for the "European Theater of Operations" during WWII.
41. Ivan Glen Speer, Author's Interview.
42. John P. Cooper Jr., *The History of the 110th Field Artillery*, (Baltimore: Maryland Historical Society, 1953), p. 119, hereafter referred to as Cooper, *110th F.A.*; Eckenrode, "D-Battery, 110th AAA," p. 33.
43. Cooper, *110th F.A.*, p. 122-23. These Propaganda Shells were used around July 9-10.
44. Ivan Glen Speer, Author's Interview.
45. Bradley, *Soldiers' Story*, p. 342.
46. *Life*, August 14, 1944, p. 21, 23.
47. Bradley, *Soldiers' Story*, p. 342. Others were credited with similar devices and some tanks had single or double prongs on the front designed to punch a hole into a hedgerow to insert explosive charges.
48. The 29th Infantry Division consisted of three regiments, the 115th Infantry Regiment, the 116th Infantry Regiment, and the 175th Infantry Regiment. The 115th and 175th were mostly Maryland National Guard units while the 116th was mostly Virginia National Guard units.
49. Cawthorne, *Fighting Them on the Beaches*, p. 211.
50. The total casualties of killed, wounded, or missing would be equaled six months later in the Battle of the Bulge.

51. Eckenrode, "D-Battery, 110ᵗʰ AAA," p. 33-34.
52. Ibid.
53. Ibid., p. 35; Reiver, "Reiver's Retrievers," p. 6. Cheney and his quad-50 were assigned to gun #1 of D-Battery.
54. Elmer Potzmann, Author's interview.
55. Forman, "Memories," p. 19.
56. Edds, "Memories,", p. 8; Cohen, "Memories," p. 1. McNair would become the highest ranking Allied officer killed in Europe.
57. Cawthorne, *Fighting Them on the Beaches*, p. 212.
58. James Chase, "Memories;" James E. Chase, letter to Elmer Potzmann dated May 11, 1995; James E. Chase, Letter to the Author; Terry Bye, Author's Interview; Henry Thake, Author's Interview.
59. Ibid; Edds, "Memories," p. 8. Weller and Bridges were both from Missouri. They are both buried at the National Cemetery at Normandy. Lt. Coates eventually survived but suffered disabling fractures and other severe wounds. In addition Capt. Chase's injuries resulted in total deafness in one ear. Both he and Coates were eventually hospitalized for extended periods of time in England as well as U.S. Army hospitals back in the States and placed on inactive status in March 1946.
60. Ivan Glen Speer, Author's Interview.
61. Glover S. Johns, Jr., *The Clay Pigeons of St. Lo* (Mechanicsburg, PA: Stackpole Books, 2002), p. 228; *Life*, August 14, 1944, p. 21, 23; Marie-Louise Osmont, *The Normandy Diary of Marie-Louise Osmont, 1940-1944*. (NY: Random House, 1994), p. 62.
62. Edds, "Memories," p. 7; Cohen, "Memories," p. 1.
63. William A. Gushurst, Letter to Author.
64. Lou Azrael, Baltimore *News-Post*, as quoted in Balkoski, *Beyond the Beachhead*, p. 275.

Chapter 7

1. Soll was taken to a field hospital where his hand was operated on and then flown back to England where he remained in the hospital at Swindon for 4 to 5 months. He later returned and was assigned to work in a "repo-depo," where he equipped new recruits being sent to the front.
2. Eckenrode, "D-Battery, 110ᵗʰ AAA," p. 38.
3. Cooper, *110ᵗʰ F.A.*, p. 123; Richard Holmes, *The D-Day Experience, From the Invasion to the Liberation of Paris* (London: Carlton Books, 2004), p. 43.

4. Gardner, *D-Day*, p. 39.
5. Nigel de Lee, "The Breakout," in *D-Day, Operation Overlord, From the Landing at Normandy to the Liberation of Paris*, edited by Bernard C. Nalty, (NY: Smithmark, 1993), p. 182, hereafter referred to as Nalty, *D-Day*.
6. Ibid., p. 208.
7. Cawthorne, *Fighting Them on the Beaches*, p. 213.
8. Ivan Glen Speer, Author's Interview
9. Eckenrode, "D-Battery, 110th AAA," p. 37-38. The city was totally destroyed. It was never rebuilt but some of the ruins was left as a memorial to the war.
10. Henry Thake, Author's Interview.
11. Ibid.
12. Ibid.
13. Ibid. The confused or angry soldier shooting at the pilot was later reprimanded and transferred out of the battery. Captain Sisson and several non-coms got in a jeep and went to pick the pilot up. Thake, Carroll and the other soldier—whose name Thake could not recall—later received medals for their action.
14. Eckenrode, "D-Battery, 110th AAA," p. 38-39.
15. Ibid., p. 38.
16. Ibid., p. 39.
17. Ibid.
18. Trevor N. Dupuy, *The Military History of World War II*. 18 vols. (NY: Franklin Watts, 1962-1965), Vol. 2, p. 26-27, hereafter referred to as Dupuy, *Military History of World War II*. Lt. Gen. Omar N. Bradley had been placed in command of the newly formed 12th Army Group on Aug. 1, 1944 and on that date Lt. Gen. Courtney H. Hodges was placed in command of the U.S. First Army. Later known as the "Falaise Gap," it was closed on August 18. A total of 50,000 German troops were captured, at least 10,000 were killed in the fighting to escape the trap, and reportedly somewhere between 20,000 to 40,000 escaped.
19. Eckenrode, "D-Battery, 110th AAA," p. 40.
20. Reivers, "Retrievers," p. 7.
21. Ibid.
22. L. James Thieriault, Author's Interview.
23. Eckenrode, "D-Battery, 110th AAA," p. 41.
24. Ibid.
25. Forman, "Memories," p. 19-20.
26. Roger Cirillo, "Pursuit to the Seine," in Nalty, *D-Day*, p. 213; Ivan Glen Speer, Author's Interview; Capt. Jules Reiver maintained that

being one of the first American units to enter Paris was another reward his battery received—the first being the publicity and interview involving journalist Ernie Pyle—because of being the first American unit to shoot down an enemy aircraft on French soil ("D-Day Recollections," p. 4). Entering on the 24th, though, was on his own initiative.

27. Larry Collins and Dominique LaPierre, *Is Paris Burning?* (NY: Simon and Schuster, 1965), p. 255, hereafter referred to as Collins and LaPierre, *Is Paris Burning?*; Roger Cirillo, "Pursuit to the Seine," in Nalty, *D-Day*, p. 213.
28. Ivan Glen Speer, Author's Interview
29. Gardner, *D-Day*, p. 39-40; Commendation issued to 110th AAA Gun Battalion (Mbl), dated May 10, 1945.
30. Edds, "Memories," p. 11; Commendation issued to 110th AAA Gun Battalion (Mbl), dated May 10, 1945.
31. Eckenrode, "D-Battery, 110th AAA," p. 42.
32. Pyle, *Brave Men*, p. 313-14.
33. Theodore "Ted" N. Noel. Author's Interview.
34. William Walton, "The Liberation of Montmartre," *Life*, Sept. 11, 1944, p. 38.
35. Eckenrode, "D-Battery, 110th AAA," p. 42; Charles Cawthon, "July, 1944: St. Lo," *American Heritage*, June 1974, p. 83.
36. Don Whitehead, "Allies Enter Paris, August 25," *AP* Aug. 25, 1944, *Twentieth Century America: A Primary Source Collection from the Associated Press*. Vol. III, WWII 1939-1945. Alan Brinkley, ed. (Danbury, CT: Grolier, 1995), p. 149. The FFI was the Forces Francaises de l'Interieur, (French Forces of the Interior).
37. Edds, "Harvey's Story," p. 11.
38. Harry Pasku, *Memories of World War II, Battery B, 110th AAA Gun Bn.*
39. Nelvin M. Tyree, 441st AAA (AW) Bn.Bty. D, Letters addressed to wife and parents, one dated Aug. 30, 1944 and one dated Sept. 7, 1944. "Saland" loosely translated means "dirty person."
40. Forman, "Memories," p. 20; Johnson, "Franklin Johnson Papers," p. 5; Eckenrode, "D-Battery, 110th AAA," p. 44; Porte de Montrouge is a south-central suburb of Paris. The right turn was made on Brune Boulevard at Cite University where they set up in Parc de Montsouris.
41. Edds, "Harvey's Story," p. 11; Wisniewski, "WWII," p. 45. Battery B was set up about 3-4 miles east of A-Battery.
42. William A. Gushurst, Letter to Author. The rail yard was in the Ivry sur-Seine district of Paris, about 15 miles east of the Battery A & B positions.

43. Ibid.
44. Forman, "Memories," p. 20.
45. Edds, "Memories," p. 11.
46. Eckenrode,"D-Battery, 110th AAA," p. 44; Collins and LaPierre, *Is Paris Burning?*, p. 340.
47. Reiver, "Reiver's Retrievers," p. 7.
48. Ibid., p. 8.
49. Ibid.
50. Ibid.
51. Eckenrode, "D-Battery, 110th AAA," p. 30.
52. Reiver, "Reiver's Retrievers," p. 6. Colonel Munford was commander of the 18th AAA Group.
53. Ibid.
54. Ivan Glen Speer, Author's Interview.
55. Eckenrode, "D-Battery, 110th AAA," p. 45.
56. Ibid., p. 45-46.
57. Ibid., p. 46.

Chapter 8

1. *Life*, Vol. 17, No. 10 (Sept. 4, 1944), p. 19.
2. David P. Colley, *The Road To Victory, The Untold Story of World War II's Red Ball Express*, (Washington, DC: Brassey's, 2000), p. xiv, 47-48, hereafter referred to as Colley, *Road To Victory*; Ivan Glen Speer, Author's Interview; Wayne Edmondson, Author's Interview; Gardner, *D-Day*, p. 40.
3. Ivan Glen Speer, Author's Interview.
4. Ibid.
5. Colley, *Road To Victory*, p. 19-23, 49-50, 108.
6. Ivan Glen Speer, Author's Interview.
7. Colley, *Road To Victory*, p. 50 and 108; Ivan Glen Speer, Author's Interview.
8. Colley, *Road To Victory*, p. 52.
9. Ivan Glen Speer, Author's Interview.
10. The record tonnage of 12,342 was made on August 29. The official dates of existence for the Red Ball Express was Aug. 25, 1944 to Nov. 16, 1944 although some transporting after that date was done. During that time, a total of 412,193 tons of supplies was transported. (Colley, *Road To Victory*, p. xiv).
11. Eckenrode, "D-Battery, 110th AAA," p. 47.

12. Edds, "Memories," p. 73; Harvey Edds, Letters to Author.
13. War Dept., *Pocket Guide To The Cities of Belgium and Luxembourg* (Washington, DC: GPO, 1944), p. iii; Eckenrode, "D-Battery, 110th AAA," p. 47.
14. Eckenrode, "D-Battery, 110th AAA," p. 47; Edds, "The Josee Story," p. 1. The 12th Army's other big supply center was behind the First Army's right flank at Verdun.
15. Edds, "The Josee Story," p. 1.
16. Ibid.
17. Ibid.; Edds, Letters to the Author.
18. Forman, "Memories," p. 23.
19. Edds, "Harvey's Story," p. 12; IFF is a reference to "Identification Friend or Foe" radar equipment.
20. Eckenrode, "D-Battery, 110th AAA," p.48.
21. Ibid.
22. Parrish, *Encyclopedia of World War II*, p. 1547; Jozef Garlinski, *Hitler's Last Weapons* (NY: Times Books, 1978), p. 171 and 225. A total of 1,096 V-1s and 27 V-2s fell on Liege.
23. Ivan Glen Speer, Author's Interview.
24. John Batchelor and Ian Hogg, *Artillery* (NY: Charles Scribner's Sons, 1972), p.73-74, here- after referred to as Batchelor and Hogg, *Artillery*; Parrish, *Encyclopedia of World War II*, p. 1547; Garlinski, *Hitler's Last Weapons*, p. 225.
25. Ivan Glen Speer, Author's Interview.
26. Batchelor and Hogg, *Artillery*, p. 73-74; Parrish, *Encyclopedia of World War II*, p. 1547; Forman, "Memories," p. 22.
27. Garlinski, *Hitler's Last Weapons*, p. 171; Colley, *Road To Victory*, p. 172; Gardner, *D-Day*, p. 40.
28. Bradley, *Soldier's Story*, p. 432-33; Eckenrode, "D-Battery, 110th AAA," p 48-49. The meeting was on October 14. The battalion was transferred out three days later, on October 17.
29. Ibid.; Edds, "Memories," p. 13.
30. Roger N. Hutchinson Jr., Battery C, 109th AAA Gun Bn., in letter to his family dated Oct. 17, 1944. In Author's possession.
31. Ibid., letters dated Nov. 3 and Nov. 8, 1944, in Author's possession.
32. Bradley, *Soldier's Story*, p.439-440.
33. Persistently bothered by this report off and on over the years, Edds made numerous inquiries in the mid-1990s and finally located a family who put him in touch with Josee. Edds was able to inform his battery at a reunion in 1995 that although a number of buzz bombs had indeed hit in the area of the Scevenels home, Josee *had not* been killed.

"We hid in the basement of our home," she advised. By then a widow, she sent him an updated photo of herself and they continued to corresponded for some time.

34. Reiver, "Reiver's Retrievers," p.2.
35. Ivan Glen Speer, Author's Interview.
36. Ibid.
37. Ibid. The family name of the caretakers was DeCreppe. Many of the GIs of Battery-D corresponded with the family, including Robert and Margarette, years after the war; some as late as fifty years later.
38. Forman, "Memories," p. 23; Eckenrode, "D-Battery, 110th AAA," p. 51.
39. Eckenrode,"D-Battery, 110th AAA," p. 51.
40. Ivan Glen Speer, Author's Interview
41. Ibid.
42. Ibid.; Reiver, "Reiver's Retrievers," p.2.
43. Ivan Glen Speer, Author's Interview.
44. Ivan Glen Speer, Author's Interview; Wayne Edmondson, Author's Interview; Reiver, "Reiver's Retrievers," p.2. "I knew nothing of this until a year or two after the War," advised Julius Reiver. Army authorities continued sending him bills for the coal for several years, insisting he admit making the original requisition so proper restitution could be made.
45. Ivan Glen Speer, Author's Interview; Eckenrode,"D-Battery, 110th AAA," p. 50-51; Edds, "Memories," p. 13.
46. Ibid.

Chapter 9

1. Charles Whiting, *Siegfried, The Nazis Last Stand* (NY: Stein and Day, 1982), p. 131, here- after referred to as Whiting, *Siegfried*.
2. Terry Bye, Author's Interview.
3. Forman, "Memories," p. 23; Harold W. Mueller, Author's Interview. During the next several days two armored divisions, two airborne divisions, and regiments and combat commands from other infantry and armored units would be shifted to meet the intensified German attacks which rapidly began to form an expanding "bulge" in the U.S. First Army front line thus causing the battle to become known as the "Battle of the Bulge," so named by Winston Churchill.
4. "After the Battle of Normandy," Peiper once noted, "my unit was made up of young fanatical soldiers. A good deal of them had lost parents, sisters, or brothers during the bombing raids. They had seen

for themselves the total destruction of the German people, their homes and workplaces; their hatred was such that I could not always keep them under control." There was no evidence that he ever tried.

5. David Jordan, *Battle of the Bulge, The First 24 Hours* (London: Amber Books, 2003), p. 166; Michael Reynolds, *The Devil's Adjutant, Jochen Peiper, Panzer Leader* (NY: Sarpedon Publishers, 1998), p. 76-78, hereafter referred to as Reynolds, *The Devil's Adjutant*; Michael R. Craddock, "Kampfgruppe Peiper," *Stars and Stripes*, December 20, 1992, p. 22. "Burp Gun" was a slang term used by G.I.s in reference to the low-pitched fast-action sound made by the German 9mm Schmeisser MP-40 machine pistol.

6. *Army and Navy Journal*, February 24, 1945.

7. Edds, "Memories," p. 13-14; Wisniewski, "WWII," p. 50; Ivan Glen Speer, Author's Interview. As soon as he could, Edds took the girl back to her grandparents' home nearby, where she had been staying. Of course, they were overjoyed at her safe return and proceeded to excitedly thank him, hug him and kiss him. It was later determined, in the confusion around this area, some of these strafing runs were made by our own planes.

8. Ivan Glen Speer, Author's Interview.

9. Charles Whiting, *Massacre At Malmedy* (London: Leo Cooper, 1971), p. 43-44, hereafter referred to as Whiting, *Massacre*; Craddock, "Kampfgruppe Peiper," *Stars and Stripes*, December 20, 1992, p. 22; Reynolds, *The Devil's Adjutant*, p. 87 and 98.

10. Hugh M. Cole, *The Ardennes: Battle of the Bulge* (Washington, DC: Office of the Chief of Military History, Department of the Army, 1965), p. 260-264, hereafter referred to as Cole, *The Ardennes*; Reynolds, *The Devil's Adjutant*, p. 88-93; Whiting, *Massacre*, p. 49-56. Some were still able to flee from the field after the Germans left but then died later. A few others did manage to survive the ordeal and made it back to the American lines to report the incident.

11. Forman, "Memories," p. 23.

12. Frank Wisniewski, "Memories," p. 1; Wisniewski, "WWII," p. 50-51.

13. Whiting, *Massacre*, p. 59.

14. Eckenrode, "D-Battery, 110th AAA," p.53; *Army and Navy Journal*, February 24, 1945.

15. Eckenrode, "D-Battery, 110th AAA," p.53.

16. Cole, *The Ardennes*, p. 337-340; Reynolds, *The Devil's Adjutant*, p.147.

17. Ivan Glen Speer, Author's Interview.

18. Reynolds, *The Devil's Adjutant*, p.145; Ivan Glen Speer, Author's Interview.

19. Bob Hall, *Memorable Bulge Incidents* (Arlington, VA: VBOB, 1995), p.1.
20. Reynolds, *The Devil's Adjutant*, p. 145.
21. Eckenrode, "D-Battery, 110th AAA," p.54; Julius Reiver, "The Battle at the Gas Dump," p. 2. The official designation of this Gas Dump on the military map was "K-6707."
22. Reiver, "The Battle at the Gas Dump, p. 2-3.
23. Eckenrode, "D-Battery, 110th AAA," p. 56-58; Reiver, "The Battle at the Gas Dump," p.3-4.
24. Eckenrode, "D-Battery, 110th AAA," p. 58.
25. L. James Theriault, Author's Interview.
26. Letter of Commendation, Unit Citation, from Headquarters 49th AAA Brigade, Brig. Gen. E. W Timberlake to Lt. Col. William F. Curren Jr., 110th AAA Gun Bn., dated May 10, 1945, p. 2.
27. Reynolds, *The Devil's Adjutant*, p. 91 and 151.
28. *Army and Navy Journal*, February 24, 1945.
29. Blunt, *Inside the Battle of the Bulge*, p. 45.
30. Ivan Glen Speer, Author's Interview; Forman, "Memories," p. 23; Harold Mueller, "Battle of the Bulge Memories," p. 1; Harold Mueller, "Massacre at Malmedy, Belgium," p. 1; Harold W. Mueller, Author's Interview.
31. Kenneth Lang, "Memories of World War II, Battery B, 110th AAA Gun Bn.;" Wayne Edmondson, Author's Interview; Ivan Glen Speer, Author's Interview; Nelvin M. Tyree, various letters to his family, dated 9/7/44, 10/10/44, 10/13/44, 11/18/44, in author's possession.
32. Mueller, "Battle of the Bulge Memories," p. 1; Harold W. Mueller, Author's Interview; The G.I.'s little finger on his right hand was nearly severed. When he was sent back to a field hospital, the doctors wanted to amputate. He refused and insisted they stitch it up. He returned to the battery with a wrapped hand soon afterwards.
33. Harold W. Mueller, Author's Interview; Elmer J. Potzmann, Author's Interview; Blunt, *Inside the Battle of the Bulge*, p. 81.
34. Eckenrode, "D-Battery, 110th AAA," p. 58-59; Ivan Glen Speer, Author's Interview; Reiver, "The Battle at the Gas Dump," p. 1, 3-4; Technically, the 110th AAA Battalion as part of the 49th AAA Brigade, was under the 82nd Airborne Division and that is why one of its officials awarded the medals. Although Army officials knew that the details of the article was wrong, it apparently continued to promote the story and use the publicity. The fact that troops of the 526th Armored Infantry Battalion did set fire to some of the gasoline from the Francorchamps dump the day before simply added to the confusion. In 1965 a similar scene was portrayed in the movie "Battle

of the Bulge," staring Henry Fonda. It even found its way into the Army's official history, *The Ardennes*, by Hugh M. Cole (p. 266) published that same year, but most historians now agree it never happened—a German unit was never driven back or defeated by a wall of fire at the gas dumps. Instead, it was simply "a fire-fight!"

35. Gardner, *D-Day*, p. 46-47; Clinton Gardner, Letter to Author.
36. Edds, "Memories," p.14; Forman, "Memories," p. 23-24; Gardner, *D-Day*, p. 48-49; Clinton Gardner, Letter to Author.
37. Mueller, "Battle of the Bulge Memories," p. 1.
38. Ivan Glen Speer, Author's Interview; Reynolds, *The Devil's Adjutant*, p.114 and 121; Cole, *The Ardennes*, p. 278-79; Trevor N. Dupuy, David L. Bongard, and Richard C. Anderson Jr., *Hitler's Last Gamble, The Battle of the Bulge, December 1944-January 1945* (NY: Harper—Collins, 1994), p. 12-13; Mueller, "Battle of the Bulge Memories," p. 1; Harold W. Mueller, Author's Interview. Although easily confused with "grief" for the American forces, "Greif" is German for Condor. The operation was under the direction of Waffen-SS Otto Skorzeny, the commando officer of the 150th Panzer Brigade.
39. Ivan Glen Speer, Author's Interview; Constance McLaughlin Green, Harry C. Thomson, and Peter C. Roots, *The Ordnance Department: Planning Munitions For War.* (Washington, DC: Office of the Chief of Military History Department of the Army, 1955), p. 306; Ivan Glen Speer, Author's Interview; Terry Bye, Author's Interview; Harold W. Mueller, Author's Interview.
40. Ivan Glen Speer, Author's Interview.
41. Harold W. Mueller, Author's Interview.
42. L. James Theriault, Author's Interview; Edds, "Memories," p.15.
43. Forman, "Memories," p. 24; Jerome Varrato, *Middletown* (CT) *Press*, December 11, 1994, p. 6; Harold W. Mueller, Author's Interview.
44. Forman, "Memories," p. 24; Ivan Glen Speer, Author's Interview.
45. Edds, "Memories," p.15.
46. Ibid.
47. Ibid.
48. Eckenrode, "D-Battery, 110th AAA," p. 60; Arthur Hubbard, "Battery-B Memories," p. 1.
49. Blunt, *Inside the Battle of the Bulge*, p. 61; Edds, "Memories," p.16.
50. L. James Theriault, Author's Interview.
51. Ivan Glen Speer, Author's Interview; Wayne Edmondson, Author's Interview.
52. Eckenrode, "D-Battery, 110th AAA," p. 60.
53. Edds, "Memories," p.16.

54. Mueller, "Battle of the Bulge Memories," p. 1; Eckenrode, "D-Battery, 110th AAA," p. 61.
55. Forman, "Memories," p. 24.
56. Robert Goralski, *World War II Almanac, 1931-1945*, (NY:Bonanza Books, 1981), p. 375; "Battle of the Bulge Facts," (Arlington, VA: Veterans of the Battle of the Bulge, 1994), p. 1-2.

Chapter 10

1. Harold W. Mueller, in *Everyday Heroes of the Battle of the Bulge in WWII*, (St. Louis, Mo: Veterans of the Battle of the Bulge, St. Louis Gateway Chapter, 2002), Taped interview; Forman, "Memories," p. 25-26.
2. Morning Reports, Battery D, 110th AAA Gun Battalion (Mbl), dated February 28, 1945; Eckenrode, "D-Battery, 110th AAA," p. 62.
3. Johnson, "Franklin Johnson Papers."
4. Ibid.
5. Ibid.
6. Morning Reports, Battery A, 110th AAA Gun Battalion (Mbl), dated March 2, 1945; Morning Reports, Battery D, 110th AAA Gun Battalion (Mbl), dated March 2, 1945; Eckenrode, "D-Battery, 110th AAA," p. 62.
7. Eckenrode, "D-Battery, 110th AAA," p. 62.
8. Ibid.
9. Ibid., p. 62-63.
10. Ibid.
11. Ivan Glen Speer, Author's Interview.
12. Ibid.
13. E. Paul Semmens, "The Hammer of Hell, The Coming of Age of Antiaircraft Artillery in WWII," *Air Defense Artillery*, January 2000, p. 43-45; Ken Hechler, *The Bridge at Remagen* (Missoula, MT: Pictorial Histories Publishing Company, 2001), p. 159.
14. Eckenrode, "D-Battery, 110th AAA," p. 63.
15. Ibid.
16. Ibid.
17. Ivan Glen Speer, Author's Interview.
18. Eckenrode, "D-Battery, 110th AAA," p. 63.
19. Morning Reports, dated March 12, March 13, and March 14, 1945.
20. Ibid.
21. Eckenrode, "D-Battery, 110th AAA," p. 64.
22. Ibid.
23. Terry W. Bye, Author's Interview.

24. Sidney Olson, "The Germans Crumble in the West," *Life*, March 19, 1945, p. 25. "Jerry" or "Jerri"was a British reference or nickname for German soldiers picked up by American G.I.s. who also referred to them as "Krauts." Jerry is an old British term for a chamber pot; kraut was a reference to the belief the Germans ate a lot of sauerkraut.
25. Robert Goralski, *World War II Almanac, 1931-1945* (NY: Bonanza Books, 1981), p. 382-86.
26. Elmer J. Potzmann, Author's Interview.
27. Eckenrode, "D-Battery, 110th AAA," p. 64.
28. Ivan Glen Speer, Author's Interview; Wayne W. Edmondson, Author's Interview.
29. Eckenrode, "D-Battery, 110th AAA," p. 65.
30. Ibid.
31. Ibid.
32. Ibid., p. 66.
33. Ibid.
34. Arthur William "Bill" Nelson, Author's Interview.
35. Forman, "Memories," p. 29; Ivan Glen Speer, Author's Interview; Eckenrode, "D-Battery, 110th AAA," p. 67. Many of the battalion brought these weapons home as war souvenirs. Forman still had his into the mid-1980s and Speer still had his in 2005. Later a rifle manufacturing plant was found by D-Battery and they all got German sniper rifles and Headquarters battery dispensed two Nazi daggers to each of the battery from a factory they came across.
36. Eckenrode, "D-Battery, 110th AAA," p. 67.
37. Cohen, "Memories," p. 2.
38. Forman, "Memories," p. 29.
39. Forman, "Memories," p. 30; Eckenrode, "D-Battery, 110th AAA," p. 68; Ivan Glen Speer, Author's Interview. The Weilburg-Kuback area is about midway between Bonn and Frankfurt.
40. Ivan Glen Speer, Author's Interview; Wayne W. Edmondson, Author's Interview. Glen apparently didn't realize that the castle referred to was actually on the Lahn River, which flowed directly into the Rhine, just 2.5 miles away.
41. Eckenrode, "D-Battery, 110th AAA," p. 68.
42. Forman, "Memories," p. 32-33.
43. Harvey W. Edds, Author's Interview; Harvey Edds, Letter to Author.
44. Edds, "Memories, p. 17; Harvey Edds, Letters to Author.
45. Forman, "Memories," p. 32.
46. Edds, "Memories, p. 17; Harvey Edds, Letters to Author.
47. Ibid.

48. Gardner, "Memories,"p. 1; Dan Mackie, "The Rest of the War Paled Beside This," *Valley* (White River Junction, VT) *News*, April 22, 1995; Gardner, *D-Day*, p.55-59.
49. Ivan Glen Speer, Author's Interview.
50. Ibid.
51. Ibid.
52. Ibid.
53. Ibid. Harold E. Acheson, 19, of Wayne County, Iowa, KIA August 13, 1944.

BIBLIOGRAPHY

PRIMARY SOURCES
Published Material

Barnes, John. *Fragments of My Life with Company A, 116ᵗʰ Infantry Regiment.* Holland Patent, NY: JAM Publications, 2000.

Baumgarten, Harold. *Eyewitness on Omaha Beach.* Jacksonville, FL: Pvt. Prt., 2000.

Bayerlein, Fritz. "Invasion, 1944." *The Rommel Papers.* Edited by B.H. Liddell Hart. NY: Harcourt, Brace and Company, 1953.

Beacham, Edmund G. "Fortieth Anniversary of D-Day June 6, 1944, A Physician Re-members." *Maryland State Medical Journal*, Vol. 33, No. 6 (June 1984).

Bernstein, Walter. *Keep Your Head Down.* NY: Viking Press, 1945.

Blunt, Roscoe C. Jr. *Inside The Battle of the Bulge, A Private Comes of Age.* Westport, CT: Praeger Publishers, 1994.

Bradley, Omar N. *A Soldier's Story.* NY: Henry Holt and Company, 1951.

Braziller, George. *The 133ʳᵈ AAA Gun Battalion.* Munich, Germany: R. Oldenbourg, 1945.

Bulge Bugle. Arlington, VA. Vol. 1 No. 1 to Vol. XV No. 1 (Feb. 1982 to Feb. 1996).

Camp Edwards, Headquarters. *Daily Bulletin.* Various issues, April-December, 1943.

Capa, Robert. *Slightly Out of Focus.* NY: Henry Hold and Company, 1947.

Cawthon, Charles R. "July, 1944: St. Lo," *American Heritage*, Vol. XXV, No. 4 (June, 1974).

Chapman, Robert B. *Tell It to the Chaplain.* NY: Exposition Press, 1952.

Davies, Owen T. Interview. "At Omaha," Dee Ann Shaw, ed. *The Daily World* (Aberdeen, WA) Nov. 11, 2001.

Dohmann, George W. "Suddenly I Knew I Was Hit, A Medic in Normandy." *American History Illustrated*, Vol. IV, No. 3 (June 1969).

Edds, Harvey. "50 Years of Wondering, Alive and Well," *The Bulge Bugle*, Vol. XV, No. 1, (February 1996).

Eisenhower, Dwight D. *Crusade in Europe*. Garden City, NY: Doubleday, 1948.

_____. *The Papers of Dwight D. Eisenhower, The War Years*. Vol. 3 and 4. Edited by Alfred D. Chandler. Baltimore: John Hopkins Press,1971.

Eustis, Morton. *War Letters of Morton Eustis to his Mother*. Edited by Edith Morton Eustis. NY: Spiral Press, 1945.

Gach, Gene. *In The Army Now*. NY: Dodd, Mead & Company, 1942.

Gaige, Richard. *Me and the Army*. NY: American Artists Group, 1943.

Gardner, Clinton C. *D-Day & Beyond, A Memoir of War, Russia & Discovery*. Philadelphia, PA: Xlibris Publishing, 2004.

Gaskill, Gordon. "Bloody Beach," *American Magazine*, September, 1944.

Giles, Henry. *The G.I. Journal of Sergeant Giles*. Edited by Janice Giles. Boston: Houghton Miffin, 1965.

Hargrove, Marion. *See Here, Private Hargrove*. NY: Henry Holt and Company, 1942.

Harrison, A. Cleveland. *Unsung Valor, A GI's Story of World War II*. Jackson: University Press of Mississippi, 2000.

Hemingway, Ernest. "Voyage to Victory," *Collier's*, July 22, 1944.

_____. "How We Came to Paris," *Collier's*, October 7, 1944.

Hogan, Harry and Don McGrath. *This Army Stuff*. NY: Coward-McCann, 1942.

Kahn, E. J. Jr. *The Army Life*. NY: Simon and Schuster, 1942.

Kelakos, Michael G. *"The Forty-Niners," Unit History of the Headquarters and Headquarters Battery, 49th AAA Brigade, December 1, 1942 to May 9, 1945*. n.c.: 654th Engineer Bn., Third U.S. Army, 1945.

Lingg, James T. "WWII Memoirs of James T. Lingg." n.c.: Pvt. Pub., 1988.

Marsden, Michael H. E. *Khaki Is More Than A Color*. Garden City, NY: Doubleday, Doran and Company, 1943.

Marshall, S. L. A. "111th FA Bn on D-Day," *Field Artillery Journal*, Vol. 35 (Jan. 1945).

New Jersey Bell Telephone Company. *Your Camp Kilmer Guide*. NJ: Trenton, 1943.

Olson, Sidney. "The Germans Crumble in the West," *Life*, March 19, 1945

Osmont, Marie-Louise. *The Normandy Diary of Marie-Louise Osmont, 1940-1944*. NY: Random House, 1994.

Panter-Downes, Mollie. *London War Notes, 1939-1945*. Edited by William Shawn. NY: Farrar, Straus and Giroux, 1971.

Patton, George S. Jr. *War As I Knew It.* Boston: Houghton Mifflin, 1947.

Pyle, Ernie. *Here Is Your War.* NY: Lancer Books, 1943.

————————. *Brave Men.* NY: Henry Holt and Company, 1944.

Raaen, John. *Beyond Valor: In Their Own Words, the Personal Stories of America's World War II Veterans.* Edited by Patrick K. O'Donnell. NY: The Free Press, 2001.

Rommel, Erwin. *The Rommel Papers.* Edited by B. H. Liddell Hart. NY: Harcourt, Brace and Company, 1953.

Rommel, Manfred. "The Last Days." *The Rommel Papers.* Edited by B. H. Liddell Hart. NY: Harcourt, Brace and Company, 1953.

Samuels Ltd. *Visitors Guide To London with Large Map.* London: Geographia, 1944.

Scarangella, Joseph H. *Battery "A" History, Battery "A" 137th Gun Battalion.* n.p., n.d. (circa December 1944).

Schultheis, Everett P. *Battery "B," 467 AAA AW Bn. 1944-1945.* n.c.: pvt. ptd., circa 1989-1990.

602nd Ordnance Base Armament Maintenance Battalion. *Newsweak.* Vol. 1, No. 1 to Vol. 1, No. 22 (April 6, 1945 to Sept. 8, 1945).

Smith, Albert H. Jr. "D-Day: Forty Years Plus One." *Infantry.* Vol 75 (May/June 1985)

Smith, Walter Bedell. *Eisenhower's Six Great Decisions.* NY: Longmans Green, 1956.

Speidel, Hans. *Invasion 1944.* Westport, CT: Greenwood Press, 1950.

————————. *We Defended Normandy.* London: Michael Jenkins, 1951.

Spencer, Henry G. *Nineteen Days in June 1944.* Kansas City, MO: Lowell Press, 1984.

Stradling, John S. *Johnny.* Edited by Harriet J. Stradling. Salt Lake City: Bookcraft, 1946.

Sugarman, Tracy. *My War.* NY: Random House, 2000.

Thompson, Paul W. "D-Day on Omaha Beach." *Infantry Journal.* Vol. LVI, Vol. 6 (June 1945).

301st Ordnance Regiment. *Cracked Crab.* Vol. 1, No. 1 to Vol. 1, No. 12 (April 1946 to March 1947).

Veterans of The Battle of the Bulge. *Memorable Bulge Incidents.* Arlington, VA: VBOB, Inc., 1995.

————————————————. *VBOB Gateway Newsletter.* St. Louis Gateway Chapter, St. Louis, Missouri, various issues Vol. V, No. 1 (Jan/Feb. 1997) to Vol. XII, No.5 (Sept.-Oct. 2004).

————————————————. *Everyday Heroes of the Battle of the Bulge in WWII.* St. Louis Gateway Chapter, St. Louis, Missouri, 2002.

———

Vincken, Fritz. "Peace on Earth, Good Will Toward (Seven) Men, An Unsolved Mystery of The Bulge." *The Bulge Bugle*, August 1995.

Wertenbaker, Charles C. "Beachheads of Normandy, The Big Days," *Life*, June 19, 1944.

Whitlow, Louie. *Battery C, 132nd AAA Gun Battalion, 1943-1946*. New Bedford, MA: privately published, 2001.

U.S. Government Manuals, Pamphlets, and Publications

U.S. Dept. of Army, Chief of Ordnance. *American Army Vehicles of World War II, Official U.S. Encyclopedia of Tanks, Trucks & Other Military Vehicles*. Andover, NJ: Portrayal Press, n.y. Reprint, originally published as *Catalogue of Standard Ordnance Items, Re- stricted-Confidential*, March 1, 1944 by GPO, Washington, DC.

_____, Special Services Branch. *1000 and 1 Questions about Camp Edwards*. MA: Camp Edwards, 1943.

_____, Special Services Branch. *Camp Kilmer*. NJ: Camp Kilmer, 1943.

_____, Special Services Branch. *A Short Guide to Great Britain*. Washington, DC: GPO, 1943.

_____, Information and Education Division. *France*. Washington, DC: GPO, 1944.

_____, Information and Education Division. *French Phrase Book, TM30-602*. Washington, DC, GPO, September 28, 1943.

_____, Information and Education Division. *Pocket Guide To Paris and Cities of Northern France*. Washington, DC: GPO, 1944.

_____, Information and Education Division. *Reims* [France]. Washington, DC: GPO, 1945.

_____, Information and Education Division. *Pocket Guide To The Cities of Belgium and Luxembourg*. Washington, DC: GPO, 1944.

_____, Information and Education Division. *Germany*. Washington, DC: GPO, 1944.

_____, Information and Education Division. *German Phrase Book, TM30-606*. Washington, DC, GPO, November 30, 1943.

U.S. First Army. *Combat Operations Data*. Governor's Island, NY: GPO, 1946.

U.S. War Department. *Army Life, FM21-13*. Washington, DC: GPO, August 10, 1943.

_____. *So You Got A Furlough?* Washington, DC: GPO, June 13, 1944.

_____. *Basic Field Manual: Protective Measures, Individuals and Small Units, FM21-45*. Washington, DC: GPO, March 10, 1943.

_____. *It's Your Head—Keep It!* Natick, Mass.: U.S. Army, nd.

_____. *Basic Field Manual, First Aid For Soldiers, FM21-11.* Washington, DC: GPO, April 7, 1943.

_____. *Enemy Capabilities For Chemical Warfare.* Washington, DC: GPO, July, 1943.

_____. *Basic Field Manual, U.S. Rifle Caliber .30 M1, FM23-5.* Washington, DC: GPO, July 30, 1943.

_____. *Individual Score Book for the Rifle, AGO-82.* Washington, DC: GPO, July 1940.

_____. *Thompson Submachine Gun, Cal. .45, M1, TM9-215.* Washington, DC: GPO, October 10, 1942.

_____. *Basic Field Manual, Grenades, FM23-30.* Washington, DC: GPO, June 15, 1942.

_____. [Aircraft] *Recognition Pictorial Manual, FM30-30.* Washington, DC: GPO, June 1,1943.

_____. *Antiaircraft Artillery Field Manual, Fire Control, Guns, FM4-121.* Washington, DC: GPO, December 22, 1943.

_____. *Antiaircraft Artillery Field Manual, Service of the Piece, 90 mm AA Gun On M1A1 Mount, FM4-126.* Washington, DC: GPO, June 30, 1943.

_____. *90-mm Antiaircraft Gun, Materiel M1 and M1a1, TM9-370.* Washington, DC, 1942.

_____. *Twin Cal. .50 Machine Gun Mount M33 and Multiple Cal. .50 Machine Gun Mount M45, TM9-223.* Washington, DC: GPO, July 15, 1944.

_____. *Driver's Manual, United States Army: Expert Driving Keeps 'Em Rolling, TM10-460.* Washington, DC: GPO, May 6, 1942.

_____. *Principles of Automotive Vehicles, TM10-510.* Washington, DC: GPO, October 1, 1943.

_____. *Basic Field Manual, Motor Transport, FM25-10.* Washington, DC: GPO, March 12, 1942.

_____. *Standard Military Motor Vehicles, TM9-2800.* Washington, DC: GPO, March 6, 1943.

_____. *Ford Model GP: Maintenance and Repair, TM10-1101.* Washington, DC: GPO, 1941.

_____. *1/4-Ton 4X4 Truck (Willys MB and Ford GPW), TM9-803.* Washington, DC: GPO, February 22, 1944.

_____. *Tractor, High Speed, 18 ton, M4 Series, TM9-785.* Washington, DC: GPO, November, 1943.

_____. *Engine and Accessories and Torque Converter for High Speed 18 Ton M4 and 38 Ton M6, TM9-1785A.* Washington, DC: GPO, March, 1944.

Periodicals

Air Defense Artillery
American History Illustrated
American Heritage
American Legion
American Magazine
American Veteran
Antiaircraft Artillery Command
Army and Navy Journal
Army Times
Bulge Bugle
Camp Edwards (MA) *News*
Camp News (Camp Edwards, MA)
Cape Cod Standard-Times
Cape Cod Times
Coast Artillery Journal
Colliers
Daily World (Aberdeen, WA)
DAV
Des Moines (IA) *Register*
Erie (PA) *Times-News*
Evening (Uniontown, PA) *Standard*
Falmouth (MA) *Enterprise*
Field Artillery Journal
Honolulu Star-Bulletin
Infantry
Infantry Journal
Life
Los Angeles Times
Middletown (CT) *Press*
Military History
Military Review
Newsweek
New York Times
Retired Officer
St. Louis *Post Dispatch*
Saturday Evening Post
Springfield (MA) *Journal*
Stars and Stripes

Time
VFW
Watch on the Rhine
Wayne County (IA) *Republica*n
World War II
Yank

Unpublished Material

Interviews, Documents, Diaries, Manuscripts, and Letters
Battery B, 110ᵗʰ AAA. Accumulated typed manuscript pages of memories of Camp Edwards, the *Queen Mary*, and the five major battles as provided by various members of the battery.

Bye, Terry. Various interviews and correspondence between August 17, 2002 to May 2005. Accumulated war and service records, military documents, personal papers, letters, and photographs.

Chase, James E. Various correspondence from September to October 2002.

Dunshee, Carl A. Various interviews in May 2005.

East, Marvin R. "Curly." Interviews and various correspondence during December 2003 and May 2005.

Eckenrode, Joseph B. "History of D-Battery, 110ᵗʰ AAA Bn." Typed 77-page manuscript.

Edmondson, Wayne. Various interviews and correspondence between June 15, 2002 to Jan. 31, 2004. Accumulated war and service records, military documents, personal papers, letters, and photographs.

Edds, Harvey. "Memories of World War II, Battery B, 110ᵗʰ AAA Gun Bn." Typed 75- page manuscript.

_____. "The Josee Story." Typed 7-page manuscript.

_____. Various interviews and correspondence between Oct. 5, 2002 to Jan. 4, 2004. Accumulated war and service records, military documents, personal papers, letters, and photographs.

Ferriss, Franklin. "Defeat of the 1ˢᵗ SS Panzer Division, Adolf Hitler," OCMH MS A-924. "30ᵗʰ Inf. Div., Ardennes, 16-25 Dec 44."

Forman, John (Jack) A. "World War II Memories." Typed 37-page manuscript. Personal Memories, incidents, and history of A-Battery, 110ᵗʰ AAA Bn.

Gardner, Clinton C. Correspondence during November and December 2002.

Gushurst, William A. Correspondence during February 2004, interviews in May 2005, and accumulated war service records, military documents, and photographs.

Hubbard, Arthur. Interview in May 2005; Provided various publications, photos and records of and about the 110th AAA Gun Bn. Mbl., including various history, members information and insights.

Hutchinson, Roger N. Jr. A member of Battery C, 109th AAA Gun Bn. Mbl. An accumulation of 125 wartime letters written home from Camp Edwards, England, France, and Germany, that include eyewitness accounts about St. Lo, Paris, Battle of the Bulge, etc.

Jones, Sergeant L. "Defense of Spa Gas Dump," OCMH MS C-924.

Kania, Leo C. "A Memoir of the 110th A-A-A Gun Battalion: 1943-1945." Typed manuscript.

_____. Accumulated war and service records, military documents, personal papers, Letters, and related material. Interviews in May 2005.

Kosicki, Lillian E. "1937—The Beginning—The Trumpet." A 12-page typed and bound manuscript about the author's husband, Edward Kosicki, bugler for Battery-B of the 110th AAA, including his war and service record, from memory, stories passed along, and his diary.

Lashier, Charles "Neil." Various interviews in May 2005. Accumulated photographs.

Libby, Clyde R. Various interviews and correspondence between Aug. 1, 2002 to July 4, 2003. Accumulated war and service records, military documents, personal papers, letters, and photographs.

Mueller, Harold W. Various interviews and correspondence between August 15, 2002 to May 2005. Accumulated war and service records, military documents, personal papers, letters and photographs.

_____. "Battle of the Bulge Memories, T-5 Corporal Harold Mueller, 110th AAA, 90MM MBL. GUN BN. BTR C." Typed manuscript.

_____. "Massacre at Malmedy, Belgium." Typed Manuscript.

Nelson, A. William "Bill." Various interviews and correspondence between Nov. 6, 2003 to May 2005; Accumulated war and service records, military documents, personal papers, letters, and photographs.

Noel, Theodore "Ted" N. Various interviews in May 2005.

Peterson, Henry J. "Henry Peterson's Life Story." Typed Manuscript.

Potzmann, Elmer J. Various interviews and correspondence between August 2, 2002 to July 2004; Accumulated war and service records, military documents, personal papers, letters and photographs.

Reiver, Julius. "The Battle at the Gas Dump." Typed Manuscript of personal memories Regarding Battery D, 110th AAA Gun Bn, defense of Fuel Dump K-6707 during the Battle of The Bulge.

_____. "Reiver's Retrievers—Battery D, 110th AAA Gun Bn (Mbl)." Typed manuscript of memoirs.

_____. "D-Day Recollections." Typed Manuscript of additional details to memoirs.

Speer, Ivan Glen. Family papers, letters, photographs; Accumulated war and service records, military documents and memorabilia.

_____. Oral History: Various interviews between September 30, 1996 to September 30, 2002; Tape-recorded interview consisting of 3 ninety-minute cassette tapes—two recorded on September 23, 1997 and one recorded October 3, 2001—and 1 Video and audio tape of June 6, 2001, and various follow-up interviews through 2005.

Speer, Lloyd Rex. Family papers, letters, and photographs.

Speer, Lonnie R. Family papers, letters, and photographs.

Thake, Henry F. Various interviews and correspondence between July 24, 2002 to July 2004. Accumulated war and service records, military documents, personal papers, letters, photographs and memorabilia.

Theriault, L. James "Jim." Various interviews and correspondence between July 27, 2002 to May 2005.

Tyree, Nelvin M. A member of Battery D, 441st AAA Gun Bn. An accumulation of 117 wartime letters written home from various training camps, as well as England, France, and Germany, that include many first-hand observations and battle-action accounts.

Way, Dwight N. Various interviews in May 2005.

Way, Norman R. Various interviews in May 2005.

Wisniewski, Frank T. "What I Can Remember Of WWII, 1942-1945, 110th AAA Gun Battalion." Bound and typed manuscript of 55 pages with photos and maps.

Woolson, Richard "Dick" Various interviews in May 2005.

National Archives, Washington, D.C.
Stanley Bach papers. Typed Manuscript.
Cleaves A. Jones papers. Typed Manuscript.
RG337—Army Ground Forces, 1942-1945.

National Archives and Records II, Modern Military Reference Branch, College Park, MD
RG331—Records of Allied Operational and Occupational Headquarters, World War II.
RG407 Section 3—Records of the 110th AAA Gun Battalion (Mbl), 1944-1945.

National Personnel Records Center, Military Personnel Records, St. Louis, MO
Organizational Records Unit:
Morning Reports, D Battery, 110th AAA Bn.
Morning Reports, C Battery, 110th AAA Bn.
Morning Reports, B Battery, 110th AAA Bn.
Morning Reports, A Battery, 110th AAA Bn.
Morning Reports, Hdqs. Battery, 110th AAA Bn.

U.S. Army Military History Institute, Carlisle Barracks, PA
Omar N. Bradley. Papers.
Louis B. Hershey. Papers.
Bob L. Sales. Papers.
John R. Slaughter. Papers.
Robert A. Rowe Collection:
Robert E. Garcia. Interview transcript.
James E. Gary. Papers.
Orlando T. Grimes. Papers.
Glenn E. Gibson. Papers.
W. W. Jones. Papers.
Theodore L. Lamb. Interview transcript.
Veterans Survey Project:
Edmund Beacham. Papers
James J. Caivano. Papers.
Joseph H. Dougherty. Papers.
William B. Gold. Papers.
Fletcher Harris. Papers.
John Hooper. Papers.
Evermonte Huffman. Papers.
George A. Kobe. Papers.

Weldon L. Kratzer. Papers.
William H. Lewis. Papers.
Charles J. Lillis. Papers.
Edward J. Regan. Papers.
Charles H. Schreyer. Papers.
Walter P. Shawd. Papers.
110th AAA Battalion, World War II Survey Collection:
Harold W. Mueller (Battery C).

National D-Day Museum, Peter Kalikow World War II Collection, New Orleans, LA
Joseph S. Blaylock, Sr. Oral History Transcript and Papers.
Edward Gilleran. Oral History Transcript and Papers.
Warner H. Hamlett. Oral History Transcript and Papers.
Michael Kruglinski. Oral History Transcript and Papers.
John Pellegren. Oral History Transcript and Papers.
Samuel Reali. Oral History Transcript and Papers.
Sidney A. Salomon. Oral History Transcript and Papers.
Everett Schultheis. Oral History Transcript and Papers.
James Shearhouse. Oral History Transcript and Papers.

University of Connecticut, Storrs
Franklin E. Johnson. Interview transcript. (110th AAA, Battery B).

University of Texas, Austin
John A. Forman. Accumulated war and service records, military documents, personal papers, letters, photographs and memorabilia (110th AAA, Battery A).

Imperial War Museum, Lambeth Road, London, U.K.
Sound Archive, All-Saints Annex, Austral Street
B.B.C. Archive, 1939-1945, SR 1604/H/C

SECONDARY

Adler, Bill, with Tracy Quinn McLennan, eds. *World War II Letters*. NY: St Martin's Press, 2002.
Allen, Peter. *One More River, The Rhine Crossings of 1945*. NY: Scribner's Sons, 1980.
Allen, Thomas B. "Untold Stories of D-Day," *National Geographic*, June 2002.

Allsup, John S. *Hedgerow Hell: L' Enfer Du Bocage*. Bayeux, France: Editions Heimdal, 1985.

Alm, Ray. *Beyond Valor: In Their Own Words, the Personal Stories of America's World War II Veterans*. Edited by Patrick K. O'Donnell. NY: The Free Press, 2001.

Ambrose, Stephen E. *The Supreme Commander: The War Years of General Dwight D. Eisenhower*. Garden City, NY: Doubleday, 1970.

——————. *Citizen Soldiers*. NY: Simon & Schuster, 1997.

——————. "They Were There, D-DAY, 1944," *American History Illustrated*, Vol. IV, No. 3 (June 1969).

Bailey, Ronald H. *The Home Front: U.S.A.* Alexandria, VA: Time-Life Books, 1977.

Balkoski, Joseph. *Beyond the Beachhead, The 29th Infantry Division in Normandy*. Mechanics- burg, PA: Stackpole Books, 1999.

——————. *Omaha Beach, D-Day, June 6, 1944*. Mechanicsburg, PA: Stackpole Books, 2004.

Batchelor, John and Ian Hogg. *Artillery*. NY: Charles Scribner's Sons, 1972.

Becker, Marshall O. *The Amphibious Training Center, Study No. 22*. U.S. Army Ground Forces, Historical Section, Washington, DC: GPO, 1946.

Bisset, James. *Commodore: War, Peace and Big Ships*. Sydney, Australia: Angus & Robertson, 1961.

Bliven, Bruce Jr. *The Story of D-Day, June 6, 1944*. NY: Random House, 1956.

Blumenson, Martin. *Breakout and Pursuit*. Washington, DC: Office of the Chief of Military History, Department of the Army, 1961.

——————. *The Duel for France 1944*. Boston: Houghton Mifflin, 1963.

Brake, Fred E. "A Soldiers' City Rises From the Dust," *The Quartermaster Review*, Vol. 20, No. 5 (March-April 1941).

Brinkley, Douglas, and Michael E. Haskew, ed. *The World War II Desk Reference*. NY: Grand Central Press, 2004.

——————. *New York Times Living History, World War II, The Axis Assault, 1939-1942*. NY: Henry Holt and Company, 2003.

——————. *New York Times Living History, World War II, The Allied Counter- offensive, 1942-1945*. NY: Henry Holt and Company, 2003.

Brinkley, Alan ed. *Twentieth Century America: A Primary Source Collection from the Associated Press*. Vol. III, WWII 1939-1945. Danbury, CT: Grolier, 1995

Brinkley, Douglas, and Ronald J. Drez. *Voices of Valor, D-Day: June 6, 1944*. NY: Bulfinch Press, 2004.

Butler, Daniel Allen. *Warrior Queens, The Queen Mary and Queen Elizabeth in World War II*. Mechanicsburg, PA: Stackpole Books, 2002.

Cavanagh, William C. C. *A Tour of the Bulge Battlefield*. UK: Leo Cooper, 2001.

Cawthorne, Nigel. *Fighting Them On The Beaches, The D-Day Landings June 6, 1944*. London: Arcturus Publishing Ltd., 2002.

Cirillo, Roger. *Ardennes-Alsace*. Washington, DC: Center of Military History, United States Army, 1994.

Close, Ian, ed. *D-Day, Invasion of Hitler's Europe*. n.c.: Phoebus Publishing Co., 1975.

Cochran, Alexander S. Jr. "Failure At The Bulge," *Military History*, December 1984.

Colby, Elbridge. *Army Talk: A Familiar Dictionary of Soldier Speech*. Princeton, NJ: Princeton University Press, 1942.

Cole, Hugh M. *The Ardennes: Battle of the Bulge*. Washington, DC: Office of the Chief of Military History, Department of the Army, 1965.

_____. *The Lorraine Campaign*. Washington, DC: Office of the Chief of Military History, Department of the Army, 1950.

Colley, David P. *The Road To Victory: The Untold Story of World War II's Red Ball Express*. Washington, DC: Brassey's, 2000.

Collins, Larry and Dominique LaPierre. *Is Paris Burning?* NY: Simon and Schuster, 1965.

Commemoration Committee, *"Fact Sheet: Ardennes-Alsace Campaign."* Washington, DC: HQDA, SACC: Pentagon, Room 3E524, 1994.

Cooper, John P. Jr. *The History Of The 110th Field Artillery*. Baltimore: Maryland Historical Society, 1953.

Craddock, Michael R. "Kampfgruppe Peiper, A Young, Ruthless German Officer Spearheaded the Battle of the Bulge." *Stars and Stripes*, December 30, 1992.

Crismon, Fred W. *U. S. Military Tracked Vehicles*. Osceola, WI: Motorbooks International, 1992.

Dedmon, Rad. "From Massachusetts to Normandy, Capt. William C. Goodwine and the 18th AAA," *Military History*, January 1998.

Dupuy, Trevor N. *The Military History of World War II*. 18 vols. NY: Franklin Watts, 1962-1965.

_____ and David L. Bongard and Richard C. Anderson Jr. *Hitler's Last Gamble, The Battle of the Bulge, December 1944-January 1945*. NY: Harper Collins, 1994.

Dzwonchyk, Wayne M. And John Ray Skates, eds. *A Brief History of the U. S. Army in World War II*. Washington, DC: Center of Military History, United States Army, 1992.

___

Edds, Harvey. "Myth Of The Ardennes, Documentary Evidence Debunks Many Popular Concepts of the Nazis' Bold Counter Stroke," *The Bulge Bugle*, Vol. XV, No. 1, (February 1996).

Eisenhower Foundation. *D-Day, The Normandy Invasion in Retrospect.* Lawrence: University Press of Kansas, 1971.

Eisenhower, John. *The Bitter Woods: The Battle of the Bulge.* NY: G. P. Putnam's Sons, 1969.

Forty, George. *U.S. Army Handbook, 1939-1945.* UK: Alan Sutton Pub. Ltd., 1995.

_____. *World War II AFVs: Armoured Fighting Vehicles & Self-Propelled Artillery.* London: Osprey, 1996.

_____. *Patton's Third Army At War.* London: Ian Allan Ltd., 1978.

Fowler, Will. *D-Day, The First 24 Hours.* Miami: Lewis International, 2003.

France, Department of Tourism. *D-Day In Normandy.* Paris: Ministere Des Travaux Publics Et Des Transports Commissariat General Au Tourisme, 1994.

Frank, Reinhard. *Ford At War.* Atglen, PA: Schiffer Publishing, 1993.

Frank, Stanley. "First Stop—Omaha Beach," *Saturday Evening Post*, 1946.

Garlinski, Jozef. *Hitler's Last Weapons, The Underground War against the V1 and V2.* NY: Times Books, 1978.

Gawne, Jonathan. *Spearheading D-Day, American Special Units in Normandy.* Paris: Histoire & Collections, 1998.

Goldstein, Donald M., Katherine V. Dillon, and J. Michael Wenger. *D-Day Normandy, The Story and Photographs.* NY: Brassey's (US), 1994.

Gollancz, Victor. *What Buchenwald Really Means.* London: Victor Gollancz Ltd., 1945.

Goodman, Jack. *While You Were Gone: A Report on Wartime Life in the United States.* NY: Simon & Schuster, 1946.

Goolrick, William K. and Ogden Tanner. *Battle of the Bulge.* Alexandria, VA: Time-Life Books, 1979.

Goralski, Robert. *World War II Almanac 1931-1945.* NY: Bonanza Books, 1981.

Green, Constance McLaughlin, Harry C. Thomson, and Peter C. Roots. *The Ordnance Depart- ment: Planning Munitions For War.* Washington, DC: Office of the Chief of Military History Department of the Army, 1955.

Gregory, Ross. *America 1941, A Nation at the Crossroads.* NY: The Free Press, 1989.

Hackett, David A., ed. *The Buchenwald Report.* Boulder, CO: Westview Press, 1995.

Harrison, Gordon A. *United States Army in World War II, ETO, Cross-Channel Attack.* Washington, DC: Office of the Chief of Military History, Department of the Army, 1951.

Hart, B. H. Liddell, ed. *The Rommel Papers*. NY: Harcourt, Brace and Company, 1953.

Hastings, Max. *Overlord, D-Day, June 6, 1944*. NY: Simon and Schuster, 1984.

Hearn, Chester G. *The American Soldier in World War II*. Osceola, WI: MBI Publishing Company, 2000.

Hechler, Ken. "The Capture of the Remagen Bridge," *Military Review*, Vol. XXVI (July 1946).

Hechler, Ken. *The Bridge at Remagen*. Missoula, MT: Pictorial Histories Publishing Co., 2001.

Hogan, David W. *Northern France, The U.S. Campaigns of World War II*. Carlisle Barracks, PA: U.S. Army Center of Military History, 1994.

Hogg, Ian V. *Anti-Aircraft: A History of Air Defense*. London: Macdonald and Janes's, 1978.

_____. *The Guns: 1939-45*. NY: Ballantine Books, 1970.

_____. *Anti-Aircraft Artillery*. Marlborough, UK: Crowood Press, 2002.

Holmes, Richard. *The D-Day Experience from the Invasion to The Liberation of Paris*. London: Carlton Books, Ltd., 2004.

Humes, Ted. *A Guide to the Atlantic Wall and D-Day Beaches*. Phoenix: Corporate West, 1984.

Infantry Journal. *The World at War 1939-1944*. Washington, DC: U.S. War Department, February 1945.

Johns, Glover S. Jr. *The Clay Pigeons of St. Lo*. PA: MSPC Books, 1958.

Jordan, David. *Battle of the Bulge, The First 24 Hours*. London: Amber Books, 2003.

Keegan, John, ed. *Who Was Who in World War II*. NY: Thomas Y. Crowell Publishers, 1978.

_____. *Six Armies in Normandy*. NY: Viking Press, 1982.

Kennett, Lee. *G.I.: The American Soldier in World War II*. NY: Scribner's Sons, 1987.

Kirkpatrick, Charles E., ed. *Defense of the Americas, The U.S. Army Campaigns of World War II*. Carlisle Barracks, PA: U.S. Army Center of Military History, 1991.

Kluger, Steve, ed. *Yank, The Army Weekly*. NY: St. Martin's Press, 1991.

Levin, Harry. "The Great Crusade." St. Louis *Post-Dispatch*, June 8, 1994.

Linderman. Gerald F. *The World Within War, America's Combat Experience in World War II*. NY: The Free Press, 1997.

MacDonald, Charles B. *The European Theater of Operations, The Siegfried Line Campaign*. Washington, DC: Office of the Chief of Military History, Department of the Army, 1963.

_____. *A Time For Trumpets: The Untold Story of the Battle of the Bulge*. NY: William Morrow & Co., 1985.

Maddocks, Melvin. *The Great Liners*. Alexandria, VA: Time-Life Books, 1982.

Man, John. *The D-Day Atlas*. NY: Facts On File, 1994.

Mansoor, Peter R. *The G.I. Offensive In Europe*. Lawrence: University Press of Kansas, 1999.

Marsh, Robert W. "Mistakes and a Language Barrier Changed the Course and History of the Battle of the Bulge." *World War II*. Vol. 15, No, 4 (November 2000).

Martin, Ralph G. *The G.I. War, 1941-1945*. Boston: Little, Brown and Company, 1967.

Mauldin, Bill. *Up Front*. NY: World Publishing Company, 1945.

Mayer, S. L., ed. *Signal, Hitler's Wartime Picture Magazine*. NY: Prentice-Hall, 1976.

Mayo, Lida. *The Ordnance Department: On Beachhead and Battlefront*. Washington, DC: Office of the Chief of Military History, Department of the Army, 1968.

McCombs, Don and Fred L. Worth. *World War II; 4,139 Strange and Fascinating Facts*. NY: Wing Books, 1983.

McElfresh Map Company. *LeHavre To Cherbourg: Normandy at D-Day, June 1944*. NY: Earl B. McElfresh Map Company, 2004.

Merriam, Robert E. *Dark December, The Full Account of the Battle of the Bulge*. NY: Ziff-Davis Publishing, 1947.

Miller, Russell. *Nothing Less Than Victory; The Oral History of D-Day*. NY: William Morrow, 1993.

Morison, Samuel Eliot. *History of United States Naval Operations in World War II, Vol. XI: The Invasion of France and Germany, 1944-1945*. Boston: Little, Brown & Company, 1959.

Nalty, Bernard C., ed. *D-Day: Operation Overlord, From the Landing at Normandy to the Liberation of Paris*. NY: Smithmark Publishers, 1993.

Neillands, Robin and Roderick de Normann. *D-Day, 1944, Voices from Normandy*. London: Weidenfeld and Nicolson, 1993.

Ninth Armored Division. *The Bridge*. n.p., n.d.

O'Donnell, Patrick K., ed. *Beyond Valor: In Their Own Words, the Personal Stories of America's World War II Veterans*. NY: The Free Press, 2001.

Palmer, Robert R. And William R. Keast. *The US Army in World War Two: The Procurement and Training of Ground Combat Troops*. Washington, DC: Office of the Chief of Military History, Department of the Army, 1948.

Parker, Danny S. *Battle of the Bulge: Hitler's Ardennes Offensive, 1944-1945*. NY: DaCapo Press, 2001.

Parrish, Thomas, ed. *The Simon And Schuster Encyclopedia of World War II.* NY: Simon and Schuster, 1978.

Pogue, Forrest C. *The European Theater of Operations, The Supreme Command.* Washington, DC: Office of the Chief of Military History, Department of the Army, 1954.

Poller, Walter. *Medical Block Buchenwald, The Personal Testimony of Inmate 996, Block 36.* NY: Lyle Stuart, 1961.

Reynolds, Michael. *The Devil's Adjutant: Jochen Peiper, Panzer Leader.* NY: Sarpedon, 1995.

Ruppenthal, Roland G. *The European Theater of Operations, Logistical Support of the Armies.* 2 Vols. Washington, DC: Office of the Chief of Military History, Department of the Army, 1953.

Ryan, Cornelius. *The Longest Day; June 6, 1944.* NY: Simon & Schuster, 1959.

Sawicki, James A. *Antiaircraft Battalions of the U.S. Army.* 2 Vols. Dumfries, VA: Wyvern, 1991.

Scharnberg, Ken. *Voices: Letters from World War II.* Nashville: Premium Press America, 1993.

Sears, Stephen W., ed. *Eyewitness to World War II.* Boston: Houghton Mifflin, 1991.

Semmens, E. Paul. "The Hammer of Hell, The Coming of Age of Antiaircraft Artillery in WWII," *Air Defense Artillery*, January 2000.

Shilleto, Carl and Mike Tolhurst. *A Traveler's Guide to D-Day and the Battle for Normandy.* NY: Interlink Books, 2000.

Smart, Don. "Terror at Honsfeld," *World War II*, Vol. 16, No. 4 (Nov. 2001).

Smith, Chard P. *He's in the Artillery Now.* NY: Robert M. McBride & Company, 1943.

Stanton, Shelby L. *Order of Battle, U. S. Army, World War II.* Novato, CA: Presidio Press, 1984.

Steinhoff, Johannes and Peter Pechel and Dennis Showalter. *Voices From the Third Reich, An Oral History.* Washington, DC: Regnery Gateway, 1989.

Stouffer, Samuel A., Edward A. Suchman, Leland C. DeVinney, Shirley A. Star, and Robin M. Williams, Jr., eds. *The American Soldier, Adjustment During Army Life.* Princeton, NJ: Princeton University Press, 1949.

_____. *The American Soldier, Combat and Its Aftermath.* Princeton, NJ: Princeton University Press, 1949.

Sweeney, Michael S. *From The Front: The Story of War.* Washington, DC: National Geographic, 2002.

Thornton, Willis. *The Liberation of Paris.* NY: Harcourt, Brace & World, 1962.

Time, ed. *D-Day: 24 Hours That Saved the World.* NY: Time Books, 2004.

Tout, Ken. *Roads To Falaise, Cobra & Goodwood Reassessed.* UK: Sutton Publishing, 2002.

U.S. War Department, Historical Division. *Omaha Beachhead (6 June-13 June 1944).* Washington, DC: Office of the Chief of Military History, Department of the Army, 1946.

_____. *St.—Lo (7 July-19 July 1944).* Washington, DC: Office of the Chief of Military History, Department of the Army, 1946.

Vanderveen, Bart H. *The Observer's Fighting Vehicles Directory, World War II.* London: Frederick Warne & Co. Ltd., 1969.

Wardlow, Chester. *The Technical Services, The Transportation Corps: Movements, Training, and Supply.* Washington, DC: Office of the Chief of Military History, Department of the Army, 1956.

Warlimont, Walter. *Inside Hitler's Headquarters.* NY: Praeger, 1966.

Weinberg, Gerhard L. *Germany, Hitler & World War II.* U.K.: Cambridge University Press, 1995.

Whiting, Charles. *Massacre at Malmedy.* London: Leo Cooper, 1971.

_____. *Siegfried: The Nazis Last Stand.* NY: Stein and Day, 1982.

_____. *West Wall: The Battle for Hitler's Siegfried Line.* UK: Spellmount, 1999.

Wilmot, Chester. *The Struggle for Europe.* London: Colins, 1950.

Wilt, Alan F. *The Atlantic Wall 1941-1944, Hitler's Defenses For D-Day.* NY: Enigma Books, 2004.

Winter, C. W. R. *The Queen Mary.* NY: W. W. Norton & Co., 1986.

Works Progress Administration. *Iowa.* American Guide Series. NY: Viking Press, 1938.

_____. *Massachusetts.* American Guide Series. Boston: Houghton Mifflin, 1937.

_____. *New Jersey.* American Guide Series. NY: Viking Press, 1939.

INDEX

4th Signal Bn., 155;
99th Infantry Battalion of the Army
    Security Force, 188, 193, 199;
125th Cavalry, 188, 199;
23rd Chemical Battalion, 188;
80th Smoke Generating Company,
    188;
509th Military Police Battalion, 188;
3597th Quartermaster Truck Company
    Bn., 175;
Battle of the Beaches, 11-15, 99-123, 124-
    127, 132-133, 136-138, 150.
Battle of the Bulge, 16, 185-186, 187-215,
    217.
Battle of the Hedgerows, 138-143, 150,
    described, 125, 126, 138.
Baumgarten, Harold, 99.
BBC (British Broadcasting Corp.), 91.
"Bed-Check Charlie," 127.
Belfort Gap, 167.
Belgium: 167, 171, 172, 174, 177, 178,
    186, 201, 210
    Andrimont, 195;
    Antwerp, 174, 175, 186, 187;
    Bastogne, 204, 209;
    Baugnez, 190, 214;
    Blanchimont, 191;
    Bullingen, 189, 190, 214;
    Butgenbach, 190;
    Cour, 200;
    Creppe, 179, 180;
    Dinant, 211;
    Eupen, 190;
    Francorchamps, 190, 191, 192, 193,
        200, 214, 285
    Givet, 211;
    Honsfeld, 187, 214;
    Jemeppe, 172;
    LaGleize, 192, 195, 196, 199, 200, 211,
        214, 215;
    LaReid, 193;

Liege, 171, 172, 173, 174, 175, 179,
    180, 181, 182, 187, 188, 189;
    Ligneuville, 189, 190, 214;
    Malmedy, 187, 189, 190, 191, 193, 200,
        201, 204, 205, 206-207, 210, 211,
        212, 213, 214, 232
        bombings of, 205-207, 211,
        casualties, 206, 207, 211, 213, 214,
        massacre of US POWs, 190, 214;
    Mista, 191;
    Mont, 214;
    Monthouet, 198;
    Namur, 187;
    Ostend, 175;
    Parfondruy, 214;
    Pepinster, 176, 178;
    Renardmont, 214;
    Rochefort, 204;
    St. Vith, 187, 190, 204, 207, 209, 210;
    Schonberg, 204;
    Spa, 179, 180, 181, 187, 188, 189, 190,
        192, 193, 195, 199, 200, 211, 215,
        216, 217;
    Stavelot, 189, 190, 191, 192, 193, 199,
        200, 201, 204, 207, 211, 212, 214;
    Ster, 214;
    Stoumont, 192, 193, 194, 198, 199, 200, 232;
    Trois Ponts, 192, 207;
    Verviers, 176, 178, 179, 180, 181;
    Waimes, 190.
Bellendoorn, Holland, 225.
Billette, Pierre, 159.
Birdwood, Lord William, 70.
Blanford Camp, 82.
Blaylock, Joseph S. Jr., 97.
Blunt, Roscoe C., 133.
Bocage region, 116, 126, 136, 138, *see also*
    Hedgerows.
Boksanski, William J., 189.
Booby traps, 136, *see also* Land mines.
Born, Lester K., 49, 121, 132.

Bott, Ormal, 19.
Bradley, Omar N., 15, 103, 136, 141, 146-
147, 150, 154, 167, 172, 176, 178,
179, 279.
Brammann, Dick, 105, 119.
Brassard, Ray, 40, 43, 81, 87, 212.
Breit, Ernest F., 197, 198, 205.
Brennan, James, 87.
Bridges, Donald, 146.
British Second Army, 154, 167.
British 21st Army Group, 154.
Broadsands, 82.
Brown, Norman, 85.
Brown, Philip, 85.
Buchenwald Concentration Camp, 233,
234.
"Bucky" (vehicle name), 87.
Buntemeyer, Eddie, 232.
"Burp" gun, 187, 284.
Bush, Thomas E. 265.
Butts, Walter R. Jr., 199.
"Buzz Bomb Alley,"174, 175.
Buzz Bombs, see German: V-1.
Bye, Terry, 40, 83, 185, 226.

Café Bodarwe, 190.
Cahman, Reinhart H., 265.
Camp Callan, 49.
Camp Davis, 49.
Camp Dodge, 21-23, 260, described 21-22.
Camp Edwards, 25-26, 28, 29-53, 74, 226,
described 28, 29.
Camp Grant, 235.
Camp Kilmer, 53-56, 235, described 55, 58.
Camp #72, SS POW prison, 232.
Camp Wellfleet (see Wellfleet).
Canadian First Army, 154, 167, 216.
Capa, Robert, 101.
Cardigan Bay, 77.
Carroll, Walt, 152, 153.
Cawley, Mrs. Frederick L., 70.

Cawthon, Charles R., 142.
CC-2, 90.
Chafee, Jairus, 85.
Chase, James E., 49, 83, 84, 85, 107, 108,
110, 119, 146.
Cheney, Leo, 81, 144, 213.
Christ, Ostuf, 195, 198.
Churchill, Winston, 97, 283.
Ciaburri, Daniel H., 64, 65, 119.
Clapp family, 70.
Clear, Willian, 53.
Clegg, Leo, 54.
Coates, Barrett, 146, 234.
Coffey, Chase C., 109.
Cohen, Lester, 57, 63, 110, 117, 118, 145,
147, 230.
Cohen, Stanley B., 206.
Cole, Roland S., 120.
Collins, J. Lawton, 149.
Colliver, Billie, 61, 67, 232, 267.
Colmar Pocket, 183.
"Comet," 143.
Connors, John, 229-230.
Cook, Bob, 31, 40.
Corbitt truck, 45, 50, 73, 75, 76, 78, 79.
Corps:
III, 221, 223;
V, 75, 98, 132, 133, 135, 142, 186, 187,
189, 190;
VII, 132, 145, 146, 150;
VIII, 145, 185, 186, 187, 189;
XIX, 142, 143;
Corydon, Ia., 18, 20.
Cosmoline, 73.
Couturier, Al, 84, 85.
Cranford Hotel, 70.
Culin, Curtis G., 140-141.
Cunningham, Chris, 135.
Curran, John, 84, 85.
Curren, William F. Jr., 49, 108, 109, 155,
156, 163, 182, 188, 198, 236.

313

Revere Beach, 43, 44.
Rhine River, 183, 204, 216, 220, 221, 222, 223, 224, 226, 227, 231.
Rhino ferry, 113, 119, 273.
Richts, O. Charles (Peter Rabbit), 41, 42, 53.
Robinson, George W, 120.
Roer River, 216, 219, 220, 222.
Rommel, Erwin, 15, 125.
Roosevelt, Franklin D., 18, 56, 59-60, 228.
"Ruth," 87.

Sabatino, Bernard J., 103.
Sales, Bob L., 12, 13.
Salidas, Charles L., 48.
Salm River, 192.
Sauer pistol factory, 230.
Sausage Camps, 85-86.
Saverne Gap, 178.
Scarangella, Joseph H., 33.
Scevenels, Josee, 173, 179, 282-283.
Schade, Henry, 84.
Scotland:
    Airdrie, 67;
    Bathgate, 67;
    Edinburgh, 67;
    Glasgow, 65, 67;
    Gourock, 66;
    Greenock, 66;
Scott, Lawrence E. Jr., 120.
SCR-584 Artillery AA radar, 74, 75, 82, 93, 137, 177, 185, 188.
Seine River, 159, 160, 167.
Selective Service, 18-19, 21.
Shore, Dinah, 157.
Showalter, Bill, 235.
Siegfried Line, 167, 178, 204, 211, 216, described, 178.
Silverman, Theodore H., 49.
Simons, Donald R., 48.
Simpson, William H., 176.
Sisson , Richard D. (Dick), 70, 156-157.

Sites, John W., 39, 42, 45, 263.
Skyline Drive (the St. Vith-Diekirch highway), 187, 204.
Slapton Sands, 75.
Slaughter, J. Robert, 12, 13.
Slaven, George, 54.
Smith, Roy W., 49.
Smith, Walter Bedell, 95.
Soll, Delwin D. 83, 84, 85, 136, 149.
South Camp, England, 68.
Speer, Dewey O., 18, 20, 21, 48, 53, 235.
Speer, Elsie M., 18, 20, 21, 235.
Speer, Gerald, 20.
Speer, Ivan Glen, 14, 16, 17, 40, 43, 48, 49, 54, 58, 94, 112, 113, 115, 131, 132, 133,137, 168, 178, 193, 212, 228, 234, 235, quoted: 11, 18, 19, 21, 23, 24, 31, 34, 37, 38, 39, 41, 42, 43, 44, 45, 47, 48, 50, 51, 52, 53, 56, 57, 59, 60, 62, 63, 64, 66, 67, 69, 71, 72, 73, 74, 75, 76, 77, 78, 79, 80, 82, 88, 89, 90, 96, 98, 99,105, 109-110, 113-114, 116-117, 123, 128, 131-132, 138, 139, 141, 146- 147, 151, 157, 158, 165, 168, 169, 170, 174, 175, 179, 180, 181, 182, 189, 193-194, 201, 204, 207, 208, 209, 212, 213, 223, 228, 231, 234, 235-236.
assisting girls in Paris, 164-165;
threatened with court-martial, 165;
first time backing gun into place, 45;
forcing truck off road, 73;
M-4 front hitch request, 141;
preference for M-4 rubber tracks, 79-80;
tent fire, 72.
Speer, Lloyd Rex. 18, 48, 53, 235.
Spotter Cards, 69.
Statistics, 13, 14, 17, 91, 97, 124, 132, 136, 143, 145, 162, 163, 167, 170, 174-175, 184, 185, 186, 187, 212, 215, 226, 236, 272, 279,

Battle of the Bulge, 215;
D-Day, 13, 14, 124-125;
110th AAA Gun Bn, in WWII, 236;
Paris liberation, 162, 163;
Red Ball Express, 170;
Rhine River drive, 226;
Remagen bridge defense, 222, 226, 227;
Siegfried Line fighting, 184-185;
Stein, Mark, 206.
Stevensky, Stanley, 63.
Stoumont Station (railroad depot), 194.
Strand Palace Hotel, 69-70.
Stroud, William F., 48.
Supple, Lt. Col., 49.
Switzerland, 176, 178, 184.

Tackitt, Grayson (Bull Durham), 40, 43, 112, 114, 137, 264.
Tank Destroyer Battalions:
612th Tank Destroyer Bn, 188;
823rd TD Bn., 193, 194, 195, 200;
843rd TD Bn., 189.
Tank units: 140, 141.
9th Armored Group, 199;
2nd Armored Div., 140, 145, 149;
3rd Armored Div., 145, 150;
4th Armored Div., 149;
9th Armored Div., 220;
1st Mechanized Infantry Div., 145;
70th Tank Battalion, 102;
27th Armored Infantry, 220;
526th Armored Infantry Battalion, 200, 207, 285;
14th Tank Battalion, 220;
743rd Tank Battalion, 195, 198, 200.
Thake, Henry, 40, 81, 120, 152-153, 234.
Thake, Walter, 40, 120, 136.
Thames River, 67.
Theriault, Donald, 156.
Theriault, L. James (Buster), 63, 156, 193, 198, 212, 263.

Tidlund, August, 53.
Timberlake, Edward W., 109, 127, 157, 182, 189, 221
Tobery, George P., 121.
Tonfanau Firing Point, Wales, 75, 77.
Tyree, Nelvin M., 161, 201, 202.
Tywyn, Wales, 77.

U.S. Air Command, 143, 144.
U.S. Air Force:
Eighth Air Force, 144, 147, 206, 210;
82nd Airborne Div., 205, 209, 210, 285;
Ninth Air force, 92, 147;
101st Airborne Div., 209;
153rd Liaison Squadron, 188.
U.S. Army, 26, 27, 28, 29, 30-49, 50-52, 69,
Artillery training, 37-38, 45, 47;
Basic Training, 30-48, 261, 262, 263;
clothing issue, 26-27, 30, 177;
drill sergeants, 33, 39-42;
equipment issue, 26;
infiltration course, 38;
M-1 training, 30, 36;
machine gun training, 37, 47;
mechanics school, 49;
obstacle course, 35;
phonetic alphabet of WWII, 29;
rations described, 51-52;
training methods of WWII, 29-39, 69;
winter clothing issue, 26, 177.
U.S.O., 44, 70, 157, 180, at Buzzards Bay, 44.
Utah Beach, 88, 132, 133.

Varrato, Jerome, 210.
Vesledahl, Donald S., 265.
Vire River, 135, 139, 146.
Von Kluge, Gunther, 154.
Vosges Mountains, 178.

Wade, W. L., 101.
Walther gun factory, 230.